"The lights of Hanoi were beautiful," Donohue recalled later. "Suddenly, just beyond them, the Navy planes had the sky over Haiphong Harbor lit up like the Fourth of July with flares."

Donohue was now two miles from Son Tay.

It was 2:18 Saturday morning, November 21, Hanoi time. The most important five seconds of Marty Donohue's life were coming up, after 16 years and 6,300 hours in the cockpit of a helicopter.

He would be the first man over Son Tay Prison. At treetop level, moving at only a few knots' forward airspeed, Apple Three would fly between the two guard towers on Son Tay's west wall. The Gatling gun—like cannons, one mounted in each side door, would open fire and spew out a cone of converging tracer bullets at 4,000 rounds a minute to knock out the guard towers and then a guard barracks just outside the gate on the east wall. Donohue was not to fire on the guard tower at the gate. Beneath it, the Defense Intelligence Agency had warned him, was the cramped hutch where prisoners were often tortured or kept huddled in solitary. If that guard tower came crashing down, it might kill one of the POWs they were trying to rescue.

Just as the prison came into sight, the sky above Son Tay exploded in brilliant light. . . .

Books published by The Ballantine Publishing Group
are available at quantity discounts on bulk purchases for
premium, educational, fund-raising, and special sales use.
For details, please call 1-800-733-3000.

THE
RAID

The Son Tay Prison Rescue Mission

Revised and Updated

Benjamin F. Schemmer

BALLANTINE BOOKS • NEW YORK

A Ballantine Book
Published by The Ballantine Publishing Group
Copyright © 1976, 1986, 2002 by Benjamin F. Schemmer

www.ballantinebooks.com

ISBN 0-345-44696-8

Manufactured in the United States of America

First Ballantine Books Edition: July 2002

OPM   10   9   8   7   6   5   4   3   2   1

With everlasting thanks and all my love
to the Lithuanian Princess, my wife,
ELIZABETH T. SCHEMMER,
who brought me a new and joyous life after
all my doctors had declared me near dead

Contents

Prologue   1

ONE   Son Tay Prison   6

TWO   "Polar Circle"   24
    Fort Belvoir, Virginia   24
    SACSA   34
    The "Tank"   48
    Arlington Hall Station   52
    The Plan   60
    Fort Bragg, North Carolina   67

THREE   "Ivory Coast"   75
    Volunteers   75
    Assets   92
    Cuba?   99
    Range C-2   103
    Bullets, Blowtorches, and Bolt Cutters   112
    The Ivory Coast Yo-Yo   124
    Carriers and CAS Agents   139
    Leaks and Lost Messages   143
    The Oval Office   162
    The Cigarettes   169

FOUR   "Kingpin"   187
    Takhli Royal Thai Air Force Base   187
    Udorn Royal Thai Air Force Base   197
    Yankee Station   203

Son Tay 208
The National Military Command Center 232

FIVE   Disarray 240
The Pentagon Press Room 240
The Halls of Congress 246
Public Relations 254
Postmortem 264

SIX   Hoa Lo Prison 282

Epilogue 303

Author's Note 321

APPENDIX I   The Son Tay Prisoners 329
APPENDIX II   The Son Tay Raiders 332
APPENDIX III   The Son Tay Awards for Valor 340
APPENDIX IV   The Son Tay Planners 343
APPENDIX V   Who *Was* at the "Secondary School"? 345
APPENDIX VI   Nagging Questions 352
APPENDIX VII   The Special Operations Warrior
                Foundation 354
APPENDIX VIII   Fallen Warriors 356

Bibliography 357
Index 363

Illustrations

Photographs

Colonel Simons and members of his assault group during their final equipment check, moments before launching on the Son Tay rescue mission

A low-level aerial photograph of Son Tay Prison (Department of Defense)

Teledyne Ryan's "Buffalo Hunter" (Teledyne Ryan)

Lockheed's SR-71 reconnaissance aircraft (Department of Defense)

Aerial photograph of the mid-1970 flood at Son Tay (Department of Defense)

Model of the Son Tay compound built by CIA (CIA photograph)

MC-130 "Combat Talon" with UH-1 in draft position off left wing and two HH-53s in draft off right wing

Army Brigadier General Donald D. Blackburn (United States Army Photographic Agency)

Army Colonel E. E. Mayer

Army Lieutenant General Donald V. Bennett and Air Force Major General Richard R. Stewart

Air Force Lieutenant Colonel Warner A. Britton (*Airman* magazine)

Army Lieutenant Colonel Joseph R. Cataldo

Army Lieutenant Colonel Elliott P. Sydnor

Air Force Major Frederic M. Donohue

Army Captain Richard J. Meadows

Three Son Tay raiders

Colonel Arthur D. "Bull" Simons before the Pentagon press corps

The Chinese officer's belt which Captain Udo H. Walther "confiscated" at the "Secondary School" just south of Son Tay Prison

Ceremony to decorate the Special Forces soldiers and airmen (Department of Defense)

"Unofficial" shoulder patch of the Son Tay raiders

Bull Simmons being decorated by President Richard M. Nixon

An SR-71 reconnaissance photo taken immediately after the raid

Maps

American POW Camps Outside Hanoi   193
Routes of Son Tay Assault Force (Ann Oinas)   194
Target Area Tactics (Ann Oinas)   195
The Assault on Son Tay   196

Illustrations

The North Vietnamese "rope trick"   8

The prisoner's arms were repeatedly cinched up until the elbows were forced together. Sometimes "hell cuffs" were applied at that point—handcuffs that were put on the upper arms and pinched as tightly as possible to cut off circulation. The resulting pain was extreme. If the prisoner was not broken by this time, his arms were rotated until the shoulders dislocated. As the artist, Lt. Cdr. Mike McGrath, a POW for six years, would later write, "Words could never adequately describe the pain, or the thoughts that go through a man's mind at a time like this."

Drawing by Lt. Cdr. Mike McGrath from his 1975 Naval Institute Press book, *Prisoner of War: Six Years in Hanoi.*

Cigarettes provided the POWs   175

Prisoners were allowed three cigarettes a day, but had to bow each time a guard dispensed them. Many POWs gave up smoking so they wouldn't have to bow or because the brand of cigarettes given them was so rancid. Others took up smoking to combat sheer boredom.

Drawing by Lt. Cdr. Mike McGrath from his 1975 Naval Institute Press book, *Prisoner of War: Six Years in Hanoi.*

President Nixon's note to Defense Secretary Melvin Laird   183
President Nixon's note to Defense Secretary Melvin Laird, written the night before Laird authorized the final "Go!" in spite of last-minute intelligence that the camp might well prove empty.

Prologue

Eight days before Thanksgiving of 1970, President Richard M. Nixon met in the White House Oval Office with four of his closest advisers to hear one of the most dramatic briefings of his presidency. It was Wednesday morning, November 18, a cold and cloudy day so bleak in Washington that the National Weather Service would record only four-tenths of an hour of sunshine all day long.

Nixon was deep in conversation with National Security Adviser Henry A. Kissinger, Central Intelligence Agency Director Richard M. Helms, Defense Secretary Melvin R. Laird, and Secretary of State William P. Rogers, when Admiral Thomas H. Moorer, Chairman of the Joint Chiefs of Staff, was ushered in precisely at 11:00 A.M. The tall, soft-spoken Moorer greeted the President, nodded to the other men with a warm yet businesslike smile, and opened a large map case full of 20- by 30-inch briefing charts. As he set them up on an easel between the President's desk and the overstuffed chairs and sofas which flanked the Oval Office fireplace, Rogers noticed the Top Secret designation on the charts' cover sheet. Of all those present, he was the only one for whom the subject of Moorer's briefing would be a total surprise. The United States' Secretary of State was about to learn for the first time that an "invasion" of North Vietnam had been planned for months.

Nixon laid his ever-present yellow legal pad on an end table beside his chair, a sign for Moorer to proceed. Moorer opened his briefing book, a carefully tabbed, three-ring black binder with the words "Top Secret—Chairman's Eyes Only" stamped in gold on the cover. "Mr. President," he began, "the code name for this operation is 'Kingpin.' It provides for a raid on North Vietnam to be conducted by Army Special Forces personnel assaulting the Son Tay prisoner-of-war camp, 23 miles west of

Hanoi, in Air Force helicopters assisted by a Navy air diversion near Haiphong. The most advantageous period for this undertaking is between November 21 and 25."

Standing beside the easel, Moorer uncovered a large map of North Vietnam to pinpoint the location of the Son Tay compound. He then unveiled charts and detailed diagrams of the compound itself and the surrounding area. He calmly described the compound's layout and said, "This is the only confirmed active POW camp outside Hanoi, Mr. President. The Son Tay camp has a prisoner population of 70 Americans. Of these, 61 have been tentatively identified by name and service: 43 Air Force, 14 Navy, 4 Marines . . . We propose," Moorer said, "to rescue them all."

As Moorer began to describe how the rescue mission would be timed and executed, Kissinger quietly picked up a phone; within minutes, his deputy, Major General Alexander M. Haig, entered the Oval Office and took the chair farthest from Moorer's briefing charts. Flipping through the charts one by one, Moorer took 18 minutes to relate the details of the raid. Despite the "Pentagonese" in which the briefing was written, his proposal was full of drama, rich in detail. He knew the subject well, and referred only sporadically to his briefing book.

Finally Moorer paused; he had a flair for dramatic effect. Then he spoke very slowly: "The ground commander is positive that the operation will succeed, Mr. President."

The President, one participant at the briefing would recall, was lapping it up "like an eight-year-old at his first cowboy movie." He told Moorer, "Sounds great, Tom. What else?"

Moorer gave a short intelligence summary which focused on the "threats" that would present the operation with its greatest risks. Then he paused again: "A final word, Mr. President. If resources in support of this operation reveal that the enemy may have determined our objective, the operation will be canceled." He let the word "canceled" sink in.

"Damn, Tom, let's not let *that* happen," Nixon said. "I want this to *go.*"

During the briefing, Moorer realized, the President had scribbled only a few notes on the yellow legal pad at his side. That was good, Moorer thought; he'd kept the President's attention and there wouldn't be many questions. Nixon had only two. He asked when Moorer had to have a final decision. Then he asked what cover stories had been devised in case the raid failed.

The raid on Son Tay had been postponed once before, for political reasons. But now Nixon said, "How could anyone *not* approve this?" Then he told Moorer, "Tom, I know you guys have worked months on this. I want these POWs home too . . . Hell, if this works, we could even have them here for Thanksgiving dinner, right here at the White House."

Five days later, it was Moorer's turn to listen to a briefing, this time by the Secretary of Defense standing in front of 55 newsmen at the Pentagon. It was Monday, November 23, a dark, cold and not very friendly day in Washington.

The Pentagon press corps knew that a big story was about to break. That morning, the daily news briefing known as the "eleven o'clock follies" had been postponed until 3:30. By then, so many rumors had spread around the pressroom that there was a "full house" waiting when Melvin R. Laird strode into "the studio," the newsroom just off the Pentagon's Mall Entrance. He was accompanied by Moorer and two officers unfamiliar to the "regulars" who covered the Department of Defense for the nation's newspaper and radio/TV networks. One was Leroy J. Manor, a slim, suave Air Force brigadier general; the other was Army Colonel Arthur D. Simons, a gruff, barrel-chested, mean-looking rock of a soldier whose blouse bore an array of parachutist and combat infantryman badges, six rows of decorations and campaign ribbons, three distinguished unit citations and the shoulder tab of the famous World War II 6th Ranger Battalion.

Laird stepped to the microphone and told the reporters that he wanted to give them details of an "operation that took place north of the 19th Parallel this past weekend." A raid, he announced, had been made on a prisoner-of-war compound "approximately 20 miles west of Hanoi." Its purpose was to rescue "as many of our prisoners as possible." Laird then introduced Manor and Simons to the Pentagon press corps. Three minutes and two seconds into his carefully worded briefing, he delivered the punch line: "Regrettably," he said, "the rescue team discovered that the camp had recently been vacated. No prisoners were found."

Laird talked for two more minutes, describing some general

details of the raid. Finally he opened the press conference to questions. He turned most of them over to the two officers flanking him. General Manor had been the overall commander of the raid, Colonel Simons had led the assault on Son Tay; but because of "security," they weren't allowed to add much detail, even though the reporters had a flock of questions. Apparently the raid itself was a success: no American lives had been lost. But the question uppermost in the reporters' minds went unanswered. Why were there no prisoners at Son Tay? Twelve minutes and five seconds into the press conference, a reporter summed up a conclusion every journalist in the studio had reached by then. "On whom do you blame the intelligence failure?" he asked.

At 4:12, Laird cut off any further questions with, "Thank you very much, gentlemen." That was the end of the Son Tay press conference—and the opening page of a news story that was to dominate the papers for weeks.

The next morning, an eight-column banner headline across the front page of the *Washington Post* read:

U.S. Raid to Rescue POWs Fails

About one-third of the paper's front page was devoted to the raid on Son Tay. Three of the other nine articles on that same page fleshed out the story:

Incursions by U.S. Raise
New Peril for Nixon Policy

Paris Session Canceled
as Reds Protest Raids

Senators
Appalled
at Forays

Many of the news stories that followed were off the mark. There were several details of the raid that the Pentagon did not want made public, and some which it did reveal would prove to be untrue. As a result, a host of questions remained unanswered. Was the raid on Son Tay a daring and courageous mission—worth the risk, even though it failed to rescue a single American prisoner of war? Or was it, as many editorials suggested, a foolhardy and provocative act which needlessly endangered the lives of the raiding force and invited retaliation on the POWs who still remained in North Vietnamese prisons? How and why was the raid planned? What actually happened during the 27 minutes that the raiding force spent on the ground in a remote—and empty—POW camp deep in the heart of enemy territory? How had the Pentagon been able to obtain such detailed intelligence about the names and number of POWs held captive at Son Tay? Why was the camp empty? Why didn't the Pentagon learn that the camp had been vacated before the raid was launched? Or did it? And if so, why wasn't the raid canceled? Was the raid an act of desperation by a government and military machine that had been frustrated at almost every turn in the war in Vietnam? Or was it a useful card in the Byzantine game of power politics? Was the raid on Son Tay a failure? Or did it, in the end, achieve an ironic success—or, as in most complex situations, was it a mixture of both?

The raid on Son Tay was an archetypical event of the Vietnam War, a complex political and military operation that encompassed the ponderous bureaucracy of the Pentagon and the White House, the rigidly compartmentalized work of and sometimes counterproductive rivalry between America's various intelligence agencies, meticulous planning and training, and, finally, the incredible bravery of the men who carried out the mission. But in a very real sense, the raid on Son Tay was the highlight of the last three years of that traumatic decade called Vietnam. From early 1969, when America began withdrawing its forces from Vietnam, until early 1973, when 566 American POWs were finally released by North Vietnam, the Viet Cong, and Communist China, there was only one purpose left in the war. America spent 20,683 lives and over $62 *billion* in those five years to achieve what a small party of brave men tried to do at Son Tay—bring those prisoners home.

ONE

Son Tay Prison

In North Vietnam early in 1970, Air Force Captain Wes Schierman was fighting for his life in a cold, dingy, cramped prison just west of a small town called Son Tay Citadel. For weeks he had been gasping for every breath of air. His fellow prisoners watched him "almost die" several times, unable to help him, outraged when the guards ignored their cries to get him a medic.

The men at Son Tay had learned that flying over North Vietnam was not an easy way to earn a living. So had hundreds of other POWs held captive elsewhere in North Vietnam.

Navy Lieutenant (j.g.) Everett Alvarez, Jr., was the first American to find out what a North Vietnamese prison was like. His A-46 jet light attack aircraft was one of two planes shot down in 1964 during the August 5 retaliatory strikes over Haiphong Harbor ordered by President Johnson after the Tonkin Gulf incidents. As Southeast Asia exploded into a full-scale but undeclared war in 1965, air strikes over the north mounted rapidly, averaging about 70 planes a day. So did the number of planes shot down and Americans taken prisoner. By the end of that year, 60 American pilots and 3 air reservemen were held captive. They were the "lucky" ones. Most of the aircrews in planes that were shot down, almost one plane every other day in the north, never lived to see the inside of a North Vietnamese prison. In 1966, 223 planes a day were hitting the north—but the North Vietnamese had built up the heaviest air defenses ever seen in the world and their gunners shot down an American airplane about eight out of every ten days. That year, 84 more Americans found themselves in "Heartbreak Hotel," that part of Hoa Lo Prison, the huge old French jail in downtown Hanoi, where North Vietnam took new captives for their first weeks of interrogation—and torture. Hoa Lo was aptly named—in Vietnamese, it meant "the place of the cooking fires."

By the end of 1967, air strikes over North Vietnam were averaging close to 300 planes a day. And almost daily, one of them fell mortally crippled from the skies over Hanoi, Haiphong, or the Vietnamese panhandle above the Demilitarized Zone. Despite heroic efforts, search and rescue (SAR) helicopter crews were able to recover less than 13 percent of the airmen shot down during this entire period. Pilots who bailed out over the sea, between Yankee Station in the Gulf of Tonkin and Dixie Station off the northern part of South Vietnam, stood a much better chance of being rescued. So did airmen shot down over land in South Vietnam, Laos, or Cambodia. But the odds were not very good over North Vietnam. Chances were almost nine to one that pilots who got "smoked" there would die—or end up a prisoner.

Every other day that year of 1967, the most intensive and costly of the air war in the north, another American airman was taken prisoner. By the time President Johnson ordered a total bombing halt over the north on October 31, 1968, 143 more planes had been shot down and 197 more Americans had been thrown into North Vietnamese prisons. Somewhere outside those prisons, and possibly in them, another 917 Americans were missing in action. In all, North Vietnam had bagged 927 planes and 345 prisoners by late 1968 when flights over the north were limited to reconnaissance sorties.

Many of the men shot down over North Vietnam were in grave trouble before they even hit the ground. Under normal circumstances, over 90 percent of crewmen who have to bail out of an airplane land uninjured. Over North Vietnam, it was a different story. Seven of every ten men who lived to tell what happened suffered injuries so severe when they ejected that they were incapable of even *trying* to escape or evade capture after they hit the ground.

Flying under great stress in skies full of exploding flak, missiles and small arms fire, already drained of reserve energy after a flight to the target that had lasted over an hour, sometimes two hours, these men were pushing their planes, and themselves, to the outer boundary of safe "design limits." Many of the planes were flying at 400 knots or faster when their crews had to eject. In some cases, the planes were in a dangerous nose-down attitude, screaming toward impact with the ground. In other cases, they were also rolling, tumbling out of control—or just plain disintegrating. Sometimes traveling at supersonic speeds, the men had to strain against four to eight times the force of gravity, their bodies pressed against their seats or the sides of the cockpit as they struggled to eject.

Ejection seats ("life support systems," as airplane designers call them) were not designed very well for those extreme conditions. Once a crew member pulled or pushed the eject handle, he was supposed to be shot out of the airplane (usually by a 37mm cannon shell beneath the seat) into a "smooth ballistic trajectory" until his parachute opened automatically and the seat fell comfortably away while he prepared for a parachute landing. It didn't happen that way in North Vietnam. Ten percent of the men reported extreme difficulty in even locating or activating their ejection controls. Others found it impossible to get "squared away" in their seats when the time came to "punch out." Improperly positioned to eject, 40 percent of the men experienced "flailing"—spinning through the air out of control, a tumbling mass of arms and legs torn by near-supersonic forces.

Fighter-bomber pilots were supposed to fly with their shoulder straps "locked," to restrain them in their seats even under heavy gravity forces. But most of the aircrews over North Vietnam loosened those shoulder straps—so they could relax a bit

on the long flight, bend over their backseat radar scopes, read the bomb sights better as they rolled into the target, or look over their shoulders to check for enemy MIGs. Once their planes were hit, there was too little time to actuate the locking mechanism that tightened their shoulder straps and positioned their bodies to eject. Twenty percent of the men broke their elbows and arms or knees on the sides of their cockpits, or suffered other "major injuries," because American technology had not devised a way for those shoulder straps to be pulled taut automatically a split second or two before the ejection charge went off.

The men who had been injured during ejection had no hope of evading their captors. Even those who ejected and landed safely were usually captured very quickly. They were robust, tall, very white or very black Americans and they were very conspicuous in a land of 21 million short, thin Orientals. It took North Vietnam only three weeks to pick up the longest evadee. A Navy pilot, he decided to head inland instead of toward the coast, hoping to reach a friendly CIA outpost on the Laotian border. But the North Vietnamese found his flight helmet and tracked him down with dogs. It took them only 12 days to nail the second-longest evadee, Colonel George E. Day. He was a forty-year-old "half blind" F-100 pilot who lost his eyeglasses when he ejected on August 26, 1967. But he escaped soon after being captured, even though his right arm was broken in three places, his left knee badly sprained and his body numb with pain from his initial torture. He almost made it across the Demilitarized Zone. How he thrashed about the rice paddies and stumbled through the hills and jungle of North Vietnam that long before being caught again was something even he can't explain, except that he wanted to get home "very badly."

Captured quickly, their bodies broken and bleeding before they hit the ground, pummeled by irate, overexuberant villagers worked into a frenzy of hate by local political cadres, spat upon and beaten on their way into Hanoi's Heartbreak Hotel, the Americans were ill-prepared for what followed.

Torture.

Torture of the most inhuman, crudest kind. It wasn't sophisticated. It just hurt—beyond comprehension, beyond the limit of human endurance. The most common form was going "on the ropes." After their initial interrogation periods, when most prisoners were beaten savagely but gave only the "name, rank and serial number" required by the Geneva Convention, these debilitated men found their captors impatient—but effective. Their arms were bound behind them until wrists, then elbows, touched. A rope was looped through the bonds, pulled up behind their necks, strung over a hook or bolt in the ceiling, and pulled taut until their arms were raised behind their backs to the point where their shoulders were often literally pulled out of their sockets.

The men were left to hang there. Until they talked. Some held out for a week or ten days.

Once a prisoner talked, he was finally fed. A typical meal was a bowl of insipid pumpkin or cabbage soup. Often it was infested with vermin. For one four-month period, the prisoners' diet consisted of two bowls daily of unspiced, boiled cabbage soup—240 consecutive bowls of it, nothing else. Diarrhea, dysentery, scurvy, beriberi, and hepatitis were forever present in the bare, unventilated cellblocks.

Hoa Lo Prison was the "Devil's Island of Southeast Asia." Built by the French 40 years earlier, it was known intimately by many of North Vietnam's highest officials. Some of them had been imprisoned there as long as 10 to 12 years, by the French and then the Japanese.

The prison stank. Years of urine, blood, vomit, and feces permeated every crevice. Rats and long flying cockroaches were Hoa Lo's real landlords; the North Vietnamese guards were just the caretakers. Mice, spiders and ants were all over, mosquitoes so profuse that one prisoner said of his first night there, "The insects nearly carried me off." American POWs dubbed Hoa Lo the "Hanoi Hilton."

Other parts of Hoa Lo were filled with North Vietnamese civilian convicts. Some were children only fourteen years old. When they were brought into the courtyards for "exercise," the Americans could see through their cell windows that many of the children were chained together.

Rules for the POWs were strict: no whistling, singing, or talking. Just silence. As the prisoners tried to communicate, they learned quickly that their captors spent much of the time looking for excuses to punish them. Catching the men communicating was a favorite excuse.

The 345 Americans held prisoner by 1970 had bailed out in the prime of their lives. The "average" POW—if the word "average" can be used for men who were to endure what they did—was only about thirty-two years old, a captain in the Air Force or a Navy lieutenant, married and the father of two young children. About 85 percent of them had flown more than 15 missions over the north when their "number came up."

One of the unluckiest prisoners of all was Captain Richard P. "Pop" Keirn, shot down on July 24, 1965, the seventh Air Force crewman bagged in the Vietnam War. A B-17 copilot in World War II, Keirn had been shot down on his eighteenth mission over Germany and spent nine months as a POW. An F-46 pilot in Vietnam, he was shot down on his eleventh mission in Southeast Asia. Keirn experienced almost ten years as a prisoner of war. After his release in 1973, he would joke that the Air Force had become much smarter; it was impossible, he said, to find a pilot dumb enough to fly with him. Asked to compare captivity in Southeast Asia with his experience in World War II, Keirn said, "Captivity in Germany was rough, but at least I was treated like a human being. Captivity in North Vietnam was unreal, unbelievable, not of this world."

Air Force Lieutenant Colonel Robinson Risner became a prisoner on September 16, 1965, while flying an F-105 over the north. A Korean war ace with 109 combat missions and eight MIGs, he had been shot down over North Vietnam six months earlier but managed to make it to the coast and bail out over the water. An SA-16 flying boat plucked him out of the water while the other planes in Risner's flight strafed the North Vietnamese boats rushing from shore to capture him. The crew which saved him was on its first combat rescue mission and could barely get its plane airborne.

Time magazine wrote up the mission; Risner's picture was on the cover. When he was shot down again, he came "to regret that *Time* had ever heard of me." The more senior a prisoner was, the more "famous" or the more important, the more impatient the North Vietnamese were to break him, to have him confess his "crimes against the North Vietnamese people" in front of visiting peace groups or foreign newsmen, to hammer him into submission as an example to other prisoners that there was no use resisting because their senior officers had already talked.

Risner was to spend seven and a half years in captivity. The "distinctive character of imprisonment in North Vietnam," he would report, "was the suffocating monotony. . . . Bodies built for movement were confined to closetlike boxes. Active minds were forced to be idle with the numbing nothingness of four walls in a dingy little cell. Men trained to fly sophisticated machines at incredible speeds and breathtaking heights were caged like animals. . . . But worse than that, no people to be close to."*

Navy Lieutenant John M. McGrath had a rough bailout when his A4-C was shot down on his 179th mission in Southeast Asia. By the time he hit the ground, his left arm was broken and badly dislocated; he also had two fractured vertebrae and a broken left knee. In their haste to rip off his boots, the North Vietnamese militiamen who captured him hyperextended his broken knee six times; en route to Hanoi, frenzied villagers twisted his injured leg and dislocated the same knee. McGrath was "sure" he would not reach Hanoi alive. He did— but soon wished he *had* died. During his initial interrogation, the North Vietnamese dislocated both his right shoulder and right elbow. They denied him medical treatment, but when he begged them to shoot him, he was told, "No, you are a criminal! You haven't suffered enough."**

The men suffered.

Their families suffered almost as much. It's hard for a woman not to know whether she's a wife or a widow, for a son or daughter not to know if their father is dead or alive. It happened not to just a few hundred, but to *thousands* of families. For every 12 men who were killed in Southeast Asia, there was another man listed as a POW or MIA. At one time or another, 3,307 American families had a husband, father, or son who was either "missing in action" or held as a "prisoner of war." Three years after the Paris peace agreements that terminated American involvement in Vietnam, fewer than one in four of these men had been accounted for.

Carroll Flora's wife was typical of those kept in limbo so

The Passing of the Night: My Seven Years As a Prisoner of the North Vietnamese by Colonel Robinson Risner. New York: Ballantine Books, 1973.

**Prisoner of War: Six Years in Hanoi* by Lieutenant Commander John M. McGrath. Annapolis, Md.: Naval Institute Press, 1975.

long, not knowing if a husband was alive or dead. Sergeant First Class Carroll Flora became missing in action on July 21, 1967, during an Army Special Forces night action. For six years, his wife didn't know if he had been killed, captured, or was still trying to evade capture in the jungles and hills of Laos. She never received one letter from him, or he from her. On Saturday, January 29, 1973, 2,017 days after he was listed as MIA, the North Vietnamese released his name in Paris as one of the prisoners who would be returned home. Flora was only one of 53 men released about whom North Vietnam had given out no information whatsoever during the entire time they were held prisoner.

Some families knew that a husband or father had been captured or seen in prison, but never got a letter from him or knew if he was getting theirs. Even though North Vietnam eased many restrictions on POW mail from 1970 to 1973, 95 of the 566 prisoners released in 1973 had never received a letter from home; 80 families had never received a letter from the prisoner.

For still other POW/MIA families, there was the agony of knowing that a husband or son had been taken captive but was seriously wounded, and that North Vietnamese medical treatment was primitive and torture frequent. Of every 100 men taken prisoner, 11 were to die in captivity. The Commander-in-Chief, Pacific, Admiral John S. McCain, Jr., lived with this kind of agony for five and a half years. His son, John S. McCain III, a Navy attack pilot, was shot down over Hanoi on October 26, 1967, just three months before his father was named to command all of the Army, Navy, Marine, and Air forces prosecuting the Vietnam War. Young McCain was known to have been seriously wounded when his plane was hit. His wingman saw the North Vietnamese fish him out of a lake in downtown Hanoi, apparently unconscious. In August of 1969, two prisoners who were released early by North Vietnam reported that McCain was near death, tortured beyond the believable limit of human endurance. He had been given only enough medical care to stay alive, sometimes in a semicomatose state, and had been held in solitary for the past 15 months.

His captors knew who McCain's father was, and the North Vietnamese had offered him an "early return" in July of 1968. Jack McCain, however, declined—and was tortured repeatedly because he refused the chance to go home. His fellow prisoners begged him to accept the offer; they were afraid he would die if not given better medical care. But McCain didn't want the North Vietnamese to propagandize his "groveling" for an early release, as he felt sure they would, while fellow POWs languished in Hanoi's cells.

The prisoners suffered all the more knowing the anguish and uncertainty their families were going through. Bent by brutality, dispirited because they had "talked," weak from malnutrition, suffering from primitive or nonexistent medical attention, confined in solitary—some men for as long as four years, one Navy captain for 58 months—tortured when caught trying to talk with their fellow prisoners, it was a miracle that the POWs retained their sanity. Some didn't.

The night he was moved to Son Tay, December 19, 1969, Air Force Major Elmo C. "Mo" Baker thought he might have lost his. He had been a prisoner for two and a quarter years, shot down on his 61st mission over the north on a strike against the Bac Giang bridge 28 miles northeast of Hanoi. Bac Giang was not a target pilots liked to visit very often; photo interpreters had counted 138 guns around it. Baker had flown against it the month before and won the Distinguished Flying Cross for knocking the bridge out. But the bridge served one of the only two railroads coming down from China, and because it was vital to North Vietnam's supply system, it was quickly repaired. Colonel Bob White led a new F-105 attack against the bridge; Baker led the roll in to the target. The "golden beebee" caught up with Mo Baker that day, August 23, 1967.

Baker was thirty-five years old, a tall, soft-spoken native of Kennett, Missouri, who got his bachelor of arts degree from Syracuse and a master's degree in electrical engineering just before going to Vietnam. When he ejected, his F-105 was porpoising and Baker broke his left thighbone in a painful fracture. As his parachute neared the ground, he could see and hear North Vietnamese all around him. He had no chance for escape or rescue. The North Vietnamese took him to Hanoi by helicopter, straight into Heartbreak Hotel. His introduction to North Vietnamese "culture" was excruciating: instead of the usual torture, the guards twisted his left foot, first one way, then another, rotating it almost three-fourths of a circle each time.

Three weeks after his initial interrogation, Baker's leg was finally set in Bac Mai Hospital. He stayed there 30 days, then was sent to the "Plantation," the "show" prison in Hanoi where visiting peace delegations were often taken. The prisoners hated those visits: they got "tromped up" before a delegation came, and again after it left. Baker was used as a prize exhibit to show that the POWs were getting "hospital care." He met his first delegation, headed by peace activist Tom Hayden, on October 11, 1967. The North Vietnamese, of course, didn't tell the visitors that the thighbone Mo Baker had snapped while ejecting was used for torture for three weeks before they finally "repaired it," and that it now had a radial fracture as well.

The North Vietnamese had a list of 17 questions they knew visiting delegations would always ask, and the prisoners were "instructed" beforehand on how to answer. If a prisoner "got on a preaching stump" or was too recalcitrant, the North Vietnamese had a stock answer: "You shall know pain."

Baker's cellmate at the Plantation was Air Force Captain Larry E. Carrigan, shot down the same day he was. Carrigan was picked to meet some visitors from the Women's Strike for Peace. Instead of admitting contrition for his "criminal acts" against the North Vietnamese people, he told the group he was proud to be an American pilot. After the delegation left, his captors hung him "on the wall" and Carrigan knew pain. Ropes bound tightly around his wrists were hoisted through two eyebolts on the wall until he hung there like a crucifix. One of his arms came out of its socket. The pain Carrigan knew from that one session would last for five years.

Twenty-seven months after their shootdown, on December 9, 1969, a guard came into their cell late one night and told Baker and Carrigan to "roll up"—gather their few belongings and roll them up in their rice pad blankets. It was a "scary thing" for the POWs, being moved to another camp, usually at night, always on short notice. There was never enough time to collect the carefully hidden homemade pencils, paper, nails, or pieces of string and wire that they hoarded like treasure and used to communicate from cell to cell or in some other ingenious way.

The guards blindfolded Carrigan and Baker, tied their wrists to each other, and threw them into a minibus along with several more prisoners. Guards were put between groups of the POWs to make sure no one lifted a blindfold or talked. The North Vietnamese didn't want them to see who the other prisoners were or where they were headed. But Carrigan and Baker managed periodic peeks through their blindfolds. They could see they were headed west. As the bus rumbled on, Carrigan told Baker, "I think we're going to Laos." That bothered them; they were sure that prison in Laos would be even worse than Hanoi. Baker dispelled the idea with a curt, "You're crazy, Carrigan." Another 30 minutes went by, but the bus still headed west. Carrigan lifted his blindfold again and told Baker once more, "I think we're headed for Laos." Baker told him to "quit smoking opium." Thirty minutes later, Baker managed to lift his own blindfold. The bus was in open country and still rumbling west. He blurted out involuntarily: "Sweet Jesus, I think we're going to Laos."

Late into the night, the bus turned off a road and stopped in front of a steel gate. Carrigan and Baker were led through it. All they knew was that they were a long, long way west of Hanoi. They found themselves in a small compound courtyard roughly 140 by 125 feet. In it were three small buildings: one of them was to their left, in the southeast corner; the other two buildings adjoined each other just inside the compound's north wall. They were taken to a cell in one of them, the building on the right, and locked up with Air Force Major Irby D. Terrell, Jr., a January 1968 shootdown who had been on the bus with them. It was the first time they'd had another roommate in 837 days of captivity.

The building they were housed in was called the Opium Den; it contained three other three-man cells. The building beside it was known as the Beer House and the one farther away, in the compound's southeast corner, as the Cat House. Baker noticed that the walls of his building were made of brick and mortar; they would carry sound real well. Each of the three new inmates put an ear to one wall. Baker was "astonished" to hear that "it was alive, humming with tapping conversations." They decoded the loudest tapping: "Two guys just came into the Opium Den. One is bald-headed."

Baker hit the wall solidly with his elbow; the "Ka Thump" was a standard warning signal, an order to be obeyed instantly—"guards coming" or "stop communicating." The walls fell silent.

Baker then "initiated comm"—"Shave and a haircut, two bits," he tapped, meaning "I want to communicate." He tapped out the code: "I am Major Elmo Baker," and then added, "the bald guy." He tapped again: "Just arrived from the Plantation with eleven others. Where are we?" He got an immediate response from the camp's senior ranking officer (SRO), Navy Lieutenant Commander Render Crayton, a February 1966 shootdown. "You're at Camp Hope, near Son Tay Citadel. It's isolated as hell out here. Eleven men have just been moved out."

Suddenly, communications was interrupted by another sharp "Ka Thump" from somewhere. The "V"—North Vietnamese—had "heard the walls vibrating"; guards began patrolling, and they looked agitated. Son Tay fell silent. Baker and the new arrivals wondered what lay ahead for them in this godforsaken prison outpost.

That Thursday morning, December 11, 1969, Baker and his cellmates awoke early. The day was bright. A stern guard told them, "This is a *working* camp." He took them outside. Baker was given a steel pipe about a foot long and told to break up a pile of old bricks. They would be used, Baker learned later, for the foundation of a new interrogation building. Baker was elated: "They couldn't have given me a better telegraph key!" And he was outside, in fresh air, basking in the cool sunshine. The compound was even smaller than he had pictured it in the dark and everyone would be able to hear him.

He started pounding on the bricks, "sending out the news." He described and named the new prisoners, then told that Neil Armstrong had walked on the moon. The guard was so pleased over his industrious prisoner that he brought Baker a new pile of bricks. Baker pounded out a new message, "This guy don't read code," and announced that a turbine-powered car had led the Indianapolis 500 for 197 laps. Signals from the Beer House told him it was great: none of Son Tay's holdover prisoners had heard that. Almost half of them were 1965 and 1966 shootdowns, the rest 1967; none of the prisoners were 1968 or 1969 captives. The camp, Baker learned in turn, had become active on May 24, 1968, when 20 POWs were moved there from Hoa Lo Prison; on July 18, 1968, another 20 men were moved in. The last group of 15 had moved in on November 28, 1968.

Captain Wes Schierman was one of that last group. He had been a prisoner of war for over three years. Shot down on August 28, 1965, he was the eleventh Air Force pilot to be taken

captive in North Vietnam (of 312 finally released in 1973).*
Like the other POWs, Schierman had been moved from one
camp to another—first from Heartbreak Hotel to another part
of Hoa Lo, then to a camp near Ap Lo in the country far to the
west of Hanoi which the prisoners quickly dubbed the "Briarpatch." Late in 1968, Schierman was moved to still another
camp, this time to the shabby little compound called Son Tay. It
was not a bright or cheery place, but the sun broke out that
Thanksgiving Day of 1968 and the prisoners decided to nickname their new home Camp Hope.

Compared with Hoa Lo and Briarpatch, Son Tay was "great"
in one respect. There were as many as ten prisoners in some of
the cells. Most of the POWs had spent their captivity in solitary
or with only one or two cellmates, listening to the cries of a fellow American being tortured in a nearby interrogation room,
wondering how soon their turn would come again for the same
agony. At Son Tay, they were able to see and talk to each other.
It was "a new world."

"The new companionship was unbelievable," Navy Lieutenant (j.g.) Ralph Gaither would say of the changed circumstances. "We were able to share knowledge and help each other
over the rough spots. We could have fellowship in church services, in games, in shooting the bull."** Like Wes Schierman,
Gaither had been a prisoner for five years; a 1965 shootdown,
he was the fortieth American to be taken prisoner in North
Vietnam (of those eventually released in 1973).

Gaither's F-4 Phantom had been hit on October 17, 1965; he
spent his first 15 months of captivity in solitary, initially in
Heartbreak Hotel, then in a prison on the southeast edge of
Hanoi called the Zoo. His cell there was lit 24 hours a day by a
glaring, bare lightbulb, and he was kept in handcuffs after getting caught cutting a peephole at the bottom of his cell door.
On December 1, 1965, he was moved to the Briarpatch. There,
still in solitary, Gaither became deeply depressed. Through the
tap code, he asked his fellow prisoners for help. From a cell

---

*Thirteen additional Air Force men were released in Hanoi after being brought
there for release—one from China, seven from Laos, and five from South Vietnam.

**With God in a POW Camp, by Lt. Cdr. Ralph Gaither, as told to Steve Henry.
Nashville, Tenn.: Broadman Press, 1973.

next door, an Air Force officer and POW he had never met, Wes Schierman, established contact and kept talking to Gaither. Schierman helped him get through "a deep spiritual crisis."

Gaither got his first roommate on January 20, 1967, after 460 days of captivity. But three weeks later he was moved back to the Hanoi Hilton, and from there he was moved again for three months to the Hanoi power plant; Ho Chi Minh had made good his threat to "chain" POWs to the power plants if they were ever attacked by U.S. air strikes, and they were now being targeted regularly. It was a flagrant violation of the Geneva Convention agreements, which specified that prisoners of war would not be held near a target area and that POW camps would be clearly marked. On October 25, 1967, after two prisoners nearly escaped from a little camp called Dirty Bird on the other side of the power plant, Gaither and most of the prisoners were moved back to the Hanoi Hilton.

A year later, on Thanksgiving eve, 1968, Gaither was moved without explanation again—to Son Tay. There he found that one of his roommates was a former neighbor from an adjoining cell in Briarpatch, that unseen, friendly "voice" who had helped him through his crisis almost three years before—Wes Schierman. Another cellmate was John Frederick, a forty-six-year-old Marine Corps chief warrant officer. Shot down on December 7, 1965, while flying as radar intercept officer, he was one of the last Marine Corps warrant officers still on flying duty. An avid fisherman like Gaither, the two became fast friends. Raised on an Illinois farm, proud of having "carved life out of earth" with his own hands, Frederick dreamed of retiring from the service and buying a small farm. He never got to buy that farm. He would die in a North Vietnamese prison.

Life at Son Tay was "pretty quiet" compared to other prisons. But the torture continued. Wes Schierman was one of three cellmates who "caught it" time and again. So did Marine Corps Captain Orson Swindle, a 1966 shootdown who was the senior man in their cell. They had what the North Vietnamese called "bad attitudes." Their refusal to stand at attention or to bow to their captors sent them repeatedly to the interrogation room. There, they were made to sit on stools for days on end, legs clamped tightly in irons, never allowed to sleep. After one grim session, Julius Jayroe was taken back to his cell exhausted, his ankles and feet cruelly swollen from the leg irons. A day later, the camp commander had the gall to invite him to join some North Vietnamese officers for tea. It was September 2, 1969. They were going to celebrate North Vietnam's National Day. Jayroe curtly refused the luxury and the North Vietnamese cut their party short. Once again, he had "won" and made his captors lose face. It was a small victory but an important factor in maintaining the POWs' morale and self-respect. Word of the incident quickly passed from one cell to another and each of the prisoners "stood a little taller." They knew they were "beaten but not broken."

Periodically, the North Vietnamese would move the senior ranking prisoner out of Son Tay. It usually happened whenever the "V" were displeased because prisoners were being obstinate in their interrogation sessions or caught in a lot of infractions like not bowing to the guards, or communicating between cells. Jayroe was SRO when Ralph Gaither moved into Son Tay late in 1968. By the time Mo Baker arrived in December of 1969, Render Crayton was SRO, but the North Vietnamese found him so uncooperative that in the last months of 1969 they stuffed him into "the Oven," a punishment cell beneath the east guard tower whose roof was too low for a man to stand up. It had a metal door that faced south and became so hot in the sun's rays that the men dared not touch it. Then they froze at night. They kept Crayton inside that hellhole for two months before shipping him back to Hanoi that December or in January 1970. Marine Corps Major John H. "Howie" Dunn, a December 1965 shootdown, took over from him, but Dunn was shipped out in May of 1970. Lieutenant Commander Claude D. "Doug" Clower, a prisoner since mid-November 1967, then took over as the senior American in Son Tay Prison.

Like all SROs, Clower had the prisoners tabulate and keep current a mental "data bank" of every American any prisoner had seen alive on North Vietnamese soil. By May of 1970, there were 347 names on the "corporate" list. Mo Baker had all of them in his data bank. And Clower kept encouraging the men to pass on every shred of information they could garner on the lay of the land outside those compound walls.

The prisoners at Son Tay got to spend more time outside than in other camps because the North Vietnamese were enlarging the compound, building a new interrogation room and a small kitchen–dining hall for the guards. Before Mo Baker arrived and began his enthusiastic assault on the brick pile, Ralph Gaither and the other POWs had been put to work building a new compound wall, about 60 feet beyond the north wall that lay just outside the Opium Den and Beer House. The interrogation room Mo Baker was breaking up bricks for and another small cellblock were being built just inside the new wall.

The North Vietnamese were improving Son Tay in other ways. They had the prisoners plant two steel pipes to hold poles for a volleyball net—so the guards could play, not the prisoners. One day, Air Force First Lieutenant Richard C. Brenneman, a November 1967 shootdown, brashly shimmied up the volleyball pole, right in the middle of the compound, and took a look outside the walls. It was "pretty obvious," a big "no no." A guard in the tower by the front gate spotted him. The North Vietnamese were "irritated." They threw Brenneman "under the tower"—a favorite form of torture at Son Tay. Brenneman was locked up in the small shack for thirty days, baking by day, freezing at night, choking in the stench of his own excrement. Also known as "the Tank," it was the same cell where Crayton had been locked up. This was "Dog" Brenneman's second punishment tour there. It was like living inside a metal drum, which the Vietnamese guards would bang regularly with the butts of their AK-47s. The guards hauled him out only long enough to beat him when he refused to admit that he had climbed the pole on anything but a whim. Brenneman took it well, but finally got an order from the camp's SRO to write an apology to the North Vietnamese before they broke him and extracted something critical, like the real purpose of his trip up the pole, or communication methods and codes. Brenneman wrote the note. It said something harmless like "I'm sorry I was a bad boy," and the camp commander ordered him to be released.

Brenneman wasn't the only climber. Whenever they saw the guards in the towers dozing off, the POWs would climb the compound wall for a quick look at the area outside. They got away with it often enough to piece together a mental mosaic of the countryside around them. They were in the middle of a farming area, surrounded by rice paddies and irrigation ditches. A few hundred yards to the south, there was some kind of a canal. It flowed from a river which ran to the north just outside the compound's west wall. There was a pumphouse where they intersected. One POW swore that it had a skull and cross-bones on it, but others passed it off as an odd mud smear, the kind of image clouds seem to form. It didn't make any sense; it was incongruous for the North Vietnamese to be painting a skull and crossbones on anything.

The winters in Son Tay were the hardest. The camp was primitive, cold, and damp. Very damp. The Song Con River flowed by just outside the compound wall, often so high that the compound came near to flooding. Medical care was cruelly lacking and the prisoners were weak from years of malnutrition and torture.

Wes Schierman developed asthma problems. They became so severe in the winter of 1969 that he almost died. He would gasp for breath, sitting up night after night for weeks at a time to keep from smothering in his own phlegm. In April of 1970, even though life in prison had "eased" considerably for most of the prisoners in the preceding six months, Schierman was again fighting for his life. The sound of his gasping for breath filled his fellow prisoners with terror because they were so helpless to aid him. When they asked the guards to get medical help for him, their pleas were ignored. Sometimes Schierman could not even get up enough strength to take the occasional bath the prisoners were allowed and always looked forward to as a luxury. Yet his fellow POWs never heard him complain.

During their long months of captivity, the prisoners at Son Tay thought mainly of going home. Escape, they knew, would be impossible. But the camp's location in an isolated farming area gave them another idea. Rescue. Yet who the hell knew they were there? American reconnaissance aircraft flew over the north almost every week, photographing installations with walls around them. But from the air Son Tay might pass for a barracks, a farm compound, or a schoolyard. The prisoners de-vised a plan.

On work details in the prison yard, the POWs dug ditches and moved rocks under the watchful eyes of the guards. The guards did not notice that the rocks and dirt from the excava-tions were piled up in odd ways. The prisoners were put to work digging a new well, since the old one in the compound had dried up. The POWs dug and dug; they never reached water level, but the dirt was piled up very carefully. Allowed to dry their laundry in the prison yard when the sun came out, the prisoners hung up their clothes in an unusual way.

One day the camp's auxiliary generator, which was located just outside the compound and powered the lights around the compound wall, failed. The North Vietnamese couldn't get it to run. They asked if any of the prisoners knew anything about machinery. It was an excellent opportunity to pick up more intelligence about the area outside the compound. Air Force First Lieutenant Gerald Venanzi persuaded camp authorities he was an expert on generators, and he was taken outside the compound one night to fix it. He fixed it so it would run about only 20 percent of the time. He spent hours with the North Vietnamese debating what else was wrong with it, arguing over how to repair it, and explaining how they could get it running again. But he was always careful to leave out an essential step or two. Finally, they persuaded him to take another look at it; that night Venanzi made his second reconnaissance outside Son Tay, this time with new instructions. He also fixed the generator so it would *never* run again.

TWO

"Polar Circle"

Fort Belvoir, Virginia

Fifteen miles from the White House, on the Potomac River just south of Mount Vernon, Air Force Technical Sergeant Norval Clinebell and his bosses were sure he had made a "breakthrough." They were working their usual Saturday morning stint in the heavily secured, isolated compound that housed the Air Force's 1127th Field Activities Group at Fort Belvoir, Virginia. Not many people knew what went on inside the high chain-link fences that sealed the 1127th off from the Army Engineer Center in the northern part of the sprawling, 9,237-acre post. A big 5- by 8-foot sign inside the gate said only, "1127th USAF FAG." One of the unit's men used to complain about it: "My Army friends keep asking why we need such a big cage to hold the 1,127th queer caught in the Air Force."

The 1127th was, in fact, an "oddball" unit, a composite of special intelligence groups who "conducted worldwide operations to collect intelligence from human sources." The men of the 1127th were "con artists." Their job was to get people to talk—Russian defectors, North Vietnamese soldiers taken prisoner in South Vietnam, anyone who might have information and was willing to "sing." In addition, the 1127th processed intelligence on American prisoners of war and designed programs to help downed airmen evade capture or escape from prison. The latter work went on in a small section called the Evasion and Escape Branch. Two of its members had been prisoners themselves. Personnel assigned to the branch were dedicated to their work, good at it—and frustrated by it. They knew there were more than 462 American POWs in Southeast Asia, 80 percent of them held captive in North Vietnam. Over half of the POWs had been imprisoned over 2,000 days, longer than any serviceman had ever spent in captivity in any war in America's history. Some, they knew, had died; others were near death, and all the POWs were being held in conditions so primitive and brutal that they sometimes wondered if any of them would return home sane.

The date was Saturday, May 9, 1970. Twelve days before, President Nixon had launched the invasion of Cambodia. It was not going well; about all the White House could announce was the discovery of 65 tons of rice in the Fish Hook area of the SVN/Cambodian border. Earlier that week, four students at Kent State University had been shot to death by National Guardsmen called out to control a campus protest against the war; 11 others had been wounded. The day before, 75,000 protesters had demonstrated at the White House, which the Secret Service decided to seal off by a bumper-to-bumper ring of buses borrowed from the D.C. Transit Company. Early that Saturday morning, a sleepless President drove to the Lincoln Memorial to mingle with the protesters, mostly college students, in a gloomy, drizzling rain. He talked with them about football, then the war. Their "dialogue" lasted almost an hour. Later that day, two of Henry Kissinger's deputies mounted their own protest by resigning from the National Security Council staff.

The invasion of Cambodia had torn America apart. About the only issue the country wasn't divided on was the POWs and MIAs. Everyone wanted them home. But there wasn't much prospect of that happening soon. In Paris, the North Vietnamese had made it clear that the prisoners were hostages. They would be released only when the United States pulled all of its forces out of Vietnam. President Nixon's withdrawal program was under way, but there were still 428,000 American servicemen in Southeast Asia. Nine hundred and twenty of them would be dead before the month of May was out, 4,291 others wounded in action, about 20 taken prisoner; 25 more would be missing in action.

Information on where those prisoners were held, and where the missing might show up, had the Pentagon's highest intelligence priority and became one of the nation's top ten Key Intelligence Questions. The intelligence community had gathered reams of "input" from a variety of sources, but useful, "hard" information was difficult to come by. One of the steps taken early in the war was to photograph regularly every installation in North Vietnam with a wall around it. That made a sizable target list, however, in a country where almost every family raised pigs and chickens and didn't want them running loose in the middle of a nation short on food, and where almost every school had its own closed-in compound.

There were, of course, many sources of intelligence besides reconnaissance photographs: enemy propaganda films, news releases and broadcasts; and the interrogation of defectors and enemy prisoners of war, which had proved especially valuable when a captured North Vietnamese turned out to have a brother or cousin or brother-in-law who was a guard in one of the POW camps. In one case, a previously unknown prisoner, Air Force Captain Willis E. Forby, had been positively identified when a North Vietnamese soldier taken captive in the south revealed that he had captured Forby when he was shot down early in the war, September 20, 1965. Sometimes information came from foreign visitors to North Vietnam or members of American protest movements allowed to visit there. Other tidbits were passed along, often purposefully gathered for the United States, by military attachés and diplomats stationed in Hanoi from friendly and neutral nations—and occasionally, even from an unfriendly one. Another source was mail from the POWs themselves, when they were allowed to write those cruelly short and uninformative letters home. Only about half the prisoners were being given that privilege, however. Finally, there were the nine Air Force and Navy prisoners who had been released by North Vietnam after several months to several years of captivity. But that was a rare occurrence; and in mid-1970, almost a year had passed since the last three came home: Apprentice Seaman Douglas B. Hegdahl, Navy Lieutenant Robert F. Frishmann, and Air Force First Lieutenant Wesley L. Rumble, had been released.

Late in 1966, efforts had begun in earnest to exploit every such source of intelligence on a systematic basis. At that time, the Air Force alone had 264 men down in North Vietnam, but only 29 of them were known to be POWs, including one man shot down over the South China Sea who was being held prisoner in China. The other 235 were "missing in action." North Vietnam announced very few captures. It had become evident that Vietnam was going to be a repeat of Korea, with the enemy refusing to make systematic reports on the identity, location, and treatment of its American prisoners as required by the accords of the Geneva Convention, which, contrary to many impressions, North Vietnam had signed in 1959.

In October of 1966, at the urging of the Air Force Casualty Branch, a small, informal meeting of intelligence specialists and casualty representatives from all of the services took place, its purpose to find new ways to collect POW and MIA data, and better ways to analyze it. There were two immediate goals: one was to identify those held prisoner so that the concern and anguish of their families could be somewhat alleviated. The other was to locate the POW camps and place them "off limits" to Air Force and Navy planners who were targeting the "Rolling Thunder" bombing campaign in the north. Yet while every effort was made to avoid hitting known camps, the campaign itself made a grim contribution to the POW problem. In November of 1966, for instance, 7,257 planes had bombed North Vietnam with 11,142 tons of explosives. Over 20 of the planes never made it back.

The meetings quickly grew both in size and frequency, from "as needed" to at least weekly. The group normally met every Friday morning, at first in the Air Force's Pentagon personnel center, then in more formal sessions chaired by the Central Intelligence Agency (CIA). By August of 1967, it was formally chartered as the "Interagency Prisoner of War Intelligence Committee"—IPWIC—and headed by the Defense Intelligence Agency (DIA). At times the meetings included as many as 20 or 25 people, representatives from each of the military services (Belvoir's odd Air Force unit, the 1127th, for instance, had two full-time members, sometimes more), the CIA and the DIA. The State Department, the FBI, the Secret Service—and even the Treasury Department and the United States Post Office participated when required. Treasury, for example, was called in when a few POW wives began getting letters asking, "Please send me $20 so I can buy some fruit" or "$50 for vegetables." When they tried to send the money, they were told it was illegal. Neither North Vietnam nor the United States had formally declared war, but North Vietnam was an "enemy" and the Foreign Assets Control Regulations administered by the Treasury Department prohibited "all unlicensed transactions by Americans with North Vietnam," including payment of any kind for "accommodations or for services." Treasury and the

Post Office finally found a way for the wives to get international postal money orders to some of the prisoners, but it took special approval from Congress. A Marine Corps officer who was a member of IPWIC was nevertheless against having the money sent. At one meeting, he protested, "I'm damned if we'll let anyone send money to help North Vietnam's war effort." He calmed down when an Air Force member suggested that if $50 would help North Vietnam win, the war had already been lost.

The Post Office also worked with international postal authorities on ways to expedite POW mail to and from Hanoi. But as of mid-1970, almost three-quarters of the mail reaching the POWs got to them not through postal channels, but was hand-carried by peace activist Cora Weiss, cochairman of the Committee of Liaison with Families of Servicemen Detained in North Vietnam. The last mail received *from* the POWs by post had arrived from Hanoi on May 13; from then on, Hanoi saw to it that Cora Weiss was the *only* conduit through which the families could communicate.

Gradually, as IPWIC spelled out new "collection requirements" and priorities and took a closer look at the data it already had, its work began to pay off. Late in 1968, for instance, information from enemy prisoners, visitors to Hanoi, and the first three American POWs to be released by North Vietnam indicated that Americans were being held in a "walled installation" located "approximately 30 miles west of Hanoi." At that time, four POW camps in the north had been located and identified. Three were in Hanoi proper; the fourth was 25 miles to the west. The physical characteristics of the fourth camp, however, did not match the rough description of the camp supposedly five miles farther west. Nor did the presence of "walls" offer much help. Practically every walled installation in the north deemed capable of holding POWs had been photographed; many of them were located in an area that could be loosely described as "approximately 30 miles west of Hanoi."

Members of IPWIC worked hard to pin that camp down. But the DIA had an impossible load of other intelligence requirements, from new Russian intercontinental ballistic missile sites to new Soviet ballistic missile submarines, from new tank parks in East Germany to Chinese atomic bomb tests in Sinkiang Province, from increased construction of Egyptian air defenses opposite the Suez Canal to Viet Cong rice caches in

Cambodia. For the DIA's senior member of IPWIC, it was only one of two dozen other top-priority assignments.

Nor did he always have the best help in the world. Both the DIA and the CIA were almost suffocated by intelligence data, but it was the men who collected it, not the men who analyzed it, who were getting promoted. Blocked from promotion in jobs analyzing data, many of the bright, senior civilians in the intelligence community spent a lot of time working their way into transfers to posts where they could collect it—and, they hoped, a promotion as well. The net result, as a senior staff member of the National Security Council would sum it up, was that "95 percent of the U.S. intelligence effort has been on collection, and only 5 percent on analysis and production."

New civilian talent shied away from the intelligence agencies, which simply could not compete with the rest of the federal government in enticing aboard the "big brains" who might bust open the intelligence logjam. The DIA, for example, had 3,088 civil service employees, but only 15 "supergrades." The 776-man National Highway Traffic Safety Administration, in contrast, had 36 supergrade billets. A job as an intelligence analyst—or "spook"—was a dead end.

On the military side, the situation was equally bad. Not until 1973 would a single Army colonel or Navy captain assigned to the DIA be selected for promotion to general or admiral. The DIA was a graveyard. It was an environment that was hardly conducive to producing brilliant analysis. Notwithstanding the dedication of some very hardworking people, pinpointing the location of North Vietnam's POW camps suffered accordingly.

At Fort Belvoir, a few men in the 1127th Field Activities Group devoted almost full-time to unraveling the reams of raw data from the DIA and the CIA. Finally, on May 9, 1970, Norv Clinebell was pretty sure he had discovered something "hot" on that POW camp west of Hanoi. He was an intelligence technical specialist, an old hand at the game who had worked in Laos long before overt American operations began there. Just under six feet tall, slightly overweight with receding blond hair, close to retirement, Clinebell was known for his patience even when things didn't fit together right away. His work was like trying to cook a three-star French dinner out of garbage, but he stuck to it. Late in April, he had started to assemble various tidbits of information, both old and new. There were *two* camps west of Hanoi. He was sure of it. And within a short time he had identified one of them; it was at Ap Lo, 31 miles west of North Vietnam's capital. But a close comparison of old and new reconnaissance photos of the area revealed much more, Clinebell thought. He went to his boss, Colonel George J. Iles, and asked if he could "bounce some ideas" off him.

Iles headed the 1127th's Programs Division, of which the Evasion and Escape Branch was part. He had more than an average interest in his work: he had been a POW himself in World War II, shot down over Italy in a P-51 Mustang. Together Iles and Clinebell laid out the bits and pieces, everything they knew, the "total take" from the intelligence community—and their own latest, if small, collection of raw data. They came up with an almost simultaneous discovery.

The jigsaw puzzle seemed to fit. If their analysis was correct, there were *two* POW camps west of Hanoi: the one at Ap Lo, and another nearby in a walled compound just west of the provincial capital called Son Tay. Until Clinebell compared old and new reconnaissance photos of the area, no one had noticed that the Son Tay compound was being enlarged; there was a new wall and a new guard tower in the northwest corner. Through an ingenious code spelled out in hieroglyphics on the ground, someone in that camp had revealed that there were 55 prisoners at Son Tay. Six of them were calling for an urgent rescue mission; they had devised a desperate plan that, Iles and Clinebell felt, might just work—if it was acted upon quickly.

Iles and Clinebell asked two men for their assessment. One was Colonel Rudolph C. Koller, the 1127th's commander; the other was Claude Watkins, a retired Air Force master sergeant back in service as a civilian intelligence specialist in Iles's Evasion and Escape Branch. Both Watkins and Iles were members of IPWIC. Like Iles, Watkins was inordinately interested in his work. He had been a prisoner of war in World War II for 15 months, a B-17 waist gunner shot down in a raid over Germany. He had spent from 1950 until that May 9, 1970, meeting, with the exception of one year, totally immersed in POW affairs. Koller, a tall, jovial, crew-cut officer, also cared deeply about the POWs. Many were fellow airmen, not just statistics in an intelligence report. Thus, Koller and his men were much more personally involved with the POWs than higher echelon intelligence analysts from the CIA and the DIA. It was not surprising that when the White House had asked for a full POW "update," the 1127th was picked to give it, not the DIA or the CIA. By December of 1972, Watkins was to give one briefing, "Captivity in Southeast Asia," 364 times in all parts of the world. It was updated every week. American peace negotiators in Paris thought it was "gangbusters."

Koller had given men like Iles and Clinebell the license they needed to do a near-impossible job with imagination. And when they came to him with information about Son Tay—and the request for an urgent rescue mission—he went to the telephone, called the Pentagon, and asked Major General Rockly "Rocky" Triantafellu, Air Force Assistant Chief of Staff for Intelligence, if they could meet with him early the next morning. He had something "hot."

Claude Watkins worked late that night putting together a briefing and making the necessary "flip charts" to spell out what Clinebell and Iles had unraveled. He was excited.

Son Tay—located on the Song Con River where it flows into the Red River as it bends east toward Hanoi—had been identified a year and a half earlier as the possible location of a prison compound. A North Vietnamese soldier captured near the Demilitarized Zone had revealed that his battalion had bivouacked near the site on its way south. Sent to draw water for his platoon from a well outside the compound, he had seen several prisoners working in the open courtyard. He was "pretty sure," but not positive, that they were Americans. Now Iles and Clinebell had come up with reconnaissance photos of Son Tay that showed it must be a *very* important place: there was a *brassiere* hanging on a clothesline just outside the compound's east wall, one of them noticed under a magnifying glass. Vietnamese women are not very big breasted, and most of them were far too poor to afford a brassiere in any case. "Somebody *really* important lives here," they concluded. Scrutinizing every inch of the film, they soon realized there was new construction at Son Tay. Watkins also noticed he had never seen POW uniforms hung up to dry inside a compound the way those in Son Tay were arranged. Some were spread on the ground and seemed to spell out the code words for "SAR"—a search and rescue mission. It also seemed as if some POWs had tromped out the letter "K" in the dirt in one corner of the compound. "K" was a code letter for "Come get us."

There was more. Clinebell had unraveled a message the prisoners had worked at for months to get back to the States through a new version of their "tap code." It called for the rescue of six POWs—fast. The prisoners had managed to communicate where the pickup should be made, a spot just far enough from the compound to be workable. They had even made known who the six men were; one of them was in "pretty bad shape."

"Jesus," Watkins thought as he worked on his briefing charts that night at his home in Reston, Virginia, "someone really worked to spell it all out." Then the thought struck him, "God, what if they've been caught?" He drank a beer with his wife, Millie, and asked her to wake him up no later than six the next morning. And would she explain to their son, Kelley, that they would have to postpone working on that go-kart? It might be a long day.

It was.

Rocky Triantafellu was convinced the 1127th Field Activities Group had something. As soon as he saw how positively the reconnaissance photos and the hieroglyphics designed around the tap code seemed to confirm the request for a pickup, he called in other specialists. "Christ knows, we've waited long enough for something like this," he told Koller. Triantafellu could hardly believe how clearly the prisoners had drawn the Pentagon a veritable road map for a daring and desperate escape. Son Tay was located approximately eight miles northeast of Mount Ba Vi in the foothills approaching Laos. Objects arranged by the POWs in the compound suggested an arrow pointing to the west and the number "8." The prisoners were calling for a pickup at Ba Vi. Clinebell had speculated that work parties from the camp were sent there on certain days of the week, perhaps to chop hardwood for the camp's kitchen fires, perhaps for timber for whatever was being built inside the compound. Triantafellu was convinced the rescue would work. He asked Koller to call Arlington Hall Station, the DIA's annex three miles from the Pentagon. He wanted Navy Captain John S. "Spots" Harris and some of his POW specialists to hear the briefing. Harris headed IPWIC. Meanwhile, Koller was told to begin work on a rescue plan.

Harris brought his team to Triantafellu's Pentagon office

early on Monday, May 11. Some of them weren't impressed, a few of the participants recall. One told the Air Force team it was "all a bunch of shit." He conceded that there was a camp near Son Tay and that Clinebell had a "hard lock" on 55 prisoners in it. But he thought that the Air Force interpretation of a bunch of photographs and that odd message calling for a rescue was a "pile of crap."

Nevertheless, the Air Force team was "positive" it was right. Triantafellu and Koller were convinced that a rescue should be attempted. They were concerned about the POWs at Son Tay. Why had the North Vietnamese put them in such a remote, isolated camp? Why weren't they locked up in downtown Hanoi, where most of the prisoners were known to be held? Triantafellu wondered if these were the "basket cases"—the prisoners who were most seriously injured, the most tortured, or ones who had gone insane. That would explain why the North Vietnamese wanted them out of Hanoi, far out. That way, there would be no risk of a visiting peace delegation seeing them. Triantafellu felt that if peace activists like Ramsey Clark or Jane Fonda or Cora Weiss ever saw how badly some POWs had been treated, they might "turn around 180 degrees." All they saw were the "showcase" prisoners, men who had been beaten into submission before their visits, or the few POWs who were cooperating to save their own hides—and sanity. North Vietnam would go to any length, Triantafellu knew, to keep those peace delegations from realizing how few prisoners were getting such "humane" treatment and what torture the others were still enduring.

But finding prisoners was Triantafellu's job; *rescuing* them was someone else's. He decided to take Koller, Iles, and Watkins to Room 4D1062 to see Brigadier General James R. Allen, Deputy Director for Plans and Policy under the Air Force Deputy Chief of Staff for Plans and Operations. Allen was impressed by their evidence; some of the participants recall that he got "real excited," calling in one of his key planners for covert operations, Colonel Norman Frisbie. After the meeting, Allen told Frisbie to "go hide somewhere for a week" with another planner, Lieutenant Colonel Lawrence Ropka, Jr., and come up with a solution for getting inside Son Tay Prison without killing all of the POWs. Allen wanted to go for all the prisoners there, not for just the handful that might make it to

Mount Ba Vi. Tall, lean, serious, with a long face and sense of humor that didn't often show, Allen was known as a "doer, not a ration-drawer." He was not the kind of general who needed a big staff study to prod him into gear, but a major rescue operation deep into North Vietnam was "way out" of his authority. Impatient with the rituals and delays of bureaucracy, Allen asked his boss, Lieutenant General Russell E. Dougherty, for permission to take the issue up with a small group in the Office of the Joint Chiefs of Staff. On Monday, the 25th of May, he took Koller, Iles, and Watkins downstairs to a little-known office in the Pentagon basement, Room 1E962.

SACSA

Not many of the 27,840 people who worked at the Pentagon in 1970 knew what the acronym "SACSA" meant. Fewer still had any inkling of what the group really did. It was headquartered in the prestigious "E" ring just beneath the office of the Chairman, Joint Chiefs of Staff. Five United States Capitol Buildings could rest comfortably within the Pentagon's walls and two and a half Washington Monuments could be stretched end to end across the same space, so proximity to the "E" ring executives was an important indication of where an individual or office stood in the military hierarchy's "pecking order." SACSA stood pretty close to the top.

SACSA was Donald D. Blackburn, a sandy-haired, 6-foot, 180-pound Army brigadier general, the "Special Assistant for Counterinsurgency and Special Activities" to the Chairman, Joint Chiefs of Staff. He looked far younger than his fifty-three years, and after greeting Allen, Koller, Iles, and Watkins that Monday morning, he picked up the telephone to ask a fifth man to join them from down the hall. This was Army Colonel E. E. "Ed" Mayer, a tall, stocky North Dakota–born clandestine operator who looked like an affable, mild-mannered Midwestern farmer, but one whose patience should not be tested unnecessarily. There was something in his bearing that hinted he could break the average man in two with a sudden whack of his forearm. Mayer headed a small group in SACSA called the Special Operations Division. His work never made the newspapers; for one thing, it took far more than a Top Secret or "Q" clearance to find out what Special Operations did.

The five men sat down around a conference table. Then Allen asked Watkins and Iles to go through the briefing they had prepared for General Triantafellu, showing how the 1127th had positively identified prison compounds at both Ap Lo and Son Tay, and how they had pieced together the urgent request to rescue six prisoners held captive at Son Tay.

The briefing over, Allen told the group that he thought the men could be rescued. He wanted to know if Blackburn could arrange for a clandestine agent to be put into the area. Contrary to many impressions, agents in most of North Vietnam were a military responsibility, not the CIA's, and their missions were "laid on" and controlled by SACSA. Early in the sixties, President Lyndon Johnson had limited the CIA's coverage to the western part of North Vietnam within 15 miles of the Laotian border. The CIA had a number of operating sites there and some coverage into North Vietnam was a natural fallout. But organizing the rescue would be largely the responsibility of SACSA.

One plan seemed simple. Rescue helicopters with a small Army Special Forces team would stand by only 105 miles away from Son Tay at one of the CIA's border stations in northern Laos. Meanwhile, the SACSA agent would infiltrate the area around Mount Ba Vi, find out when and how often the work party from Son Tay was there (if that's how the prisoners were getting to Mount Ba Vi), and when the situation "looked propitious," call in a rescue team. He could signal for a rescue on a small radio that Allen was pretty sure the North Vietnamese couldn't monitor. Two beeps would mean: "Come get us. They're here." One beep: "Come get me. They ain't here. I've been watching a week and they're not around." If he signaled for helicopters to come in and bring some prisoners out, Allen said, the whole operation would come off very quickly: less than half an hour from "Beep-beep" to when six American prisoners of war would be in friendly hands and on their way to an American base in Thailand.

Several factors seemed to favor the operation. North Vietnamese radar might pick up the helicopters coming in from Laos, but the enemy air defense system would have little time to react. Mount Ba Vi was in a remote area of the country, outside the heavy flak coverage, and the main threat to either the prisoners or the rescue force would be small-arms fire from guards accompanying the work party. The agent could help mark a landing zone for the helicopters, alert the prisoners that a pickup was imminent, and perhaps even help overcome the guards if necessary.

Allen and Blackburn discussed the idea in more detail. If the operation succeeded, six POWs could be brought back to the United States within a week, two at the most. And besides recovering six Americans who obviously needed help fast, they felt the rescue would pay off in several other ways at this juncture in the war. The Paris peace talks were stalemated; the POWs were North Vietnam's strongest bargaining chip. Rescuing some of them would focus even stronger world attention on the POW/MIA tragedy—and pressure North Vietnam to negotiate more seriously toward release of the others. Unlike the nine POWs released earlier by North Vietnam, the rescued POWs might be permitted to talk publicly about conditions of their captivity. Few of the POWs whom the North Vietnamese had so far released had been badly treated, although they reported knowing that others were undergoing brutal torture, some to the point of death. Coming from a rescued prisoner instead of a released one, news of North Vietnamese brutality would have a tremendous impact. World opinion might then persuade North Vietnam to treat the prisoners more humanely.

But Allen's idea of busting into Son Tay and bringing out *all* the prisoners appealed to Blackburn and Mayer even more. Frisbie's quick study had even suggested the possibility of landing one helicopter inside the compound. Blackburn asked to look at the aerial reconnaissance photos again. The two camps Koller's men had identified were in isolated parts of North Vietnam and looked like the most vulnerable of any POW camps located so far. Perhaps they could hit both Son Tay and Ap Lo in the same raid.

But a larger rescue operation posed some real, big problems. Even if Blackburn thought one was feasible, he pointed out, it was out of his purview. It was something the Joint Chiefs of Staff would have to decide. During World War II, 29 years earlier, a regimental or division commander could have okayed such a mission on the spot. But this was the Vietnam War: the decision to attempt to rescue American prisoners in North Vietnam would probably have to be made in the Oval Office of the White House, 9,500 miles from the battle zone.

Blackburn told Allen he would talk to the Chairman of the Joint Chiefs of Staff personally. He would get back to Allen just as soon as possible, the next morning at the latest.

Claude Watkins left the room disappointed. He too wanted to get more than six prisoners back—but he had a vague sinking feeling that a larger rescue operation would "slow things up."

Watkins was right. There were several problems connected with the rescue plan that Blackburn and Mayer couldn't talk about. Chief among them were the effects of the bombing halt over all of North Vietnam ordered by President Johnson in 1968. The military no longer had the authority to mount special operations or agent "insertions." Its authority was now limited to mounting immediate rescue attempts if a reconnaissance plane or one of its armed escorts was shot down. President Johnson had also forbidden any missions to resupply the CAS teams ("Controlled American Sources," as the agents were known) that were operating in North Vietnam at the time. Nine teams, 45 carefully trained Vietnamese, had been simply abandoned. For months, about all they were told in guarded radio messages was to "hang in there"; there were "problems with resupply," but they were being "worked out." It was one of the biggest, most secret tragedies of the Vietnam War. Reconnaissance flights and propaganda leaflet drops were still being flown over the north regularly—but not one CAS resupply mission. In time, some of the men had been picked up by the North Vietnamese; a few had defected; others had simply died, more than a few of outright starvation. Ironically, one of the last CAS teams to remain in contact had set up a "safe site" on Mount Ba Vi, guarded for the U.S. by North Vietnamese soldiers who were, in effect, "double-dipping." It was one of several hilltops in Laos and North Vietnam which aircrews were told to try to reach, if shot down, so they could be "exfiltrated." Just a few months before Allen's visit, SACSA finally lost contact with the CAS team there.

Blackburn and Mayer had pointed out, before the meeting with Allen and his men broke up, that even if SACSA could get an agent request approved now, insertion would be difficult and the timing uncertain. Often CAS agents were parachuted into the north in conjunction with search and rescue missions; that way, the planes flying them in wouldn't attract undue attention. But no air strikes were being flown over North Vietnam in May of 1970, planes weren't being shot down, and there were no SAR missions to use for a cover. They couldn't point out, of course, that recruiting new CAS teams had become very difficult since President Johnson left the last nine of them "twisting in the wind."

Moreover, Blackburn and Mayer weren't sure if the six POWs expected to reach Mount Ba Vi on a work detail or after escaping from Son Tay. They were very leery of attempted POW escapes. They knew of six such attempts. All had failed. Some of the POWs had been killed trying to escape; all of the others had been recaptured, and some of them later tortured. One had apparently been tortured to death. In some cases, Mayer had worked hard to foil escapes which, he had learned, the prisoners were planning. Several POWs got word out of one camp, for instance, that they would "bust out" in two months, steal a boat or make a raft, and float down the Red River at night toward Haiphong Harbor. They had devised signals so they could be picked up en route. Ed Mayer agonized over that one, but finally got a message into the camp telling the POWs not to try: the Red River had just been mined.

Without detailing all of these problems, Blackburn and Mayer had agreed with Allen that something should be done. And Blackburn was the man who could do it. Brigadier generals didn't normally pick up the telephone and ask to see General Earle G. Wheeler, the Chairman of the Joint Chiefs of Staff. But as SACSA, Blackburn had special access when he needed it; if he had something "hot," he could get in to see Wheeler without going "through channels." It was a ticket he didn't punch unless necessary. On May 25, however, he and Mayer left his office soon after Allen had departed and walked upstairs to Room 2E873. There, 30 yards off the Pentagon's imposing River Entrance, Blackburn asked the colonel who guarded the chairman's "inner sanctum" to see General Wheeler on a priority matter. They were admitted immediately.

In Wheeler's office, Blackburn and Mayer told the chairman in three or four minutes of the new prisoner intelligence that the group at Fort Belvoir had put together. Then they described the possibility of inserting an agent and launching a rescue mission to pick up six POWs on Mount Ba Vi. But, they pointed out, if the rescue was hastily mounted and botched, it would compromise chances of a follow-up mission to later rescue the other prisoners. Blackburn and Mayer then pitched Allen's alternative plan: a larger, more carefully planned raid to rescue all of the prisoners at Son Tay, perhaps even those at Ap Lo.

"Jesus Christ, Don," Wheeler said, "how many battalions is this going to take?" His reaction was a natural one. The last thing "Bus" Wheeler needed on May 25, 1970, hard on the heels of President Nixon's controversial Cambodian "incursion," was an invasion of North Vietnam. Moreover, at this juncture in the war, American combat deaths in Vietnam were still averaging over 500 a month. May 1970 would be a particularly bad month: 754 Americans were to die in hostile action, and another 166 would be dead from other causes. The Army's strategic reserve was down to its lowest number of deployable battalions since World War II.

Wheeler's question didn't bother Blackburn. He knew that the chairman was one of SACSA's strongest supporters. A summary compiled soon after Wheeler left office would show that close to a third of all the actions he had recommended to the Secretary of Defense for approval involved "special operations" handled through SACSA channels. During the McNamara era, however, the Secretary of Defense had not even responded to about 25 percent of the proposals.

Blackburn told the chairman he wasn't thinking in terms of battalions, but of a small group of Special Forces volunteers. With that reassurance, Wheeler asked Blackburn to think about it for a while, and get back to him as soon as possible with a recommendation. But there was another problem. Wheeler had been Chairman of the Joint Chiefs since mid-1964, just before the Tonkin Gulf incident. Worn by the war and his own ill health, he was just weeks away from retirement. He wanted Blackburn to brief his successor, Admiral Thomas H. Moorer, before the planning went too far.

With a green light from Wheeler, Blackburn and Mayer swung into action. They passed the word to only a few people that the chairman had asked for a high-priority feasibility study of a sensitive special operation. But first, they needed more intelligence about North Vietnam's POW camps. They went to see two senior general officers at the DIA, who "got the picture" quickly. The next day, Tuesday, May 26, Blackburn and Mayer were told that "DIA will handle the intelligence briefings." The operation was too important and sensitive to be based solely upon intelligence input from any one service or agency, and the DIA had some unique intelligence sources not available to the 1127th or Allen.

The second "Jesus Christ, Don," came the next day. On Wednesday, May 27, Blackburn went to his superior, Air Force Lieutenant General John Vogt, the Joint Chiefs' Director of Operations, or J-3, and told him that he had a "requirement" to put together a quick, prisoner-rescue feasibility study for the chairman. "Jesus Christ, Don," Vogt exploded. "Don't you ever tell your own boss what's going on?"

Blackburn wasn't the type of officer who tried to cultivate "Brownie points" by running in to his superiors with tidbits of information they didn't need at the time; he preferred to fill them in after the groundwork had been laid. But some of his superiors felt that he just didn't like bosses and operated "solo" a bit too often. It was a natural fallout of Blackburn's determination to keep his "access lists" small. The more people who knew about his kind of work, the greater the danger of inadvertent leaks or compromises. Just as important, the more people who were privy to his special operations, the more officers he had to "coordinate" with, any one of whom might try to second-guess or object to his proposals. Few senior officers on the Joint Staff understood his brand of warfare; fewer still were enthusiastic about it.

After his initial explosion, Vogt, a burly officer who looked like a Russian Cossack, asked Blackburn how soon he could have a recommendation for Wheeler. Blackburn said he and Mayer would get back to Vogt by Monday, June 1. "There goes Memorial Day weekend," Mayer thought to himself when told of the deadline. Home from Vietnam only since April, he was looking forward to some time with his family, and Memorial Day weekend would be their first real holiday together. As events transpired, he would also spend the July Fourth weekend and Labor Day working on the Son Tay raid.

Blackburn and Mayer were under a whirlwind deadline. For the normal "action officer," working a proposal through the Joint Staff was like swimming through tapioca. But SACSA had a unique license to work free of bureaucratic restraints. And Blackburn was in his element; a POW raid deep into enemy territory was right up his alley.

Donald D. Blackburn was a rare breed of soldier. Florida-born and -educated, he had been sent to the Philippines soon after being commissioned in 1940. When the Japanese attacked Pearl Harbor, he was serving as an adviser to a Filipino infantry battalion in northern Luzon. When Corregidor fell in May of 1942 and the Japanese overran Luzon, he and a handful of other officers refused orders to surrender. Instead, they evaded capture and took to the bush. Blackburn spent the rest of the war helping to organize 20,000 Filipino guerrillas, eventually commanding one of their five regiments. The unit was made up of his favorite warriors, Igorot headhunters.

When American forces landed on northern Luzon on January 9, 1945, 235,000 well-equipped Japanese troops were defending the island. Blackburn's headhunters fought hard behind the lines. By the time the Philippines were declared reconquered, on July 5, 1945, 24 Japanese had died for every American lost. It was a remarkable kill-to-kill ratio since the attacker seldom loses fewer troops than the defender. Nevertheless, Blackburn left the Philippines with nagging questions about the Army's sledgehammer way of winning wars. One incident illustrated why.

There was an important road junction and Japanese airstrip at the town of Aparri. Ordered to seize them, Blackburn and his guerrillas crossed the Cagayan River at night, met only light opposition, and by dawn held both objectives. Blackburn rushed back to his headquarters to radio the good news to his superiors. A message was waiting when he arrived: a battalion combat team of the 11th Airborne Division was going to capture Aparri. "But we have already captured Aparri," Blackburn radioed back.

It was going to be a "public relations attack," he learned with astonishment, complete with photographers. Blackburn and his men were asked to act as "extras" in the farce. According to a later account of the incident:

The guerrillas were bewildered but good-natured about it. They cleaned up the airstrip they had captured, and ruffled up the cogon grass they had trampled to make it look nice and fresh for the photographers. Then they took up positions from which they could defend the airstrip just in case any Japs returned. These positions were carefully concealed so that the paratroops, who had not been informed that they were capturing a town that had already been taken, would not mistake the guerrillas for Japs.*

The next morning, while Blackburn and his men watched from their hiding places, gliders of the 11th Airborne descended on Aparri, hitting the ground in "crunching collisions that left many of the men hurt and scared." Blackburn's guerrillas left their hiding places to give them first aid. Sixty-one paratroopers were seriously injured in the "capture" of Aparri—none of them from bullets.

Blackburn returned to the United States a twenty-nine-year-old full colonel. The Army didn't know what to do with a colonel that young—and, presumably, "inexperienced." It sent him on a six-months' tour of Army schools with former POWs to learn something about the Army. After he had served for a year as provost marshal of the Military District of Washington, the Army decided to turn him into a "normal" soldier and sent him to infantry school. A two-year stint in the Pentagon followed by parachute training finally made him more respectable in Army circles.

In 1950, Blackburn was picked to teach military psychology and leadership at West Point. His department head, Colonel Samuel E. "Ned" Gee, had a unique philosophy: "It takes all kinds of clowns to make an Army work." Blackburn shared that philosophy and peppered his courses with grains of his own theories of combat, challenging his cadets to come up with ways of holding their casualties down, urging them to think unconventionally. More than once in the Philippines, he had found the unorthodox approach very effective.

Late in 1957, Blackburn was sent to Vietnam as senior adviser to the Vietnamese general commanding the Mekong Delta. During his tour there, Hollywood made a movie of

---

Blackburn's Headhunters by Philip Harkins. New York: Norton, 1956.

his exploits in the Philippines. But the writers took so many liberties with the story that when Allied Artists released the film, *Surrender, Hell!,* Blackburn called it the worst movie he'd ever seen. Following his tour in Vietnam, he was given command of the prestigious 77th Special Forces Group at Fort Bragg, North Carolina. When President Kennedy decided early in 1960 to send a covert military advisory group into Laos, Blackburn was told to organize it. The man he picked to head the so-called "White Star" teams was a young lieutenant colonel and World War II Ranger named Arthur D. "Bull" Simons. Blackburn already had Simons in the back of his mind as the man he wanted to lead the prisoner raid into North Vietnam—if he could get it approved.

When Vietnam erupted into a full-blown war in 1965, Blackburn was back in the covert operations business at the Pentagon. He soon returned to Vietnam to command one of the most secret and little-known units in all of Southeast Asia, "SOG." The acronym, the public was told, stood for "Studies and Observations Group." In reality, Blackburn headed the Special Operations Group. It was the OSS of Southeast Asia, a handpicked force of CIA operatives and volunteers from Army Special Forces and Air Force Special Warfare Units as well as Navy SEAL teams. Its crest sported a skull wearing a green beret in front of a burst of black and gold fire, emblematic of SOG's explosive operations. It hardly symbolized a Studies and Observations Group. Blackburn's men were never able to wear the crest on their uniforms, but inside the security of their own compounds, they sported it on beer mugs, drinking cups, ashtrays—and, Blackburn suspected, probably a few jockstraps.

SOG's headquarters in Saigon had about 90 people planning operations for its detachments outside South Vietnam. At Nha Trang, SOG had its own wing-size air detachment. A Navy element at Da Nang ran SOG's private fleet of PT boats. At a place called "Bearcat" near the village of Long Than, airborne and ground units were billeted and prepared for insertion into North Vietnam. There were 350 to 500 people in SOG's operational units, but that was just the American contingent. Another group of 400 to 500 Vietnamese "technical services" troops had been running secret "cross border" operations in Laos and Cambodia before they were combined with SOG to operate in

North Vietnam. One of the few SOG missions ever made public involved the "34 Alpha" PT boat raids on North Vietnamese coastal installations by American-trained South Vietnamese crews. Some historians suggest these raids may have triggered the Gulf of Tonkin incidents in August of 1964.

Blackburn had the ideal job for a colonel, running his private international army, navy, and air force, doing "black" work only a handful of people were cleared to know about, reporting directly to General William C. Westmoreland, the commander of United States forces in Vietnam. He was very much his own boss, and he wanted Bull Simons as one of his deputies and chief troubleshooter. But getting Simons assigned to Vietnam was not easy. Westmoreland had laid down a firm policy: colonels would not be assigned to his headquarters unless they had graduated from one of the war colleges. Simons had not been selected to attend one. His efficiency reports as a leader and combat commander were among the best in the Army, but he was a reserve officer and not rated as "general officer potential." Even with Simons's Ranger combat experience, Special Forces background, and the invaluable knowledge of Southeast Asia and of the North Vietnamese which he had gained while commanding "White Star" teams on two tours in Laos, the Pentagon had to process a special, written exception to Westmoreland's policy before he could join SOG.

Blackburn was also supposed to have, but never got, a CIA deputy. The man who objected to the idea was a covert operations specialist named William Colby. The CIA was going to run its own war, not wage one subordinate to an Army colonel. Later, Colby would head the CIA's controversial "Phoenix" operations in Vietnam and go on to become Director of the CIA.

Blackburn assumed command of SOG in May of 1965. At that juncture in the war, American advisory and combat operations were supposedly limited to South Vietnam. But Blackburn's units ranged over Laos and North Vietnam. Blackburn remembered his own guerrilla days and exhorted his teams not to risk lives needlessly. He never lost an American on the first 45 "cross border" operations that SOG mounted. He always inserted the teams by helicopter late at dusk or first light. The North Vietnamese or Viet Cong could hear them, of course, and usually knew about where the team had been landed, but the helicopters would touch down quickly in two or three places near the objective to mask the actual insertion. To foil the ambushes that the Viet Cong often set up, Blackburn told his men, "After you land, just get lost in the jungle and wait; make *them* hunt for you. When you hear them, *you* can do the ambushing."

He stopped his men from wearing the camouflaged jungle uniforms which the Army Quartermaster Corps had specially designed for such work. It was one of Simons's ideas; the suits blended beautifully with the foliage, but Simons reasoned they were a death sentence if movement was detected. "How many North Vietnamese or Viet Cong do you see dressed in jungle suits?" he reminded his team leaders when they were drawing equipment for a raid or an intelligence-gathering foray.

Experienced as they were, Blackburn's Special Forces teams were understandably nervous about going into "denied areas." Time and again, he had to convince them that it wasn't as dangerous as going on the "main line of resistance" in World War II or Korea. Still, Blackburn was worried about his men being captured; the Communists, he knew, would capitalize in propaganda forums around the world if they could prove that American combat troops were operating outside South Vietnam. So SOG made sure that Blackburn's teams mounted their more sensitive operations with old French maps, or sometimes specially made ones, which distorted South Vietnam's borders by ten kilometers or more. Blackburn reasoned that even with Russia's mapping help, the North Vietnamese could never be sure that it wasn't their maps that were wrong.

One of Blackburn's best "operators" was a young Special Forces master sergeant, Richard J. "Dick" Meadows. "A real-life Jack Armstrong," Meadows captured an entire battery of Russian artillery from a North Vietnamese storage point on one mission he led into Laos. It was being moved to South Vietnam, and was so new that the barrels and breechblocks were still packed with cosmoline preservative to prevent rust during shipment. He brought back the Russian-made fire-control equipment. Westmoreland was ecstatic; it was a first, just the evidence President Johnson needed to convince his critics that the Vietnam conflict was no longer a quiet little internal revolution, but a full-blown war being fought by North Vietnamese troops equipped with Russian supplies. Westmoreland asked to meet Meadows personally and was surprised to find a seasoned soldier who looked in his early twenties. He subsequently awarded Meadows a battlefield commission, the first one of the Vietnam War and one of only two which "Westy" was to award in four years as commander of American forces in Vietnam.

During the time that Blackburn commanded SOG, from May 1965 to May 1966, American troop strength in Southeast Asia soared from 22,000 "advisers" to more than eight divisions and a quarter of a million men. Thus, Westmoreland's attention, and the Pentagon's as well, was focused on the massive buildup of conventional forces, with the sprawling logistical base needed to support them. The military operations which everyone watched most carefully involved equally conventional land combat.

SOG's unorthodox operations never made the headlines, of course, because of their secrecy, but seldom did its work figure in the overall strategic planning for the Vietnamese conflict. Covert operations were too far down on everyone's checklist. Besides, they were closely controlled out of the Pentagon, and Secretary of Defense Robert McNamara seemed content to direct the conflict from Washington; while Westmoreland, critics said, was bent on winning the war with a few good old-fashioned cavalry charges.

Yet some of SOG's operations had a profound impact on the North Vietnamese. In one ingenious operation, SOG's covert specialists shut down North Vietnam's fishing industry for six months. To do it, SOG's PT boats picked up every fisherman they could find in the waters off North Vietnam from Vinh to the DMZ. The roundup went on for weeks. Close to 1,000 fishermen were kidnapped and brought to Phoenix Island near Da Nang, one of SOG's most secret installations. There, they were treated royally, but their captors explained that next time it might be different. Because North Vietnamese political leaders often used fishing boats to send contraband weapons and supplies to the south, it might be necessary to sink the boats, and some innocent fisherman might be killed. Perhaps, they were told, it would be best not to fish for a while, or not to fish too zealously—just enough to provide for each fisherman's immediate family. Then, by way of apology for the inconvenience, all the captured fishermen were given baskets of presents that contained sewing kits, cloth, fresh meat, vegetables, cigarettes, spices, garden seeds, sandals, small garden tools, pocket-knives—and transistor radios tuned to a single, preselected frequency.

After a final sumptuous meal, each fisherman was taken back north and put to sea near his home, floating ashore in the huge wicker baskets which the North Vietnamese used as combination dinghies and life preservers. Sometimes the baskets were so laden with presents they would barely float.

SOG operatives realized that the trick was working when they began picking up "double dippers"—fishermen who had been captured before and were willing to risk being captured again for another boatload of presents. Others, however, took the hint, for in South Vietnam, newly captured North Vietnamese soldiers were heard to complain that their diet had fallen off before the long march south. For one thing, there had been very little fish. They didn't understand it. The South Vietnamese units that had captured them were eating fish; sometimes it was even served to the prisoners. If there were fish in the south, there had to be fish in the north. Why weren't the North Vietnamese people getting any?

Blackburn believed strongly in the efficacy of such unorthodox operations. They cost few casualties, wore on the enemy psychologically, discouraged his soldiers, distracted his attention, diverted his resources, kept him off balance, sapped his energy—and were deniable. Back in Washington after his tour of duty in Vietnam, he urged his Pentagon superiors to try more of them. By May of 1970, the war was past its peak of American involvement. Since April of 1969, 115,482 Americans had left Southeast Asia; "Vietnamization" was well under way. Yet 11,527 Americans had died in Southeast Asia that year, and 3,279 so far in 1970. Hundreds of POWs still languished in prison. On May 20, 1970, Navy Lieutenant Everett Alvarez, Jr., had spent his 2,120th day of captivity in the north; in the south, Major Floyd J. Thompson, an Army Special Forces officer from Ed Mayer's old unit, had been a prisoner for 2,250 days. Blackburn felt something dramatic could be done to get North Vietnam to negotiate seriously toward the return of American prisoners and, just possibly, its own disengagement in the south. Nixon's Cambodian invasion was a conventional military operation which seemed designed to fail; Blackburn wanted to try something on the North Vietnamese that would really "rattle their cage."

What he had in mind was a series of unannounced, unpublicized, unorthodox operations by small forces, like taking out the Lang Chi hydroelectric dam on the Red River, 65 nautical miles northwest of Hanoi. Built with Soviet equipment and technical assistance, it was the showpiece of Soviet–North Vietnamese solidarity, the Aswan Dam of Southeast Asia. The dam was nearing completion. Its three turbogenerators would turn out 108,000 kilowatts of electricity, more power than North Vietnam had ever generated. A platoon of Special Forces men, Blackburn felt, could knock out the generators easily— and get back safely. The operation, moreover, would be "deniable." Hanoi wouldn't dare admit that American forces were operating with impunity in North Vietnam's heartland, able to destroy overnight a key installation that had taken years and close to a billion dollars to build.

Blackburn wanted to raise hell in Hanoi's backyard—just as the Viet Cong had done in the south. He knew that he could knock out that dam. Every soldier who wore a Ranger tab on his shoulder had participated in just such a practice mission as his graduation exercise. Special Forces troops often practiced similar raids, just as they trained from time to time disabling the locks of the Panama Canal. A raid on the Lang Chi Dam, and other operations like it, could become an important bargaining lever, Blackburn felt, and far more effective than the recent "cavalry charge" into Cambodia. But he needed a hunting license.

The Son Tay raid might give him one. If he could show the Joint Chiefs how vulnerable North Vietnam was to the kind of foray he had in mind; if he could get the President's attention; if people would quit asking questions like, "Jesus Christ, how many battalions?" If they would let him go north, in style, just once . . .

The "Tank"

Blackburn and Mayer made their June 1 deadline. At three o'clock that afternoon, they reviewed several rescue alternatives with Vogt and Lieutenant General Donald V. Bennett, Director of the DIA. Their briefing—vugraphs, maps, and all—lasted about 45 minutes. It spelled out several principles for an operation they called "Polar Circle." The code name had been picked at random by a Pentagon computer loaded with thousands of similar phrases. It was the first of three code names the operation would have by the time the raid was launched.

By now, Bennett's analysts had expanded significantly on the breakthrough made by the Air Force's 1127th Field Activities Group. Throughout the preceding week, working with Koller, Iles, Clinebell, and Watkins, DIA's POW and photo-interpretation specialists had been running back and forth to a little-known building in downtown Washington only a few blocks from the Capitol called "Building 213." Even that guarded designation appeared unobtrusively only two or three times in the Department of Defense's entire 437-page-thick telephone directory. It was the National Reconnaissance Office, an agency so secret at the time that merely mentioning its name to anyone without a precise "need to know" could mean years in the federal military prison at Fort Leavenworth, Kansas. There, as well as in a suite at the Pentagon that housed DIA's "Directorate for Collection and Surveillance," and in the specially secured offices of the DIA complex at Arlington Hall Station near the Pentagon, Bennett's analysts had been scrutinizing new high-altitude SR-71 photographs of the countryside west of Hanoi. They weighed their assessment of those photos against other new "input" and confirmed beyond doubt the existence of POW camps at both Son Tay and Ap Lo. Some of their confirmatory information may have come from two unlikely sources. One was South Vietnam's vice premier, Air Marshal Nguyen Cao Ky. He was from the town of Son Tay and still had relatives there. Another was a Saigon entrepreneur known as "Mr. Trinh." A dissident North Vietnamese who had fled to the south, he had once "served time" in Son Tay Prison, and based in Saigon, he occasionally came up with an interesting tidbit of what was going on in the north. It all added up to "pretty certain proof" that 50 or so Americans were being held at Son Tay, perhaps as many as 100, given the way the compound had been enlarged in the past year.

Reviewing rescue possibilities with Vogt and Bennett at the Pentagon that Monday morning, Blackburn and Mayer advised against the original plan to insert an agent in the area who would call for a pickup east of Mount Ba Vi. If the operation was botched, or even if it was successful, it would blow chances of rescuing all of the prisoners held at Son Tay and Ap Lo. Blackburn and Mayer thought that both camps looked isolated enough to be promising targets for a major POW rescue.

One option they suggested involved launching a small, fairly simple raid into Son Tay from CIA sites on the Laotian border, 105 miles away. The sites were close enough so that helicopters would not have to refuel in flight to or from the objective. The monsoon season had set in up north and weather would make in-flight refueling a tricky proposition. Two or three extra helicopters would be standing by in Laos while the raid was under way. They could be called in to take out the extra prisoners, or to mount a search and rescue effort if any assault helicopters were shot down or forced to land inside North Vietnam. The compound at Son Tay looked just big enough to land a small assault helicopter inside the walls; that might permit a rescue party to break into the prisoners' cells before the North Vietnamese could react and hold the prisoners hostage or possibly even shoot them.

Another option would be to launch from Thailand, Blackburn and Mayer said; but that would entail a larger, more complex operation. In-flight refueling would be needed and the timing of the operation would be even more dependent upon precise weather predictions. Meteorologists had told them the first good weather "window" would not come before October. In either case, the raid should probably be made at night, Blackburn said. But weather would be the key factor, and much more meteorological data had to be analyzed to recommend the best combination of weather and moonlight. Weather uncertainties during the present monsoons ruled heavily in his mind against an immediate effort.

There was too much risk of a compromise, Blackburn felt, to launch the raid on a "standby basis" from Laos. He respected the enemy's intelligence system too much. He knew that the North Vietnamese and Viet Cong often had gained advance warning of B-52 raids launched from Guam, 2,400 miles away. It was possible that the North Vietnamese would learn that helicopters had been positioned on the border in northern Laos. They would sense that "something was up" as the helicopters waited for the weather to break, and might alert their warning systems and tighten defenses accordingly. "When you operate against a sophisticated intelligence system," Blackburn said, "don't hedge: be sure."

Blackburn also suggested the possibility of drawing North Vietnam's attention away from Son Tay with a Navy diversionary strike launched over Haiphong from the Tonkin Gulf. In the back of his mind, he wanted an operation that would have a 95 to 97 percent chance of getting in and out without a loss, not a 20 percent chance of jeopardizing the prisoners.

Vogt and Bennett agreed with Blackburn's assessment. The next step was to present their proposal to the Joint Chiefs. Blackburn recommended a two-phase approach. First, he would pull together a "feasibility study group" of about 25 people and be ready to report to the Joint Chiefs on about July 15. Phase two, the raid's detailed planning, training, and execution, would follow. Vogt thought 25 people was too large a group to be "cut in" at this early stage and reduced the study group's size by half. But he wanted the planning to move faster; he changed Blackburn's deadline to June 30.

The following afternoon, Tuesday, June 2, Blackburn and Mayer briefed General Wheeler. He was enthusiastic. "I don't see how *anyone* could say 'No' to this operation," he said. He wanted to know whether his successor, Admiral Moorer, had been "clued in." Blackburn told him that they had briefed Moorer last Friday, the 29th, though in much less detail. Wheeler said he felt it was time to let all of the Joint Chiefs and the Secretary of Defense know that a major POW rescue was being considered. He asked that a JCS briefing be scheduled before the week was out, when he would be leaving for Europe on his last visit to NATO as chairman of the Joint Chiefs of Staff.

On Friday, June 5, at one o'clock in the afternoon, Blackburn and Mayer were in "the Tank," the gold conference room where the Joint Chiefs of Staff met almost daily. It was the first time in nine months at SACSA that Blackburn had been called into the Tank to brief all of the Joint Chiefs. Mayer made the presentation; Blackburn spent most of the time "just watching the faces" of the five senior officers present; together, they wore 19 stars. None of them had much to say, although as the briefing unfolded, Blackburn thought some of the members were looking at him "like I was smoking marijuana." But the "Chiefs" agreed that SACSA should proceed with an in-depth feasibility study of how to bring home all of the prisoners from Son Tay and Ap Lo.

Given the way things were done in the Pentagon, however, Blackburn and Mayer would have to run through their briefing several more times before they could even start the study the Joint Chiefs had just approved. Right after lunch the following Monday, June 8, they briefed the service Deputy Chiefs of Staff for Operations in a session that lasted about an hour. Each DCSOPS (pronounced DESSOPS) had his own special warfare division from which SACSA could draw whatever personnel, equipment, and funds were needed to mount the raid.

The next day Blackburn and Mayer met at CIA headquarters in Langley, Virginia, with the director's Special Assistant for Southeast Asia Matters, George Carver, and his deputy for prisoner-of-war affairs, Richard Elliott. SACSA and Carver's office worked together on an almost daily basis; Elliott had served with Blackburn in SOG and with Mayer on IPWIC. Blackburn asked Carver for someone from the CIA to meet regularly with his feasibility study group. He told Carver that one option still to be considered was launching the raid from "Site 32," a key CIA border post west of the targets. Carver agreed to support the study.

Blackburn had his hunting license. He and Mayer now had the approval, cooperation, and resources they needed to plan a major POW rescue mission. But over two weeks had passed since that mission was first proposed, and it seemed to Blackburn and Mayer that they had spent most of their time "briefing" and "coordinating." In the way that JCS proposals normally proceed, they knew that was pretty fast work. But was it fast enough?

Arlington Hall Station

The first thing Blackburn needed to plan the raid on Son Tay was more intelligence than IPWIC or the 1127th had in their files about prison camps in North Vietnam. It would have to come from the Defense Intelligence Agency, and getting it wouldn't be easy.

The DIA was housed in an 87-acre, fenced-in, well-guarded complex at Arlington Hall Station, Virginia, a residential area that some real estate agents called the "Pentagon's bedroom." DIA's critics suggested it was so named because whenever a crisis broke, the agency was caught napping. When Lieutenant General Donald V. Bennett got word late in 1969 that he would become director of the DIA, the first question he asked himself was, "Am I being brought in to preside over a funeral?"

For half a year, the DIA had functioned without leadership. Its director, an Air Force lieutenant general, had not been in the office for six months; he was a very sick man. DIA's deputy director, a Navy vice admiral, had been in the office only one week between May and October of 1969. The rest of the time, he too, was on sick leave. The number-three man, an Army major general who served as DIA's chief of staff, had retired on May 1, 1969, but had not been replaced. DIA's fourth-ranking officer was an Air Force major general who refused to take over and continued running his own directorate as if the front office were still open for business.

The leadership vacuum wasn't the only problem Bennett inherited. The DIA's reputation stank.

On every new assignment in his twenty-nine-year Army career, Bennett, a 6-foot, 3-inch West Pointer, always seemed to find himself in a cage with a new tiger. As he flew to Washington to be sworn in as the agency's new director, he knew that Vietnam would be in the forefront of his problems. His wavy, short-cropped hair was salt-and-pepper gray when Defense Secretary Melvin R. Laird administered his oath of office as the nation's top military intelligence officer. Within a year, the raid on Son Tay would turn his hair white.

Bennett's first task had been to take inventory of DIA's problems. It proved to be a very long list. Heading it was the agency's lousy reputation. On New Year's Eve of 1968, DIA's copy of an urgent message from the NSA had been misplaced on a clipboard. It warned of intercepting North Korean communications suggesting the spy ship *Pueblo* might be seized. The message was found over three weeks later, after *Pueblo* had been captured and its men imprisoned.

Later that same year, the Soviet invasion of Czechoslovakia caught the intelligence community completely by surprise, despite an obvious seven-week buildup of Soviet troops on the Czech border. The CIA, the NSA, and the National Reconnaissance Office were equally at fault, but the DIA took the brunt of the blame. In fact, the DIA continually found itself in the middle of some dispute within the intelligence community; it usually wound up on the losing end.

The DIA's estimates weren't always the best, but they weren't the worst. They were just the best publicized—probably by the CIA. It was a clever way of deflecting potential criticism of, or too many questions about, the CIA's own work. And the CIA was in the driver's seat. It enjoyed a much closer dialogue with the White House and controlled the ultimate fabric of U.S. intelligence. By law, the CIA director was also the director of Central Intelligence for the President. Theoretically, every member of the intelligence community—the DIA, the CIA, the State Department, the NSA, sometimes the FBI—had an equal say with the CIA in the production of national intelligence. But the CIA jealously guarded its prerogative to "polish" the intelligence sent to the President. What ultimately reached the President's desk was the daily Central Intelligence Bulletin, a document edited by the CIA. Only rarely were dissenting views ever mentioned in it, and then only by footnote.

When disagreements surfaced between the DIA and the CIA, they weren't easily resolved. The CIA had too much clout. CIA Director Richard Helms had the President's ear whenever he needed it. By contrast, until Don Bennett came aboard no director of the DIA had ever sat in on the chairman of the Joint Chiefs of Staff's daily briefing, the early morning session where "no holds were barred."

The DIA had other problems. One was a complicated charter which saddled it with so many conflicts of interest and fractionalized responsibilities that Solomon couldn't have managed the organization. Formed in 1961 at the direction of Robert McNamara, the DIA served two masters. On the civilian side, its director was the secretary of defense's chief intelligence adviser; on the military side, the DIA served in place of a J-2, or intelligence branch, for the Joint Chiefs of Staff. On many occasions the secretary of defense and the Joint Chiefs had diametrically opposed views of what they needed to hear from the head of military intelligence, and the DIA had to come up with an analysis to support both sides of the argument. It was an impossible assignment.

Most of its assignments were. For one thing, except for the military attachés the DIA handled at embassies around the world, the agency was totally dependent upon "input" from other sources: intelligence reports from the Army, Navy, Air Force, or Marine Corps units in the field, or raw data from the CIA, the NSA, and the National Reconnaissance Office. The DIA didn't have *one* man of its own in South Vietnam.

The agency was not lacking in raw data. Far from it. At times there were 1,700 cables a day coming into its "indications center." But the agency had trouble recruiting the talent necessary to sift through that mass of information; other civilian and military departments of the federal government could offer better pay and promotion opportunities. Many of the attachés, for instance, were on their last assignments before retirement. Soon after he took over, Bennett fired 38 of them "outright" for "incompetence."

Yet with all these problems, Bennett knew that there were a host of questions his analysts would have to answer if a raid on Son Tay stood any chance of success. The odds were against the raid. Except in the Civil War, despite scores of tries, there had never been a successful rescue of American prisoners from a POW camp during all the years of America's military history. The closest to success was an armored thrust by General George Patton's 3rd Army into Germany to liberate a camp in which Patton's son-in-law was held captive. The "raid" succeeded, but on their way back to friendly lines the rescuers ran into a German ambush and suffered frightful casualties.

Despite the odds, Bennett was determined to give Blackburn and his planners the sharpest intelligence mosaic the DIA had ever produced; they would need it to bring the Son Tay POWs home. The men he put in charge were DIA's best. One was the agency's Deputy Director for Intelligence, Air Force Major General Richard R. "Dick" Stewart. Aggressive, demanding, a hard worker and tough boss, Stewart was DIA's top intelligence officer. One of his subordinates at the time was Army Colonel Thomas C. Steinhauser, who headed DIA's Operational Intelligence Division. Steinhauser would describe Stewart as a "24-hour-a-day general," a "really hard-nosed sonovabitch" who was determined to put professionalism back into the DIA's product.

Navy Captain Spots Harris, head of DIA's Production Support and Resources Office in Building B at Arlington Hall Station, also joined the DIA team supporting Blackburn's planning syndicate. Harris was more of a bureaucrat or manager than an intelligence expert. But as head of IPWIC, he was a logical focal point to coordinate DIA's work on a prisoner-of-war rescue. He wasn't as flexible or quick to react as some of the Son Tay planners might have liked. But he was a good "front man" and cared very much about the raid. At one time, when he thought the CIA was holding some key intelligence too close to its chest, Harris was said to have told a CIA deputy director: "If I find out you've held back on one dot of information that will help free those prisoners, I'll personally commandeer a cruiser, sail it up the Potomac and blast this fucking building off the map."

Harris arranged for some of DIA's brightest people to work on the Son Tay raid. One of them was a GS-17 named John T. Hughes, a civilian supergrade who was DIA's Deputy Director for Collection and Surveillance. Hughes worked out of Room 2D921 in the Pentagon, overseeing the agency's work with the National Photographic Interpretation Center in "Building 213." A former Army enlisted man, Hughes was "hip" on photo interpretation. He cultivated contacts with firms like Kodak, Hycon, Fairchild Instruments, Perkin-Elmer, and Itek, pushing them to produce better lenses, better cameras, higher-resolution film. He was not just an expert on photo interpretation, but on briefing what the photos meant. He became famous in the intelligence community in 1962 when he uncorked Russia's installation of medium-range ballistic missiles in Cuba.

For the Son Tay raid, Hughes would have even better collection tools at his disposal: Lockheed's "Big Bird" multisensor reconnaissance satellite; Lockheed's SR-71 reconnaissance plane, a black monster that flew three times faster than the speed of sound and higher than 80,000 feet above the earth, a system so complex and sophisticated that over 400 maintenance man-hours were needed to ready it for every hour in the air; Teledyne Ryan's "Buffalo Hunter" low-altitude reconnaissance drones; and lastly McDonnell Douglas's RF-4 reconnaissance planes that flew either at low or high altitude.

Finally, there were weather and communications intelligence experts whom the DIA could call on from within the services or the National Security Agency to support the Son Tay planners. Altogether the DIA team was an impressive one.

It had to be. Without intelligence—accurate intelligence—the raid had no chance for success.

Don Blackburn convened his 15-man feasibility study group at Arlington Hall Station on Wednesday morning, June 10. It met in one of DIA's more secure facilities; nevertheless the room had been "swept" by a counterintelligence team just before the meeting to make sure that it wasn't bugged. Seven of the group's 12 officers were Air Force, three were from the Army, and one each from the Navy and the Marine Corps. Air Force Captain James A. Jacobs and Marine Corps First Lieutenant James A. Brinson represented the DIA. Army Sergeant Major Donald M. Davis was the only noncommissioned officer in the group; and there were two civilian secretaries, Frances L. Earley, a GS-8 from SACSA, and Barbara L. Strosnider, a GS-6 from Air Force intelligence.

Chairing the group's first meeting was Army Colonel William C. "Clint" Norman, a Special Forces veteran from SACSA who, in one officer's words, had been "the best team commander Fort Bragg has ever seen." Soon after the group began meeting however, Norman went on an ordinary leave for almost a month. He had planned it for some time. But Blackburn and Mayer were miffed; when Norman returned, he was no longer on the study group.

Air Force Colonel Norman H. Frisbie took over as the senior member at the group's later meetings. Assigned by the Air Force Plans and Policy Directorate, Frisbie was quick, gregarious, and "a strong runner" when it came to "getting things done." But in the interests of getting the job done, Frisbie took into his confidence a few officers who had no "need to know," and that became a point of irritation for Blackburn and Mayer.

After Clint Norman went on his leave, the Army's senior member of the study group became Lieutenant Colonel Thomas F. Minor, assigned from the DCSOPS Directorate of International and Civic Affairs. As planning for the raid unfolded, Minor was to prove himself invaluable. Slight of build, soft-spoken, prematurely gray, he was a "detail" man more than a broad-gauged planner. Asked to describe him, one officer said unkindly, "He was the messenger to Garcia, the guy who could always get us what we needed from the Army, always charging around the Pentagon. But there were times you had to know which stairwell he was headed for to make sure he didn't get sidetracked en route." The same officer added, "Minor really knew how to make the Army move."

Keith Grimes was stationed at the Air University, Maxwell Air Force Base, Alabama, when he received orders early in June to report to Washington for "extended temporary duty." He was one of the officers whom Blackburn and Mayer had asked the Air Force to detail by name. Grimes was a lieutenant colonel and meteorologist, and they had worked with him often in Southeast Asia. His weather predictions had always been "uncanny." Throughout the months ahead, he was to play an increasingly key role in the raid.

The noncommissioned officer in the group, Army Sergeant Major Donald M. Davis, was detailed from the 6th Special Forces Group at Fort Bragg. Six feet tall, he was the movie image of a "Green Beret" type, lean, mean, hair cropped so short he looked almost bald. Another member detailed from Fort Bragg was Major Boyd F. Morris, assigned from the headquarters of the John F. Kennedy Special Warfare Center. He was to prove himself one of the raid's sharpest planners.

Only one man in the group would actually end up going on the raid, Air Force Lieutenant Colonel Warner A. Britton. A soft-spoken, Alabama-born veteran helicopter pilot with receding gray hair and gold-rimmed glasses, he looked more like a college math professor than someone who had flown into North Vietnam on a host of hairy rescue missions. Detailed from Headquarters, Aerospace Rescue and Recovery Training Center at Elgin Air Force Base in Florida, Britton later was to recruit most of the helicopter crews who would fly into Son Tay.

There were three Air Force intelligence and operations experts in the study group: Lieutenant Colonel Lawrence Ropka, Jr., Major Arthur A. Andraitis, and Captain John H. Knops. They were all pros. Ropka, the group's senior operations officer, was quiet, enthusiastic but subdued, poised and confident. He enjoyed everyone's respect. His cohorts called him an "inspiring guy." If there was "one real brain" in the Son Tay planning group, they said, it was Larry Ropka. Many of the changes that evolved in the original concept and some of the most important operational details of the raid were his ideas. Blackburn later said of him: "He generated complete confidence in whatever he told you"; because "he had gone through the staff procedures mentally, he commanded respect by the composition of his thoughts and their presentation, and you didn't have to look over his shoulder." He was something of a contrast to other planners who were equally imaginative, but more impetuous and whose "wild-ass ideas" gave Blackburn and Mayer occasional heartburn. They felt they could "give Ropka his leash and let him go." Ropka was sincerely convinced that the Son Tay operation *could* go, *should* go, and *would* go.

Andraitis was one of the top planners in Air Force intelligence, assigned from the "Multisensor Branch" of the Imagery and Data Management Division in the Air Force's Directorate of Intelligence Systems. Scholarly, slim, he was described as probably *"the* top photo interpreter in the Washington area."

Knops was young, very junior to the people he was working with daily. An intelligence specialist, he was not shaken by rank. He was "confident and ready to stand up and be counted any time." A "nitty-gritty guy who understood the big picture," he also knew every detail of the North Vietnamese warning system just as if, one member of the group later remarked, he had been sitting in a North Vietnamese radar room and "knew exactly when everyone there took a leak." If you had to get forces into the north undetected, Knops knew how to "thread the needle." Blackburn later described him this way: "A problem solver, he had a knack of foreseeing the problems and difficulties that could 'blow safe entry,' and he came up with logical ways to counter them. He knew that operational perfection on the part of the guys going in there wouldn't do any good if the intelligence behind them wasn't just as good." Blackburn called him "the shining star of the entire intelligence group."

SACSA's feasibility study group met days, nights, and weekends, and throughout its work, Colonel Rudolph Koller and Claude Watkins were called in regularly from Fort Belvoir's 1127th Field Activities Group. One outside civilian also worked closely with the group, but on an ad hoc basis—Dick Elliott from the CIA. Nevertheless, Blackburn and Mayer were concerned by the extent to which the CIA would be involved. First, there was the need for all the intelligence they could get; second, it still looked as if the raid might have to be mounted from one of the agency's border sites in Laos. When Blackburn and Mayer advised General Wheeler of this, he suggested that he sign a letter to Director Richard Helms, asking the CIA's all-out support for the rescue mission. Mayer drafted a short letter, one paragraph long; Wheeler signed it on Friday, June 19. Helms wrote back on June 25. He pledged the agency's full co-operation but said that his people were already working with the feasibility study group. Wheeler, unaware that Blackburn and Mayer had visited the CIA the day before the study group first met, seemed surprised that the agency was so deeply involved in planning such a closely held JCS operation.

The deadline for the preliminary feasibility study—June 30—came and went. Ten more days would go by before the Son Tay mission was again taken up with the Joint Chiefs of Staff. Early July of 1970 was a time of musical chairs for the military hierarchy, full of such distractions as retirement ceremonies, speeches, and welcoming parties. On Wednesday, July 1, Admiral Thomas H. Moorer was succeeded as Chief of Naval Operations by Admiral Elmo R. Zumwalt, Jr., the youngest CNO in naval history, who had been selected over 60 admirals much more senior to him. On that same day, President Nixon signaled Hanoi that America was ready to resume serious peace negotiations by appointing David Bruce, one of the country's most experienced and respected diplomats, to head the United States negotiating team in Paris. On Thursday, July 2, "Bus" Wheeler retired from military service and a grueling six years as Chairman of the Joint Chiefs of Staff during the longest, most divisive, and third-bloodiest foreign war in American history.

The Plan

On Friday afternoon, July 10, Admiral Moorer presided over one of his first meetings of the Joint Chiefs of Staff. A major item on the agenda was Don Blackburn's recommendation for a mission to rescue the American POWs at Son Tay. Briefed about the raid almost a month and a half earlier, Moorer was in favor of it, like his predecessor. He wanted some "focal point, something dramatic," to give the country a different, more positive perspective on the war. Rescuing some of those prisoners—or at least trying to—might do the trick. "If we could get 50 or 60 of those boys back in the United States," he thought, "and let them tell in their own words what had happened to them, it would throw a new light on the character of the North Vietnamese." And he wanted to let the POW families and wives know that the people in the Pentagon were doing more than just wringing their hands.

Moorer, moreover, felt a personal identification with the POWs and MIAs. A few days after Pearl Harbor, 29 years earlier, he too almost became a prisoner of war. He was piloting a two-engine Catalina PBY amphibian patrol plane near a Japanese-held base in the Netherlands East Indies when it was attacked by Japanese fighters. Wounded during the engagement, Moorer managed to ditch his badly damaged and burning aircraft safely downwind. He helped evacuate the crew into life rafts and they were soon spotted by a Philippine freighter. But two hours after the freighter picked them up, it too was sunk by Japanese planes. For the second time in one day, Tom Moorer found himself in a life raft. Determined not to be taken prisoner or let his men die, he improvised a small sail and alternately sailed or rowed the raft to Melville Island off Australia. There, an Australian submarine chaser finally rescued him and his men.

Twenty-six years later, on June 28, 1967, Tom Moorer was listening on the radio to an air strike over North Vietnam when he heard one of his best friends get shot down. The man was Commander William P. Lawrence, commander of VF-143, the F-4 attack squadron of the aircraft carrier *Constellation*. For five years, Bill Lawrence had been Moorer's executive officer and senior aide. Moorer looked upon the five foot, ten inch tall, quiet, young officer from Tennessee almost like a son; Lawrence was the one person Tom Moorer could confide in. It had been six months since Lawrence had left the Pentagon to take command of his attack squadron, and Moorer, flying from Saigon aboard a small Navy passenger-cargo plane to the *Constellation* off Yankee Station in the Gulf of Tonkin, was looking forward to a good, long visit.

His plane was about one hour away from Yankee Station when Moorer's pilot asked if he wanted to listen in on some radio traffic; a large "Alpha Strike" was approaching its target just south of Haiphong. Moorer moved up to the cabin, took over from the copilot, and put on the headphones.

Then he heard Bill Lawrence get shot down. For the next 45

minutes, he listened in silence as a massive rescue effort got under way. It failed. As his plane turned to land on the *Constellation,* Moorer heard a downcast rescue helicopter pilot report that a North Vietnamese gunboat had fished Bill Lawrence out of Haiphong Harbor.

Now, more than three years later, Lawrence was still in a North Vietnamese prison camp, and Moorer heard Blackburn's proposals with more than passing interest. He could listen to a briefer with an intensity that some found unnerving. His dark eyes seemed to focus like two laser beams to dig way inside someone's mind. Yet he could be so calm and impassive that critics would describe him as a military robot—but one who wore his four-star uniform well. In his relaxed moments, Moorer was disarming, a good companion. He took his golf game seriously. He hated to lose, but he was a good loser—at golf; he didn't want to lose those prisoners at Son Tay.

By this time, DIA's "make" on Son Tay was so detailed that 61 prisoners had been identified in the camp, by name and service. There might be more, but Bill Lawrence was definitely not one of them. The DIA had also learned that the camp at Ap Lo was now empty, and Blackburn's original idea of busting both camps was scrapped. But Moorer was concerned; raids could backfire, even if they succeeded. What would success or failure at Son Tay mean to the prisoners like Bill Lawrence who were left behind, he asked? In his own mind, he knew "their treatment was pretty God damn severe" and reasoned "it would be hard to get much worse."

Bennett agreed; the question had worried him, too, and he had asked the CIA for its assessment. The job was given to Ken Brock, Dick Elliott, and William Miller, CIA's top POW specialists. One of the people whose views Brock had sought out was a young Vietnam specialist on the National Security Council staff, Dolf Droge. A towering, craggy-faced giant, Droge had served three tours in Vietnam and Laos with the Agency for International Development. He spoke Vietnamese fluently and probably understood the culture and people better than some of South Vietnam's own leaders. Brock couldn't tell Droge that a raid on Son Tay was being planned, but he asked a hypothetical question: "What would North Vietnam do to the other prisoners *if* one of the camps were raided and a bunch of POWs rescued?" Droge didn't hesitate a second before answering that, succeed or fail, it would be "the greatest thing America could do" for *all* the prisoners. Their treatment, he predicted, would improve dramatically and instantly. Brock sometimes wondered if Dolf Droge was nuts. He didn't buy that optimistic assessment. Instead, he turned in a three- or four-paragraph analysis concluding that there would be a "general tightening of security" for four or five months following a raid, but no reprisals on the prisoners left behind. The North Vietnamese, Brock and his cohorts reasoned, would look for much more specific targets for their hostility than POWs who hadn't concocted the operation.

Another problem which Moorer, Bennett, and Blackburn discussed was whether to keep the raid a secret, even if it succeeded. One of the reasons for the raid was to increase American clout at the Paris peace talks. Why not alert Ambassador David Bruce, the American negotiator in Paris, before the rescue was launched? Then the instant aircraft were on their way back with prisoners, Bruce would be notified and would ask to meet with his North Vietnamese counterparts immediately. "Let's make a deal," he would propose. "You don't want to admit that we got into North Vietnam and rescued 61 prisoners. We could really make headlines telling the world about their bad treatment. But we won't. We won't make any fanfare. We won't even tell about the rescue—*if* you agree right now to immediate and regular International Red Cross inspections of *all* the POW camps." The Joint Chiefs even considered letting North Vietnam claim credit for *releasing* the prisoners, since it would be impossible to keep their return under wraps for very long.

As the Joint Chiefs listened to SACSA's briefing, the rescue of those 61 men sounded more and more feasible. Blackburn seemed confident as he outlined the overall concept. He then turned the briefing over to Norm Frisbie, who covered the feasibility study group's plan in detail. It was obvious from the data Frisbie presented that Don Bennett's spooks were bringing together the kind of intelligence needed for the raid to be plausible.

Low-altitude photos taken by an unmanned Buffalo Hunter reconnaissance drone and high-altitude photos taken from an SR-71 confirmed that the camp was isolated and active. It was located in an area surrounded by rice paddies, at least a mile from the closest civilian habitations at Son Tay city to the southeast.

Although the prison was isolated, there were several North Vietnamese military installations within a few miles. In all, the DIA and the CIA estimated that as many as 12,000 North Vietnamese troops were located within ten to 15 minutes' driving time, but that was under normal daytime conditions. The primary threat would be from three installations within ten kilometers of the target, to the south of Son Tay, and from troops billeted in Son Tay city. The DIA had identified them as elements of the 12th Infantry Regiment. The Son Tay artillery school was the closest military installation housing enemy personnel. Frisbie showed the Joint Chiefs the approach routes from the school to the target. In addition, there was the Son Tay Army Supply Depot with about 1,000 supply personnel, but it was about 20 minutes away under normal daytime driving conditions. Finally, there were about 500 troops and 50 trucks at an air defense installation to the southwest; in daytime, they could react within 20 or 25 minutes.

There was only one other facility near Son Tay Prison. About 500 yards south of it, across a small canal, was another compound of about the same size. On Frisbie's maps of the area, intelligence specialists had it labeled "Secondary School."

The camp at Son Tay, Frisbie explained, consisted of two separate portions, a recently enlarged, walled compound and an administrative support area, including guard quarters, outside the east wall. Bennett's analysts estimated that only 45 North Vietnamese were housed there, including a few dependents. There was only one power and telephone line in the area and it terminated at a communications headquarters building just outside the main gate.

The prisoners were thought to be housed in four large buildings inside the compound. Three guard towers along a seven-to-ten-foot wall marked the corners of the prison. It was 185 feet from the north to south wall and 132 feet from the east wall to the west wall. Two of the towers were on the corners of the west wall, where the camp adjoined a river. The third tower was at the main gate on the east wall. Photo interpreters had spotted a small hut beneath it and by comparing photos taken at different intervals, even verified that POWs were occasionally shoved into it. Apparently it was where the prisoners were punished in a form of outdoor solitary confinement reminiscent of the Japanese tin oven in *The Bridge on the River Kwai*. That's where Lieutenant Commander Render Crayton had spent his last two months at Son Tay and where Air Force First Lieutenant Richard C. "Dog" Brenneman had been confined twice.

Photo reconnaissance had also spotted prisoners in the compound's open courtyard. It was small, the unobstructed portion hardly as big as a volleyball court. There were trees almost 40 feet high, just inside the wall, but there appeared to be enough of a clear area for a small UH-1 "Huey" helicopter to land inside the compound with a six- or eight-man assault team. If that could be done, some of the rescuers could get into the cellblocks before the guards could react. Outside the south wall, there was a clear area large enough for several larger helicopters to land with the rest of the raiding force. They would blow a hole in the wall so that more men could rush through the opening to release the prisoners and guide, or carry, them out. Some of the POWs, the DIA knew, were very sick men. While the main assault was under way, another part of the raiding force would take care of the guards in the prison's support area and set up blocking positions on a road east of the compound to prevent reinforcements or reaction forces from reaching the area. The ground force would total only about 50 men. Other helicopters would fly in with the raiding force but land farther away in some rice paddies, on call to touch down at Son Tay and help evacuate the prisoners.

The raid would be launched at night for maximum surprise and to lessen the chance of the helicopters being detected as they flew into North Vietnam. Parachute flares would be dropped over the camp seconds before the first helicopters set down to blind the guards (the raiders would wear protective goggles) and let the helicopters land safely.

All of this would have to happen very fast. Blackburn had calculated that North Vietnamese troops from the Son Tay artillery school could get there in as little as 30 minutes. This assumed 12 minutes for them to be alerted, grab their weapons, and board trucks before racing up that road. On this basis, the plan called for the whole raid to be over in 26 minutes. The helicopters would be airborne and headed for Laos by the time the first truck driver spotted that breach in the wall of Son Tay Prison.

When Blackburn and Frisbie finished their briefing, there were quite a few questions. Most of them came from the new

Chief of Naval Operations, Admiral Zumwalt. None of his questions focused on the raid, but on whether it was necessary. Was Blackburn sure that every possible avenue had been explored in the Paris peace talks to get the prisoners released? Was there anything else the United States could do to negotiate with Hanoi on the treatment of the POWs, or to get better information on the MIAs? One of those present at the meeting (not Blackburn) later remarked, "You can describe Zumwalt's questions this way: they would have been great at the White House or over dinner with Henry Kissinger, but at that meeting, they were just plain irrelevant. He acted like a drone."

The questions from Army Vice Chief of Staff General Bruce Palmer were probing and to the point. He wanted to know how sure Blackburn was that he could get the raid in, and out, without putting more soldiers or airmen in some North Vietnamese prison. Palmer later recalled just one impression he got from Blackburn's answers: "You know, that sonovagun really convinced me; he was going to pull it off."

Blackburn explained the raid's timing. It was all weather-dependent. Monsoon rains and the risk of compromise, going in from CIA border stations in Laos, argued against an early launch; weather experts agreed that late October or November would offer the safest launch windows. Moreover, the moon would then be just high enough above the eastern horizon to give the helicopters good visibility on the 100-plus-mile flight from the Laotian border to Son Tay, yet low enough to reduce the possibility of their being detected.

The Joint Chiefs of Staff approved Blackburn's final recommendations. More detailed planning would be needed; then a joint task force would be trained to execute the raid on Son Tay.

Blackburn wanted to lead the raid, with Ed Mayer as his deputy. But his boss, John Vogt, told him that his job was to plan the raid. He'd have to pick someone else to command it. Blackburn was let down but not surprised. For one thing, he knew his name was on a special list which proscribed him even from traveling to certain "high risk" areas; he had too many clearances on too many operations and he knew too much about too many intelligence sources. So did Mayer.

Vogt nevertheless called Mayer a few days later. "I owe you an explanation," he said. "I know how intense you guys are about this. I know how much you and Blackburn would like to lead it. But it's going to take months to get this raid ready. If I could let you do it, we wouldn't need you on the Joint Staff." He did not have to explain that their sudden absence would also raise too many questions he didn't want people to ask.

Fort Bragg, North Carolina

At Fort Bragg, North Carolina, on Saturday, July 11, 1970, Army Colonel Arthur D. "Bull" Simons was busy cataloging his collection of ancient Vietnamese brassware—spittoons, chamber pots, snuffboxes, dragon heads—a veritable horde of antiques. A big man, he was the spitting image of Telly Savalas, except that Simons had a thin wisp of hair. There was one difference. Bull Simons didn't *act* mean; he *was* mean. An officer who served under him twice in Laos described him as "the only man I know who genuinely hates people." Underneath that gruff surface, however, Simons was a very sensitive man.

The phone rang. It was Don Blackburn. He and Ed Mayer were flying to Fort Bragg on Monday. Could they all get together? Bull Simons didn't know it, but he was about to make his fourth trip to Vietnam.

After he hung up, Bull's wife, Lucille, remarked quietly, "Don Blackburn? Every time he gets in touch with you, there's bad news. Don't tell me you're going to get mixed up with *him* again!"

Simons went back to his Vietnamese brassware. He knew the history of every piece, some of them centuries old. But brassware wasn't all that he collected. He had his own arsenal, an armory of pistols, rifles, and submachine guns that would be the envy of any gun buff. In Panama years before, his officers used to kid that "the Bull" had enough arms in his attic to mount his own invasion of Cuba. For relaxation, he loaded his own ammunition. At Fort Bragg, Bull kept five or six cases of black gunpowder on the second floor of his quarters. He often took his guests up there and went about loading shells as they talked—puffing away on a cigar, oblivious of the long ash that always needed flicking.

Blackburn and Mayer landed at Fort Bragg around 10:30 Monday morning, July 13. They had two objectives. One was to find out if Simons was available to command the raid on Son

Tay, without revealing to him that it entailed a prisoner rescue or a mission into North Vietnam. Second, they had to select a training site, either Fort Bragg or Eglin Air Force Base in Florida. The overall mission commander would come from whichever service provided the training site; that would ease a lot of administrative problems and minimize the kind of inter-service "coordination" that might compromise the raid. If Fort Bragg was selected, an Army officer would be the mission commander with an Air Force deputy. If Eglin was picked, there would be an Air Force commander with an Army deputy. SACSA would make the decision.

Simons met Blackburn and Mayer for lunch at the Fort Bragg Officer's Open Mess. Bull Simons, they knew, had suf-fered a slight stroke before the tour in Korea from which he had recently returned to serve as supply officer, or G-4, of the XVIIIth Airborne Corps. Both were relieved to see how well he looked. When Blackburn asked him how he was really doing, what kind of shape he was in, Simons told them casually he was back up to 250 push-ups a day. Blackburn looked at him and suspected it might be more like 800.

Over lunch, Blackburn asked Simons if he would be inter-ested in leading a "very sensitive mission." It might be "kind of rough," he suggested. Simons knew enough not to ask what it was; if Blackburn was involved, it had to be interesting. "Hell, yes," he answered, "let's go. I don't need to know any more about it." There was no discussion of a raid, no mention of North Vietnam. Instead, the three began to talk about personal-ities, what kind of men Simons might want to have with him. A few officers came to mind immediately, men they had all worked with before. Some of them, they realized, wouldn't "fit" because they were on orders to Vietnam or Germany or had just been assigned to new posts in the United States. Re-calling them or canceling their orders would raise too many questions. Several names were agreed upon, however: Sydnor, Meadows, Petrie . . .

After lunch, Blackburn and Mayer told Simons they'd be back in touch; but it might be a while, they cautioned. As they said good-bye, it was clear to them that Bull Simons would lead the raid. Whether he or someone else would be the overall commander would hinge on other factors.

Before they had left the Pentagon, Blackburn and Mayer

were convinced that Fort Bragg would be the ideal training site. The sprawling 130,698-acre reservation was the home of the Strategic Army Corps; joint Army and Air Force training exercises were regular events and one more wouldn't raise undue attention. Pope Air Force Base was located nearby. All over the reservation, and in outlying areas where the Army leased additional land, people were used to the oddball training programs that Fort Bragg's Special Forces teams and the 82nd Airborne Division conducted regularly. There was a secure compound built for just such purposes. Moreover, Bragg was where most of the ground force volunteers would come from. The Air Force Special Warfare Center at Eglin Air Force Base—a vast 464,980-acre complex in the panhandle of northern Florida—offered some advantages. It had access to 44,000 square *miles* of Gulf waters for test ranges undisturbed by commercial air traffic. And it was the home of the Aerospace Rescue and Recovery Training Center as well as USAF's Special Operations Wing. Most of the helicopter crews and C-130 refueling tankers would come from those two units. But on the whole, Blackburn and Mayer favored Bragg.

After leaving Simons, they called on the commander of the Special Warfare Center. They explained that they had to pick a site for training a special force, many of whose members would come from Fort Bragg. They needed a secure area to house special intelligence assets and some very sensitive planning. Could they use the area which had been built at Smoke Bomb Hill some years earlier for just such a contingency?

"No way," the commander, a major general, told them. His Personnel Records Section and Judge Advocate General's Office had just moved into that compound. It would "disrupt everything." But he suggested an alternative: how about the communications shack on Chicken Road near Camp Mackall? There were some empty World War II wooden barracks available there. Blackburn and Mayer explained again—without really explaining—that this was for an operation of the highest national priority. The major general wouldn't budge.

In disgust, without even visiting Eglin Air Force Base, Blackburn and Mayer flew directly back to the Pentagon. Mayer drafted a brief message for Admiral Moorer to sign: Eglin Air Force Base would be the training site for what was now to be called the "Joint Contingency Task Group" (JCTG).

The message directed the Air Force to designate a mission commander. Henceforth, the operation would have a new code name, "Ivory Coast." The point of contact for JCS coordination would be Colonel E. E. Mayer in SACSA.

Meanwhile, Blackburn went to see General Palmer, Army Vice Chief of Staff. He told Palmer that he wanted to name Bull Simons as JCTG's deputy commander and to lead the raid. Palmer knew of Simons's reputation as a combat leader, and as a special operations expert since World War II. But he told Blackburn, "Jesus, I don't know if I can go along with that. Didn't Simons have a massive heart attack about two years back?" It was a slight stroke, Blackburn said, but he and Mayer had just visited Fort Bragg and Simons was back on parachute status and doing 250 push-ups a day. Even with the stroke, Blackburn told Palmer, "Simons is ten times better than anyone else."

Palmer had confidence in both Blackburn and Mayer. Blackburn's guerrillas had once bailed Palmer's soldiers out of a hot spot in the Philippines when he was a division chief of staff; Mayer won one of the two Silver Stars Palmer had awarded during American intervention in the 1956 Dominican Republic crisis. Palmer looked at the list of about ten men Blackburn and Mayer had drawn up. He put a check mark and his signature by Simons's name.

Blackburn was relieved. That choice, he felt, would increase the operation's chance of success by a wide margin. His path and Bull Simons's had crossed time and again for almost 28 years. Blackburn believed that Simons could do almost anything—and the two had a bond of mutual trust and respect so strong that, Blackburn felt, Simons would do the impossible if Blackburn told him it was important enough.

Simons's nickname was appropriate. At fifty-two, he looked like a bull—huge shoulders on a 5-foot 11-inch, 190-pound frame that seemed carved from granite. He had a lot of distinguishing features: a thick neck, receding hairline, bushy eyebrows, a wide, hawklike nose, big ears. Deep creases curved from either nostril around his mouth and down to his chin.

Those who knew him called Simons fearless. "Death is not that far away from me by other causes," he used to say. But there was a big difference between being fearless and being careless; as he put it, "I didn't want my people to get their ass shot off for nothing." That's what leaders were for, to not let that happen. The object of any operation, Bull believed, was "to kill the other sonovabitch, not your own people." He was not interested, however, in "body counts" and once told his men, "If I find one of you counting any bodies, I will break your neck right where you are standing." "Take only those losses that are unavoidable," was his philosophy, "if you can't smart your way out of it." And soldiers, he felt strongly, were "entitled" to leadership from men who could "smart their way out of it."

Leadership, Simons believed, wasn't as complicated as service schools made it sound. "Small unit combat is a pretty simple business," he later said of his work. "The guy who carries the gun wants to know what the hell kind of a man you are and he wants to know you're there with him—not up front, necessarily, but that you know your business, you've got control of the sonovabitch and if the thing really goes sour that you are going to be there with him when it's time to have it out."

He had been in enough firefights to accept the blood of battle as "an occupational hazard"; war, after all, was "a miserable business to begin with." But Simons believed in soldiering: "If history is any teacher," he once said, "it teaches you that when you get indifferent and you lose the will to fight, some other sonovabitch who has the will to fight will take you over."

Simons became a soldier in 1941, commissioned as an artillery second lieutenant out of ROTC from the University of Missouri. He liked artillery and he liked animals, so he asked to join a "pack artillery" outfit. He was in the 98th Field Artillery when it was sent to New Guinea. The "grizzly old sergeants" in it knew their business, he thought, so he kept his mouth shut. "For the first 60 days out there," he later said, "all I saw in front of me was a long line of mules' asses." Then one day he noticed that the mules' loads weren't riding right and the animals were getting chafed by shifting ammunition cases and bouncing 75mm gun barrels, breechblocks, and mounts. Simons barked at one of the sergeants to "pull that mule out of the column and fix his load. It's not riding right." The sergeant "damn near fainted"; he thought Simons was a deaf-mute. Simons would later joke that his first order in combat was telling a sergeant how to make a jackass more comfortable.

The pack artillery was not effective in New Guinea and the battalion was disbanded. By then, Simons was in command of one of its firing batteries, and when he learned that the Sixth Ranger Battalion was being formed and needed some very mobile artillery, he took his battery into the Sixth Rangers.

Simons commanded "B" Company of the Sixth Rangers in the invasion of the Philippines. He landed on an island in Leyte Gulf three days before the invasion began, taking in a team of Navy men and "5,000 pounds of God damn electronic gear" to help blow the electronic mines with which the Japanese had sown the channel. The next night he had to get his company to another island to knock out a radar station. All they could find for the assault was "a bunch of God damn canoes" and a Philippine guide, who "was smart enough to jump out" as soon as they left shore. All the canoes sank, "the whole God damn outfit." But Simons stole more canoes, landed on the wrong island, carried his canoes to the other side, and paddled on to the objective. By that time, another force from the Sixth Ranger Battalion had landed to take out the radar site, "but they had some strange orders, got a couple of guys killed and decided to pull back."

Simons decided to knock off the radar site. He had only 15 men left of an 80-man company. But at two o'clock in the morning, he led them up a cliff on the backside of their objective. "It took an hour and a half to climb that cliff," Simons later recalled, "by our fingernails, you know. I mean straight up." As they reached the top, Simons saw "a young Japanese gentleman about to take down his drawers and take a crap." He was about ten feet away. "It was too bad." Simons shot him, and then he and his men proceeded to blow up the radar station.

About a month later, Simons's Rangers were emplaced on a hill near Aparri, ready to provide covering fire for Don Blackburn's guerrillas as they seized the Japanese airstrip that would later be "captured" by the 11th Airborne. But the two officers didn't meet until years later.

In 1957, Simons was stationed at Fort Bragg. The senior officer of the post, a lieutenant general commanding the Strategic Army Corps, noticed that he had earned a degree in journalism at Missouri and made him the public information officer. Simons hated the job and hated the press. They could be "conned." "The press hasn't done very well for the American soldier," he would explain later. As Fort Bragg's go-between with the fourth estate, he found the press lazy: "They never asked the crucial questions." After a year in "purgatory," he asked his boss for mercy and was posted to the Special Warfare School. By then, Don Blackburn was commanding 77th Special Forces stationed at Bragg and had just returned from his first tour in Vietnam. He put Bull Simons in charge of a battalion-level "C" team. The two men, both advocates of unorthodox warfare, became fast friends.

Early in 1960, Blackburn got word to organize a clandestine group to go to Laos for six months to train a Laotian army. The CIA had originally been assigned the mission, but it wasn't working. Blackburn picked Simons to recruit a new force. They were code-named "White Star" teams. Simons took 107 men to Laos. Before they left, he told them all, "You are going to lose your manhood. Some dumb sonovabitch from the jungle is going to tick you off. But you're going to keep your mouth shut and take it."

Simons and his men left Fort Bragg in July; when they arrived in Laos, no one could tell him whom he was supposed to train or what to train them for. But there was so much ferment in the country, so much military activity from North Vietnamese cross border operations, and so little muscle in Laos's military force (it was mainly a palace guard) that some kind of army was obviously needed. Simons decided to build one. When the government wouldn't recruit any volunteers, Simons kidnapped them. His men roamed all over the country, impressing thousands of Meo tribesmen uprooted by the turmoil in their land. He put them in compounds behind barbed wire, fed them, clothed them—and gradually taught them to soldier. They were eager to learn; life had a purpose and they were even being paid. Bull Simons kidnapped 12 battalions of "volunteers," and they proved to be such tough opposition that North Vietnam soon lost much of its appetite for the cross border raids that had torn Laos apart and almost toppled its government. When Simons's six-month tour of duty was up, he brought every member of his White Star teams back to the States alive. One of his deputies on that mission later recalled: "I would follow Bull Simons to hell and back for the sheer joy of being with him on the visit."

After Laos, Simons headed a large Special Forces contingent

in Panama, then joined Don Blackburn's Special Operations Group in Vietnam. In executing SOG missions, Simons refused, in his own words, to "live with some of the restraints put on me." But, he would add, "I got away with it only because I didn't make any mistakes." He knew that if he got caught, "they'd get some other conductor for the trolley car and throw my dead body off the back." When Bull Simons undertook an operation, Blackburn later recalled, the research and planning behind it were "meticulous." He didn't believe in "foolhardy frolics." But he also came to believe that "the more improbable something is, the surer you can pull it off." This was the man that Blackburn picked to lead one of the most improbable missions of the war in Vietnam—the raid on Son Tay. The research and planning would be superb, and he was sure that Bull Simons could "pull it off."

By one of the great ironies of the Son Tay raid, on the day after Bull Simons was picked to lead it, the prisoners there were moved to another camp. A few weeks earlier the well inside Son Tay had dried up. Then the worst monsoon rains in years hit North Vietnam. The prisoners didn't know that just outside the compound, the Song Con River was flooding water to within a foot or two of the west wall. Indeed, one prisoner, Air Force Captain Jon A. Reynolds, would recall later that only days before the move, he was being punished by spending a few days at the bottom of the well—and that it was dry. But very clear, high-altitude aerial reconnaissance photos taken at the time showed that the camp was near being flooded.

The move from Son Tay was orderly, almost casual, not the kind of "panic move" the prisoners would experience later. The guards had ordered them a few days before to take down the clothesline, then the volleyball net and posts. The next day, they loaded hogs and chickens aboard some trucks. Then they were told to take inventory of their dishes and blankets. Finally, they were ordered aboard buses. That night, July 14, 1970, they were all driven to a converted Army barracks at Dong Hoi (also known as Dan Hoi), 13 miles to the east. The prisoners immediately named the place Camp Faith.

THREE

"Ivory Coast"

Volunteers

At Eglin Air Force Base, Brigadier General Leroy J. Manor was fishing on a Saturday morning when he got a phone call on his "brick" from his boss, General William W. "Spike" Momyer, commander of Tactical Air Command, telling him, "You're needed in Washington Monday morning." Manor asked him deferentially, "Why?" Momyer said he didn't know—and he probably didn't care. He was not an enthusiastic backer of special operations. In Vietnam, while commanding 7th Air Force, he had banned the Australian-style bush hats worn by his 14th Air Commando Wing and told its commander he was going to "educate you guys back into the Air Force." He was to pack enough luggage to spend several weeks in Washington and fly up by special courier plane the next morning; another plane picked up Colonel Simons at Pope Air Force Base, North Carolina, near Fort Bragg, and flew him to Washington. Both had been told they would be met at Andrews Air Force Base, driven directly to the Pentagon, and briefed by Brigadier General Donald D. Blackburn, the JCS SACSA.

Manor and Blackburn had never met, but they knew of each other, and Manor had a good idea of what SACSA was all about. As commander of the Air Force's Special Operations Force at Eglin, the forty-nine-year-old New York–born officer trained the unconventional warfare teams which supported SOG operations in Southeast Asia. His students included American and Vietnamese airmen, Cambodians, Thais, and occasionally a few Laotians. Their subjects covered everything from jungle defoliation and leaflet drops over North Vietnam to the clandestine insertion of special infiltration teams. Moreover, for three years Manor had been at the Pentagon as the Air

Force's top briefing officer on Southeast Asia. He knew there was a lot more to the war in Vietnam than the "search and destroy" sweeps, body counts, and fighter-bomber missions which made up most newspaper accounts of the fighting there.

Like Bull Simons, Manor had seen a lot of combat—345 missions in World War II and Vietnam, 275 of them in Southeast Asia, where he commanded the 37th Tactical Fighter Wing at Phu Cat. Their reputations differed, however. In the Army, Bull Simons was respected as a combat leader, but he was a renegade whose work often made his superiors somewhat uneasy. In the Air Force, Roy Manor was a precise organizer who quickly won the full confidence of his superiors. Simons was outspoken, Manor quiet. Both were competent, dedicated, serious men, but they were different breeds of cat.

Their flights to Washington were uneventful, but soon after arriving at the Pentagon, Manor and Simons heard about the raid on Son Tay. Blackburn and Mayer told Manor that he would be in overall command, the "manager"; Simons would be the deputy commander and lead the raid itself. Blackburn and Mayer would handle the coordination in Washington, where one of their main jobs would be to keep people "off their backs" so Manor and Simons could concentrate on recruiting, equipping and training the force, and executing the mission. Whatever they needed, they would have the highest priorities the Joint Chiefs of Staff could provide. In fact, Manor would later be handed a letter by the Air Force Chief of Staff, General John D. Ryan. It was addressed to the Air Force's major commanders and directed them to give Manor their "full support" on a "No questions asked" basis.

After Manor and Simons reviewed the operational concept which Blackburn's feasibility study group had presented to the Joint Chiefs of Staff, both men felt confident the raid could be pulled off. But there was a lot of work to be done, much more detailed planning was needed, and success or failure would depend largely on the quality of intelligence behind them. At a meeting with Bennett, Stewart, and Harris of the DIA, they were relieved to hear that whatever they needed, whenever they wanted it, the DIA would "lay it on." Manor and Simons would get the best intelligence the DIA, the CIA, the NSA, and the National Reconnaissance Office could offer.

NSA's specialty was electronic surveillance; Manor knew

how vital its work would be in selecting penetration and escape routes for his aircraft. North Vietnam juggled its air defenses regularly. Firing batteries were moved, communications frequencies changed, and the effective radar coverage varied from week to week. But there was one problem: not once during the Vietnam War had NSA's electronic intercepts picked up one word about the location of prisoners of war. There were thousands of reels of tape in NSA's vaults: the "Encyclopaedia Britannica" on North Vietnamese radio and telephone signals—and specious power line transmissions as well. But in all those intercepts, there wasn't a microsecond of data on the POWs that hadn't already been publicly broadcast in some propaganda forum. Thus, Manor and Simons were told, they would be almost totally dependent on photographic reconnaissance for the intelligence so vital to the success of the raid.

Some last-minute, new information might be developed through other sources, but it was not likely. Occasionally, there was a useful tidbit in mail from POWs, but the letters were weeks and sometimes months out of date. Manor's and Simons's best intelligence would come from photographs taken by the high-flying SR-71s and the low-altitude drones. The SR-71s' long focal length "technical objective cameras" produced fantastic photos. Taken from higher than 80,000 feet, they were sharp enough to let a skilled interpreter count the exact number of people moving around in a cramped compound. But sometimes SR-71 missions produced nothing but photos of cloud puffs directly over a target. The drones could fly under those clouds but had to be used sparingly; too many low-altitude Buffalo Hunter flights near an isolated target like Son Tay might tip off the North Vietnamese that something unusual was up. And Buffalo Hunter assets were scarce, so there was no way to saturate North Vietnam with decoy flights to mask the real objective. Moreover, weather would be bad over the north in the weeks ahead, and that would also limit the effectiveness of photo reconnaissance flights.

Manor and Simons had another problem. If the raid was to be launched in the first favorable weather window in October, they would have to work fast. They agreed with Blackburn on a rough timetable. They would immediately fly back to Eglin and Fort Bragg to recruit their nucleus of volunteers and specialists. Then on Saturday, August 8, they would reconvene in Washington with their handpicked deputies for five days of detailed planning. A special security section would be organized by that time to develop cover stories and handle the counterintelligence measures necessary to prevent a leak. While the planning group was meeting, Manor and Simons would send a small team to Eglin to pick a training site and prepare it for their men to begin training early in September. The planners would have a training plan ready by August 20, and the actual operations plan laid out by August 28. Training would begin by September 9 and had to be finished by October 6. Most of the photo reconnaissance missions would be programmed in that interval. If everything went as planned, the raiding force should be ready to deploy by October 10, in time to launch the raid during the first good weather window, anticipated between October 20 and 25. It was a tight schedule, but as Roy Manor and Bull Simons left Washington to return to their home bases, they were confident they could make it.

Back at Eglin, Manor began to pick his key subordinates. He called in one of the Air Force's top helicopter pilots, Lieutenant Colonel Warner A. Britton, the operations and training officer at Eglin Air Force Base for the Aerospace Rescue and Recovery Service. Britton had been on Blackburn's feasibility study group, so he was well clued in on the mission which lay ahead. Manor asked Britton if he would volunteer for the raid. Britton told him "Yes" without hesitating. Manor believed in delegating authority; he trusted the instincts and judgments of his "operators," the men who would be in the cockpits instead of the command post. He asked Britton to select the helicopter crews that would land Bull Simons and his men in Son Tay. Britton told Manor that he personally would fly one of the ships.

One of the first men Britton recruited was Lieutenant Colonel John Allison, a forty-four-year-old Jolly Green Giant veteran who commanded one of the HH-53 flights at Eglin's training center for the Aerospace Rescue and Recovery Service. Allison signed on immediately. But Britton had a difficult time with another "volunteer"—Lieutenant Colonel Herbert R. Zehnder. He couldn't give Zehnder any details about the mission, just that it would involve a lot of training and night flying. Zehnder had been an enlisted man for ten years; he had heard the advice "Never volunteer for anything" too often. He told

Britton "No." But Zehnder had the experience and guts Britton needed. The forty-six-year-old pilot had set a long-distance record in 1967, flying an HH-3 helicopter nonstop from New York to the Paris Air Show. He had also flown counterinsurgency missions in Vietnam for a year; in sometimes hairy jungle pickups he had saved the lives of 84 people. Britton finally "talked" him into volunteering.

Allison and Britton would fly two of the helicopters that landed Simons's assault force at Son Tay; Zehnder would be the copilot of the third one. A fourth pilot, Major Frederic M. "Marty" Donohue, would also play a key role, but he was recruited later. Donohue would fly the first helicopter over Son Tay, a gunship that would knock out the guard towers. At the moment, however, he was on another special mission, preparing to fly the world's first trans-Pacific helicopter flight. Britton decided that Donohue had enough on his mind getting ready for that. The historic mission took place on August 15–24, when Donohue flew 8,739 miles on a great-circle route from Eglin Air Force Base, over Alaska, Japan, and the Philippines to Saigon, with 13 HH-53 refuelings along the way by four-engine HC-130 tankers. When he returned to Eglin, he deserved a long rest. Instead, Britton met him as soon as he stepped off the plane, asked him into the base operations office, and, as Donohue put it, "closed the door—which was highly unusual."

Donohue had flown 131 missions in Southeast Asia, four of them rescues in North Vietnam. At thirty-nine, this lean Californian had logged almost 6,000 hours as a helicopter pilot, as much as and possibly more than any other pilot in the world. He had been the helicopter launch site recovery commander at Cape Kennedy on the Apollo space launches. Behind that closed door, Britton could tell Donohue only that he was needed for a "challenging mission" that would involve a lot of night flying. Donohue replied that he wanted to be "in on it."

Manor would acknowledge later that while his Air Force people were all volunteers, just like Simons's, many were "selected" and a lot of his planes were borrowed from different locations to keep people confused. Among them were an MC-130 Combat Talon crew from the 7th Special Operations Squadron in Germany; five A-1 pilots from his own command at Eglin plus another five recalled to the States from Vietnam for some unspecified temporary duty; some HH-53 pilots from

Tactical Air Command plus some from Military Airlift Command's rescue forces in the Pacific area; and one HH-3 pilot from Pacific Air Forces and one from TAC. He wanted the most proficient aircrews around but made sure that some of them were up to date on current procedures in Southeast Asia.

His Combat Talon pilots and navigators would be key to the operation's success. The four-engine planes would be modified with new communications gear and special "forward-looking infrared" pods that had been used before only by the CIA. The aircraft would serve as "guide dogs" for the whole force, "crawling on the grass" in radio silence toward Hanoi, as Lieutenant Colonel William A. Guenon, Jr., the lead MC-130 pilot, would later describe their tactics.

The lead navigator of one MC-130, Major John Gargus, was chief of radar instruction at Detachment 2 of the 1st Special Operations Wing, located at Pope Air Force Base next to Fort Bragg, North Carolina. He was selected in part because he had served as a Combat Talon mission planner flying clandestine missions into North Vietnam out of Nha Trang in South Vietnam. He was intimately familiar with and had worked closely with Texas Instruments trying to fix the shortcomings of the new APQ-115 terrain-following radar that had been installed on all MC-130s by Lockheed Air Service in Ontario, California. The system performed so erratically that some crews were afraid of it. Lieutenant Colonel Cecil Clark, one of his predecessors at Nha Trang, would become the electronic warfare officer aboard Gargus's plane. Both had a good feel for the terrain and past reactions of North Vietnamese defenders to nighttime intrusions into their heavily defended airspace, having already flown many such clandestine missions.

In the weeks ahead, Gargus would make endless mathematical calculations and use reams of graph paper plotting new maneuvers showing how Manor's planes might weave their way to the target at low level through mountainous terrain in dead-of-night blackout conditions.

As Manor and Britton were rounding up their volunteers at Eglin, Bull Simons corralled his at Fort Bragg. The first two men he wanted were Lieutenant Colonel Elliott P. "Bud" Sydnor, Jr., to serve as his overall deputy and ground commander during the mission, and Captain Richard J. "Dick" Meadows, to head the compound assault team. Both were stationed at the Infantry School, Fort Benning, Georgia. Simons, Meadows, and Sydnor knew each other well. At the time Simons and Blackburn were in SOG in Vietnam, Meadows was the Special Forces sergeant who had captured the first North Vietnamese artillery pieces in Laos; and when Westmoreland awarded him the first battlefield commission of the Vietnam War, it was Simons who pinned on Meadows's bars. Simons and Meadows had served on many missions together, none of which Simons would discuss in detail. "If we had asked permission for some of them," he later explained, "Westmoreland would have fainted." One of them, Simons claimed, was "the most beautiful operation of the Vietnam War." It involved an "almost impossible" situation. But Meadows was "a steady boy" and he pulled off a "beautiful show—it was slick, I mean really *slick!*" Another time, Meadows and Simons had taken a small Special Forces team, only about 18 men, and recaptured a major CIA outpost in Laos that the North Vietnamese had overrun and operated from with impunity for almost two months. They "cleaned it off."

Meadows had also served under Simons in Panama. There, but after Simons had left, Meadows helped pull off an operation called "Black Palm." It was a training exercise, to hone Special Forces teams in covert operations and train Panamanian National Guardsmen defending the locks. One of Blackburn's officers flew down and personally briefed the governor of the Canal Zone; he said that small teams would be operating within a ten-day period and gave him a list of seven potential targets, most of them locks along the canal. The governor briefed his troops on the period of the "threat" and the target areas; and the Panamanians quickly picked up one of the Special Forces teams and locked them up in jail. By the next morning, the men had escaped. Twenty-four hours later, the governor was told that if he had divers inspect one of the locks, they would find dummy explosives wired to the flotation chambers that gave buoyancy to the huge lock doors. Meadows's team, which had just escaped from jail, had planted them.

Simons knew that Son Tay would not be Dick Meadows's first visit to North Vietnam. In 1968, after Blackburn had left SOG, Meadows was serving his third tour in Southeast Asia. A team of CAS agents got into "a real pickle" deep in North Vietnam, at a site known as "Eagle" between Hanoi and Haiphong. Meadows was sent in from an aircraft carrier to rescue them. He arrived too late. But he got himself and his men out safely. "I can't say too much about that man," Ed Mayer would later remark. "He's truly a *great* soldier: he's not just heroic, he *performs!*"

Elliott Sydnor was "lean, mean, five foot, ten inches tall." Mayer described him as "gung-ho, brilliant, competent, sensible, fearless, a great team player." Blackburn called him a "mummy. You ask him to do something and he doesn't react. He just *does* it." In combat, he was "fantastic: the tougher things get, the cooler he becomes. *Nothing* flusters him. I've never seen another soldier like him in my life." Like Meadows and Simons, Bud Sydnor believed in Blackburn's line of work. "People in the rear area should never feel comfortable," Simons later said. "The idea is to discomfort the sonovabitch as much as you can."

Sydnor would joke years later about having "volunteered" for the mission: "Some *volunteer,*" he laughed. Colonel Simons flew to the Columbus Airport outside Fort Benning, Georgia, and met Sydnor in the parking lot there. It was a "very short meeting," Sydnor would recall. Simons told him "there was 'something happening' that was good for the U.S., good for the Army, and good for Special Forces. Further, it would be done by volunteers only. He asked, 'Did I want to be part of it?' " Sydnor had worked for Simons in Laos for nine months on the White Star mission in 1960 and 1961 and admired him as "something special as a leader," a man who reminded him of his father, a veteran of World War I in France and a farmer who had taught Sydnor "the value of hard work and never quitting." Sydnor said, "Yes." Simons left. Shortly thereafter, Sydnor received orders to temporary duty with the Joint Chiefs of Staff for four months. "No one ever really *asked* me to 'volunteer'," he would note. The power structure at Fort Benning tried to talk him out of leaving on an unspecified mission, worried that the recent War College graduate would be "jeopardizing [his] career on some foolish fling. Since I did not know anything yet," Sydnor would muse later, "I had no way to rebut that notion." When he told his wife, Jean, that he and Meadows had to drive to Fort Bragg to work with Simons for a while, she rejoined, "You're not going to get mixed up with *those* two again, are you?"

Simons needed one other senior officer, a doctor. Blackburn's feasibility study group had listed one as essential to the mission. Many Special Forces troops were well-trained medics, but the raid needed a full-fledged doctor, not only to help in the final planning but to be on the raid and care for the prisoners—or Simons's men, if something went wrong. Simons asked the Army Surgeon General to recommend a "combat-type" doctor, but he couldn't tell the Surgeon General what for.

One day early in August, a lieutenant colonel named Joseph R. Cataldo walked into Simons's office. He told Simons, "I'm Doc Cataldo. I hear you need a doctor." Simons asked him if he knew why. Cataldo said no, but that he was available. He had been chief surgeon for the Green Berets at Fort Bragg, graduated from the Command and Staff College at Fort Leavenworth, and had just been reassigned to Washington. He and his wife, Lee, were getting settled with four young children in a home in Alexandria, but the Surgeon General had sent him to Fort Bragg to see Simons about some kind of "special assignment."

The two had never met, but Cataldo was just what Simons needed. He was new to Washington and his absence wouldn't raise too many questions. He knew what special operations were like; he was parachute-qualified, had worked with Green Berets in the field, and he "spoke my language pretty well," Simons later recalled. The only question in his mind was, "Would Cataldo volunteer?" He told Cataldo bluntly that a prisoner-of-war rescue was being planned that would involve a raid deep into North Vietnam. The "risk would be great," Simons said, and he needed a doctor to go along. That was about it. Would Cataldo volunteer? Cataldo told him, "I'm your surgeon."

Simons was surprised. "There was the word 'Surgeon' on my damn personnel check list," he would recall, "so I put a check mark next to it, asked Cataldo how to spell his name, and said to myself, 'No shit: well, now we've got one of those.' "

People described Doc Cataldo differently. One of the Son Tay planners would call him "intense, earnest, dedicated but a self-centered publicity seeker." Simons bridled at that description. "Cataldo *is* a funny guy," he said, "but I want to tell you something: you couldn't get a *captain* to volunteer for that mission. Sure, they'd be happy to come down and help with the training or give the shots and that bullshit—but go into North

Vietnam? *Forget* it!" Simons almost bit through the plastic tip
of a cigarillo as he continued: "So here a *lieutenant colonel*
walks in and volunteers. The man's got a career worth a hundred thousand dollars a year ahead of him. He really had it
made, close to retirement if he wanted, ready to make a bundle
in private practice. So I have reservations about anyone who'd
run Cataldo down. The guy *is* hyper-aggressive. Some people
don't care for him. But some people don't care for me either
and I really don't give a shit, to tell you the truth. He had the
guts to do the job and furthermore he was intensely interested
in doing it well. I really don't give a damn about motives, to tell
you the truth. I don't know why Doc Cataldo volunteered.
From *his* view, the risk was great. But he volunteered. Just remember *that*."

Simons had to be discreet in choosing the rest of his force.
Through company first sergeants and unobtrusive notices in
Fort Bragg's daily bulletins, word went out that Colonel Arthur
D. Simons was looking for volunteers. Those interested were to
report to the post theater. Simons's reputation on the post was
almost a legend; shortly before lunch one day, close to 500 men
showed up to hear what he had to say. It wasn't much.

Without disclosing any details, Simons told them that he
needed men for a "moderately hazardous" mission. There
would be no extra money involved, meaning no "TDY allowance" for temporary duty away from home station. That
was it. Anyone who was interested should report back to the
theater after lunch with his company "201 jacket"—personnel
folder. Simons would personally interview every man who volunteered. Those who weren't interested needn't worry; Simons
would make damned sure that no one took roll of who came
back and who didn't.

During lunch, a lot of soldiers speculated about Bull Simons's idea of a "moderately hazardous" mission. That afternoon, only half of them were back. Simons spent the next three
days interviewing every one of them. He had Cataldo and two
sergeant majors with him; they screened every man's service
background and medical records. Cataldo gave each a quick
physical. Nine men were turned down because they were overweight, even though they were Green Berets. Eleven men had
psychiatrists' notations in their medical jackets of enough concern to disqualify them. Some had pregnant wives; Simons

ruled them out because he couldn't risk men with "extraneous worries" on their minds.

Daniel D. Turner, a Special Forces B Detachment commander, combat veteran, and (by his own description) "a young, obnoxious captain," was one of those who showed up. Simons asked him, "Why are you here?" Turner told him, "Sir, I've been here nine months and I'm bored. All I've seen 'em do here is pick up pinecones." Years later, Turner would recall that he too was never really invited or asked to volunteer; he was just selected.

While Simons probed their combat qualifications and assessed their physical condition—he was looking for soldiers strong enough to *carry* the prisoners out of Son Tay if they had to—Doc Cataldo taunted them to see how quickly they could be provoked under stress: "I see here that your liver is enlarged. What's the matter, soldier, got a drinking problem?" Many of their questions were designed to cloud the real nature and location of the mission, questions like: "Can you ski?"—"Have you ever had scuba training?"—"Do you get seasick easily?"— "How long can you walk in the desert without water?"—"Do you sunburn easily?"—"Are you anti-Semitic?"—"Any problem living in crowded confines with a lot of garlic-loving Lebanese allergic to showers?" Simons and Cataldo selected 15 officers and 82 enlisted men. About one-third of them had served under Simons before and he "knew" at least half of them. Six had never been in combat before, but Simons liked their "mettle." Ten of the men would be backups or alternates for roughly a 50-man assault force; the others would make up the support detachment.

On Saturday, August 8, the JCS message that Ed Mayer had drafted for Moorer's signature in mid-July was sent to unified and specified commands around the world. It told of a "Joint Contingency Task Group" under Manor and Simons's command and dubbed the operation "Ivory Coast." There was no hint of what Ivory Coast was all about. By that time, Blackburn had also moved his staff from Arlington Hall Station to a secure DIA complex in the Pentagon's basement.

Two days later, on August 10, Manor and Simons met again with Blackburn in Washington. Simons had brought Bud Sydnor along, took him into the JCS complex, showed him "four or five sheets of paper and some photos." Sydnor would recall that Simons told him, "That is the mission order and that's where we're going. Let me know if you think the plan is feasible—in about 30 minutes." Sydnor found it "the simplest, most complete plan that I had ever seen."

Simons confided in Sydnor that he planned to be on the ground with Sydnor's raiders, as opposed to in the air above the objective. "I don't plan to put men on the ground without being there myself. But I will not interfere with your running of the ground force." It was a refreshing contrast to the way operations were being run in South Vietnam, where company commanders led their troops on the ground but were second-guessed by battalion commanders circling in helicopters above them who were supervised by brigade commanders flying above them, often micromanaged by division commanders who were in still higher orbits and sometimes dictated platoon-level tactics.

Then Manor and Simons met with the people Blackburn had convened as the Ivory Coast Planning Group. There were 27 people present at the meeting, along with 13 others who made up "SACSA's Administrative Support/Augmentation Group." Two of that group would not appear on any Pentagon records of the meeting: Dick Elliott and Robert Donohue from the CIA. The planning group, Blackburn explained, would meet from Monday through Friday to review and modify plans for the raid. Thenceforward, the final, detailed planning would be up to Manor and Simons at Eglin Air Force Base. Blackburn and Mayer would "run interference" for them and coordinate at the JCS level from the Pentagon.

Of the 38 planners, 11 were from the 15-man feasibility study group Blackburn had formed on June 10. Among the new faces present, besides Manor and Simons, were Cataldo, Meadows, Navy Captain William M. Campbell from the Chief of Naval Operations' office, and a "wad of intelligence types." One of them was the "Blue Max," a counterintelligence expert and Army major named Max E. Newman. Another was Air Force Lieutenant Colonel John E. Kennedy from the Pacific Air Defense Analysis Facility. He was NSA's expert on the North Vietnamese air defense network. Navy Captain Spots Harris headed DIA's four-man contingent. Of those present at the meeting, four would end up flying into Son Tay.

One of the first decisions Manor and Simons agreed on at the meeting was to send representatives to Eglin to select a training site for Simons's force and begin arranging the needed logistical support. On Wednesday and Thursday, while planning group meetings were still under way in Washington, their representatives chose Eglin's Auxiliary Field Number 3. History was repeating itself: the Doolittle Raiders had trained nearby 28 years earlier. It was an isolated, vacant cantonment used by Air Force ROTC students. There were enough parking aprons at the field to handle the helicopters, six barracks for troop billets, a theater and other classroom space, a small post exchange and snack bar, a mess hall and motor pool, and a headquarters building with barred windows that could be used for a classified operations center. Nearby was plenty of unused range area in the flat, wet Florida scrubland. Blackburn's feasibility group had proposed—and Simons agreed it would be essential—that a mock-up of the Son Tay compound be built so that the assault could be rehearsed under terrain conditions as close to those in North Vietnam as could be found in the United States. Florida's thin pine and cottonwood trees were about the same height as those inside Son Tay Prison, although the foliage wasn't as thick.

As the planning group discussed details of that nature, however, counterintelligence personnel cautioned against building the complete, realistic replica that Blackburn and Simons had in mind. Too much detail would prematurely reveal the nature of the target to the raiders and the new construction would be difficult to explain to casual observers. More important, the "spooks" pointed out, Russian photographic satellites passed over Eglin Air Force Base regularly. Like their American counterparts, Soviet photo interpreters presumably were trained to take a close look at any new construction on a military base. Cosmos 355 was passing over Eglin twice every 24 hours at that time, at an altitude of about 70 nautical miles. From that distance, U.S. Big Bird satellites could take photographs that would let a skilled interpreter spot a new outhouse in the middle of Siberia. Its heat-seeking infrared sensors could even tell how often it was being used. Every 13 days or less, the intelligence analysts knew, Cosmos's film payload was "deorbited" and examined for just such evidence. Often, Russia had two such satellites in orbit at any one time, thus shortening still further the interval before a Son Tay mock-up might be detected. Moreover, a Soviet trawler was operating in the Gulf of Mexico, clearly on an electronic intelligence-gathering mission. There was no way to mask from radar the extra flights that would be going in and out of Field Number 3; and the training couldn't be conducted in complete radio silence, although codes and frequencies could be changed. The flights and radio traffic might give the trawler enough of an "indicator" to warrant having Cosmos 355, or a specially launched satellite, take a closer look at Eglin Auxiliary Field Number 3.

But Simons wasn't about to train his men for a raid into North Vietnam with a Fort Leavenworth "map exercise." So the planners decided to build a mock-up that could be dismantled during the daylight hours. They could use two-by-four lumber and target cloth for the compound walls and buildings. Gates, doors and windows could be painted on or cut into the cloth. Thus, the Son Tay compound could be "rolled up" and stored out of sight; the two-by-fours could be lifted out of their holes and the postholes covered by lids to conceal the camp's outline. Daylight training would be limited to those four-hour-a-day periods when the satellite was not in position to photograph the area.

For cover purposes, Simons would tell his men the mock-up was a "village" they might have to fight in. But he wanted that mock-up ready fast. He had most of the information he needed to do the job. Blackburn had asked the DIA to arrange a comprehensive photo reconnaissance study of the entire target area. It was handled by the CIA and completed in August. Blackburn had also contacted Milt Zaslov of the NSA, who coordinated the Pentagon's more important requests for special electronic intelligence. Thus, DIA's "target folder" on Son Tay now filled several file drawers. In them were a special set of large-scale maps of the objective area, printed in only a few copies (1 inch on the map would equal 50,000 inches on the ground); large- and small-scale photo mosaics from Son Tay to the Black River, 65 miles to the west; special photographs showing each turning point on the route from Laos into the target; and mosaics of the objective itself in two scales, 100 and 200 meters to each grid square. The planning group knew the location of every building, every wall, every ditch, and every tree in the Son Tay compound; and within days of its first meeting in

Washington, 710 6-foot-long two-by-fours and 1,500 yards of target cloth would arrive at Auxiliary Field 3. Elsewhere at Eglin, huge trees would be dug up and transplanted to conform exactly, with respect to the mock-up, to the positions of the trees the helicopters would have to fly over to land Simons's assault team within the walls of the compound.

Equal attention had been paid to the intelligence details necessary for the long flight from Laos to and from the target area. Recent SR-71 and drone coverage, the planning group was told, showed "no major changes" near the objective, although a new early warning/ground control intercept training site was identified 3.3 nautical miles southeast of the prison, and there were more trucks and vehicles than usual south and west of the objective.

The planners were told one other thing: photos taken since June 6 showed Son Tay Prison to be "less active" than usual.

Some very odd American "air strikes" were under way over northern Laos to the west of Son Tay as Blackburn's planning group discussed the "decreased activity" which had been noted at the prison. Manor would note later in the JCS after-action report that "Other intelligence satisfactorily explained these changes." But he did not elaborate, even in the Top Secret document, on what that "other intelligence" was—or if he was even told. For Manor and the other Son Tay planners were apparently unaware that the "changes" meant Son Tay Prison was not just "less active"; it was empty. Nor were they told that the "changes" may have been triggered by those odd air strikes over Laos that were part of an ultrasecret program called "Operation Popeye."

Operation Popeye was only one of several code names for "weather modification activities" conducted by the Department of Defense and the CIA during the war in Vietnam. Information on those operations was held in a "special channel," access to which was so limited that five years after the raid, the head of one intelligence agency would explain that he wasn't "scared" discussing the subject, he was "just shivering over it." For the suggestion would be made that the prisoners some Americans were trying to rescue from Son Tay were moved out of the target in July of 1970 because of a flood caused by covert rain-making missions which other Americans were flying nearby.

But because Operation Popeye—and its related activities—ranked among the most closely held secrets of the Vietnam War, the Son Tay planners, and the men who would go on the raid, were not told of that possibility.

The rainmaking program had been conducted under different code names: "Operation Compatriot," then "Intermediary," and when those were "uncovered," Operation Popeye. The program lasted from March 1967 to July 1972, and it was not a small deal. It involved 2,602 sorties, almost as many fighter-bomber missions as were flown over North Vietnam in all of 1970 and 1971. The purpose of the program was "to increase normal monsoon season rainfall," using air-dropped silver and lead iodide cloud-seeding units. This, it was hoped, would slow the infiltration of supplies down the Ho Chi Minh Trail by "softening road surfaces, causing landslides along roadways," and "washing out river crossings." Because the North Vietnamese were using the Laotian streams that fed the Mekong to float supplies to the south—usually in barrels, which just "bobbed" when bombed—another purpose of the program was to turn the streams into "raging torrents." An even more highly classified part of the weather modification program was handled by CIA teams in northern Laos who dumped tons of "emulsifier" on trails and riverbanks wetted by the extra rain. The emulsifier turned the trails into impassable, slippery pools of quicksand, while riverbanks collapsed and compounded the flooding.

At the time of the bombing halt ordered by President Johnson, on November 1, 1968, all "seeding operations within the boundaries of North Vietnam were terminated and never reinstituted." But operations over Laos, and in Laos, intensified.

All of the 1969 seeding operations were flown over northern Laos, in a small target area contiguous to the border of North Vietnam. Most of the area was due west or southwest of Hanoi—and Son Tay. In 1970, the seeding area was enlarged to include the eastern part of southern Laos; but the target area west of Hanoi—and Son Tay—was also doubled. That year, 277 such sorties were flown; the planes dropped 8,312 "seeding units," the third highest number in any of the six years that Operation Popeye was under way. And most of the missions were flown between March and November.

Did those missions cause a flood at Son Tay, or so worsen the floods that normally occur that time of year in western North

Vietnam that the prisoners had to be moved? For reasons unknown, the vital figures for 1970 are no longer available. But they do still exist for 1971, and in June of that year 16 inches of rainfall were recorded in the hills of Laos west by southwest of Son Tay; 7 of them, Pentagon analysts would calculate, were "induced" by Operation Popeye. Yet most of the 1971 missions were flown far to the south in the Laotian panhandle, whereas more of the 1970 missions were concentrated to the north, in the area west and southwest of Son Tay Prison. It rained like hell in northern Laos and North Vietnam in 1970.

The world's best weathermen would be hard-pressed to explain why it rains hard somewhere one year and not the next. But if Operation Popeye had anything to do with the heavy summer rains over Laos and the July flood at Son Tay Prison in 1970, not many people would have been aware of it. The Defense Department would estimate that in the six years the cloud-seeding missions were flown, only 1,400 people were ever cleared to know of them. That included all of the aircrews and "supporting personnel" who flew or launched the 2,602 sorties involved, and loaded 47,409 "seeding units" aboard Popeye's airplanes. Any way the numbers are divided, they averaged out to only about 230 people who were cleared to plan, load, and fly about 435 missions every year. Popeye was a *very* "close hold" operation.

A list supplied by the Pentagon would later reveal that the "Director, CIA and limited supporting staff" were made privy to the operations. The list also revealed that 14 other agencies or offices "were informed in varying degrees as to operation and scope." They ranged from the "Joint Chiefs of Staff" and "limited members of the staff of the Office of the Secretary of Defense" to the "Director of Defense Research and Engineering." There was no mention that the DIA was informed, although it must have been; and while it was the DIA that would have informed the Son Tay planners, it would become evident that some of the key DIA analysts supporting the operation were not cleared to know of Operation Popeye. Nor did the CIA always inform the Joint Chiefs of all it was doing in its "private fiefdom" in Laos.

The situation was so complex—and so intentionally vague—that it would raise a host of questions about the Son Tay raid. Did some senior members of the intelligence community know in July or early August that the prisoners at Son Tay had been moved? Were they moved because of a flood caused by American rainmaking operations; and if so, were the Son Tay planners not told of the move because they were not cleared to know about Operation Popeye? Those questions would not even be asked until long after the Vietnam War was over. In August of 1970, the Son Tay planners knew only of "decreased activity" at the prison compound. And in the weeks ahead, the men who would actually mount the operation would be confronted with very unusual weather conditions. Roughly "five years of typhoons," Manor would write in the JCS after-action report, "moved into the area of North Vietnam, South Vietnam and Laos" in the two months preceding the raid. The area was experiencing its "worst weather" in years. It meant that obtaining last-minute intelligence from photo reconnaissance flights would be extremely difficult. It meant that timing the raid would be difficult. Did it also mean that a Top Secret American operation was inadvertently endangering both the lives of the POWs in North Vietnam and the lives of the soldiers and airmen who were about to attempt their rescue?

Assets

No one at Strategic Air Command Headquarters, Omaha, Nebraska—or anywhere else in SAC—was cleared to know anything about the Son Tay raid. Yet SAC would have to provide the bulk of the intelligence on which Manor and Simons would depend. SAC refueling crews, as well as its communications relay aircraft, would also support the raid.

As Blackburn's planning group continued its August 10–14 meetings, a "package" of seven Buffalo Hunter reconnaissance drone launches was put at Manor's disposal to give his task group last-minute "prisoner verification" and "positive identification of the enemy order of battle." At least as many high-altitude SR-71 missions would be available, but photo interpreters would depend on the drone photos to verify the small-scale coverage from the SR-71s' ultralong focal length "technical objective" cameras, which covered a swath ten nautical miles wide on the ground.

SAC crews would fly both sets of missions, but no one in

Omaha knew why. Nor would SAC's photo interpreters be told what to look for. After the raid, Roy Manor was to recommend "that in the future, if SAC reconnaissance assets are used, one officer in the SAC Reconnaissance Center Intelligence Requirements Office be briefed on the operation." He went on to explain that "Some difficulty was experienced in coordinating the JCTG reconnaissance requirements with the SAC Reconnaissance Center at Offutt Air Force Base as none of the SAC personnel were cleared for this operation." A "more intimate knowledge of the requirements," he suggested, "would aid considerably in obtaining the desired coverage."

There was another difficulty. Due to a quirk of the military bureaucracy, SAC was responsible for all high-altitude reconnaissance (satellites, U-2s, and SR-71s), but only *part* of the Air Force's low-altitude reconnaissance program. SAC was responsible for "remotely piloted vehicles (RPVs)" or drones—the Buffalo Hunters—and flew these unmanned low-altitude reconnaissance missions over North Vietnam; but the Tactical Air Command (specifically, 7th Air Force in Saigon) planned and flew all of the *manned* low-altitude recce missions there, usually with RF-4s or RF-101s. The mixed bag of responsibilities drove Pentagon planners up the wall on missions as complex and sensitive as the Son Tay raid—especially when the JCS Reconnaissance Office couldn't tell either SAC, TAC, or 7th Air Force what the Pentagon was looking for or when the target being reconnoitered might be hit.

Part of the confusion was planned to prevent leaks; part of it was accidental. But at SAC headquarters, a young lieutenant colonel named John Dale was perplexed; as head of drone reconnaissance for SAC, he was "laying on" a "slug" of Buffalo Hunter missions over a part of North Vietnam no one had paid much attention to for years. And his hunters weren't bagging anything. Seven "shots" would be flown between early September and late October; at least two were downed by North Vietnamese gunners and four had "mechanical failures" caused by weather, operational, or maintenance problems.

One of these, ironically, was flown on July 12, two days before the prisoners were moved. Two of the American POWs, Mo Baker and Larry Carrigan, were in the prison courtyard, saw the drone approaching and waved frantically to tell the outside world, "We're here, we're here." But something went wrong, and of the 127 million Buffalo Hunter photos of North Vietnam which fill the DIA's files today, none came from that mission.

The last Buffalo Hunter shot was a perfect launch. It was supposed to bring back photos taken from treetop level, just above the walls of Son Tay Prison, to show "the height, color, eyes and facial expressions" of every man in Son Tay Prison. The photographs were superb. But the carefully programmed drone banked an instant too soon and the perfect pictures it produced were of the horizon beyond Son Tay. When he saw them, DIA Director Don Bennett would recall, "I cried for two days." For all he could tell from the imagery, Son Tay could have been empty—or full of a visiting delegation of rice farmers.

The intelligence community agreed that flying more missions near the camp at low level could tip off the raid; it was decided to "depend upon our high-level penetrations for the remaining photos." The SR-71s would fly out of Kadena Air Force Base, Okinawa, but the film would be rushed to DIA's photo interpreters in SAC's 67th Reconnaissance Technical Squadron at Yokota Air Force Base Japan, then back to Washington for a closer look. Since the DIA men assigned to SAC were not cleared to know of the raid, the interpreters in Yokota would look for changes in North Vietnam's air defense system and new military deployments over the ten-mile-wide swath covered by the SR-71s' photo track. They did a good job. As one user of their product said later, "They located every gun barrel within 50 miles of that place." Only the DIA photo interpreters assigned directly to Manor's Joint Contingency Task Group would "read" what was going on at Son Tay itself, but it was not all that easy. Because of the unusual weather in that part of Southeast Asia in mid-1970, the objective was often covered by clouds or cast in heavy shadows.

At the DIA, Bennett and his deputy Dick Stewart decided it was time to call on other "assets." The possibility of "inserting" a CAS agent near the objective was revived, someone who could "bicycle down the road" outside Son Tay, arrange to have a flat tire or break his drive chain, take a quick glimpse or two inside that front gate, listen for an American voice.

The 1968 ban on agent insertion and resupply had been partially lifted by President Nixon. Bennett went to see Admiral

Moorer. The insertion, he suggested, should be timed so that the agent would be in, and hopefully out, long before the raid was scheduled. Moorer agreed. He ordered Bennett to check with CIA and "investigate the desirability of injecting a CAS team," but on a *very* "close hold" basis.

Asked, "What came back?" Moorer would later recall: "Objections." In a country and closed society like North Vietnam, he would explain, "a white person stands out like a box. But you could never be sure whether you can trust the Vietnamese, if you had to go in there with a non-American agent. And it could reveal the fact that you were zeroing in on that point. The concern revolved around the chance that the North Vietnamese might find out about the raid and lay an ambush." Asked if he was "aware before the raid that a CAS team or agent had gone in," Moorer would pause: "No. I don't think there was one there." He would add, however, "There may have been one close to it [Son Tay] out of Laos, but the team didn't provide any information. Operations of that nature were going on up and down the North Vietnamese border, but they didn't contribute anything, as I recall, to the Son Tay raid."

Bennett's recollection would be more specific: "We did put an agent in." It was done "about two months" before the raid, but according to Bennett, he found out "nothing." Asked if the agent was recovered, Bennett would reply, "I don't know. That wasn't my end of the business. You know, we never could find out much when they were threshing around up there."

Perhaps because the operation was "close hold," or perhaps because the agent discovered nothing, Blackburn was not informed of what the CIA and the DIA had done. Apparently, even Admiral Moorer was not informed of the particulars of the operation. An "asset" that had originally been discarded because it might jeopardize the security of the raid was being used—without the knowledge of the man in charge of planning the mission. Blackburn would not learn that a CAS agent might be "threshing around" Son Tay until shortly before the raid was launched.

There was another "asset" known only to a handful of officials in the entire U.S. government. He was North Vietnamese, a "middle-level" but "well-informed" bureaucrat in Hanoi. His name was Nguyen Van Hoang, a senior official in the research office of the North Vietnamese Enemy Proselytizing Office, the group concerned with administration and supervision of the POWs and their detention areas. Its "research" office, and Hoang in particular, dealt with POW interrogations. Cheerful, eloquent, and well liked—by his associates—Hoang was close to fifty years old and tall for a Vietnamese, 5 feet 10 inches. His most distinguishing features were his light skin, short dark hair, and thick eyebrows; he looked like North Vietnam's version of John L. Lewis.

For more than a year since Ho Chi Minh's death, the United States had been cultivating Nguyen Van Hoang through a contact in Hanoi called "Alfred." When the Buffalo Hunter shots "crapped out," the DIA arranged for requests to be made of Nguyen for information about Son Tay and, to mask too specific an interest in that target, other POW camps as well. It was a request that would bring much more positive results than the CAS agent insertion. But Blackburn and Mayer knew nothing about that "asset" either.

With hindsight, five years after the raid, military intelligence officials would admit there was one "ace card" they had failed to play: acoustic and seismic sensors to "spike" the camp at Son Tay. These were being used widely to "seed" the trails in southern Laos at the time, with results the Air Force claimed to be "spectacular" in directing air strikes to choke off North Vietnam's resupply of the south.

Don Blackburn had been intimately involved in the early development of the sensors. Soon after he returned from SOG in 1966, he was abruptly taken off the NATO Military Committee and assigned to a newly formed agency called the "Defense Communications Planning Group." Its job was to design and build the "electronic fence" or "infiltration barrier" with which Defense Secretary McNamara hoped, with grandiose optimism, to isolate South Vietnam. Blackburn's job at DCPG was Assistant Deputy Director, Intelligence and Evaluation, and as the sensors were developed and tested, he gained some appreciation for their potential. Later, as SACSA, he was briefed regularly on the intelligence they produced and the operations they triggered. By that time, McNamara had left the Pentagon and his "electronic fence" had been scrapped; but the sensors developed by DCPG were replacing clandestine "trail watchers" in Laos to the point where "every fourth bush on the Ho Chi

Minh Trail had an antenna in it." As one Air Force officer put it later, "We wired the Ho Chi Minh Trail like a drugstore pinball machine and we plugged it in every night."

The operation was called "Igloo White," and by mid-1970, it was beginning to pay off. In January of 1971, for instance, airmen flew 25 percent fewer strikes over Laos than they had in January of 1970, but destroyed four times more cargo. The sensors were so good that an air attack against a convoy moving at night or a truck park camouflaged in the daytime destroyed about half of the trucks and cargo. Some 320 tons of North Vietnamese supplies a day were coming into Laos; only ten tons survived to reach South Vietnam.

All kinds of sensors were used. Two of them were acoustic. "Spikebuoy" was a free-fall acoustic device which buried itself in the ground after it had been dropped by helicopter, transport aircraft, or jet fighter-bombers. "Acoubuoy" was another acoustic sensor, but it was dropped by parachute and hung up in the jungle canopy. A third was a seismic sensor, "Adsid," a small free-fall device that looked like a thin mortar shell. This, too, buried itself in the ground, but a small antenna resembling a tropical plant remained above ground. A fourth sensor, "Acousid," combined acoustic and seismic features. It was free-fall, similar to Adsid, but it transmitted audio pickups of command from electronic "triggers" relayed by a high-flying EC-121R. The converted Lockheed Constellation relayed the sensors' signals to an "Infiltration Surveillance Center" at Nakhon Phanom in eastern Thailand. There, it took two IBM-360-65 computers to analyze all the signals coming in from the sensor fields. Over Laos itself, a "Lightning Bolt" C-130 command ship could monitor the signals in "real time" and direct strike aircraft or AC-123 "Black Spot" and C-130E "Surprise Package" side-firing gunships against the most lucrative targets.

There was one drawback. As even more sophisticated sensors were added to the electronic arsenal, an increasing number of the "targets" turned out to be water buffaloes, not North Vietnamese trucks—until the "bedbug breakthrough."

The Army's Limited Warfare Laboratory at Aberdeen Proving Ground, Maryland—a group Blackburn helped get started—had a "people sniffer" program. The object was to develop a sensor that could pinpoint people, not just truck engines or trembling ground. A gamut of technological devices was tested, but again, mechanical systems could not distinguish human beings from tigers or water buffalo. Bedbugs could. The Limited Warfare Lab tested all kinds, but Mexican bedbugs worked best: they had 20 percent more range. They could sense a human being at about 150 yards' distance, wet season or dry, and "got agitated as hell." The bedbugs were literally glued to phonograph needles hooked to a vibrating crystal wired to a tiny transmitter. The Pentagon soon had Mexican bedbugs glued to phonograph needles all over Southeast Asia.

What the CIA needed in Son Tay was a bedbug; but in mid-1970 the device had not yet been perfected. The acoustic sensors had, but Blackburn would later admit that he never thought of using them; he was leaving intelligence up to the spooks. And, he remarked candidly, "I didn't want to know *too* much. Doubts I didn't need. I needed a license to 'go.' " But in retrospect, he said he would have "spiked" the camp, and to mask the real objective, the Air Force could have seeded every other rice paddy in North Vietnam.

Asked about the feasibility of using sensors, DIA's Dick Stewart would say, "That's a hell of a good question." He recalled that "The idea was discussed," but North Vietnam had never been spiked and "I guess we didn't push it hard enough. We have to hold ourselves to blame because we didn't. You can say, 'Well, Christ, we should have done it.' "

When Manor and Simons flew back to Florida after their August 10–14 planning meetings with the spooks, they talked about a model that Mayer had introduced them to. Her name was Barbara. Mayer had described her as "quite handsome, amply endowed, impeccably put together." When Simons saw her, he had to agree. "Barbara" was a $60,000 table-size replica of the Son Tay compound, built by the CIA in June at Mayer's request, precise in detail and rigged with special viewing devices. Through them, Simons's men would be able to see the compound exactly as the ground before them would look the night of the raid. By varying the light in the optical viewers, the camp would appear to be lit by a quarter- or half-moon, by flares, or in near-total darkness. Simons had seen similar models on other operations, but none quite this elaborate. He wanted his men to know the target in such detail that, between studies of the model and practice assaults on the Son Tay mock-up at Eglin, every member of the assault force would be able to fight his way into the POW cells even if he was blind, deaf, drunk, and wounded.

Cuba?

Cuba weighed heavily on Marty Donohue's mind. Air Force training for the Son Tay assault began on Thursday, August 20, and by the time Donohue had returned from his trans-Pacific HH-53 record-setting flight and joined the other helicopter and C-130 crews recruited by Warner Britton, they were well into the program. Much of their flying was done over water in the Gulf of Mexico, just south of Eglin Air Force Base. The rest was done at very low level, in terrain-hugging flights which twisted and turned over the mountains of northern Georgia and Tennessee, then back through the flat scrub pines of the Florida panhandle at treetop level. Often they were accompanied by a flight of aging A-1 propeller-driven attack planes, lumbering but maneuverable, tight-turning monsters left over from the Korean War, which usually escorted the Jolly Green Giant helicopters on their Southeast Asia rescue missions.

Donohue had no idea what they were training for. Few of the men did. There was a lot of night flying, refueling practice, and close formation work with the lumbering Sikorsky HH-53 rescue helicopter and its smaller HH-3—sometimes the even smaller Army UH-1 Huey. The latter two usually flew tucked into "draft" formation behind the four-engine, turbine-powered, propeller-driven Lockheed C-130s. Everyone wondered what kind of mission Britton and Manor had dreamed up; but from the duration of the training flights—and reports that the Soviets might be building a submarine resupply base at Cienfuegos in Cuba—Donohue became convinced that Ivory Coast involved a helicopter assault in Cuba.

It all seemed to fit. As HH-53 training progressed, Donohue noted, the flights lasted longer and longer, from just under two hours at first until finally just over four hours in duration. From Eglin, it was roughly 1,000 nautical miles to the southern coast of Cuba, about nine and a half hours' flying time in an HH-53 at its best airspeed. But a raid from Eglin to Cuba was impractical; the actual mission would probably be launched from the huge Tactical Air Command complex at MacDill Air Force Base, south of Tampa. That was the base from which strikes against Soviet missile installations would have been flown in the 1962 Cuban missile crisis. MacDill was about 520 nautical miles from Cuba, roughly five hours' flying time one way in an HH-53; but if the planes landed to refuel on the ground at Homestead Air Force Base south of Miami, the trip to Cuba would run three to three and a half hours. The "profiles fitted"—three and a half hours, lots of over-water flying, a hill-hugging, low-altitude penetration across Cuba's Santa Clara mountain range, then "Bang!" to knock out those sub pens in Cienfuegos.

Other crews in the training program shared Donohue's conviction. Cuba would be the target. They were only about 9,500 miles off.

Donohue's calculations were accurate in one sense, however. During the raid on Son Tay, the HH-53s would be airborne exactly 3.4 hours en route to the target. But there wouldn't be much flying over water, only a few rivers and lakes in Laos and North Vietnam. The three and a half hours would be spent bending around hills and mountains on winding routes the DIA and the NSA had mapped out to hide the penetration into Son Tay through precisely located blind spots in Chinese and North Vietnamese radar coverage. Every turn was carefully timed to offset the scanning intervals of enemy radar antennae.

The training flights at Eglin were long—but not monotonous. Some of them were just plain "hairy." The C-130s, for instance, were operating at the extremes of their capabilities—at what aeronautical engineers call close to the "dead man's curve." Three C-130s would take part in the raid. One, a rescue HC-130, would assist in the early phases of navigation and refuel the helicopters over Laos. The other two would be specially equipped "Combat Talon" C-130s, with precise, new navigation equipment and forward-looking infrared systems (never used before) which had been matched against intelligence "tracks" giving the IR signature of every turning point along the routes into the target. One of these Combat Talons would lead the assault force of five HH-53s and either one HH-3 or UH-1 into Son Tay Prison and drop flares over the camp. The second would guide the supporting A-1 strike force through and under the enemy radar net. The crews of the two Combat Talons had to practice switching roles and formations, however, in case one of them was shot down or had to "abort" en route because of mechanical failure. That was not an unlikely possibility, but it was also not the least of the problems.

Major Irl L. Franklin of the Air Force's 7th Special Operations Squadron and Lieutenant Colonel Albert P. Blosch of Detachment 2, 1st Special Operations Wing, had flown a lot of MC-130 missions—but none like these. The normal cruise speed of an MC-130 at low level is about 250 knots; Blosch and Franklin were now trying to keep theirs airborne at 105 knots—roughly ten knots above the airplane's "stall" speed. They had to fly that slow because the HH-3 and UH-1, one of which would land the compound assault team inside the walls of the prison, couldn't fly any faster. Nor did they have enough power to carry their own precise navigational gear plus the assault team, and a more powerful, bigger helicopter couldn't be used because the clearing inside Son Tay was so small. The MC-130 Combat Talon "mother ships" would have to be like seeing-eye dogs for the long flight into Son Tay; and both helicopters were so underpowered for the mission that they would have to fly "in draft," tucked in close enough behind the MC-130s' wings to be "sucked along" in the planes' vacuum just the way some formula race-car drivers race behind frontrunners on early laps to conserve fuel and gain speed. At 105 knots, a fully loaded HH-3 or UH-1 was at the "upper boundary" of its performance envelope; at 105 knots, an MC-130 was at the rock bottom of its performance curve.

It was crazy. To fly an MC-130 that slow, Blosch and Franklin had to use 70 percent flaps, something they would normally call for only on landing. To stay airborne at that speed, they needed power on and all four engines in perfect tune. If an outboard engine were to fail in that "configuration," the MC-130's flying characteristics were "marginal." They would be too low, of course, to parachute to safety. Blosch and Franklin might avoid a crash landing—"impact"—only if they could push the throttles "straight into the firewall" fast enough to accelerate to 140 knots safe forward airspeed. And their reaction time would be tested every second of the three and a half hour flight into the target; with 70 percent flaps, the MC-130 was "unstable" and could not be flown by autopilot.

Moreover, Blosch and Franklin soon learned, "Caution must be used in making power changes or during roll in and out of turns." Leveling off from a descent in that condition was a "critical maneuver." Too much power applied too quickly would either stall the airplane or accelerate it into the ground. And at 105 knots, the MC-130s could not respond fast enough from a "nose-high attitude" for their terrain-avoidance radars to provide much of a safety margin. Yet the route to the target over northern Thailand, Laos, and western North Vietnam would involve scores of twisting, turning descents. The navigation tasks alone proved to be so complex that, midway through the training program, Manor decided to add a third navigator to the Combat Talon Crews.

The pilot of the assault force MC-130 Combat Talon, Major Irl L. Franklin, had a slug of separate problems to deal with. Once over the target, he would drop flares to light up the compound, and then release "firefight simulators" to distract, discombobulate, and demoralize North Vietnamese ground troops. But in early practice runs, some of the flares Franklin dropped were duds. Someone had shipped the Ivory Coast task force a "bad lot" of ammunition—only the first of many to arrive at Eglin Air Force Base. And in addition to their pioneering test work to find out how slow pilots could fly an MC-130 and still keep it in the air, Franklin and Blosch were also "cross-training" to deliver the flares, firefight simulators, and ground markers in case either had to abort en route.

The flying became more complex as the helicopters, MC-130s, and A-1E Skyraiders began training together. Fully loaded with bombs, rockets, and fuel, the A-1s had to fly at about 145 knots to keep from stalling; and they, too, needed an MC-130 "mother ship" to guide them into the target. Circling and S-turn tactics were devised so the planes flying at 105 knots could keep in contact with the planes flying at 145 knots. Thus, if either Combat Talon was shot down or had to abort, the motherless helicopters or A-1s could guide on the remaining MC-130E.

The aircrews practiced their weaving and twisting, ascending and descending ballet at night at treetop level, over the rugged terrain of northern Georgia and the Great Smoky Mountains, in only partial moonlight. So they wouldn't be spotted from the ground, the pilots had to hold these tight formations with cockpit instrument lights dimmed and without the usual external night navigation lights to help them keep station. The pilots tried electronic and night low-light-level binoculars, but the dimmed cockpit lights made them of little use. In the aft cabins, however, flight mechanics and gunners used them to keep track of the planes behind them. All of this flying had to be done in radio silence; and because weather was so uncertain over Laos and North Vietnam, they had to practice reestablishing contact after flying through clouds or heavy ground fog. In all, Manor's crews logged 1,017 hours in the air getting ready for the raid on Son Tay, without a single accident in the 368 sorties flown under these strenuous conditions. The men earned their flight pay. By mid-September, they were ready to marry up with Simons's men and move into the joint training phase, practicing night assaults on that "village" near Auxiliary Field Number 3.

Range C-2

While Manor's pilots were alternately sweating and freezing in the air, Simons's volunteers were merely sweating on Eglin's Range C-2. Every one of the 103 men was a well-honed Special Forces type, picked among other attributes for his physical strength and stamina. But as soon as they arrived at Eglin, Simons and Sydnor began "getting them in shape." Simons decreed that the eight-hour training day start at 4:00 A.M. and end at noon. For an hour before breakfast on the first day training began, Wednesday, September 9, Simons led them through calisthenics—six repetitions of Army Drill one, the "daily dozen" that every veteran will remember—and then a two-mile run. That day they ran for three minutes, walked for one, and then resumed running; but the exercise period advanced to a new stage every day, and the men were soon doing the daily dozen eight times and running the two miles nonstop. The first week, the training schedule was "relaxed"—seven hours a day of weapons firing, radio procedures and practice, helicopter orientation, demolition drill, patrolling, plus evasion, escape, and survival. And any day that training was completed ahead of schedule, organized athletics were programmed. Later, training started at noon to allow time for three daylight rehearsals,

breaking for supper, then reassembling for three night rehearsals.

By September 17, night training began, starting with night
firing and target recognition, both on the ground and from helicopters, with Sydnor and Meadows juggling right- and left-
handed shooters to get the maximum number of rounds into the
"high threat targets"—the northwest guard tower and the gate.
The other training ranged from cross-country movement, village surveillance, house search, demolition placement, and
house "clearing" to lessons from Doc Cataldo on how to treat
battle wounds, shock, and fractures, and to inject morphine.
Hours were spent on "raid and immediate action drills"; Meadows took the men through them step by step, beginning with
arm and hand signals.

Thumb down: DANGER—enemy or no good—prepare
weapons for firing.
*Thumb down, followed by two fingers moving and
pointing:* ENEMY in that direction.
*Hand forming a fist, pumping from belly to full exten-
sion of an arm:* AMBUSH—move away from the fist and
prepare to open fire.
Hand rotating over the head with finger pointing up:
FORM THE CLOCK DEFENSE.
Thumb up: YES—all clear—okay—prepare to move out.

Meadows's training plan had eight pages of such signals and
drills. Another training annex covered drills for firing different
types, colors, and numbers of star clusters to recall the helicopters in an emergency, the use of strobe lights to mark landing
areas, and special radio procedures for the assault teams, once
they were on the ground, to communicate with each other and
call in the strike aircraft if needed.

Simons then formed the men into three groups. The first was
the compound assault team of 14 men in all, who would land
with Meadows from a small helicopter inside the walls of the
prison. Because space was so cramped in their helicopter, they
would be armed with CAR-15s, a smaller and lighter version of
the 5.56mm M-16 which everyone else would carry. Among
the CAR-15's other features, it had a folding stock and could be
fired with the stock folded forward like a Schmeisser subma-

chine pistol. Sydnor would lead a 20-man "command and security group"; Simons would go with the 22-man "support group" led by Captain Udo H. Walther. Both would land from larger helicopters immediately outside the walls of the Son Tay compound. These teams would each have two belt-fed 7.62mm M-60 machine guns to seal off key approaches with a steady stream of tracer ammunition. On the raid, the three teams would use the call signs "Blueboy" (Meadows's assault group), "Redwine" (Sydnor's security force, led by Captain Dan Turner), and "Greenleaf" (Walther's support team, with Simons). Sydnor's personal call sign was "Wildroot." No one would remember if it was picked at random or for comic relief because some thought his hair was thinning from having worn a helmet too much of his life.

The Air Force and Army teams began jointly practicing the assault itself in earnest on Monday, September 28. Three landings or "insertions" by helicopter were rehearsed each day, three more each night. Some were dry runs, with empty weapons; others were "live-fire," with tracer ammunition, satchel charges, grenades, everything. By then, however, the men had walked, crawled, and run through the mock-up so many times that they knew where every round was going—every *friendly* round that is. The location of each man at every second during the raid was precisely predetermined; a soldier who strayed by more than a yard or a second would have been turned into a 5.56 or 7.62mm wind tunnel by friendly M-16 automatic rifle or M-60 machine-gun fire. After some of the rehearsals, Simons personally went out and counted the holes in every target—silhouettes which had been placed around the mock-up to represent standing, crouched, or dug-in North Vietnamese. He wanted them full of holes. If they weren't, the men would go through another live-fire run. There was no room for error. The attack had to be swift, violent, and lethal. Men who couldn't fire enough rounds quickly and accurately were pulled off the assault force and put in the administrative or logistics support detachment.

By now, Simons's men weren't just shooting their way through the mock-up. They were streaking into the simulated buildings, busting down doors, breaking hasps and hinges, cutting chains and shackles with blowtorches and bolt cutters—and then they took turns carrying each other out of the "village." Of Simons's 103 men, only four knew what they were really training for. To keep up the deception but prevent too much speculation, the other men were told they might have to rescue some sick diplomatic hostages at an embassy. The code name Ivory Coast suggested that the rescue would take place in the Mideast or Africa. Fearing that some of the prisoners might be insane or become irrational in the shock of the raid, Doc Cataldo had the men "resist" being carried. The soldiers learned how to cope with kicking, screaming "diplomats"—and ones too weak to lift a limb.

When the "easy" rehearsals were over, Simons began walking, then running the men through alternate plans. Plan Green would be put into operation in case his own helicopter was shot down or crashed en route. Plan Blue assumed that Meadows's compound assault team had to abort or was lost; in that case, Sydnor's team would breach the wall, clear the compound, and release the prisoners while Simons's group assumed responsibility for securing the area outside Son Tay's walls. Plan Red would be used in case Sydnor's and Cataldo's chopper failed to make it. Simons's team then would take over their functions both inside and outside the compound walls.

Again, Simons took the men through these plans in dry and live-fire exercises, in the daytime and at night, building up to the tempo and violence he expected on the raid itself. But by the end of September, Simons was worried. At night, his men still weren't getting enough rounds into the targets, and they were only two weeks away from deploying for the first possible launch window. The guard towers worried Simons most. Whichever way he juggled the ground force plan, there just weren't enough holes in the target cloth or the two-by-fours that simulated the biggest threat. He asked Manor if the towers could be "taken out" from the air—without endangering the prisoners.

Manor suggested they try an HH-53 helicopter with 7.62 "miniguns"—small, Gatling-like six-barrel cannons—firing from each side and from the rear ramp of the helicopter. If the HH-53 flew at treetop level directly over the compound and between the two towers, it might work. The helicopters carrying the assault force would follow it into Son Tay seconds after the firing pass.

Simons was skeptical. He wanted to see it done, and he wanted to see how it was done. He didn't want the cell areas sprayed with stray lead. Marty Donohue was picked to fly the gunship helicopter. Simons decided to fly with him and fire one of the guns himself. Donohue took him up, his HH-53 loaded with enough gun barrels and ammunition to slaughter a North Vietnamese division if every bullet hit its mark. A UH-1 with a searchlight mounted on it flew overhead to illuminate the mock-up just the way Son Tay would be lit by moonlight and flares the night of the raid. When Donohue, Simons, and Donohue's three gunners made their firing pass, the belly of their HH-53 just inches above some of the cellblock roofs, Simons went deaf. He had forgotten to wear his earplugs.

He couldn't hear the next day, but his eyes were working and "God, the targets were *saturated*." And to Simons's relief, there were no holes in the cloth panels laid out where the cells were supposed to be. Simons was "impressed." Donohue and his gunners were to get to practice that firing run on only one more flight before the raid.

Late at night on Tuesday, October 6, Manor and Simons took the entire force through a final, full-time, live-fire night rehearsal. Every twist and turn of the real route was flown, but over the southeastern United States instead of Southeast Asia. This last "profile" even included a one-hour flight to simulate the last-minute move Simons's men would make from their staging base at Takhli in central Thailand to the launch base at Udorn, just south of the Laotian border but 192 miles closer to the target. From there, it would be a long, circuitous 687-mile flight to Son Tay Prison and back.

Don Blackburn and Ed Mayer flew to Eglin to watch the dress rehearsal. Simons and his men were magnificent, Manor's crews the most unflappable, confident airmen they had ever seen. If all went well, the prisoners at Son Tay would be free men in 15 days. October 21, Manor and Simons had decided, now looked like the best launch date.

Simons was pleased with the rehearsal, but he was confronted by one final problem—and it was a big one. A helicopter could not land inside the compound, not as fast as he needed it to be done. The HH-3 was too big for the cramped area. Air Force pilots had tried every which way, but the fit was too tight.

The HH-3's rotor blades had a diameter of 62 feet and the helicopter was 73 feet long. But there was only 60 to 65 feet between the south latrine and the tree trunks by the POW cell buildings and only 80 feet between the west latrine and the tree in front of the building in the southeast corner of the courtyard. The crash landing would have to be made on a diagonal heading to ensure sufficient clearance for the fuselage length. But there was no way to avoid chopping down some tree limbs on a descent to the ground.

"Practicing landings on the spot in the prison courtyard mock-up would not prepare [the aircrews] for crash landing through the treetops," one of the C-130 navigators, John Gargus, would write later. "That could not be simulated at Eglin. Actual practice landings into a carbon copy of the compound with trees would [have ruined] one helicopter on each try."

The planners talked about having Meadows's team use ropes to rappel down from the helicopter into the compound, but discarded the idea quickly because it took too long, and two helicopters had been shot down in the Delta trying that.

The smaller UH-1, 14 feet shorter than the HH-3, could get in, just barely, but it held fewer troops than Dick Meadows needed. He had to have 14 men; only ten or 11 could squeeze into the Huey. The Huey had other drawbacks. It had only one engine; the HH-3 had two. Limited to 85–87 knots airspeed while fully loaded, the Huey was hard-pressed to fly as fast as its C-130 "mother bird" could fly slow. The helicopter gained forward airspeed by about 20 knots when flying in perfect draft formation just above the C-130's left wing, its fuselage centered between the wingtip and the number-one engine. But in that position the Huey's 48-foot rotor blades overlapped the C-130's left wing, requiring enormous concentration from both pilots. A slight increase in airspeed or an unanticipated course change meant the Huey could lose its drafting position and fall out of formation. Marrying back up was a daunting task, especially since the Huey pilots were flying on night-vision goggles with limited peripheral vision.

Moreover, the UH-1 was not designed for in-flight refueling. That meant Meadows's men would have to marry up with a Huey standing by at some CIA post on the Laotian border and fly into North Vietnam from there. But rendezvousing with the rest of Simons's force in the dark of night wouldn't be easy;

some radio communications would have to be established to effect the linkup, yet radio silence would be essential for security. Even launched from Laos, an extra fuel bladder had to be installed into one of the gunner's wells to give the helicopter sufficient range, further limiting space. Simons's fully battle-dressed Green Berets were cramped in like sardines. They were so jammed together that none of the four-hour training flights carried the 11-man assault force. One Huey was weighted down with the anticipated mission load and flew in the assault formation to an assembly area near the mock-up, where a second Huey picked up the 11 men and switched places for the final 12-to-20-minute run-in for the simulated crash landing. That was hairy enough, but at least Meadows's team arrived fresh and well rested enough to execute the right tactics, although it took them so long to untangle themselves and get out of the helicopter that crash landing inside the walls seemed like an iffy proposition.

The planners worried about how the assault team might perform after four hours in the air. The moment of truth came when the raiders flew their first full-dress, night rehearsal on October 6. Blackburn had insisted on watching it from inside the prison mock-up. When the Huey landed, Meadows's men lost precious seconds exiting the helicopter because of their cramped-up legs, and their dispositions were as distorted as their bodies had been tangled up inside the Huey. Blackburn got in the way of one element leader, who ran right over him and cussed him out with robust vulgarity. That full-profile exercise signaled the end of the helicopter debate.

Manor asked his helicopter pilots to try again with the HH-3. By now, Herb Zehnder and his pilot, Major Herb Kalen, knew what the real mission was and they wanted to give Meadows and his men every split-second margin possible to get into the POW cells before the guards did. They volunteered to crash-land the HH-3 inside the compound. The 62-foot rotor blades would rip into some trees on the final descent: the tree trunks were only 65 feet and 70 feet apart, respectively, at the crucial points. That would let Kalen slip the 73-foot-long helicopter into an 85-foot clearing. But with luck it shouldn't hit with too many "g's." If Meadows and his men were properly braced, spread-eagled flat on mattresses on the helicopter floor, they shouldn't be injured. It was the only solution, Meadows and

Kalen said. Simons and Manor finally agreed. Meadows would set off time-delay charges just before leaving the compound to blow up the crippled helicopter. Kalen and his two crewmen and Meadows and his assault team would fly out of Son Tay in one of the HH-53s that would lift out the prisoners. Kalen and Zehnder practiced landing the HH-3 in smaller and smaller spaces: 31 separate flights, 79½ hours. On the very last try, they got the helicopter safely into the mock-up—with very few inches to spare.

Doc Cataldo, meanwhile, had been learning how to break down doors with a fire ax. It was one of his "cross-training" jobs as he prepared to go on the raid. The other men kidded him because he was "pretty wild" with the ax; he was a much better shot with the M-16 and a .45-caliber pistol. But getting back into top physical shape and practicing busting into a jail was the smallest part of his workload.

Cataldo was worried, very worried, about the condition they would find the POWs in. He had compiled detailed medical profiles on the nine POWs who had been released by North Vietnam, and had interviewed them to learn more about the conditions of captivity in North Vietnam. He also reviewed carefully the precapture medical records of every POW suspected to be in Son Tay and weighed them against medical and psychological studies of prisoners in World War II (especially those from Japanese prison camps, "where there were severe problems") and the Korean War.

The outlook was not good.

Before his capture, the average Son Tay prisoner weighed 171 pounds, was 5 feet 10 inches tall, and was thirty-three years old. Cataldo estimated that the Americans would now be down to 137 pounds, some to 108 pounds. That was his "hopeful" estimate, based on a 20 percent weight loss; in Japanese prisons in World War II, the average weight loss had been 32 percent.

Among the 61 prisoners whom the DIA had positively identified in Son Tay, Cataldo expected that 25 would have (or have had) malaria. In varying combinations, 35 would have intestinal parasites, 15 active dysentery, 12 active tuberculosis, 12 peripheral neuritis, 4 goiter—and two-thirds of them would be suffering from primary malnutrition.

Nor was his psychological "profile" of the POWs cheerful:

The POW has heard very little noise, has had very little physical exercise, and lives in dimly lit rooms. He eats two meals per day, usually consisting of cabbage soup plus bread or rice. Fish and pumpkin occasionally supplement the diet with less than two ounces of meat per week. Sometimes a banana or some other fruit is provided. Flour and sugar cookies are rarely given to the POW. Restriction of total protein intake plus physical inactivity will cause marked muscular atrophy plus a slow reaction to stimuli.

A few POWs will maintain a strong hope for liberation, and some will have given up all hope, but the majority are probably unsure and live day to day driven only by a natural desire to survive. Therefore, for most, the sudden realization that "liberation is here" will be shocking.

How would the prisoners act when liberated? Cataldo predicted that:

Army ground forces will see stunned individuals managing a weak smile. There will be no yelling on their part. The POW will be easily fatigued, having lost so much weight and muscle mass. His night vision will be poor. There will be lesions at the angles of the mouth. The skin on the arms and legs will irritate and bruises will be evident. There may be a slight swelling of the thyroid (neck) area, and the tongue will be somewhat swollen. Speech will be slow and somewhat slurred. He will complain that his feet burn. He will bruise easily, walk unsteadily, and may be emotional and prone to some display of tears.

Cataldo had requisitioned some unique medical equipment; he would later teach Simons's men how to use it to care for the POWs on their ride home from Son Tay. One item was a special "M-5 medical kit" with a Duke inhaler set for use with Penthane, a noninflammable inhalation agent that acted as an anesthetic. Cataldo also made up kits for each helicopter with Ketamine HCL, a very fast-acting "knock-out" anesthetic; hemostats (scissorlike surgical clamps to stop bleeding); inflatable splints; and scissors and cannulas (hollow tubes) for cricothyroidectomies (an emergency operation like a tracheotomy, where a tube is inserted at the base of the throat to suck out fluids and force air into the lungs)—Cataldo was concerned about the borderline respiratory condition of POWs like Wes Schierman. To keep the prisoners warm, there were ponchos specially made by the Army's Natick Laboratories and vacuum-packed to conserve volume. There were also specially made sneakers, with "reinforced sponge insoles," using a Bata comfort shoe as a base. Cataldo had had them designed just for the Son Tay raid, and had lied like a bandit to explain why he needed them.

There were many other items of medical gear, including 100 sets of pajamas and bathrobes for the prisoners (and wounded raiders) to wear on their long trip back to the United States. Getting the Army's hospital at Valley Forge to give him 100 sets of pajamas and bathrobes involved a whole new line of lies and deception. Finally, Cataldo had ordered a lot of Heinz baby food—mashed rice—repackaged in plain sealed foil for security reasons.

Bullets, Blowtorches, and Bolt Cutters

On September 8, as Manor and Simons put their men through their paces at Eglin, a support detachment of 26 officers and enlisted men arrived at Auxiliary Field Number 3 to feed, house, and supply the Son Tay raiders. The detachment included a supply officer and two supply sergeants plus a three-man communications group. Equipping the Son Tay raiders with all the special gear they needed to bust into a prison quickly turned into a nightmare for them. It took a ream of top-priority but unexplained, sometimes oddball requisitions, and some devious improvisations. But the Sears Roebuck catalog saved the day.

After the raid, Roy Manor would hint in his after-action report that the supply section had been a little overworked. "Future operations of this nature," he said, "must include sufficient supply personnel to ensure prompt reaction to sudden requirements. The original concept of one supply officer and two supply sergeants did not provide sufficient flexibility." In hindsight, Manor would suggest that the supply section should have included "an armorer, an ammunition specialist, and a light truck driver/clerk," plus "an Air Force supply liaison sergeant well versed in Air Force supply procedures and forms," and a "Class A [finance] Agent" with "a suitable amount of cash . . . for direct local procurement"; something like $4,000, he suggested, would have saved a lot of headaches. The frustrations his three supply specialists encountered made it obvious why.

Each of the raiders, it was found during training, needed a special knife to pry open doors or barricades; it had to be similar to a machete but with a heavier blade and a sharper point. The Army's Personnel Equipment Center at Natick Laboratory near Boston had developed something close to what was needed, and Fort Benning's Ranger Department had tested it with good results. But Manor's supply crew found that even by expediting the Army's purchasing system, it would take *four months* to get the few knives the raiders needed. They then turned to a special purchase section at Eglin, asking for a similar knife which they found was available locally. Again, they were told, getting the right number would be "an extremely lengthy process." But time was pressing. They asked the base machine shop to alter standard government machetes into the desired blade. After weeks of trying unsuccessfully through the high-priority special channels set up so carefully by the Pentagon for the raid, the men got the knives they needed "in a matter of days" by relying on a local grinding wheel. Another special request came from Simons, who told the supply crew to get 250 30-round magazine clips for the raiders' M-16 rifles. Standard Army issue was a 20-round magazine, and no 30-round magazines, the supply crew was told, could be obtained through normal channels. One supply NCO tried to go directly to Colt Arms, which manufactured 30-round magazines, but then found that he still had to go back through Department of the Army headquarters before dealing with the contractor. He finally got the magazines, only to learn that the Army did not have any "load-bearing equipment" pouches for a soldier to carry them. The supply section quickly had a bunch of Claymore mine bags modified for that purpose.

Information about North Vietnamese prison layouts obtained from previously freed POWs made it clear that a variety of leg stocks, metal hasps, and locks might be encountered. The raiders needed two oxygen-acetylene emergency cutting out-fits; they had to be lightweight, simple to operate, and have a burning time of 30 minutes. The supply section searched out a number of commercial sources without success. Then the sup-ply department at the Naval Air Station at Pensacola, Florida, found that suitable gear was available through the federal sup-ply system. After it got the federally supplied outfits, however, the supply section learned that the only quick way to get the oxygen and acetylene needed for them was to go back through local civilian sources.

Bolt cutters would also be needed on the raid. The supply section found what looked like just the ticket in the federal sup-ply catalog: 36-inch bolt cutters that should have had plenty of leverage and cutting strength. But when they arrived and Si-mons's men began practicing with them, they found the metal jaws so soft that they failed to cut the ¾-inch chains and pad-locks which Simons's intelligence team told him to expect within the Son Tay cellblocks. The supply crew undertook another search and finally settled on bolt cutters of three differ-ent sizes used by local Air Force fire-fighting crews.

Simons also needed six compact, gasoline-powered chain saws, light, simple to operate, with about a 16-inch chain drive. And they had to have a waterproof ignition; it might be raining in North Vietnam. Somewhat soured by their experience with the federal supply system, the supply NCOs visited nearby hardware stores and lumber yards and bought two different models from local merchants. Both made by Skil, they weighed just over 19 pounds and cost $206.96 and $229.46, respec-tively, not including local sales tax.

Little things kept the supply crew busy, too. Some of the raiders would be carrying M-79 40mm grenade launchers and needed ammunition vests for the rounds. The vests were requi-sitioned through the federal supply system. But Simons's men found they would not work because the round they had been designed to carry was no longer in use. To fit the new, ogive-shaped round, the supply crew had to have Eglin's fabric shop modify the straps which secured the round in every pocket of each vest.

To document conditions under which American POWs were being held captive, Simons wanted some of his men to photograph the cells at Son Tay. Several of the Special Forces volunteers he selected, therefore, were also expert photographers. They recommended taking along six 35mm Pen-EE cameras. When the supply crew found that they were not available through normal supply channels, Simons's men settled on Kodak's simple S-20 Instamatic. They had "the desired ruggedness and simplicity"—but Simons would later report that the pictures they got were "worthless."

The supply section had to fill a stack of other unusual requisitions, including electrical head lamps which, Simons found, proved a nuisance when worn on the head, so he had his men hang them on their load-bearing equipment harnesses; 15 rucksacks to carry escape and evasion gear which had to be made by the fabric shop of Eglin's Special Operations Force; and three extra fire extinguishers, which would be carried in the assault helicopter that would crash-land inside the Son Tay compound. Megaphones were needed to warn the prisoners that they were being rescued and should stay calm and keep their heads down while the assault team broke into their cellblocks. Twenty raiders would be very close to exploding demolition charges and needed special ear protectors; the others needed standard earplugs so the long, noisy helicopter flight into North Vietnam would not cause them to land at Son Tay half deaf. Simons's men also needed gloves to prevent injury to their hands while locating locks to be cut. Standard summer Air Force flying gloves were decided upon; they gave a tight fit and would not have to be removed to operate weapons and other equipment.

Every man needed a set of goggles. Originally, they were to preserve night vision when the illuminating flares were set off; later, the goggles proved equally essential to protect the men from flying debris stirred up by the helicopters' rotor downwash. The goggles became a real problem. The supply team first tried standard Air Force goggles with dark amber and green lenses, but they didn't give enough protection from the brilliant flares that would light up Son Tay in the dead of night. Simons's men then tried special radiological lenses developed by the Army's Night Vision Laboratory, but they proved too hard to use. As a last resort, the supply team started combing Sears Roebuck catalogs and sporting goods stores for a solution. Finally they improvised, coating clear-lens monocular goggles from the Army's Combat Development Command with the red "Chart Pak" pressure-sensitive tape commonly used by commercial artists and military draftsmen to make charts and vugraphs. Binoculars were found for the HH-53 aircrews, who would need them while they were sitting on the ground to see if anyone was approaching their helicopters as the rescue was under way and they were waiting to be called back to extract everyone. The Sears Roebuck catalogs later proved invaluable for obtaining ideas and rough specifications for a host of other peculiar equipment needs which Simons laid in the supply team's lap.

But it was ammunition and weapons, the basic tools of an army, which gave Simons's men their biggest headaches. Simons wanted some shotguns for area fire while clearing buildings. The Army's standard 12-gauge pump shotguns, he found, fired too small a shot pattern at 20 meters. The supply crew turned to sporting goods catalogs and came up with a five-shot, automatic gun which Simons loved: the shot pattern covered a six-foot area at 25 meters but distributed enough lead to kill anyone in it.

To help mark targets, Simons wanted some 40mm white phosphorous "spotting rounds" for his M-79 grenade launchers. Their incendiary filling burned brilliantly and it was lethal as well. To its disbelief, the supply team had to go through ammunition channels all the way to the Department of the Army and finally to the CIA, only to find that no such round existed. They tested what was offered and finally decided on the 40mm White Star Cluster. But as the pace of training quickened and the number of live-fire rehearsals increased, Simons quickly exhausted the local supply. His supply crew called Fort Bragg to order more, but was told there weren't enough in the supply system. It took a phone call to the Pentagon to get Continental Army Command Headquarters to ship 250 rounds directly from the depot.

Small-arms tracer ammunition would also be used to mark targets. Simons and 50 other men would be carrying .45-caliber pistols, the standard Army sidearm dating back to World War I. But tracer ammunition for it, they found, was a "controlled item." By now, Simons's team had the highest supply priority of any Army unit anywhere in the world, but it still took special coordination with the supply manager at Joliet

Arsenal in Illinois to get the tracer rounds released from Aberdeen Proving Ground in Maryland.

In 1970, the Army was spending close to $10 million a day, one-fourth of its total budget, on ammunition for Vietnam. But as Simons's share of it began arriving at Eglin, his men found that a lot of it didn't work. To set off demolition charges, 1,000 nonelectric blasting caps had been requisitioned from Fort Bragg and shipped from Army stocks at Fort Benning. Simons's demolitionists reported that 22 percent of them misfired; that is, didn't fire or fired late. It took a written report to the Special Forces Center supply officer, coordination with the Fort Bragg post ammunition officer, and the resourcefulness of a Mr. Thomas at Fort Bragg's ammo dump to finally track down 100 caps that would go off as advertised—and they had to be shipped from a small, special stock held at Fort Stewart, Georgia.

Simons wanted some men to carry a few 66 mm light antitank weapons (LAWs) in case they had to knock out vehicles on the roads into Son Tay. Soon after the LAWs arrived, however, Fort Bragg's Thomas called with bad news: the lot shipped to Eglin had been suspended. The rounds fired reliably enough to be used for training, but not when lives depended on them. The LAW was a standard Army weapon issued in high density to infantry and tank units all over the world, but Simons's supply team had to call Joliet Arsenal in Illinois to track down 250 rounds that worked as advertised. They turned out to be located at Lone Star Ammunition Plant in Texarkana, Texas, and would have to be diverted from a shipment bound for Southeast Asia. Simons's harried supply team had to prevail upon Fort Bragg again to get the requisition filled.

Simons's growing arsenal still wasn't stocked to his satisfaction. Two kinds of satchel charges and two special demolition charges would be needed. To blast a hole in the compound wall through which the rescued prisoners could be taken to the waiting helicopters, four 30-pound satchel charges would be carried. But Simons wasn't going to rely on the standard issue; to save lives (or, as military jargon goes, "to minimize personnel exposure"), he believed that if you were going to err, err on the side of violence. Simons ordered the explosives to be "heavily overcharged." To knock out a concrete power tower just south of the target, Simons's demolitionists recommended using a five-pound satchel charge. Simons thought that was fine—and then told them to use four charges.

To blow up the helicopter that was to land Dick Meadows's assault team inside the cramped Son Tay compound, Simons's demolitionists experimented with various destruction devices; they came up with a three-pound mixture of C-4 and Thermite stuffed into a 30-inch length of 4-inch fire hose. It would be placed under the helicopter's floor in a bilge sump between the forward and aft fuel tanks. To prevent the North Vietnamese from disabling the explosives, Simons's men decided to secure them by a specially padlocked metal cover and set them off at the last minute by a ten-minute time fuse. Fine, Simons told them—but light two fuses.

To down a bridge 120 meters north of the prison, the men recommended using two satchel charges. They could be carried in individual rucksacks and swiftly hung over the two metal stringers under the bridge's treadways. From standard demolition tables, the demolitionists computed the size of the charges needed, but by now they had learned the name of the game; the charges they ordered each weighed 30 pounds, ten times what the formula provided. Simons agreed—but had them add two backup charges of equal strength.

One final, but crucial, equipment need challenged Simons's supply crew: a night sight. Twenty years after the Korean War and at least six years into Vietnam, the Army had learned that combat against an Asian enemy, especially, put a premium on night combat. Since Korea, the Army had spent $18.4 billion on research and development; since darkness covers the earth about 50 percent of the time, a good fraction of that money presumably was spent on equipment that would function when the sun wasn't shining. But in 1970 the Army, Simons found, still didn't own a rifle sight that would enable soldiers to shoot accurately in the dark. He turned to the CIA; it didn't have one either.

In "live-fire" rehearsals, Simons found to his dismay that at night even his best shooters were getting only about 25 percent of the rounds fired at 50 meters into torso-size targets which simulated enemy soldiers standing up in a foxhole. With that kind of accuracy, he would need to pre-position a small ammunition depot at Son Tay for the 26-minute assault. Simons was genuinely concerned: unless night-firing accuracy could be improved dramatically, it would take far too long to neutralize the opposition, and the lives of both the prisoners and his own men would be jeopardized by all those stray rounds.

Early in September, however, he was relieved to learn through special supply channels of a closely guarded, secretly developed, new infrared device that might do the trick. The sight was a distinct improvement over the earlier, bulky 30-pound infrared device that the Army had used with token success late in the fifties and sixties; and the new sight weighed only six pounds. Using every priority he could muster, Simons had the Army's entire supply shipped to Eglin. But when the highly classified gear was uncrated, there were only six devices. One of Simons's supply specialists joked, "Maybe they want us to take turns using them."

Those six devices, Simons soon found out, were all the Army owned. They were hand-built items, he was told, still being tested; there was "no way" more could be provided in time for the raid.

Simons challenged the men on his supply team to come up with something that 17 years and $18 billion had been unable to produce. They were wiser now; they knew that the military supply system wasn't necessarily the answer to every soldier's prayer. Nor, they had learned, did the Army's hardware specialists always know what was available on the commercial market; they were sometimes too busy reinventing the wheel, blinded by a "not-invented-here" sort of tunnel vision. Simons's men, on the other hand, cared enough to steal the very best.

They began combing what was now a small library of sporting goods catalogs, hunting magazines, and gun advertisements. One of them had a small ad from Armalite Corporation in Costa Mesa, California, for a $49.50 "Singlepoint Nite Sight." Dick Meadows had seen the sight at a gun show in California and suggested they buy it. Armalite, they knew, was the firm that had privately developed Gene Stoner's design for the M-15 rifle, the one Army Ordnance had tested superficially and then rejected in favor of its own, much heavier, arsenal-designed M-14. The Army was persuaded to retest the weapon, and again the M-15 flunked, but only because the Ordnance Corps had substituted outmoded, earlier M-14 barrels for a new design that Stoner had persuaded Armalite to adopt when it bought the rights to his gun. The tests were run again, but it took almost three more years to overcome gamesmanship and one-upmanship at the highest levels of bureaucracy before the Army reluctantly admitted that the M-14 it had spent ten years and millions of dollars to develop was a lemon. In 1963, the Army finally asked for money to reequip its Vietnam forces— and eventually, all of its troops—with the Stoner Armalite weapon. Armalite by this time had sold its rights to Colt Arms, and the redesigned weapon was finally designated the M-16.

Simons's men called Armalite on September 15, and casually asked about the availability of the $49.50 night sight and the mount that went with it. Three days later Armalite shipped one; at Eglin's request, it was sent by airmail. As soon as the package arrived, Simons's supply section quickly read the pocket-size, 16-page operator's manual. The sight, they learned, was an old Swedish invention, patented worldwide, made in Great Britain and imported to the United States by a prominent Minnesota sporting goods firm, Normark Corporation. Every serious gun buff in America, they concluded, knew about it—except the Army.

The men hurriedly tested the sight under field conditions. The system looked promising: it weighed only 7½ ounces, was only 1 inch in diameter and 6¾ inches long, and could be dropped 8 feet onto concrete without breaking. To their chagrin, Simons's supply section noted in the operator's manual that the sight had even been designed to military specifications. There were problems with the mount; it tended to wear loose and sometimes break off—but the sight worked. Simons immediately ordered 49 more.

When they arrived and were tested further by Simons's assault force, target hits increased dramatically; shot groups from every burst were much smaller; his soldiers felt more confident of their weapons. At 25 meters, even the poorest marksman could fire all rounds into a 12-inch circle at night. At 50 meters, the same shooter could put every round into an "E-type silhouette" the size of a man's torso. In daytime tests, the sight improved speed in engaging a target and in shifting fire, although it was less accurate than the standard, open M-16 sight. At night, the situation reversed. Shooters could engage targets and shift fire just as fast, but with deadly accuracy. And the raid, of course, would be conducted in the dead of night.

The supply section was now feeling its oats and assured him the mount could be fixed, somehow. Twenty-seven more sights and mounts were ordered; by the time the last shipment arrived, at the ninth hour on October 21, Simons's three-man armament laboratory told him they had a fix for the mount—"a generous use of black electrician's tape."

All this while, Simons's support detachment had to maintain and repair a small warehouse of other equipment his troops were training with or would need on the raid, including 234 radios—just for the 56-man ground force. One reason there were so many radios was that Simons wanted two complete sets of communications gear at Eglin; one was "on loan" from higher headquarters for training, the other would be used on the mission itself. Another reason was the complexity of the operation and the need for instantaneous communications between so many elements during the short 26 minutes Simons's men would be on the ground. Simons himself would need eight separate radio nets; his troops would land with four different kinds of radios.

Two of the radio nets were for ultrahigh frequency (UHF) air-to-ground transmissions. Simons would use them to call for any A-1 close support strikes his men might need, to recall helicopters to extract his force from and take the prisoners out of Son Tay, and to relay his operational reports from the objective area to Roy Manor at the Monkey Mountain command post near Da Nang, where he in turn would relay the raid's progress to the Pentagon. Two AN-PRC-41 radios would be taken on the raid for this purpose, one carried by Simons's radio operator, one by Sydnor's. A third net would be needed for Simons's forward air controllers to direct the close support strikes if they were called in. These communication requirements meant that radios used by the ground forces had to be compatible with radios in the aircraft—a detail that one might think would have been worked out by that time in the Vietnam War. But that wasn't quite the case; the dilemma required experimentation and some modifications. The main problem was a very slight overlap of frequencies between the airborne frequency modulation (FM) radios and the man-pack radios used on the ground. The overlap was only two megacycles, which, Manor noted later, "did not give us a great deal of flexibility." He would insist, ". . . however, it worked fine."

Ten AN-PRC-77 FM radios would be carried on backpacks for this purpose. Four more nets would be required by the ground force, one for each of the three groups in the force, and a fourth to receive orders from and relay operational reports to Simons. For this purpose, the ground force would carry 24 AN-PRC-88 "handy talkie" radios. Finally, each of the 56 raiders would carry the compact AN-PRC-90 survival radio, not quite as long or thick as a carton of cigarettes. The men would use these in case a helicopter was shot down or had to force-land on the way to or from the objective. If something went wrong at Son Tay itself, Simons had decided, they wouldn't be needed; but he would wait until just before the mission to tell the men why not. In all, Simons and his 55 volunteers would carry 92 radios into Son Tay—almost as many as a 794-man infantry battalion takes into combat. They would be able to communicate almost 12 times better than the average front-line soldier.

Besides these 92 radios and their training counterparts, there were 50 other radios at Eglin which Simons used for spares and for administrative control during training. Keeping all 234 radios operating was a full-time chore for the supply detachment's overworked communications supervisor and his two radio operators. They speculated that ABC's *Wide World of Sports* used less equipment to televise the Olympics. To help them, Manor and Simons finally borrowed a complete electronics repair shop from the Air Force. But it was staffed with only one full-time noncommissioned officer; four of Simons's ground force radio operators pitched in with periodic assistance, on top of their full training schedule. Somehow, the five men kept the radios operable. During the raid, every one of them would function perfectly.

Throughout the training period at Eglin, Manor and Simons were proving an old Israeli Defense Force adage: Lean forces fight best. In 1970, the Pentagon's budget showed, there were 175,000 soldiers and civilians handling "Army logistics and materiel support." Simons's six-man supply and communications section got roughly half of the gear it needed through them—but only about half of that worked as advertised. The rest they had to improvise, buy, test, repair, and maintain on their own.

Manor's mini-wing imposed its own special requirements. It needed more precise navigation gear for its MC-130s and had to borrow forward-looking infrared (FLIR) pods that hitherto had been used only by the CIA. It needed "anchor points" for its A-1s in their objective and reserve areas and decided to use napalm, a reference point that would burn on the ground; but the napalm had to burn longer than normal. Manor's logisticians designed a pallet-mounted napalm tank with a retarded drag chute that would descend almost vertically, such that the napalm would "pool" when it hit the ground and burn much longer than if spread over a long area. They found they could get it to burn for at least an hour. They needed long-burning flares and devised so-called "log flares" for the mission, similar to railroad flares, which also added to the confusion caused to enemy ground troops. Firefight simulators that sounded like machine-gun fire were specially designed for the mission by the CIA, little more than firecrackers encased in plastic and dropped by pallets from the MC-130s.

Manor's planes needed flares to drop from C-130s and the HH-53 helicopters, but they were normally launched from a device that didn't allow enough time for the flare to ignite when dropped from low altitude. His crews switched to the Mark 8 flare, which had no launcher and had to be dropped by hand. Manor also wanted a munition that his A-1s could drop to stop vehicles at night. The CBU-24 cluster bomb was considered ideal for such missions and had been certified for use by A-1s, but only when dropped from 3,000 feet or when the plane's dive was started at that altitude or higher. That was too high for the rescue mission profile because of the proximity of so many antiaircraft guns and surface-to-air missiles. Manor borrowed eight Rockeye bombs from the Navy, tested them, had them quickly certified for use on A-1s, and developed a checklist for his airmen to use them. He also needed a very-high-frequency jammer, the QRC-128, on the A-1s to jam North Vietnamese air defense communications, but the two had never been married before. Manor's support personnel borrowed a QRC-128 from Air Force Logistics Command, tried it on an A-1, and found that it worked well. He borrowed more of them and had three A-1s modified in-theater to use them.

The Ivory Coast Yo-Yo

While Doc Cataldo was practicing ax marksmanship, the other Son Tay raiders were perfecting entry into and escape from a "village." Sydnor had them rehearse their alternate plans time after time—contingencies should one of the three helicopters carrying the ground force not arrive when or where it was supposed to—and he made them practice the plans week after week.

Manor and Simons found their "spare time" filled with chores to "coordinate" the operation. They visited everywhere from the White House to Army and Air Force headquarters in Saigon, flying back and forth from Eglin so frequently that at times they must have felt the Pentagon had strapped them to the end of a yo-yo. Blackburn and Mayer worked hard to front for them and "run interference" as much as possible, but many of the problems required Manor and Simons's personal presence.

Soon after he was put in command of Ivory Coast, Manor flew to Scott Air Force Base near St. Louis. There, he talked personally with the commander, Military Airlift Command (MAC), and showed him the letter from the Air Force Chief of Staff ordering support of the Joint Contingency Task Group on a "no questions asked" basis. MAC would handle medical evacuation of the prisoners from Thailand back to the States. Manor had to arrange for MAC's C-141 Starlifters to be ready on a moment's notice, without anyone—including MAC's commander—knowing what for. Moreover, all of Manor's helicopter crews were from MAC's Aerospace Rescue and Recovery Service, as were the HH-53 and HH-3 aircraft he was training with at Eglin. The helicopters that would actually be used on the raid would have to be "drawn down" at the last minute from rescue assets already in place in Southeast Asia. It was becoming increasingly clear that timing of the raid would depend upon the weather—and the Air Weather Service worked for MAC.

A similar visit had to be made to Tactical Air Command headquarters near Norfolk, Virginia, since the fixed-wing MC-130s and A-1s were TAC assets. Manor also hand-carried the "no questions asked" letter to the commanding general of the Air Force Systems Command (AFSC) at Andrews Air Force Base near Washington. There would be some very new and sensitive navigation and communications gear aboard many of the airplanes, some of it so new that it was still almost in the experimental stage. Special support would be needed from AFSC to install and maintain that gear; some of it had never been installed before on the kinds of planes Manor would be using. The equipment included GRC-128 very high frequency jammers for the A-1s; they would be used to disrupt voice commands from North Vietnam's ground control intercept controllers to vector any MIG fighters sent against the assault force. New forward-looking infrared navigation systems designed by Texas Instruments would be used aboard the MC-130 Combat Talon mother ships. These FL-2B FLIR sets were complex to install, maintain, and operate—to the point where it would take the full-time attention of an extra navigator to identify checkpoints en route to the target and pinpoint the objective itself. New Rockeye road denial/anti-vehicle bomblet dispensers would be needed for the A-1s; and the MC-130s would have to be modified to drop illumination flares, napalm fire bombs, firefight simulators, and log flares.

Manor, Simons, and Blackburn had other worries. On Wednesday, September 2, Max Newman—"Blue Max"—discovered a "significant unauthorized disclosure of classified information" at a bar near Fort Bragg by a "former member" of SACSA's planning group. Blackburn had the man "amputated"—quietly reassigned to another post; but he was tailed everywhere he went until the raid was over.

At about the same time, the Army's chief "special operations" planner, Brigadier General Clarke T. Baldwin, asked Blackburn about the medical evacuation plan. He suggested bringing the POWs to Tripler Army General Hospital in Hawaii. Others wanted them flown directly to the Andrews Air Force Base medical center. Blackburn wrote a note to himself: "Where will all the players be when the curtain goes up?" It was a "detail" he could iron out, but Manor would have to arrange for MAC to get the C-141s to the right destination.

In some areas, Blackburn was getting "too much help." By now his boss, John Vogt, had been promoted to director of the Joint Staff. His replacement, Army Lieutenant General Melvin R. Zais, wasn't yet "wired in" on the raid. In fact, even though Zais was the JCS director of *operations,* months would pass before he was cleared to know about the one being planned for

Son Tay. Blackburn appealed to Lieutenant General Richard T. Knowles, "the Assistant to the Chairman," to help turn down the volume and frequency of the advice and inquiries he and Mayer were getting.

In one case, for instance, a general officer who had the ear of the Army Vice Chief of Staff expressed doubt about the wisdom of landing *inside* the Son Tay compound. Blackburn heard via the grapevine that the officer was concerned about "losing" a helicopter in Son Tay. When he got wind of this idle chatter, Blackburn invited the officer down to the specially cleared SACSA rooms and suggested they "talk things out." It was an amicable meeting. The officer told Blackburn he had "just been thinking out loud." Then he asked if Blackburn had thought about the cost of the helicopter that might have to crash-land inside the compound and be destroyed. He suggested using the smaller Army UH-1 Huey, which cost about $350,000, instead of the larger Air Force HH-3, which cost almost a million dollars.

Blackburn exploded: "Jesus Christ, if it's a question between saving seconds and lives or using a god-damned Huey because it's cheaper, we're worrying about the wrong problem." He was aghast. In six years of the Vietnam War, over 3,000 helicopters had been shot down or destroyed; and here was an American general officer, privy to the Son Tay rescue, worrying about losing one more. This kind of nitpicking, distraction, and doubt came up often, but it had to be resolved. The last thing Manor and Simons needed, Blackburn knew, was to have their attention diverted from training for the raid to sweep off "sawdust" from termites in the Pentagon. He realized how right Vogt had been in his decision to keep SACSA intact and let someone else lead the raid.

There were other, more substantive problems: deception plans to cover the task force's deployment from Eglin to Southeast Asia; special communications during the raid linking Manor and Simons with the National Military Command Center; "little things" like picking the right code word to "execute"; whether or not a formal JCS operations order was needed to "legalize" the raid.

The Son Tay rescue would be the first major military operation in American history conducted under direct control of the Office, Chairman, Joint Chiefs of Staff. The key intermediate headquarters, Commander-in-Chief, Pacific, would be "informed" and directed to "support" the operation—but not to perturb it or redesign it. One three-star general, when finally "read in" on the raid, questioned that it should be directed from the Pentagon. He asked Blackburn if it shouldn't be handled through Strike Command, the Army–Navy–Air Force headquarters at MacDill Air Force Base, Florida, set up early in the sixties to train and deploy joint tactical forces for overseas contingencies. The suggestion was about as useful as teats on a bull. STRICOM, as it was called, was as far removed from Southeast Asian matters as Walter Mitty was from reality. John Vogt told the officer to leave Son Tay alone and get back to work on other JCS problems.

At their end of the bureaucracy, Manor and Simons had their own troubles. A month after they were picked to lead the mission, on Wednesday, September 16, they were called before the Joint Chiefs of Staff for a status report. At three o'clock that afternoon, Manor briefed the chiefs on the "technical concept," reported the plan was feasible, and said his force would finish training and be ready to deploy by Thursday, October 8. He recommended that the rescue be made on Wednesday, October 21.

Just over a week later, on Thursday, September 24, Manor was called back to Washington to discuss the raid with Defense Secretary Laird. CIA Director Richard Helms was present at the briefing. Manor again recommended the October 20–25 launch window. Laird said he would have to "defer approval" pending "coordination with higher authority."

After World War II service aboard a destroyer in the Pacific, where he was wounded and won the Purple Heart, and after 18 years on the House Defense Appropriations Subcommittee, Laird was a seasoned expert on defense matters, widely respected for his soft-spoken and unique understanding of the military. But given the situation in 1969, the Secretary of Defense was "a very unpopular figure in the U.S.," he would recall later. And with strong personalities like Nixon, Kissinger, and Haig in the White House and diplomatic second-guessing on every front from America's ambassadors in Vietnam, Thailand, and Laos—not to mention W. Averell Harriman's delegation at the Paris peace talks—Laird had more heavy hitters intruding on his turf than any other cabinet member.

From the moment he was sworn in as Defense Secretary on

January 21, 1969, he had put the prisoner-of-war issue at the top of his priorities. That represented a profound course change for the United States, since the Johnson administration had relegated POW matters to the State Department while the Pentagon took a backseat on POW affairs amid a mélange of interagency committees.

Moreover, the State Department's POW work fell into Harriman's portfolio, and his principal focus on the POW issue was to keep silent about it, at least publicly. In 1964 the U.S. even began referring to the POWs as "detainees" instead of as prisoners or "captured" or "interned," as had been the Defense Department's policy. The "detainee" sobriquet even applied to formal DoD press releases. (That policy remained in effect until July of 1966. In August of that year, the U.S. government counted only 45 airmen as being held prisoner in the north; later evidence would place the total at closer to 150.)

Harriman's "speak no evil" approach was formalized as U.S. policy in 1965 with a conscious decision to pursue quiet diplomacy to secure release of and better treatment for the POWs. Throughout 1966 and 1967 the Pentagon deferred to the State Department on most POW matters—efforts to gain prisoner release, attempts to persuade North Vietnam to abide by the Geneva Convention, and even on determinations of what information to provide next of kin. By 1968, Harriman's low-key approach had become gospel, lest it perturb the Paris peace talks (which were hard to perturb in any event, because they were going nowhere).

While the North Vietnamese increasingly viewed the prisoners as an asset to be exploited, both as leverage in the Paris peace talks and in the propaganda contest to turn American public opinion against the war, the Joint Chiefs of Staff and many senior Pentagon officials wanted to persuade North Vietnam that the POWs were more of a liability to them than a prize. But Harriman proved a tough adversary for those in the Pentagon who cried for more visibility—and honesty—on the POW situation.

John F. Kennedy had appointed Harriman Assistant Secretary of State for Far Eastern Affairs in 1961, a post he quickly described as "a wasteland . . . a disaster filled with human wreckage." Harriman soon negotiated the 1962 Geneva

Accords that made Laos "neutral" territory at a time when it was estimated there were 10,000 North Vietnamese troops there. An International Control Commission was established to monitor the withdrawal of all foreign troops—U.S., Russian, and North Vietnamese. The commission recorded the withdrawal of only 40 North Vietnamese, but for years Harriman fought to limit CIA and preclude U.S. military operations in the country. "In effect," Professor Richard H. Shultz, Jr., of the Fletcher School of Law & Diplomacy would record later, Harriman had "conceded Laos and unencumbered use of the Ho Chi Minh Trail to Hanoi." Harriman remained adamant about limiting U.S. operations in Laos. He was clearly out of his element in Southeast Asia, but he was a vicious and brutal bureaucratic infighter. Kennedy's national security adviser had called him the "Crocodile," referring to Harriman's bureaucratic negotiating strategy, described by his staff as "water torture: he would make the same point over and over, until his adversaries gave in." Bobby Kennedy gave him a gold crocodile; Harriman's staff gave him a silver one. They inscribed it, "from your victims."

Harriman was as intractable about bringing treatment of the POWs to the forefront of American and world consciousness as he was about leveling the playing field in Laos. Laird, on the other hand, was determined to publicize the POWs' plight and pressure the North Vietnamese into better treatment for them. He truly empathized with the POW families, met with POW wives often, helped them become better organized, and encouraged them to be more vocal. Laird became the first administration official of any stature to proclaim America would not pursue its "Vietnamization" program to the point of complete U.S. withdrawal until the prisoners were released and arrangements made to account for the missing.

Early on, he had decided that the administration needed to "go public" about North Vietnam's medieval treatment of its American prisoners. He wanted to arouse U.S. and world public opinion in a campaign to pressure the north into greater compliance with its pledges under the Geneva Convention. Ever since 1967, when Lt. Cdr. Richard A. Stratton's puppet-like movements before western television cameras in Hanoi had aroused suspicions of torture, the Defense Department had learned much more than it was allowed to reveal about the torture being inflicted on the POWs and the primitive conditions of their captivity. The horror of their incarceration became evident when Navy Commander Jeremiah A. Denton, Jr., shot down early in July of 1965, was taken before television cameras against his will in 1966 and blinked out the letters "t-o-r-t-u-r-e" in Morse code.

In March, Laird launched a formal "go public" campaign, even though Harriman had objected vociferously. Years later, Laird would reveal that Harriman had told him in February, "If you do this, you will delay the peace negotiations under way in Paris at this time." Laird said he told Harriman, "As Secretary of Defense, I *owe* these POWs the responsibility to let the public know [about their treatment]." He worked quietly to mobilize the POW families and develop a coalition with them, the national and international media, and the three military departments.

His effort reached an early peak soon after North Vietnam released three POWs on August 5, 1969. Two of them brought home an incredible memory bank, naming every single prisoner known to their fellow POWs. They reeled off many more than the 339 names the North Vietnamese had released that spring—as well as some who were thought to have been heard or spotted but who could not be confirmed and some they or fellow POWs knew had died in prison, but whom the north had never admitted holding prisoner. Laird met with the two men in Bethesda Naval Hospital (the third was being treated in California), where they made clear how bad conditions really were and what torture they and others had endured.

Seaman Apprentice Douglas B. Hegdahl had been kept in solitary confinement, for instance, for seven months. Navy Lieutenant (j.g.) Robert F. Frishmann said that Stratton had been "deprived of sleep, beaten, had his fingernails removed, and was put in a dark cell for 38 days." He had been "tied up with rope to such a degree that he still has large scars on his arms from rope burns which became infected." Lieutenant Commander John S. McCain III, although suffering from multiple fractures at the time of his capture, had endured in an isolation cell for over a year. "Medical treatment" was meant to keep prisoners alive, not to heal them. Prisoner appearances before foreign delegations were coerced; statements that their treatment was humane were extorted. "If they don't have state-ments of humane treatment, they have ways of getting them."

Laird decided that the public needed to hear this firsthand account. He went on record in a memorandum to the White House, saying he intended to hold a press conference with them: "If the Department of Defense does not publicly deplore North Vietnam's treatment of prisoners, we in effect would be condoning their actions." On September 2, the two Navy men let it all hang out after being introduced by the reading of a statement from Laird. The press conference was held at Bethesda Naval Hospital, where they were still being treated. They said that, despite North Vietnamese threats of reprisals against their fellow prisoners if they divulged the truth about their treatment, they had been tortured repeatedly, had led the same miserable everyday existence as other inmates, and had credible knowledge of the harsh treatment most POWs had re-ceived. What was especially poignant was that Hegdahl, who had become a prisoner after he fell off (or was blown off) the deck of his destroyer when its six-inch guns unexpectedly opened fire at night, had been ordered to accept early release against his violent objections. One of those who recognized what a prodigious memory Hegdahl had, who had insisted he return home, and who had helped coach him in memorizing the names of other POWs, was Stratton. Hegdahl's list also pro-vided the first confirmation that some Americans taken pris-oner in Laos were being held in Hanoi.

Hanoi's cruel treatment of American prisoners gradually be-came a front-page issue and soon punctuated the op-ed pages. By late 1969, North Vietnam's treatment of the POWs began to improve. History may never know how much of that stemmed from Ho Chi Minh's death that September or from the public furor ignited by Laird's go-public policy, but it certainly caught the attention of the North Vietnamese.

At their September 24 meeting the following year, Laird did not tell Manor that intensive, last-minute diplomatic efforts were under way to secure the release of the prisoners, or that if they failed, he was about to ask the President to approve the raid. But he agreed that it was finally time to brief "CINCPAC," Admiral John S. McCain, Jr., on the operation that Washington was about to execute in his backyard.

Late the next day, Friday, September 25, Blackburn and

Mayer told McCain, the "Grand Old Man of the Pacific," that they were ready to launch a raid on Son Tay. They briefed him in detail—including who was known or thought to be held there. McCain knew that his son, taken prisoner three years earlier and savagely beaten by the North Vietnamese, would be one of the POWs "left behind" whether Ivory Coast succeeded or failed. Blackburn and Mayer read in his eyes the anguish of a "concerned father" but the resolve of a very courageous man. McCain told them he appreciated the implications of their proposal. He would do everything in his power to help the operation succeed. He agreed that to preserve security, only one other person in his headquarters should be told of the mission, his Chief of Staff. McCain said that not even the commander of the Pacific Fleet need be told; SACSA could work directly with the commander of Carrier Task Force 77 in the Tonkin Gulf to coordinate the Navy diversion that would accompany the raid. Virtually the entire staff directing the war in Southeast Asia was to be kept in the dark about one of the most critical operations that had ever been launched in that area—to give 61 American POWs that much better chance of returning home alive.

At this stage in the Vietnam War, 20 months into the Nixon administration, there were 1,463 American POWs and MIAs in Southeast Asia. Their welfare had become the hottest issue in the country. The public compassion which the POW/MIA wives had aroused in less than a year of organized effort manifested itself in many ways. Millions of Americans, high-school youngsters as well as adults in a land bitter about the war, were wearing POW/MIA bracelets. The ½-inch-wide aluminum or copper bands carried in simple block lettering the name and date of the shootdown, capture, or disappearance of men only a few thousand of them knew; but they vowed not to take them off until "their guy" was accounted for or returned home.

Nancy Thurmond, the twenty-three-year-old wife of Senator Strom Thurmond, was leading a massive letter-writing campaign to seek more humane treatment for the POWs. Conceived by the wives in the POW/MIA League of Families, the campaign's goal was to deliver 100 tons of mail by Christmas to North Vietnam's president, Ton Du Thang, urging better treatment and release of the prisoners. Postal service officials were hard pressed to supply the millions of 25-cent stamps Americans were suddenly buying to mail letters to Hanoi.

In August, 407 members of the House of Representatives had signed their own appeal, protesting conditions under which the POWs were being held. Representative Roger Zion of Indiana tried to deliver it to North Vietnamese officials in Paris, without success—but its message got through to the White House. President Nixon dispatched astronaut Frank Borman on a 14-nation, 25-day global journey to tell world leaders how flagrantly North Vietnam was violating the Geneva Convention it had signed in 1957. Borman, one of the first three men to circle the moon on Christmas Eve of 1968, asked them to appeal to North Vietnam to let the International Red Cross become a go-between in obtaining better treatment for all POWs. He tried to contact the North Vietnamese, but failed. It had been easier to reach the moon than to reach Hanoi with a humane appeal.

When he returned to address an unusual joint session of Congress on Tuesday, September 22, Borman reported that not one foreign head of state had held out much hope of getting North Vietnam to budge. The POWs were too valuable as hostages for American withdrawal from Southeast Asia.

Diplomatic approaches to the North Vietnamese were faring as badly. Three days after Borman's address to Congress, Henry Kissinger flew to Paris to "confer" with Ambassador David K. E. Bruce on the eve of the 85th plenary session of the Paris peace talks. In reality, he was there to meet secretly for the second time that month with Xuan Thuy, North Vietnam's chief negotiator. His September trips followed four other secret missions to Paris earlier in the year, when he had met with Le Duc Tho, North Vietnam's foreign minister. Kissinger cabled a discouraging message. There was no progress on the POW issue.

On Sunday, September 27, President Nixon left Washington for his second trip to Europe and third trip abroad since entering the White House. The 12,000-mile journey would take him to five nations in nine days, it was announced, including visits to Yugoslavia, Italy, Spain, England, and Ireland. White House press secretary Ronald Ziegler went out of his way to announce that the President would also meet with Pope Paul VI and, on the same day, visit the Sixth Fleet during maneuvers in the

Mediterranean. There was no mention that Laird and Moorer would join the presidential party, but they did.

Laird briefed Nixon on the proposal to rescue the Son Tay POWs aboard the presidential helicopter while flying out to the aircraft carrier *Saratoga*. Later that day, he and Moorer told Nixon more about the mission deep inside Vietnam. The raid, they said, could be launched within four weeks, but a decision would be needed soon if the force was to deploy in time.

"Nixon cared deeply," Laird would recall later. He felt that even if the mission did not succeed, "it would dramatize our love, caring, and affection for those POWs." But at that moment, Nixon was faced with the possibility of American military involvement in the Mideast. Jordan was torn by civil war and Syrian tanks had crossed its borders. A truce negotiated the previous month between Israel and Egypt was in danger of becoming unglued. Egypt's President Gamal Abdel Nasser had died that very day. Now Laird and Moorer were proposing a new form of military involvement in Southeast Asia.

Nixon reviewed the POW situation with them, and then said that he "approved" the rescue—in principle. But he wanted them to brief Kissinger thoroughly on it before he could make a final decision on *when* the rescue should be made. As Laird and Moorer departed for a three-day visit to Greece, Malta, and Turkey, Nixon cabled for Bruce and his deputy, Philip Habib, to meet him in Ireland. He wanted their unvarnished assessment of prospects for freeing the prisoners at the conference table instead of a raid into North Vietnam, although he would not tell them one was planned. Their report would be bleak.

On another front, however, there was more encouraging and very important news. Communist China had just welcomed a proposed visit by American writer Edgar Snow. On Thursday, October 1, Snow would be invited to stand next to Chairman Mao Tse-tung at China's "National Day" ceremonies. It signaled a clear message to Washington that Mao had given his blessing to a move toward reconciliation with a bitter enemy of 25 years. That initiative had come to a screeching halt after the Cambodian invasion in April and May, but now the deadlock looked as if it had been broken.

Nixon returned to Washington on Monday, October 5, to tell the crowd of 3,000 waiting to greet him at Andrews Air Force Base that the United States was making progress "toward achieving its goals in Vietnam," and then predicted with emphasis that "events in the future will demonstrate" this.

Soon after the President's return, Laird, Moorer, Blackburn, and Manor got word that the raid on Son Tay "might" have to be postponed from October 20–25. October 24, they knew (and would remind the White House) would be the 25th anniversary of the United Nations. They did not know that on October 25, Pakistani President Yahya Khan would meet with Nixon to discuss a mid-November visit to China, in which Khan would convey Nixon's desire for "talks in Peking at 'a high level.' " Nor did they know that in the Executive Office Building, Kissinger's staff was drafting and redrafting a toast the President would make on October 26. That night, Rumanian President Ceaușescu would be honored at a White House state dinner and Nixon would hail "the uniqueness of Rumania's good relations with the United States . . . the Soviet Union . . . and the People's Republic of China." It would be the first time an American President had ever referred to Communist China as "the People's Republic of China."

If the raid was postponed, the next launch window would not occur until late November. Manor and Simons would be able to use the extra time to "fine-tune" their plan. But as the days ticked by, it seemed to some of the Son Tay planners that the raid might be canceled. To JCS Chairman Tom Moorer, "it was obvious that the President was going to approve" the raid. Yet Moorer had two concerns. There was "always a cutoff date by which you *had* to have a decision." And there was always the possibility that "they're not going to let us do this." Moorer would explain: "That was the gist of my life. In our form of government, there were always plenty of people coming forward with reasons for not doing anything. The best way of making certain you never make a mistake is never do anything." But he would also point out that Laird and President Nixon wanted to be sure "that every step had been taken" to assure success. They felt "more and more that one more month would permit 'a refinement of the training.' "

Meanwhile, "coordinating" the raid also became more refined. On Wednesday, October 7, Blackburn flew back from the full-dress night rehearsal at Eglin to brief Vice Admiral Noel Gayler, head of NSA, on the Son Tay assault. Gayler offered Blackburn NSA's full support. He lauded the "courageous effort," and was "impressed as hell" that Simons would actually land in the objective with his raiders.

The next day, Manor and Simons flew from Eglin back to Washington. This time Blackburn took them to brief the President's Assistant for National Security Affairs, Henry Kissinger. As they prepared to see Kissinger, Blackburn, Manor, and Simons met with Don Bennett and Dick Stewart of the DIA, NSA's Milt Zaslov, and CIA's Dick Elliott to assess the latest intelligence. North Vietnam continually juggled its air defense system, and one of two radars at Phuc Yen airfield, Hanoi's main fighter base 20 miles northeast of Son Tay, had been moved. They didn't know why and couldn't find out where. Blackburn was worried. Had there been a leak? Had the radar been moved to a spot where it could track the approaches to Son Tay?

The biggest threat from North Vietnamese radar would occur about 35 minutes out of the objective area, after the assault force crossed the Laotian border. There was one radar that could track them from the north. The exposed sector was a 10-to-15-degree sector east southeast of the radar. The approach of the assault aircraft would have to be precise to "thread the needle." There was no way to mask the aircraft from the radar by terrain. Closer to the objective, there was another radar that could pick them up from the south. Flying low enough, however, and along the carefully preplanned route, the C-130s, helicopters, and A-1s could mask their approach. But if they deviated too much in altitude or went off course, they could be picked up 8 to 15 minutes away from the objective. That was the reason the Son Tay aircrews had spent so much time practicing the approach, even though there was the hope that if the Navy diversion worked, the radar might be scanning in the wrong direction, toward Haiphong, not Laos.

Blackburn was also concerned about a Chinese signal intelligence antennae field high in the mountains of Laos 100 miles west of Hanoi. He asked the spooks about an air strike to knock out the installation, but they felt it would not be needed—provided Manor's force maintained radio silence until Simons was actually on the ground, and if radio messages to and from the staging bases in Thailand were kept at normal levels before the raid.

With the exception of the missing radar, it looked to Blackburn, Manor, and Simons as if the spooks had really come through; they had the North Vietnamese air defense order of battle down to a gnat's eyelash. But there was "something funny" going on at Son Tay—or not going on. By now, more than half of the programmed Buffalo Hunter low-level reconnaissance drones had been shot down or "crapped out." Intelligence on the camp was limited to what Building 213's photo interpreters could cull from SR-71 photos taken 80,000 feet or higher above the tiny compound.

Those photos were revealing. The camp looked empty.

On a good mission, if there weren't clouds over the target or too many shadows, the SR-71's technical objective camera could bring back stereoscopic photos sharp enough that, from 15 miles above the earth, the DIA could count the number of people inside the walls of Son Tay Prison. The last SR-71 mission, flown at three times the speed of sound on Saturday, October 3, came back with some very good photos—but no people.

As Manor was to phrase it in his after-action report, the missions "from 6 June through 3 October" showed "an apparent decline in track activity," with "the lightest activity" evident in the latest batch of photos. But it would be "attributed to the probability that the U.S. POWs were being kept in their cells for extended periods of time." Don Blackburn would remember "sitting around [with some DIA interpreters], talking and looking at photographs, and someone said, I vaguely recall, 'It looks like they haven't been using this.' " Simons had a similar reaction. "The photographs brought to me showed a difference in vegetation," he later remarked. Weeds were growing in the compound, and "I said to myself, 'Well, it's possible that they have restricted their movements. It's possible that they have locked them up.' " But he also thought, "It's possible they have moved them."

For Bull Simons, briefing Henry Kissinger was the "hardest part of the whole operation." It was what he later called "kind of a rarefied atmosphere for a colonel in the infantry." Only four others were present: Kissinger's deputy, Major General Alexander M. Haig, Vogt, Blackburn, and Manor. They met at two-thirty in the afternoon on Thursday, October 8, in Kissinger's office in the West Wing of the White House. The meeting lasted less than 30 minutes.

Vogt introduced everyone and Blackburn outlined the overall concept for a minute or two. Then Manor launched into the detailed briefing which he and Simons had given so many times before in the past three weeks, using a portable projector and the vugraphs they had shown to the Joint Chiefs. By that time, Simons had "heard General Manor's briefing so damn many times" that it bored him. Kissinger nodded his head "sagely" as the briefing unfolded. When Manor was through, Simons covered the ground portion of the operation; it took him only "about 2½ minutes." But as he finished, he added one comment to his "canned" pitch: "I told him that we were going to use the minimum amount of fire necessary." But, Simons cautioned, the area was too confined to avoid enemy casualties. The comment caught Kissinger's attention. He asked Simons, "What in the hell are you talking about?"

Simons explained that he wasn't going on a big hunting expedition: "We're going in there to rescue prisoners, not to blow people's heads off; but we've got to move fast and we'll use whatever fire is necessary to get the job done. But not more." For one thing, he clarified, he didn't want to alert a garrison that was on the north side of the Song Con River if it could be helped. "But," Simons said, "anybody who gets in our way is going to be dead."

"You do what you need to do," Kissinger replied. "Let us take care of the international impact; we can handle that. No one in the White House is concerned about enemy casualties. Use whatever restraint is appropriate, but whatever force is essential for the most efficient operation."

Kissinger had one important question. What if the raid failed? How sure were they that they would not just put more Americans into the prisons of North Vietnam? Blackburn told Kissinger that they could give him a "95 to 97 percent assurance of success." Manor reinforced the point; the aircrews had flown 697 flight hours and 268 sorties training for this mission. It had been rehearsed something like "170 times."

Kissinger was obviously impressed. Haig had no questions or comment.

Blackburn then mentioned his concern that a "broader assessment" might be needed of the operation, a "psychological appreciation" of its impact on the Paris peace negotiations and of how North Vietnam would treat the prisoners left behind in other camps. Kissinger cut the suggestion off. "That's not your worry. Don't get mixed up in politics. That's our worry, not yours."

His reaction "sounded good" to Simons because "that's the way it ought to be." Simons found the President's Assistant for National Security Affairs "pretty swift in the head."

Manor told Kissinger that the first good weather window would occur between October 20 and 25, with October 21 the most promising date for the raid. If that launch date was acceptable to the President, his task force was ready to deploy to its staging bases in Thailand in two days, on October 10. Actually, Manor didn't use the word "President." Instead, he said the "National Command Authority." The next suitable window, he continued, would be just before Thanksgiving. But he said that he realized there might be misgivings about conducting the raid between October 20 and 25, since the President was scheduled to address the United Nations General Assembly on its 25th anniversary, October 24, while 31 heads of state were scheduled to dine at the White House that night.

Kissinger hedged. The President was out of town, he said, and final approval would have to come from him.

As the meeting broke up, Kissinger had one final question: "Who thought this up?" Vogt and Simons replied almost simultaneously: "A lot of people have been working on it. It's been a team effort." Kissinger then offered a comment which every one at the meeting would remember. "Even if it's a 'no go,' " he said, "I want to thank you, all of you, for your imagination and initiative. Thank you for coming up with something original and imaginative."

During the drive back to the Pentagon, one participant thought to himself that there had been something odd about the meeting. Henry Kissinger had not even asked how sure they were that there were any prisoners in Son Tay.

Carriers and CAS Agents

For reasons never explained to Blackburn or Manor, the White House decided soon after the Kissinger briefing to postpone the raid. As Manor would tell a group of POWs released in 1973, three years later: "The plan was enthusiastically received but it was determined that the operation should be delayed until November, our alternate date. One reason I wanted to go in October was because I was very concerned about security. However, the delay allowed us time for further training and coordination."

On Monday, October 19, JCS Chairman Tom Moorer called Blackburn to his office and said that he and Laird would recommend a final decision to the President soon.

The following Tuesday, October 27, Moorer told Blackburn he could deploy an "in-theater coordinating staff" on Sunday, November 1, and begin to deploy the task force itself two weeks later, on Tuesday, November 10. The next day, October 28, the seventh Buffalo Hunter reconnaissance drone flew over Son Tay Prison. This was the shot that banked an instant too soon and returned "perfect imagery" of the horizon beyond Son Tay. Bennett, Blackburn, and Manor decided to "terminate" the Buffalo Hunter "effort."

Later that same day, Blackburn learned that the Navy had called off *all* of its "BARCAP" flights until November 10. These were the radar-picket aircraft that kept track of all airborne North Vietnamese MIGs and vectored U.S. fighters against them. The cancellation would leave Manor's group without "eyes and ears" for 12 days. If North Vietnam were suddenly to concentrate all its fighters at the field closest to Son Tay, it might not be known until too late. The next morning, Thursday, October 29, Blackburn asked Vogt if he would get the BARCAP missions "laid back on." But there were other flights over North Vietnam he wanted "called off." They involved C-130 "psychological operations" leaflet drops "all over" North Vietnam, plus some leaflet drops from a version of Buffalo Hunter drones flying "Operation Litterbug"—better known to the men executing them as the "Bullshit bombers." Vogt agreed; it was the wrong time to "warm up" the North Vietnamese "alert system."

Blackburn had to resolve only two other "flaps" that day. One involved the Navy, the other the CIA. Months earlier, the Navy had scheduled to replace the aircraft carrier *America* with *Ranger* on station with Task Force 77 in the Tonkin Gulf. Yet *America*'s pilots were to fly some of the Son Tay diversionary raids. Because aircraft carrier "cycling" and overhauls were so complex, such transfers were scheduled months, sometimes years, in advance. But Blackburn didn't learn of the switch until October 29. In a private log labeled "Blackburn's Eyes Only," he made an entry that day: "Strange. Am presenting need to accelerate *Ranger* and *Hancock* deployments to 19 Nov., retain *Oriskany* on station until 26 Nov. Transfer pilots and aircraft from *America* to *Ranger*?" He went to see Vogt. Vogt was stunned: "Why wasn't this thought of before?" Blackburn explained that "the requirement had been laid out early in the operational planning." But as often happened in grave matters, "something fell through the cracks." The Pentagon was a 27-year-old building; it had a lot of cracks. Vogt himself was to have handled the carrier deployments, but he had been thwarted by two problems: no one would be sure when the White House would let the raid be launched; and the planners wanted everything to look as normal as possible to the North Vietnamese.

Vogt said he would get the carrier deployments fixed. It wasn't easy. When the JCS message arrived at CINCPAC headquarters, the Commander-in-Chief, Pacific Fleet, stormed in to see Admiral John McCain's Chief of Staff, Army Lieutenant General Charles A. Corcoran. "Something odd is going on," he said. "We're getting some wild orders about switching aircraft carriers all over the Pacific and they don't make sense. What the hell is going on?"

Corcoran told him, "I've never lied to you. I'm not going to now. But I'm not going to explain. I'm just asking you to ride with me on this one. Follow the orders."

That left Blackburn with only one other onion to peel on October 29. He had discovered that the CIA was "horsing around" in his backyard.

At CIA's 213-acre wooded complex in Langley, Virginia, that morning, George Carver found himself in a dilemma. Just yesterday he had assured Blackburn that none of his agents was operating in North Vietnam. Now, Blackburn was confronting him personally to challenge that assertion. In months of planning the Son Tay raid, during 16 Saturday morning coordinating sessions with Carver's hand-picked liaison man present, Blackburn had stressed time and again his concern that some CAS agent—one of the CIA's "Controlled American Sources"—might go "threshing around up north" at the wrong time or in the wrong area, get caught, and alert the North Vietnamese warning system that something big was up. Blackburn reminded Carver of his concern and told him that he had learned, through one of his own sources, that there *was* a CAS operation now under way.

Carver had to admit it. But it was "way south" of Son Tay, he insisted, down near Route 7 on the southern border with Laos. The operation couldn't possibly affect the Son Tay raid, he protested. It was a low-key insertion; that was why he hadn't thought of it when Blackburn asked about CAS teams the day before.

CIA's track record on CAS operations up north wasn't too swift, Blackburn had long felt. Almost every agent inserted there since 1964 had been "nailed"—hundreds of South Vietnamese and some North Vietnamese whom the CIA had "turned back." Soon after he took over SOG in 1965, Blackburn had learned that some CAS teams had not been resupplied for months, and he protested inserting more agents until the CIA arranged to take care of those already there. The CIA had lost some of its best agents and risked the lives of men like Dick Meadows trying to save others; but as far as Blackburn could discern, the whole CAS effort hadn't produced a thimbleful of useful intelligence.

Yet George Carver was one of Blackburn's favorite spooks. He too believed in unconventional operations, not body counts, and had supported SACSA's work steadfastly. A former Rhodes scholar and psy-ops operative, Carver was a busy, fast-talking man. He had a lot of excess energy and he loved to pick up the telephone. Asked a question in some meeting, he would often reach for a phone to find out "right now." That's what made Blackburn worry that Carver wasn't being completely candid with him; when he asked to see exactly *where* in North Vietnam that CAS agent was, Carver didn't reach for a phone to find out. He turned into a Sphinx, not denying, not confirming, suggesting by his manner that since the operation didn't affect Blackburn, he didn't need to know about it.

Blackburn controlled his temper, measuring his words. "George, you're not leveling with me. That guy went in near Site 32 way up in northern Laos, 100 miles from Son Tay. We're getting ready to launch that raid in three weeks and now I find out that one of your guys is operating in my backyard. He could screw this whole thing up. And you didn't even tell me he was there. I'm speaking for the chairman, George; we want that guy shut down, fast. The North Vietnamese can track your guys a lot easier than we can, and *we* didn't have any trouble finding him. This is one reason I included you guys on the planning team—to stop this kind of horseshit."

Carver, Blackburn would recall, responded with the "Charlie Chan" approach—sophisticated, quiet, uninformative. He said he "would see what he could do." Blackburn was "overreacting," they were all working for the same team, et cetera, et cetera . . .

Blackburn left CIA headquarters unsatisfied, disappointed, puzzled, and concerned. *Some*thing was going on, yet the guy responsible for CIA's support of the Son Tay raid wouldn't tell him what, or why.

Five years were to pass before he finally found out all the answers. But he learned part of the reason for Carver's discomfort a few days later, from Ed Mayer. The CIA had lost Site 32. The alternate launch base for the Son Tay raid was in communist hands, and CIA's agents were fighting like fury to get it back.

Leaks and Lost Messages

On Sunday, November 1, Blackburn, Manor, and Simons left Andrews Air Force Base for Hawaii and then South Vietnam. At the same time, a small staff from the Joint Contingency Task Group flew separately to Southeast Asia to visit every wing, squadron, and base commander who would have to support the Son Tay raid. Each would be given a letter of instruction with only enough information to "perform his assigned functions." Except for the few officers whom Blackburn, Manor, and Simons would visit personally, no one else would be told the objective of the mission.

Blackburn, Manor, and Simons briefed Admiral McCain and his chief of staff in Hawaii at 10:45 A.M. on Monday, November 2. McCain was "visibly concerned, very fidgety in his chair." His concern was, of course, for those POWs who would be left behind—including his own son. But he supported the raid heartily. "It was a rough spot to place him in," one of those present thought. After their meeting, McCain offered

Blackburn, Manor, and Simons CINCPAC's "personal airplane" to fly them the 6,290 miles to Saigon. They departed
Oahu at 4:45 that afternoon for the long flight across the western Pacific.

The three men were bushed. McCain's C-118 (a military version of the DC-7) was outfitted as an executive transport and
airborne headquarters—"plush easy chairs, beds, great service,
good food, drinks"—and it was slow, about 350 miles an hour,
so they had plenty of time to catch up on their sleep. The plane
touched down at Wake Island to refuel, crossed the International Date Line, and landed at 4:00 A.M. to refuel again in the
Philippines. The next stop would be Saigon, where they would
brief General Creighton Abrams, Westmoreland's successor as
Commander U.S. Military Assistance Command, Vietnam
(MACV).

There was some work to do while they were in the air however. Just before Blackburn left Washington, Moorer had asked
him what the "impact" would be of a major bombing up north,
no longer than one day in duration, just before the raid on Son
Tay. It would be the first bombing of North Vietnam in over two
years. The White House, Moorer said, was considering it and
had proposed "tying it in" with the Son Tay rescue. Blackburn
had asked Mayer to have his assessment ready by the time he
returned, but on the flight to Saigon, Blackburn made his own
notes.

a. Bombing would have adverse impact, nationally and inter-
   nationally.
b. Might provide good excuse, if (a) is true, for NVA [North
   Vietnamese Army] to take reprisals against those left behind.
c. Would alert entire warning system.
d. We should "low key" our effort with view of obtaining maximum favorable impact; i.e., our mission is a humanitarian
   one. Bombing mission associated with this would kill this
   and raise a big stink.
e. Acknowledge White House view that if bombing took place
   before our mission, it could strengthen credibility of our
   Navy diversion.
f. But advantage would be far outweighed by the disadvan-
   tages, e.g., the adverse reactions.

Burly "Abe" Abrams, puffing heavily on his cigar, listened in silence as Blackburn, Manor, and Simons told him for the first time of the raid on Son Tay. With him was General Lucius Clay, his air deputy and the Commanding General, 7th Air Force; and Lieutenant General Welborn Dolvin who, like Abrams, was a tanker and MACV's Chief of Staff. Abrams was a man of few words. When the briefing was over, he told Blackburn, Manor, and Simons, "My God, that's a real professional job. I don't see what you've overlooked. Looks like you haven't left any stones unturned. I don't have *any* questions." Abrams then turned to Clay and asked, "Well, Lou, can you support this thing?" During the briefing, Clay's eyes had got "real big," like he was wondering, "What in tarnation, how crazy *are* you guys?" But now he told Abrams: "I'm not sure how, but we'll sure as hell manage. Sounds like we've got about ten days to get ready." Clay knew the job would not be easy, since he was in the process of removing men and equipment from every base in Southeast Asia as part of President Nixon's withdrawal program.

To attract as little attention as possible, the other JCTG officers flew to their destinations all over Southeast Asia on regularly scheduled flights and even on a "space available" or standby basis. In typical understatement, Manor reported later: "This proved to be very time-consuming and only numerous fortuitous connections made possible the completion of coordination on schedule. It is considered that dedicated airlift for this purpose would have obviated many of the problems encountered and allowed individuals more time to accomplish their tasks."

The tasks proved more formidable than Manor's after-action report would hint. Larry Ropka and four others from Manor's advance team had to visit nine air bases from Japan to Vietnam and Thailand, arranging complex final details for the raid. They all arrived unannounced and contacted air base and wing commanders of key units with perplexing, sometimes bewildering orders which caught the in-theater commanders totally off guard. Manor's people had not been allowed to use teletype or other message traffic to signal their missions. Once they arrived, they were not allowed to explain what they were doing in any commander's backyard. All they could do was hope that General Lucius Clay had discreetly passed some word to all his bases that some strangers might be showing up soon and that, once their identity from a Joint Contingency Task Force was authenticated, 7th Air Force commanders were to comply fully with their requests, no matter how odd they might be. Manor's team members could also show skeptical commanders a copy of the letter that the Air Force Chief of Staff, General John D. Ryan, had given Manor months earlier; it directed his major commanders all over the world to give Manor their "full support" on a "no questions asked" basis. Ryan had added ominously, in effect, "If you feel that you can't comply, you are to call me personally." (As it would turn out, no one took him up on the offer.)

All of this secrecy was necessary, John Gargus would explain later, because so many agencies and bases in Vietnam and Thailand had enemy agents monitoring U.S. activities. That was one reason so many rescue attempts in the south had come up empty-handed. This rescue was going to be executed by forces imported from half the world away—not all of it, as would turn out, but no one in the theater would get the big picture until the operation was ready to be launched.

Art Andraitis flew to Yokota, Japan, to coordinate the final high-altitude photography requests and personally analyze images of the Son Tay area. Keith Grimes flew to South Vietnam and Thailand to handle weather needs. Air Force Captain John H. Knops was sent to Monkey Mountain near Da Nang to arrange its use as General Manor's command post during the rescue attempt; from there he would be able to monitor all radio traffic over North and South Vietnam, Thailand, Laos, and the Tonkin Gulf, and he could communicate directly, if need be, with the National Military Command Center in the Pentagon. Lieutenant Colonel Benjamin N. Kraljev, Jr., handled other coordination needed in South Vietnam at Cam Ranh Bay and Da Nang and then in Nakhon Phanom, Thailand. Also at Cam Ranh Bay, Major William J. Kornitzer, Jr., showed up to train two HC-130p special tanker crews to refuel the HH-53s and ready their aircraft. They would train for almost two weeks but be kept in the dark about the mission until the final go-ahead.

Larry Ropka did the most traveling, hitchhiking to and then back and forth among four Royal Thai Air Bases—Takhli, U-Tapao, Udorn, and Korat. His odyssey proved particularly colorful and challenging. Ropka knew the country well from previous tours he had served there with CIA, and he was especially at home at Takhli in south central Thailand. The base commander there was in the final stages of deactivating the installation and was well into a carefully staged base closure plan when Ropka arrived to mess it up. The commander couldn't believe what this Stateside interloper was requesting, but he was impressed with Ropka's familiarity with the base facilities. Among them was a closely guarded CIA staging facility that the commander barely knew of and had just about shut down. Ropka, however, was intimately familiar with it, having coordinated its highly classified "Heavy Chain" program from the Pentagon. He said he needed the secure area reactivated, ready to house and feed over a hundred men who would be arriving in just a few days for a mission he couldn't discuss. Ropka also said he would need additional facilities for three C-130s and crews that would be landing soon. The base was about to become a hub of transportation, shuttling equipment and people to other Thai bases. Shown General Ryan's letter, the base commander cooperated fully and opened up doors he had just locked so he could expand his dwindling bedding and feeding facilities.

At U-Tapao, the southernmost air base in Thailand, Ropka had to arrange for three dedicated C-130s that would ferry raid participants from various bases to Takhli and back to their bases to do their own secretive planning. Within days of that, they would fly the raiders and their equipment to their separate launching bases just hours before their scheduled takeoffs for Son Tay. Major Richard A. Peshkin, who had joined SACSA's planning group in August, would arrive aboard the last C-130 from Eglin to brief the three in-theater C-130 crews, once they arrived at Takhli, on the whiplash missions that lay ahead for them.

Ropka also had to arrange for U-Tapao to beef up one of Strategic Air Command's specially configured radio relay RC-135Ms with four extra UHF channels. A regular RC-135M from Kadena, Okinawa, with the call sign "Combat Apple" and a mission coordinator aboard, would orbit around the clock over the Gulf of Tonkin and would have another RC-135M serving as an airborne backup. Colonel Norman Frisbie would fly aboard it to serve as the alternate Joint Contingency Task Group commander and take over if something were to prevent

General Manor from exercising command and control from his command post at Monkey Mountain's Tactical Air Control Center outside of Da Nang. These two aircraft could monitor and relay all UHF and FM communications from the Gulf of Tonkin, North Vietnam, Laos, and Thailand to Monkey Mountain. Those unusual arrangements made it obvious to some base personnel that whatever operation was brewing, it was a big one and a really big deal.

Still at U-Tapao, Ropka had to arrange for an unspecified number of the base's KC-135 refueling aircraft, which also belonged to SAC, to be ready to service the F-4s and F-105s that would be flying MIG cap and Wild Weasel cover for the mission from Korat Royal Thai Air Force Base. The final number of tankers, he said, would depend on the planning those aircrews would undertake once they were flown to Takhli and briefed on the mission. (Ten tankers would eventually be launched.)

Next Ropka flew to Udorn Royal Thai Air Force Base, close to the Laotian border in northern Thailand, to visit the 40th Air Rescue and Recovery Squadron, which flew HH-53 Jolly Green Giants. Ropka said he needed to borrow seven of the best helicopters the squadron had—without the aircrews. (In reality, Manor's task force needed only five of them. The squadron arranged nine of them ready to go.) Ropka also informed the squadron commander that Military Airlift Command would soon deliver two HH-3s from Da Nang, which would need to be made ready for a mission at an early date. On the night these helicopters would be used, Ropka added, the squadron would need to be on standby with its best crews for a possible special rescue mission. That too signaled that something really special was brewing, because the unit normally stood by for rescue missions only during daylight hours.

Still at Udorn, Ropka contacted the tactical fighter wing commander and alerted him that he would need his best-qualified F-4 crews ready for a mission that could not yet be discussed. Key crew members and planners, he said, would be picked up and flown to Takhli for instructions when the time came.

Ropka's final visit was to Korat in central Thailand, where he had to coordinate the F-105 Wild Weasel support, missions to jam and suppress surface-to-air missile launches around Son Tay, and to arrange for two EC-121T "College Eye" test aircraft (plus one C-121G to serve as a support aircraft and backup spare) to be bedded down and readied for use. The College Eyes were prototypes of an enhanced airborne early warning and control (AEW&C) system, test aircraft that were being modified at McClellan Air Force Base in California. Much of their special avionics and cryptologic gear had yet to be installed even as the planes were en route from California. Each plane was still "a delicate piece of intricate test equipment," a historian of the 552nd AEW&C Wing would later write, and extensive wiring modifications would be required after the aircraft arrived at Korat. Not even their aircrews knew why they were suddenly being sent to Vietnam for "quick reaction deployment testing." The planes with this modification had never seen combat, never been tested in an operational environment, and their unique radar and avionics systems had never been activated due to radiation problems in the continental U.S. Only theoretical calculations had been done of the electromagnetic interference they might cause. But the planes would be needed to monitor low-level aircraft activity, provide warnings of any MIG approaches, and vector F-4s against them. Theoretically, the planes could also track friendly forces with IFF equipment, distinguishing friend from foe, and could monitor and relay UHF and HF/single sideband communications. Thus, they might provide further backup for the two Combat Apple aircraft. All Ropka could tell anyone at Korat about any of their missions was that the base's key planners would be flown to Takhli shortly to be briefed on the real operation. By the time his visits at Korat were over, Ropka had been without sleep for days.

In South Vietnam, Ben Kraljev first visited Cam Ranh Bay Air Base to visit the 39th Air Rescue and Recovery Squadron. Two of its HC-130P tankers would be needed to refuel the helicopters en route to and from Son Tay. Its crews were immediately flown to Thailand to train with Bill Kornitzer, who had come from the Air Rescue and Recovery Training Center at Eglin Air Force Base. Kraljev also made arrangements for a nighttime, standby alert for a possible rescue mission, since helicopters from the assault force were expected to bring home POWs and not become involved in unscheduled rescue efforts.

Kraljev's next mission was a bit weird. He flew to Da Nang Air Base and contacted the 37th Air Rescue and Recovery Squadron. Kraljev explained that he needed to borrow two of the unit's last two HH-3 helicopters and have them flown to

Udorn, but that their crews would not be needed after that. All he could say was that it was for a very important operation about which nothing could be explained. Even though the helicopters were being phased out of service, John Gargus would later suggest that the unit's commander doubtless would not have believed Kraljev had he revealed that both helicopters would be stripped of nonessential equipment and that one of them would never return. Nor could he reveal that Lieutenant Colonel Royal C. Brown, who had disappeared from the unit months earlier for a mysterious temporary duty assignment, would be a key player in the mission about to unfold.

Kraljev then flew to Thailand to visit the 56th Special Operations Squadron at Nakhon Phanom Royal Thai Air Force Base, on Thailand's northeast border. Its A-1E propeller-driven attack aircraft normally flew cover for rescue helicopters on missions in Laos or North Vietnam. There he laid on another odd request: he needed seven of the unit's most reliable A-1Es, fully fueled and configured with special ordnance. (In fact, he needed only five of them, but Kraljev added two spares in case one or two planes might have to abort.) Kraljev told the wing commander cryptically that he was not requesting pilots to fly the planes, but that he could not explain who would be flying them, only that the requirement had to be met soon. The wing commander must have been chagrined when half the pilots who showed up to fly the planes turned out to be his own people. They had been on temporary duty in Florida for a long time.

While Manor's silver-tongued devils were reshuffling most of the air assets in Southeast Asia, Blackburn flew from Saigon back to Washington to look after other SACSA business. Manor and Simons flew by Navy plane to the Tonkin Gulf and landed aboard the aircraft carrier which Vice Admiral Frederick A. Bardshar used as "the flag" of Task Force 77. Bardshar knew "someone" was coming, but not who. He had received a high command net message* from "a friend" in CINCPAC

---

*A "high command net message" was one designed to assure delivery even when radio transmitting conditions are marginal. In this case, delivery was more important than the extra measure of security that might have been gained using a "back channel" message—which general and flag officers can send to one another on an "eyes only basis" outside regular signal channels. They are not logged in or read by the action officers who read and route operational communiqués.

headquarters; it told him only that two officers, an Army colonel and an Air Force brigadier general, would come aboard. Bardshar was to give them any help he could, but the visit and their mission were "very close hold." Bardshar was not to discuss them even with his own boss, the commander, Seventh Fleet, or with the commander-in-chief, Pacific Fleet.

Bardshar led Manor and Simons into the flag mess. He later called in two other men, Captain Alan "Boot" Hill, his operations officer, and Commander P. D. Hoskins, his intelligence officer. Together, they were to plan the Navy diversion that would mask the Son Tay raid, under a "short fuse" and circumstances that were demanding both intellectually and physically. Writing a detailed operations order for a Navy carrier air strike was like composing a symphony for an orchestra the size of the New York Philharmonic. Planning one for a major night strike to be flown simultaneously from two or three carriers was like composing a symphony for two or three orchestras that would have to perform it together without even rehearsing. And because of the "extremely limited disclosure" of the operation, Hill and Hoskins had to write a score which the musicians would see for the first time only hours before curtain time.

Blackburn was back in the Pentagon on Tuesday, November 10, to brief Moorer on the Southeast Asia trip and tell him of his concern about the proposed one-day bombing. The launch date for the raid was now about ten days away, and he tried not to think of the nightmares he had been having for weeks—"My God," he'd wake up at his home in McLean, Virginia, wondering: "What if no one's there? What if it's a 'dry hole'? What if there's been a compromise?" But there were too many other things to worry about now.

The first C-130 would leave Eglin for the objective area on Thursday, November 12. Simons and Manor had returned there to oversee the final loading of all their equipment and wish their men a safe flight. With the launch date so near, it was time to "tighten up" on security. But Blue Max came into Blackburn's office that day and told him he was concerned. There was a lot of coded traffic from CIA headquarters to its posts in Thailand and Laos; many of the messages were about the Son Tay raid.

Blackburn knew that there would have to be some last-minute traffic. CIA agents would give Simons's men their final escape and evasion briefing and there was always a chance, if the weather turned sour, that one or more of the helicopters would still have to launch from Site 32 in northern Laos. But when Blue Max showed him how much traffic was being sent, almost twice the usual average, Blackburn was alarmed. He told Moorer, who offered to call Helms and tell the CIA in no uncertain words to "tighten things up."

But the time had also arrived to let some new players in on the game. Among the first was the Pentagon's official spokesman, Daniel Z. Henkin, Laird's Assistant Secretary of Defense for Public Affairs. A longtime military journalist, and editor of the 102-year-old *Armed Forces Journal* before he joined the Pentagon public affairs staff late in 1965, Henkin was a hefty, easygoing man with graying, curly hair that looked as if he combed it only as an afterthought. He had sometimes managed to irritate the Pentagon press corps because he seemed so unperturbed by such events as the *Pueblo* capture, the Tet offensive, and the invasion of Cambodia. But a few Pentagon regulars described him as "unflappable."

When Blackburn finished briefing him on the Son Tay raid early on Thursday, November 12, Henkin thanked him almost casually and assured him that his office could "handle" the press. In Henkin's near-cavernous office in Room 2E800, halfway between the Pentagon's Mall and the River entrances, the imminent rescue of 60 to 70 American prisoners within 23 miles of Hanoi was a business-as-usual proposition. Blackburn felt almost stupid walking back to his office. Why had he been so concerned about "impact assessments" if a press expert like Henkin could take the raid in such smooth stride? Was a prisoner rescue really such small potatoes? Maybe he'd blown the raid out of all proportion in his own mind.

That same morning, Blackburn, Mayer, Manor, and Simons had another meeting with Moorer. Moorer was "great," they would recall. "I've given you a job to do," he told Manor. "You're liable now to get a bunch of requests for reports or information on one thing after the other. Ignore them." The mission came first, protocol and questions second. Moorer said he'd do anything Manor and Simons needed to ease their load in the days ahead and wished them luck.

Ten minutes after Manor and Simons left the chairman's

office, Blackburn received a call directly from Moorer. He wanted to know what the "impact" would be if the raid had to be delayed until December. "Just let me tell you," Moorer explained. "Something's happened. Laird is apprehensive. Something's up in Paris."

Blackburn was stunned, but he recovered enough to tell Moorer that a delay would be "devastating." They wouldn't have another weather window for months. The assault force was already en route to Thailand. The men were "up" psychologically. A delay or recall now would mean serious risk of compromise; you could keep a lid on things only so long, once everyone was "peaked." Blackburn noted in his private log later: "I am afraid they are looking for a rationale to call off a difficult, complex mission. Difficult to understand a turn-down of this mission unless tremendous overriding factors of which we have no knowledge. Fact that North Vietnamese may have become more amenable to POW Christmas packages doesn't constitute, to me, an overriding factor."

A few minutes later, Mayer received another call, this time from Navy Captain Harry D. Train II, Moorer's executive assistant and senior aide. Moorer needed a copy of the Son Tay briefing to take to Secretary Laird right away. Blackburn wondered what was going on. At noon, Train called him again to say that Moorer had just met with Laird, and Laird was now on his way to the White House. Blackburn asked, "What was Moorer's reaction?" "Don't worry, he was smiling," Train reassured him.

At 1:45 that afternoon, Blackburn got a phone call from Vogt. Vogt told him, "It's a 'go.' " Minutes later, Train called: Kissinger had agreed to "no bombing," and the raid was to go "on schedule." The "no bombing" decision was to change after North Vietnam shot down an unarmed low-level reconnaissance plane the next day, Friday the 13th, killing both crewmen. But Blackburn was relieved. All the work that he and the other planners had done, the weeks of grueling training the assault force had been through, would not be wasted.

Blackburn soon got more good news from another quarter. Lieutenant General Richard Stilwell, the Army's Deputy Chief of Staff for Operations, called to tell him that he had just ordered 30 days of "administrative leave" for Simons and his men as soon as they returned from the operation. Blackburn had asked Stilwell to okay it weeks ago. It was time off that wouldn't be charged to their annual leave allowance, a way of telling Simons's men that the Army knew they had worked long hours under great stress, months away from their families to get ready for a job they couldn't talk about—and from which they might not even return.

Next on Blackburn's agenda was a special intelligence meeting with the DIA and NSA spooks. They reviewed the latest SR-71 photos taken on November 2 and November 6, the first of which showed a "definite increase in activity" at Son Tay. This was believed to be the result of letting the POWs spend more time outside their cells. The "Secondary School" south of the camp had also been "reactivated." The meeting adjourned with an agreement to lay on a new set of SR-71 "tracks" that would be flown on November 13, 18, and 20, just prior to the raid.

Arthur Andraitis—DIA's photo interpreter, assigned directly to Manor's Joint Contingency Task Group—had just flown to Yokota Air Base, Japan, where SR-71 photos of the Pacific area were normally processed and interpreted. There, working in the sophisticated complex that housed SAC's 67th Reconnaissance Technical Squadron, he personally would "read out" the final SR-71 photos of Son Tay Prison. SAC's regular interpreters would cover everything outside the objective area, including the approaches from Laos, in order to look for changes in surface-to-air missile (SAM) sites, antiaircraft dispositions, and the early warning/ground control intercept stations.

To save time, the DIA had arranged for several other things to be done. It was decided to concentrate on large-scale photo coverage of the area and use only one small-scale technical objective camera. SAC was also requested to limit its other reconnaissance coverage during the period ahead to make every resource available for the special missions about to be flown to "test the responsiveness of the SR-71 to special mission requirements." Procedures for processing and interpreting the new film were radically changed as well. Unloading all of the film an SR-71 normally took was a two-hour job. DIA asked SAC if the plane could be "downloaded" in 45 minutes during the tests. The missions would all be flown out of Kadena Air Base in Okinawa by the 9th Strategic Reconnaissance Wing. As soon as the film was offloaded there, a KC-135 jet tanker would rush it to Yokota. Once the film was processed and interpreted there, Andraitis would fly the interpretation results and prints to Takhli Royal Thai Air Force Base in central Thailand by special courier plane and brief Manor's aircrews and the four men in Simons's assault team who knew what the objective was. Duplicate sets would be flown to Washington. Photo interpretation was a painstaking, mind-draining job. It took time; but every effort was being made to speed up the process.

The SR-71 missions of November 13 and 18 would be crucial. Besides large-scale photos of the objective itself, which would confirm "increased activity" at the prison, they would provide the first complete large-scale photography of the route from the Laotian border to Son Tay. This was needed to verify turning points, pick out emergency landing zones, and make sure that no additional SAM or AAA or early warning systems had been moved along the approach route. The last two "prelaunch" missions would be flown earlier in the day than usual on Friday, November 20, and on Saturday preliminary interpretation results would be phoned to Manor and the Pentagon Command Center. But at that late moment, there would only be time to look for some "mind-blowing change."

Blackburn was reassured by both the DIA and the NSA schedule and procedures. He was told that if there was one microsecond of North Vietnamese radio or signals traffic affecting the raid or any change in radar coverage or frequencies, the NSA would have them "locked in" and fed directly to Manor and Simons in Thailand. The Son Tay raid had been given the number-one priority of all electronic intelligence work worldwide. An "updated" electronic order of battle, air order of battle, and missile order of battle would be flown to Takhli on Thursday, November 19, just before the mission launched.

Blue Max was waiting in Blackburn's office when he returned from the special intelligence meeting, and this time the news was bad. He "thought" Blackburn "should know something." It looked as if there might be a "pigeon" in Son Tay, a prisoner who was "talking"—much too freely; had he given up, betrayed his fellow POWs, anxious to make his own miserable life more comfortable? Blue Max knew that Blackburn had planned to get a message into the camp forewarning the senior

officers that rescue was imminent and how to help. Now, that
plan would have to be abandoned. Blue Max wasn't sure who
the pigeon was.

That hectic Thursday ended on a more positive note. About
six o'clock that evening, Blackburn ran into Admiral McCain
in a Pentagon corridor. McCain had just seen Secretary Laird
and Admiral Moorer, and they had told him the raid on Son
Tay was "a go." McCain wanted Blackburn to know that
"whichever way it goes, I back what you're doing." On the
drive home that night, Blackburn thought long and hard about
the prisoners in Son Tay and the others who would be left behind. God, how he wished that a thirty-four-year-old naval aviator named John S. McCain III was in Son Tay Prison.

Friday, November 13, brought grim news. Six POWs were
dead. Peace activist Cora Weiss had been given their names by
the North Vietnamese front organization, the Committee of
Solidarity with the American People. All six had been carried
as POWs held in the north. Now there was an even greater ur-
gency for the Son Tay mission.

On Saturday morning, November 14, Blackburn was at Andrews Air Force Base for an early breakfast with Manor and Simons before their long flight to Thailand. They would be
leaving at 2:00 P.M. that afternoon aboard Admiral McCain's
private plane; this time it was a small, but faster North American T-39, the two-engine Sabreliner executive jet. Their principal topic of conversation was the intelligence briefing
Blackburn had received two days before, but their principal
worry was a new threat to the security of the raid that had suddenly emerged.

Early in the planning stages, wiretaps had been placed, with
the consent of all parties concerned, on the phones at Eglin
Auxiliary Field Number 3 and on SACSA's Pentagon phones.
Tapes had been made of every conversation, and from them,
Blackburn had just learned, counterintelligence teams at the
Air Force Cryptologic Depot in San Antonio, Texas, had pieced
together a disquieting "mosaic." They had figured out that a
"big operation" was about to take place. They knew it would be
in Southeast Asia. They knew that the Navy and CINCPAC
were involved, that it would happen "fast" and "at night." But
they had not been able to identify what the target was, the

specific country in which the operation would take place, or the size of the force involved.

Had there been a leak, or was it just a clever piece of deduction? As they weighed the chances of compromise, Manor and Simons decided the odds were on their side. But just before they left Andrews for the long flight to Southeast Asia, Blackburn told them that he would make one final check and alert them after they arrived in Thailand if there was a significant danger of compromise.

The next day, Sunday, November 15, as Manor and Simons were crossing the Pacific, events in Washington began to accelerate. Messages came into the Pentagon Command Center from the CIA station chief and General Abrams in South Vietnam. The CIA wanted to borrow some of the large, armed HH-53 rescue helicopters to support an operation in southern Laos which General Vang Pao's Meo tribesmen were about to run. Abrams was opposed, but he couldn't tell his CIA counterpart in Saigon why: he wanted every HH-53 in the theater available to support Manor and Simons.

By the time Blackburn and Mayer arrived at the Pentagon early on Monday morning, the 16th, JCS action officers were having a small imbroglio over the message. Their contacts at CIA were "screaming" for the helicopters; why wouldn't MACV release them? Blackburn didn't want to do *any* explaining to anyone at this late juncture; even a hint that the aircraft were "on hold" for an operation that had anything to do with SACSA, or that Southeast Asia helicopter priorities were now being decided by the JCS, was too risky. Mayer came up with the solution. He arranged for Air Force headquarters to "ground" temporarily all HH-53s worldwide because of a "potentially catastrophic technical problem." Only "safety-related test flights" were authorized, "pending further notice."

Then Harry Train called Blackburn from Moorer's office. The President wanted a "complete briefing" on the raid, tomorrow. He had invited Secretary of State William Rogers to sit in. Moorer would give the briefing right after lunch. Would SACSA prepare the necessary charts and briefing book?

Blackburn and Mayer spent the rest of Monday updating their briefing and having new vugraphs made. Their draftsman, a young Navy enlisted man named Larry Downing, worked late Monday evening getting all of them ready. The next morning,

November 17, Blackburn and Mayer checked over his work; it was a "first-class job." They delivered everything to Train, complete with Moorer's briefing text typed out in a carefully indexed, tabbed three-ring black binder with gold-imprinted letters spelling out "Top Secret" and "Chairman's Eyes Only" on the cover.

Having just arranged for the President to "learn more about Son Tay than he ever wanted to know," Mayer discovered that the raid's commanders were apparently lost. Manor and Simons had been scheduled to land at Takhli Royal Thai Air Force Base in central Thailand at 5:30 A.M. Washington time that morning, 5:30 P.M. in the afternoon local time; Manor was supposed to send a prearranged, specially coded message to the Pentagon Command Center reporting their arrival. It was now 9:30 A.M. and the message had not yet been received. Mayer had pur- posely grounded about 50 Air Force planes the day before; now he was concerned that the Navy might have accidentally lost one somewhere in the western Pacific.

Mayer spent the next hour in Room 2C945, the National Military Command Center's message section, anxiously going through all the special coded cables to see if the night duty offi- cer had misplaced Manor's message or routed it to the wrong office. There was no such message anywhere in the communi- cations center. Blackburn told his executive officer, Air Force Colonel William P. "Pat" Ryan, to keep "bugging" the message center and track down that cable. He told Mayer they'd sweat it out until three o'clock; that was when the final contingent of Simons's raiding party was due to arrive in Thailand. Manor and Simons were to send another message then, reporting that the "Joint Contingency Task Group" had "closed in" at its stag- ing base.

While Mayer and Ryan were trying to track down Manor and Simons, Blackburn met with NSA's Zaslov to try to track down the source of the information about the raid that had been picked up by Air Force counterintelligence at San Antonio. They reviewed the tapes of the Pentagon-Eglin phone taps at length. Zaslov concluded there was no cause for concern; neither the location or nature of the target nor the timing of the raid could be put together from the fragments of conversation on the tapes.

Blackburn didn't tell him how relieved he really was that the

NSA found no cause for alarm over the phone leaks. A month before, a counterintelligence officer had come to Blackburn's office to say that some information had been compromised on a phone call from the Pentagon to Eglin. Blackburn himself had placed the call, but his impromptu "waffling" and double-talk on the phone hadn't worked: a piece of potentially serious information had been overheard, taped, and logged in by Air Force security as a fairly big disclosure—and Blackburn was the violator.

Norm Frisbie, Blackburn was told, had learned of the leak and had passed word of the goof to his superiors. The counterintelligence officer had then told Blackburn that he had to advise General Palmer, the Army Vice Chief of Staff, of the security violation. Blackburn readily agreed he should. Then he called Frisbie and asked him to get back to work on the raid. Other authorities would assess the impact of Blackburn's goof.

Despite Zaslov's reassurance, Blackburn was concerned about the leak. Later that afternoon, Mayer found him in his office "despondent as hell." They discussed Blackburn's careless slip, and Mayer told him it was a "bunch of smoke," careless but "sure as hell" nothing that would compromise the raid. Yet Blackburn was profoundly disturbed. He had gone to extraordinary measures to compartmentalize the planning and limit the "big picture" to only a few people. Not even the Commander-in-Chief of the Pacific Air Force had been "wired in." Blackburn's counterintelligence team had worked hard to have the Son Tay mock-up at Eglin torn down every time a Cosmos satellite passed overhead so that it wouldn't be detected by Russian cameras. *He* was the one who insisted on the phone taps, even on his own. Now, he had caught the "biggest blabber of all"—himself.

Blackburn left the Pentagon early that day. At home that evening he wrote out his resignation from the United States Army. After dinner he called Mayer and asked him to come over. Blackburn showed him the resignation. Mayer read it in silence, carefully, and then tore the paper up and threw the pieces into a fire blazing in Blackburn's den. "Don't forget that we're teaching ourselves to be more careful; we haven't blown anything yet," he said. "This just means we'll have to be more careful in the future, or we're likely to blow something." Then he told Blackburn to forget the incident and get some sleep so he could get his "ass back to work." Blackburn grumbled about Mayer ripping up his resignation. "If you feel so strongly about it," Mayer said, "you can write another one in the morning."

Ed Mayer had had problems of his own that day. Train had called him at 11:15 A.M. with a "complete new set of instructions" for Moorer's White House briefing. The meeting with the President was now scheduled for 2:30 P.M., but Moorer needed "new charts, more charts and different-size charts." And he needed them by 1:30 to have some time to familiarize himself with the material.

To his horror, Mayer found that the only draftsman cleared for the Son Tay operation, Larry Downing, had gone home. He was babysitting. His wife had been taken to the hospital late the night before. There was no way, he told Mayer on the phone, that he could get a replacement babysitter in time; his regular one was in school. Mayer's own children were too old for babysitters and he had no idea where he could find one. He told Train of the problem, who commented wryly, "I don't quite believe it; the deadline is 1:30. Are you telling me this thing is going to come unglued over a babysitter?"

Mayer knew he couldn't ask Blackburn to babysit, and tracking one down was the kind of "detail" that Blackburn didn't like to be bothered with. So Mayer set to work on the charts himself. Presidential briefings, he learned belatedly, had to be made up on 20- by 30-inch flip-charts, each chart split down in the middle and then taped together on the back so it would fold just right on the Oval Office easel. Mayer called in two people from the JCS graphics section. Neither one had the proper clearance. So he called them in separately, gave one man unmarked, unclassified maps of North Vietnam and layouts of the Son Tay compound, and the other a bunch of "headlines" and labels to make up.

Mayer pasted everything together himself. Soon the unclassified maps and labels became Top Secret charts of the air approaches to Son Tay Prison, and of the prison itself. By the time he finished, his draftsmen still didn't know whether they'd been preparing flip-charts of a new atomic bomb storage site or maps for a routine SR-71 reconnaissance track over North Vietnam. Mayer told them they weren't to *speak* to each other for at least a week.

At 1:20, Mayer was ready to deliver the charts when he

suddenly realized he didn't have a carrying case. Nor did the JCS graphics section. He spent the next nine minutes calling one JCS office after another and finally located a case in an office almost directly above his, the Joint Reconnaissance Center in Room 2D921. Maps and photos were its product, flip-charts its hallmark. Its director, Rear Admiral J. C. Donaldson, told Mayer he could have "any kind of carrying case SACSA ever needed."

In Room 2E873, Admiral Moorer flicked through the charts quickly without comment or question. Mayer was relieved that he had put the right labels in the right places with enough glue to keep them from falling off. But at two o'clock, the White House called: the briefing had to be postponed; Moorer was to be in the Oval Office tomorrow at eleven o'clock.

Mayer went to Blackburn's office. The Son Tay assault force was due to arrive in Thailand that afternoon at 3:00 P.M. Washington time. There should be a message confirming their arrival within minutes. Addressed to Mayer's attention, all it would read was "Electric Ray." But there was still no message from Manor and Simons. Three o'clock passed; then three-thirty. Blackburn and Mayer began to wonder not only what would happen at the White House, but where in the hell their raiders were.

Late that afternoon, Blackburn met Moorer, who was leaving the Pentagon for home at an hour much earlier than usual for him. "Can I ask how it went, Admiral, with Mr. Laird at the White House?" Blackburn said.

"Fine, Don, fine, I'd say," Moorer replied. "We'll know after I brief the President tomorrow."

Blackburn had not yet received a message from Manor or Simons, but he decided not to tell the Chairman that he'd "lost" the Son Tay raiders.

By 7:30 P.M. that evening, when Blackburn and Mayer left the Pentagon exhausted from a hectic day, the messages they had been waiting for still hadn't arrived. But Manor and Simons weren't lost; their messages were—at a relay station in Japan. Manor had sent the messages on time: one reporting his and Simons's arrival left Takhli at 5:30 A.M. Pentagon time; the second, reporting that Simons's 56-man assault force had arrived, left Takhli at 3:00 P.M. Pentagon time. But because of the special codes used, they had to be handled manually at an automatic switching station in Japan whose procedures were geared to general communications. Manor's "flash" messages didn't reach the National Military Command Center until about nine o'clock that evening. By that time, Mayer had found Simons by placing a frantic but unauthorized phone call to Thailand. "Fudging it" as best he could on the unsecure voice circuit, he verified that Simons, Manor, and their troops were indeed alive, well, and ready to raid North Vietnam.

It was just the first of a series of communication foul-ups that were to plague the Son Tay raiders.

The Oval Office

On Wednesday morning, November 18, Admiral Moorer was driven to the White House to brief President Nixon on the Son Tay raid. That day was the 80th anniversary of the launching of America's first battleship, U.S.S. *Maine*. It was also a day of decision—when, or if, to launch the raid. The admiral hoped the operation would have smoother sailing than the *Maine*.

Moorer arrived at the Oval Office at precisely 11:00 A.M. There he found President Nixon, Henry Kissinger, Melvin Laird, CIA Director Richard M. Helms, and Secretary of State William P. Rogers. After a businesslike exchange of greetings, Moorer began to set up the elaborate 20- by 30-inch flip-charts Ed Mayer had assembled in such a panic the day before. Laird had already briefed the President on the concept, but had decided Nixon should hear the "full pitch" before making his final decision. And he knew the briefing had impressed Kissinger: it was imaginative, almost entertaining.

The way Oval Office briefings were handled in 1970, Moorer would be flipping his own charts. "You don't take a 'horse-holder' to the White House," he would later joke. He hadn't had much time to look all the charts over and wondered if they were in the right order. When he was given the signal to proceed by the President, Moorer opened his carefully tabbed briefing book and began: "Mr. President, the code name for this operation is 'Kingpin.' "

Of those present in the Oval Office that morning, only Secretary of State Rogers had not been briefed about the raid before.

Yet, as Moorer began to read through the briefing book, tapping the charts with a telescoping metal pointer to illustrate the text, and occasionally adding a soft-spoken comment of his own, his audience was obviously enthralled. A few minutes into the briefing, Kissinger picked up the phone to summon his deputy, Major General Alexander M. Haig. He entered the Oval Office moments later, and he, too, listened attentively.

"This is the scenario, Mr. President," Moorer said, continuing with details of the airborne approach of Simons's assault force from Thailand to Son Tay: the precise route that had to be taken to avoid detection by enemy radar, the complex procedures of aerial rendezvous and refueling, the dangers of detection and destruction on the final leg of the flight. Moorer described the Navy diversion that would be launched over Haiphong Harbor 20 minutes before the landing at Son Tay to trigger a conventional air attack response by the North Vietnamese and distract their attention from the approach of the assault force. The President was absorbed by his description of the intricate aerial ballet that would take place over an area covering 300,000 square miles of Southeast Asia.

Unveiling a large, schematic diagram of the Son Tay Prison compound, Moorer said: "Here, Mr. President, is how the assault landing and rescue will be made." Surprise, speed, and simplicity would be the keys to the success of the assault, he said, and went on to explain in detail the air and ground tactics that had been perfected through long hours of practice at Eglin Air Force Base. Moorer then added a few illustrations of how meticulously the raid had been planned. "The ground commander is positive that the operation will succeed, Mr. President. He has personally selected every man in this mission. They are all volunteers, dedicated and free from any discernible defect. The training was thorough, definitive, and intense. The aircrews are among the best available. They were also individually selected and all aircraft commanders are volunteers."

Kissinger interrupted for the first time. "I talked with the two leaders, Colonel Simons and General Manor, over a month ago, Mr. President. Most impressive. Simons swears he can get into that camp and back safely with all of his men. He said the odds are 97 out of 100 in his favor. Someone told me they'd rehearsed this more than 100 times." Laird added that planning for the operation had been under way since May.

Moorer went back to his briefing to describe the tight security under which the planning and training stages of the operation had taken place. Special security measures would also be in force while the raid itself was under way. He assured the President that "if resources in support of this operation reveal that the enemy may have determined our objective, the operation will be canceled." The President protested that he didn't want that to happen.

Flipping to another chart, Moorer described the major threats, both from the air and the ground, to the assault force. It was clear from the intriguing details he provided about North Vietnamese defenses that the intelligence behind the raid was of the highest caliber. Moorer was able to tell the President, for instance, that four of the six qualified MIG-21 night intercept pilots at Phuc Yen, the airfield closest to Son Tay, had been redeployed to Vinh airfield, far to the south. Moreover, he pointed out, there was no night alert at Phuc Yen, so the remaining planes would be slow to react. There were four MIG-17 night interceptor pilots at the Haiphong-Tien airfield, Moorer added, but there was no night alert there either. And, he said, those planes, even if scrambled, would be committed against the Navy diversion. Finally, he noted that while MIG-17 all-weather fighters were also positioned at Kep airfield, there were "no known night-qualified pilots there."

Lastly, Moorer spoke of the objective of the mission—the POWs at Son Tay. "This is the only confirmed active POW camp outside Hanoi, Mr. President. The Son Tay camp has a prisoner population of 70 Americans. Of these, 61 have been tentatively identified by name and service: 43 Air Force, 14 Navy, 4 Marines." Lieutenant Commander C. D. Clower, U.S. Navy, "promoted to commander since capture," he said, had assumed the position of senior ranking officer. The North Vietnamese had moved the two previous SROs out in January and May, respectively, he explained. Again, the President seemed to be impressed by the precise detail which the Pentagon had on the target.

After cautioning that the weather would be a "critical factor" in the operation, Moorer concluded his remarks: "If you approve the operation, I plan to release General Manor to execute the raid any time he elects between the November 21 and 25 launch windows. That's all I have, Mr. President. Are there any questions I can fill you in on?"

The President looked up. "That was great, Tom, just the right amount of detail, not too much. Ah, I know you need a final decision as soon as possible and I plan to give you one soon. But what's the latest you can wait, without fouling Manor up?"

Moorer hoped his eyes wouldn't betray his concern. He knew the President made his decisions alone, and that he would want to check to see if Kissinger, Haig, or Laird had any private qualms. But the question implied another long hold, and this was no time for delay. The operation was too unprecedented and sensitive. Moorer responded carefully to the President's question: "Mr. President, if we miss this launch window, the earliest we could try again would be March. The right combination of quarter-moonlight and weather comes up only four or five times a year in that area. We missed one window on October 21, as you know. If we're going to make this one, I should send an 'Execute' message no later than 24 hours from now, sooner if possible. General Manor and Colonel Simons are in Thailand, ready to launch."

Moorer explained his problem: "There's a lot of last-minute activity triggered by this kind of an operation—ships, airplanes, men, special reconnaissance missions, standby search and rescue forces. It takes three days to get everything in full gear. But we don't want to start it up if we're not going to go; too many people would be asking too many questions. That could jeopardize our next chance. However, once approved by you, the operation can still be aborted at any time prior to launch or canceled and, if necessary, recalled at any time. We have prearranged code word and RED ROCKET communications to handle either a last-minute cancellation or recall."

The President replied quickly: he understood Moorer's concern. It wasn't a question of "whether" to make the rescue; that had already been decided. The only question was "when." Nixon assured Moorer that he would have a decision "very soon." But he had one more question: "What if the raid failed? Had adequate cover stories been devised?"

There were five cover stories, Moorer explained. He turned again to his briefing book. If the raid was successful but some aircraft and men were lost, the word would be simple—the results justified the risk. If somehow the operation was disclosed prior to launch, the Pentagon would say only that it involved a highly classified mission and no details would be available. If the mission had to be aborted or was disclosed after launch, the aborted venture would be described as a search and rescue effort for a downed reconnaissance airman. If the raid failed at the target or if no POWs were rescued and word got out, the line would be that intransigence of the North Vietnamese made the attempt necessary, and that results would have been worth the risk.

The President nodded. One last question. What was the earliest anyone would know if the raid had succeeded or failed? Moorer explained briefly the complex communications hookup between Simons's assault force, Manor's command post at Da Nang, the Pentagon Command Center, and the White House situation room. Washington would know within a minute or two exactly what was going on at Son Tay. The whole operation, Moorer reminded the President, was keyed to Simons being on the ground not more than 30 minutes, hopefully only 20. As soon as he called the choppers back to extract the assault force, the code word would be passed on how many prisoners had been rescued. It would take only two minutes to get the message to Washington.

"How many more POWs will we find out are dead if we wait much longer?" the President said. It was a reference to the death of six more American POWs on the list turned over by Cora Weiss on the previous Friday, November 13. The only similar list had been turned over by North Vietnam the preceding January, naming five dead U.S. airmen—all of whom, it was reported, had died before they hit the ground. But this latest list caused the Pentagon and the White House grave concern about the treatment of Americans held prisoner in the north. Two names, in particular, raised haunting questions. The first man on the list was Air Force Captain Edwin L. Atterbury. The DIA had learned that he had escaped early in 1969 in "fairly robust health," but was recaptured soon after he got "over the fence." Yet, the DIA also knew, Ed Atterbury had never been seen or heard from again by a fellow POW. North Vietnam would only report that he "died in captivity" on May 18, 1969.

Another airman on the new list was Air Force Captain

Wilmer N. "Newk" Grubb, shot down almost five years earlier, in January of 1966. North Vietnam had released five photographs taken of him after his capture. Except for a minor knee injury, Grubb looked in good health; he appeared strong, head held high. Those pictures were published in at least ten Communist countries. Although his wife, Evelyn, never received a letter from him, the photos had sustained her for almost five years, knowing he was alive and "wonderful to see." But when the list of November 13, 1970, was "clarified" by North Vietnam's representatives in Paris, they said that Newk Grubb had died on February 4, 1966, of "injuries sustained in his plane crash." That was only nine days after his capture, *before* any of the pictures of him had been published. One picture caption had spoken of how "humanely" Captain Grubb was being treated. But, if Hanoi's latest information was correct, the photo was printed days *after* he died.

The grim significance of Grubb's death was on everyone's mind in the Oval Office as the President deliberated about the proposed Son Tay rescue. Had Hanoi propagandized to the whole world the humane treatment of a dead man? Were his captors fostering thoughts of life and hope, when there was only death? Why had Hanoi let those hopes linger for almost *five years*? If Newk Grubb died nine days after his capture, North Vietnam had perpetrated a deliberate, premeditated deception of a kind that only barbarians would consider. Were the other prisoners living, or dying, an equally uncertain and cruel fate?

The President mused silently for a few moments. Finally, he asked, "How could anyone *not* approve this?" It was a rhetorical question. The President told Moorer, "Tom, I know you guys have worked months on this. I want those POWs home too. Hell, if this works, we could even have them here for Thanksgiving dinner, right here at the White House. But I don't want to put any more into those camps, either."

And, the President added, he couldn't afford any more near-riots. The march on Washington just six months earlier, after the Cambodian invasion, still haunted him. "Christ, they surrounded the White House, remember? This time they will probably knock down the gates and I'll have a thousand incoherent hippies urinating on the Oval Office rug. That's just what they'd do."

The President also wondered if Fulbright would call the raid "an invasion" of North Vietnam. "This one could hurt, Tom," he concluded. "But I know you're up for it. I'm sure we'll go; just give me a little time to mull it over. Whatever happens, good luck." He got up and stuck out his hand to shake Moorer's; it was a warm, appreciative gesture, the kind Richard Nixon wasn't too noted for.

(Years later, a historian of the war in Southeast Asia would write that Nixon had visited Son Tay in 1953, when he was Vice President, and had toured a refugee camp there.* He wrote that Nixon had spent six days visiting what the French then called the "Associated States." The French were his hosts, faring badly in their Indochina war. The author said Nixon had concluded that their failure was due to their inability to inspire the Indochinese to defend themselves against communism, in large part because the French did nothing to hide their disdain of the Vietnamese. The trip was part of an extensive Asian tour. Nixon might have forgotten about the trip during Moorer's briefing on the Son Tay raid because his itinerary had been crammed with so many stops that it had all become a blur, the details of that travel quickly forgotten. But Melvin Laird would insist that Nixon had "never visited Son Tay," that the refugee camp the French had shown him was "a hundred miles away.")

As Moorer was leaving, Haig asked him quietly if he could leave an extra copy of his briefing book for the President to review in private—charts, maps, and all. Before he left the Oval Office, Moorer quickly segregated materials to be left with the President from those he would take back to the Pentagon.

In the hallway outside the Oval Office, Al Haig approached Moorer to ask if they could talk briefly. Haig spoke very softly. "Tom, you did one helluva job. The boss was visibly moved; I can tell you that. He'll approve it." Then he paused awkwardly: "One thing, Tom. If this thing fails, maybe we could find a way to let the Old Man off the hook? He's taken nothing but bum raps on every decision he's made about Vietnam. We can't let him down on this one. You know what I mean."

Moorer drove back to the Pentagon in silence. As soon as he arrived, he asked Train to pass his thanks to Blackburn and

*The First Domino: Eisenhower, the Military, and America's Intervention in Vietnam by James R. Arnold. New York: William Morrow and Company, 1991.

Mayer for the effective changes in the charts and a well-laid-out briefing book. But what Blackburn would really want to know, Train realized, was, "Did we get a go-ahead?" Train didn't know. He decided to pass the word that Moorer was "very pleased" and they'd have a decision "shortly."

Moorer thought he knew, but he wasn't really sure. The President had seemed very positive, almost effusive in his few compliments. He'd asked only a few questions. Yet he seemed worried, apprehensive, more thoughtful than Moorer had seen him in many of their so-called decision briefs. What really bothered Moorer, however, was Haig's remark about "a way to let the Old Man off the hook."

The President made his decision rapidly. Late that afternoon he gave Laird the go-ahead for the raid. Moorer was gratified by the decision, and Blackburn and Mayer began immediately to set the necessary wheels in motion. But still troubled by that conversation in the hallway outside the Oval Office, Moorer told Blackburn: "Don, there's one thing we'd all ought to think about." He spoke in a confidential tone. "Ah, I don't think the President knows about this one."

Moorer would not recall the exchange and denied categorically that anyone ever suggested he might have to take the "rap" if something went wrong at Son Tay. But then it was not likely that he would feel free to admit any such suggestion had been made. Blackburn, however, would remember the encounter vividly and made a cryptic note of it in his personal daily log. "Moorer didn't need to tell me," he would recall later, "that if we screwed up, he would take the rap, no one else. And he was reminding me that the purpose of his White House visit that day was for only a few to know and that we might all end up keeping our mouths shut about Son Tay."

The Cigarettes

When word came late in the afternoon of November 18 that the President had approved the raid, the SACSA team swung into action. For months this was the moment Blackburn and Mayer had been working and planning for. But some anxious—and ludicrous—moments lay ahead. Mayer quickly encoded the "Execute" message from a prearranged code pad and took it to Vogt for approval. The message was brief, something very close to: "Mumbletypeg, Amputate Kingpin." But Vogt looked at it and said, "For Christ's sake, this doesn't make any sense." Mayer explained that it would when Manor looked up the pre-arranged code words. Vogt didn't believe it. There had already been one communications foul-up, and Mayer couldn't convince him there wasn't about to be another. He had to go back down to his office in the Pentagon basement, unlock a secure filing cabinet within a secure vault, take out the communications plan for Kingpin, lock up the cabinet and vault again, and hurry back to Vogt's office to show him that the message was correct. Vogt finally initialed the order; Mayer then had to take it to Moorer, who took it to Laird, who signed it. Then Moorer initialed it, and Mayer could send it, praying that it wouldn't get lost somewhere between the Pentagon and Thailand.

It left the JCS message center at 5:30 P.M. that afternoon on a RED ROCKET transmission, a special, ultrafast, direct message procedure usually reserved for the kind of international crises suggesting that World War III might be imminent.

While Mayer was flapping to get the "Execute" message approved and sent, Blackburn got bad news about weather. Typhoon Patsy had hit Manila with winds of 105 miles an hour and gusts of 140; and it was moving west at about 80 miles an hour. Satellite photos taken of the objective area showed that it was clear, but a cold front was moving toward it from China. The typhoon and cold front might converge over North Vietnam. Blackburn recalled that meterologists had sifted through years of Southeast Asia weather data to pick November 20 to 25 as a good window. Now that the President had given a final okay, it looked like they had picked dead wrong.

But there was still a lot of last-minute coordination to be done. Blackburn met with Jim Allen and Navy Captain Don Engen to resolve Air Force and Navy responsibilities for processing the prisoners, and for their medical care once they arrived home. The normal procedure for evacuating wounded men from Southeast Asia was to send them to whatever military hospital was closest to their homes. Where to take the rescued POWs, however, had spawned an interservice debate that became "one of the biggest problems" Mayer had grappled with for weeks. In this case, *every* service wanted the POWs, and each had "yakked for hours and hours, day after day," to make its case. Mayer told Blackburn the debate had become "as laughable as the second 'attack' on Aparri" in northern Luzon—all because the "POWs meant publicity out the kazoo." At one point, Mayer had proposed a compromise. There were no Army POWs at Son Tay, he reminded everyone, so the freed men should be flown first from Thailand to Tripler Army General Hospital in Hawaii—it was "neutral." Once cleared for further travel, they could be flown to the hospital closest to their homes. But the Air Force insisted that *its* POWs were going to be in Air Force hospitals, not Army or Navy ones; and the Navy wanted *its* prisoners, including the Marine POWs, in Navy hospitals, no one else's. Blackburn was determined not to let the raid on Son Tay become another public relations attack. Allen and Engen agreed with him: care of the POWs came first, not the image of their services. The three decided that after a quick physical in Thailand, the prisoners would all be flown to the closest big hospital, at Clark Air Force Base in the Philippines. Then they could be evacuated, Blackburn conceded, to the respective Air Force or Navy hospitals closest to their homes.

As Blackburn left the Pentagon around six that evening, he was concerned that the large-scale redeployment of rescue units—medical evacuation C-141 jet transports from the Philippines to stand by in Thailand as well as HH-53 rescue helicopters moving from their staging bases in central Thailand to the northern launch sites closer to North Vietnam—would "light up" the North Vietnamese warning system. When he arrived home, he was still wondering what more, if anything, could be done to prevent that system from "going hot." Then a new and bigger problem came up.

Rear Admiral James C. Donaldson was calling from the Pentagon. Donaldson was the JCS Deputy Director, J-3, for Reconnaissance. He asked Blackburn if a certain Air Force colonel, who had deployed to Thailand with Manor, was "one of your people?" Yes, Blackburn acknowledged noncommittally, the officer was; what was the problem? The officer had called Strategic Air Command headquarters in Omaha from Southeast Asia, Donaldson explained, alerting them that "the operation" might "go early" and that some refueling missions and preplanned reconnaissance tracks might have to be rescheduled. SAC's reconnaissance center didn't know what the hell the officer was talking about, but he wouldn't go into detail. SAC's reconnaissance office had called Donaldson for clarification. Donaldson wanted to know if the officer was authorized to make that kind of call on an unsecure voice circuit. He thought that any such rescheduling would come from Manor through his office.

Blackburn was livid. No, the officer wasn't authorized to tell SAC a thing, he said. So compartmentalized was the Son Tay planning that *no* one in SAC was cleared to know why it was flying all those SR-71, Buffalo Hunter, and Big Bird reconnaissance satellite missions over western Vietnam, or what the KC-135 and RC-135 missions laid on for November 20–25 were all about. SAC's officers were also savvy enough not to ask.

Blackburn asked Donaldson to stand by in the National Military Command Center, while he got back to the Pentagon as soon as he could. But before leaving home, Blackburn called Air Force Colonel Franklin C. Rice at home and asked him to meet Donaldson and him in the command center "right away." Rice had been on the Son Tay planning group to arrange everything that would have to be handled in the command center, including communications from the Pentagon to Manor, CINCPAC headquarters in Hawaii, Task Force 77, and all of the commands that would support the operation from the SR-71 reconnaissance base in Okinawa to the medical evacuation plane standing by at Clark Air Force Base in the Philippines. Blackburn told Rice that he might need a fast telephone "patch" to their "friend" overseas.

At the Pentagon, Blackburn got on the phone with Donaldson and Rice to SAC headquarters. He asked to talk directly with the officer to whom the call from Thailand had been made. He was Colonel John Clancey, the SAC reconnaissance office duty officer. Blackburn explained that he was just going to ask questions, not answer any. Did the "character in the plot" say the operation "might" go early or "would" go early? Clancey told him, "might." Did he indicate "what operation"? "No," Clancey said, that's why he had decided to call Donaldson: they couldn't figure out what was going on, much less what it was that SAC was supposed to do.

Blackburn asked Rice to get Manor on the phone right away. There was no secure voice circuit to Takhli, Rice explained, so, they would have to talk "in the clear." When Blackburn reached

Manor, he told him he had been talking with some friends in the Midwest and suggested that Manor might want to strangle one of his officers with a "piano wire" because he had been playing some unauthorized "music." All the music had done, Blackburn concluded, was confuse an audience that shouldn't have been invited to the concert anyway.

It was close to midnight when Blackburn arrived back home. He still didn't have the foggiest notion why SAC had been alerted that the operation might go "early." Nor had Manor been able to clear it up in their guarded phone conversation. He had sounded as confused and irritated as Blackburn was.

Blackburn was to get only a few hours' sleep. Shortly after 4:00 A.M. he was awakened by the phone. It was Ed Mayer calling from the Pentagon Command Center. A message had just arrived from Manor, logged in at 4:11. Simons's men and Task Force 77 were ready, but "a delay due to weather was possible." Blackburn wondered what the hell was going on; was the raid going "early" or was it going to be "delayed"?

When he arrived at the Pentagon a few hours later, Thursday, November 19, his confusion mounted. He learned that if the raid didn't go on schedule, if it was delayed just one day, it might "foul up other operations." No one would tell him what those "other operations" entailed. But if the raid had to be delayed, he was told, the President would be at Camp David Saturday and wanted to be kept "in close contact" with every development.

It was only two days from the "primary launch date"; and when Blackburn saw Moorer at eight o'clock that morning, he told him of the weather problem. All they could do now, of course, was sweat it out. But weather turned out to be the least of their problems that day. Another kind of typhoon was brewing.

Blackburn spent much of the day reviewing NSA's latest electronic intercepts; an updated "air order of battle" message was sent to Takhli, giving Manor a last-minute status report on North Vietnam's air defense system. When he returned to his office that afternoon, he learned that DIA's General Bennett was looking for him, "excited as hell, really agitated" about something, and on his way to the chairman's office.

They caught up with each other just as Bennett was entering

Moorer's suite. "Don, I've got bad news," Bennett told him. Once inside Moorer's office, he dropped his bomb: "It looks like Son Tay is empty." The prisoners had been moved.

Moorer was stunned: "Oh, my God, don't tell me that now."

The "Execute" message had gone out 24 hours before. Blackburn couldn't believe that six months of work had led to this. "Now wait a minute," he interjected, "who says so?"

Bennett said the information was straight from Hanoi.

"The word" had come from Nguyen Van Hoang. Early that week, he had met an old friend in Hanoi's Chi Lang Park, six blocks northwest of Hoa Lo Prison and four blocks from the Ba Dinh Sports Club, where they first became acquainted. Hoang's friend was "Alfred"—an "elf-in-council" or "good counselor"—the U.S. code name for a senior and longtime staff member of the three-nation International Control Commission. Set up as a result of the 1954 Geneva accords which partitioned North and South Vietnam, the ICC was powerless to enforce that armistice, but its members were occasionally very effective spies—for one side or the other, sometimes both. Twice weekly, flights carried them from Hanoi's Gia Lam commercial airport to Vientiane, Laos; there, connections could be made to Bangkok and then home for leave or "diplomatic consultations."

For years, some members of the ICC staff had tried to help American intelligence pin down the location of North Vietnam's POW camps. They worked hard at it, but with little success. Figuring that North Vietnam wouldn't allow commercial flights to fly directly over any of the outlying POW camps during their approaches into Gia Lam, they carefully noted such minute details as the time and duration of every bank and turn on the Vientiane-Hanoi flights.

In the fall of 1969, Alfred tried a more direct approach, quietly cultivating the trust of Nguyen Van Hoang. He did so at first by accidentally dropping some information Hoang's interrogators had been trying to extract from POWs, but which American officials were reasonably sure, from their debriefings of the two POWs released by Hanoi in August of that year, had not been compromised. Alfred made it sound as if some drunk, offensive American colonel had done too much bragging on a flight from Bangkok for three days of "R&R" in Hong Kong. It was, of course, a carefully planted nugget, something Hoang could report to his superiors as having pieced together from the POW interrogations. The DIA and SACSA worked carefully to make sure that the information was soon corroborated for North Vietnam's defense ministry through other sources.

After a time, Alfred became an invaluable, if infrequently seen friend of Hoang. The "research" office of North Vietnam's Enemy Proselytizing Office had been thwarted for years by its inability to obtain much hard intelligence from POW interrogations, but it was now providing an occasional gem. Hoang's humor and eloquence improved; coincidentally, harsh treatment of the POWs eased somewhat. By late September of 1970, Alfred had reported that he believed Hoang was ready for the "hook"—an outright trade of information. The opportunity arose in early November. Alfred told Hoang he would be flying home for "consultations" in a few days; in fact, he confided, it might be about a big promotion. The only thing conceivably blocking it was his foreign ministry's frustration over Alfred's inability to evoke any new response from Hanoi on the POW issue. His foreign office, like others on the "neutral" ICC, was playing both sides against the middle, trying to please Washington as well as Hanoi. In fact, Alfred noted, he had almost been "challenged" in a recent cable to report on how many POWs were really held in the north. American diplomats weren't "buying" a list of only 339 men released by Hanoi

early the previous April and were putting pressure on foreign offices all over the world to find out. Alfred mused aloud: "They must really be uptight: I bet they would give anything for a convincing answer." Hoang suggested they meet again, perhaps for a stroll in Chi Lang Park, a day or two before Alfred was to fly home.

When they met again, they enjoyed a pleasant meeting. Hoang wished Alfred success on his pending promotion and then apologized for having to break off their visit early. He had to check on some POWs who would be shown to American peace activist Peter Weiss (husband of Cora) on his visit to Hanoi later in the week. As they broke up, Hoang handed Alfred a package of Thuoc La Bien cigarettes. Alfred would remember his words vividly. "Here, you might enjoy these on your trip. They're pretty strong, so don't smoke them too fast," Hoang said. Alfred noticed that the pack was partially open. "Just wanted to make sure they were fresh," Hoang added, smiling.

He mentioned that these were a "lot better" than the Truong Son cigarettes that their guards gave the POWs, three cigarettes per day. Many prisoners had chosen to stop smoking because the cigarettes were almost rancid, others as a sign of defiance because the guards required a humiliating bow after each cigarette light was given through the small opening ("the flap") in the cell door. Some prisoners had "started smoking out of pure boredom" simply because "it was something to do," Mike McGrath would relate later.

Waiting at Gia Lam Airport the next day for his plane, Alfred casually lit up one of the cigarettes: it was awful. Besides, he didn't smoke, and Hoang knew it. Obviously, there was some significance to this pack. On arriving in Hong Kong, Alfred immediately turned the cigarettes over to a friend for examination.

Hoang's package of cigarettes was decoded in Washington by midday the following Thursday, just a few hours before Bennett met Blackburn in Moorer's office. DIA's analysts were intrigued at how clearly Hoang had used one version of the POW's own tap code to spell out the number of men held in each camp. They hoped he had not broken the other versions. But Son Tay was not on the prison list. According to Hoang's head count, most of the POWs, about 150 of them, were in a new camp never confirmed before, at a place called Dong Hoi.

When DIA's photo interpreters hauled out their most recent reconnaissance photos of the converted Army barracks at Dong Hoi, they saw that the sprawling compound had been enlarged significantly. New walls divided the complex into six quadrangles, and the guard towers were manned. At the same time, however, the photo specialists showed Bennett the latest SR-71 photos of Son Tay. Some of them were infrared imagery and revealed that the camp was active; *someone* had moved back to Son Tay.

That was Bennett's bad news, and after explaining where it had come from, he told Moorer and Blackburn that he rated this new information "B-3"—close to tops. "B" meant it was a foreign intelligence source in the field; "3" meant that the source was "usually reliable," with direct access to the information supplied.

Listening to Bennett, Blackburn was not entirely convinced that Son Tay might now be empty. He told Moorer and Bennett, "That pigeon hasn't clucked before. I don't completely buy this: I'd like to see how they arrived at that conclusion." He asked Moorer if he could report back to him at six with his own assessment. Moorer and Bennett readily agreed.

As they left Moorer's office, Bennett told Blackburn to go down to DIA's "Collection and Surveillance" center in Room 2D921 "and make my guys lay it all out for you. If you need any help, call me. But I'm afraid we're too late."

Bennett's emotion welled up as he said "too late," for there was other bad news. Whatever the situation at Son Tay, even if *all* of the prisons were about to be busted successfully, it was too late for several more American POWs. In addition to the six dead POWs whose names peace activist Cora Weiss had released on the previous Friday, the 13th, Bennett had just learned there were 11 more. Their names were on a list she had just received but was not to turn over to the government for another four days, until Monday, November 23. Nevertheless, its secret had been unlocked by DIA's and NSA's "Gamma" intercepts.

For more than a year, Cora Weiss had been a courier for the American intelligence community—but she didn't know it.

From 1969 on, every time Cora Weiss stepped off an airplane from Hanoi or from a visit to North Vietnam's peace delegation in Paris, she was placed under surveillance. The NSA also set up intercepts of her telegrams, cables, and long-distance telephone calls through the microwave stations which relayed them. She was only one of many such "targets," which also included Black Panther leader Eldridge Cleaver, actress Jane Fonda, antiwar activist Tom Hayden, and anyone else who visited North Vietnam. It was all part of the Gamma special intelligence operation run by the NSA and the DIA, and illegal as hell because it was targeted against American citizens using domestic as well as foreign intercepts. It was an elaborate, expensive procedure—and occasionally very effective. The few officers cleared to know of the intercepts had taken a "blood oath" never to utter the word Gamma.

There were about 20 different code designations for the Gamma intercepts, all four-letter suffixes like "Gamma Gilt," "Gamma Goat," or "Gamma Gyro," with the suffix designating a specific target, method, or source. One of them referred to mail openings, or the "mail cover," as the CIA preferred to call it; Cora Weiss's mail was opened regularly. Another part of this special intelligence operation was code-named "Delta," although it concerned only information picked up about Russian military operations. At the DIA, all such intercepts were handled by the "Gamma Delta officer," and information from them was classified "Top Secret (Trine)," followed by the appropriate Gamma designation. "Trine" was the highest and most sensitive of three designations for special intelligence of this nature.

What the NSA and the DIA were looking for, in Cora Weiss's case, was advance word that she had new POW or casualty lists, who was on them, which POWs and North Vietnamese officials she had spoken with or seen, and everything she had observed—but might not report to U.S. authorities. This latest intercept confirmed the desperate plight of the American POWs. Of the 17 newly known dead on her two lists, 11 were known to have been held as POWs in the north, five had been listed as missing in action there, one as missing in Laos. There was no information on the cause of their deaths.

That news made it even more imperative to find out whether or not American POWs were still being held at Son Tay. Blackburn hurried back to his own office and told Mayer to call Spots Harris at the DIA. He wanted to meet with Harris's "entire team" and personally go over "every shred" of evidence, every "stitch" of data.

It was now late in the afternoon. Mayer made the call and came back to Blackburn's office with more bad news. All of DIA's "guys" had left for the day.

Blackburn was incredulous—and mad. He picked up the phone, got Harris on the line, and told him to call everyone back. Harris suggested that DIA's team could come in "early in the morning for another look." They were probably all in traffic jams about now. Blackburn said he'd gladly wait until Harris got them into reverse gear. All Blackburn wanted was for "every swinging dick" to be back in the Pentagon as soon as Harris could round up his scattered herd; and he wanted them to bring every "thread" they had on Son Tay. If they were right and Son Tay was empty, Moorer would have to recall the raid. But if they didn't work fast enough, it might even be launched—while the nation's military intelligence experts were sound asleep in their surburban Virginia beds.

Harris got his key men back in short order. Blackburn, Mayer, and Harris looked, listened, and read as DIA's experts spelled out how they had learned the prisoners were no longer in Son Tay. They also argued about what it meant.

Mayer bought their evidence. He thought Blackburn should recall the raid. To Mayer, the new camp at Dong Hoi looked like an even more promising target; it was almost as isolated as Son Tay and there were more prisoners in it. He thought everyone should "back off" and hit the new camp in a month or two.

Blackburn said he still wasn't convinced. Hoang's message, he agreed, was unambiguous; the POWs had been moved, and the DIA knew where. But the message was from a source whose reliability, in Blackburn's view, was unproven, if not suspect. DIA's photo interpreters, on the other hand, were certain that "somebody" was back in Son Tay. The camp *was* active, much more so than it had been for weeks. They just didn't know *who* was in it.

Blackburn didn't understand how anyone could form *any* conclusions from the mess in front of him. He had Harris's people go through every method of analysis, from beginning to end. He still couldn't see, he badgered them, "how in the hell" they could make "heads or tails out of the data." He was "flabbergasted" by their interpretation. One minute they were "sure" the prisoners were gone, the next they were "suspicious" that POWs had been moved back into Son Tay.

He later recalled telling them in exasperation: "Look, you clowns, don't waffle it. I need an answer. At six, I'm going in with General Bennett to tell the chairman that they are there, or they are not there. All I want out of you guys is an answer. *Are* they there, or *aren't* they? That's all. No waffling, no explanations, no chatter, no talk. Just tell me they *are* there or they are *not* there. Because the chairman, Mr. Laird, and the President have got to decide, 'Go' or 'No go.' Are we going to go or aren't we?"

Blackburn told them he didn't have the "foggiest notion" of what that decision would be. "But I want an *unequivocal* answer," he said. "And you're not going to dream one up in your sleep. I want it based on some decent intelligence. We need answers, not a bunch of bullshit."

Blackburn was sure in his own mind what the answer should be. The raid should go. Even with doubt that the prisoners were there, but with a 95 to 97 percent confidence factor that Simons could get in and out safely, it was more than worth the try. If it turned out that POWs had been moved back to Son Tay but no attempt was made to rescue them, it would have been unforgivable—and, Blackburn feared, "we'd never be given another chance."

It was time for him to meet with Moorer and Bennett in the Chairman's office. Bennett was candid. He held a stack of cables, photos, and messages in one hand. "I've got this much that says 'They've been moved,'" he told Moorer. In the other hand was another thick folder. "And I've got this much that says 'They're still there.'"

Moorer asked him, "What do you recommend?"

"I recommend we go," Bennett said.

Blackburn tried not to reveal his relief.

"Bennett had the death warrant in his hand," he said later. "I thought, 'Damn, the whole thing's about to collapse.' Hell, I knew Bull would get in there and bring his guys back. I wanted to *go.*"

Moorer took Bennett "in tow" and headed for Room 3E880, Laird's office. There they told the Secretary of Defense that Leroy Manor was about to issue the launch order to rescue POWs from a camp which they now knew, but Manor didn't,

Colonel Arthur D. "Bull" Simmons talking with his men during their final equipment check, just before launching from Thailand for the Son Tay rescue mission.

(*Below*) A low-level aerial photograph of Son Tay Prison taken by a "Buffalo Hunter" reconnaissance drone in 1968, just after the first American POWs were moved to the cramped compound 23 miles west of Hanoi.

Teledyne Ryan's "Buffalo Hunter" reconnaissance drones were flown at treetop level over Son Tay Prison seven times before the raid. Six of the flights malfunctioned or were shot down; the last banked too soon and returned with "perfect imagery" of the horizon beyond Son Tay.

Lockheed's SR-71 reconnaissance aircraft took most of the Son Tay target photos from about 80,000 feet while streaking over North Vietnam at more than three times the speed of sound. Cloud cover prevented an accurate "readout" of how active the camp really was just before the raid.

An SR-71 reconnaissance photo of the mid-1970 flood at Son Tay caused by covert American rainmaking operations over Laos. The river rose to within a foot or two of the compound's wall, and American POWs were moved from the prison four and a half months before the raid was launched.

"Barbara," code name for a model of the Son Tay compound built by the Central Intelligence Agency and used in training the Son Tay assault force. When the prison proved to be a "dry hole," CIA officials claimed the agency had not been included in the planning for the raid.

An MC-130 "Combat Talon" with a UH-1 in draft position off the left wing and two HH-53s in draft off the right wing.

The men responsible for the raid on Son Tay were among the best military planners and intelligence experts in the Department of Defense.

Army Brigadier General Donald D. Blackburn, the Pentagon's Special Assistant for Counterinsurgency and Special Activities (SACSA)

Army Colonel E. E. Mayer, chief of the Special Operations Division of SACSA

Army Lieutenant General Donald V. Bennett (*left*), Director of the Defense Intelligence Agency, and Air Force Major General Richard R. Stewart (*right*), Deputy Director for Intelligence

The air crews and assault teams that executed the raid were Special Forces volunteers, thoroughly trained in every detail of their unprecedented mission.

Air Force Lieutenant Colonel
Warner A. Britton

Army Lieutenant Colonel
Joseph R. Cataldo

Army Lieutenant
Colonel Elliott P.
Sydnor

Air Force Major
Frederic M.
Donohue

Army Captain
Richard J.
Meadows

Three of the Son Tay raiders in full battle gear (*left to right*): Sergeant First Class Donald D. Blackard, Sergeant First Class Gregory T. McGuire, Sergeant First Class Freddie D. Doss.

Colonel Arthur D. "Bull" Simons, who led the assault on Son Tay, answers questions about the raid from the Pentagon press corps. Behind him (*left to right*): Melvin R. Laird, Secretary of Defense; Admiral Thomas R. Moorer, Chairman of the Joint Chiefs of Staff; and Air Force Brigadier General Leroy J. Manor, who commanded the overall operation.

The Chinese officer's belt and buckle that Captain Udo Walther stripped from one of the unlucky troops guarding the "Secondary School" just south of Son Tay Prison.

Defense Secretary Melvin R. Laird decorates the Special Forces soldiers and airmen who assaulted the Son Tay compound deep in the heart of North Vietnamese territory without a single serious casualty.

The "unofficial" shoulder patch of the Son Tay raiders: "Kept In The Dark / Fed Only Horse Shit."

Bull Simons being decorated by President Richard M. Nixon in a White House ceremony.

(*Below*) An SR-71 reconnaissance photo taken immediately after the raid. The assault force discovered that the areas thought to be a "Secondary School" and an "Unidentified (U/I) Light Industry" complex were more heavily defended than the Son Tay POW camp itself.

BRIDGE

SON TAY POW CAMP (POST-ASSAULT)

SON TAY POW CAMP

SON TAY CITY

U/I LIGHT INDUSTRY

SECONDARY SCHOOL

FOOT BRIDGE

might be empty. Moorer and Bennett told Laird the prisoners were "gone," but that it was his opinion they "might have been reintroduced" into Son Tay.

Moorer said that in spite of the doubts, he and Bennett thought the mission should proceed. Laird's senior military assistant, Air Force Brigadier General Robert E. Pursley, would recall later that it was getting well into the evening. "Without one second's hesitation, Laird said, 'Absolutely, go!' He didn't flinch; he just said, 'Go!' "

Long after the raid was over, Ed Mayer would remark, "It was probably the toughest decision that Laird ever had to make."

Laird was keenly aware that the mission was fraught with uncertainty. He had been conscious of that well before the latest gloomy intelligence reports. More than anyone realized, Laird had been keeping Nixon abreast of the POW situation and plans for the possible rescue mission. Unbeknownst to most others, he and the President had met alone in the Oval Office to discuss the "raid and snatch" operation after a National Security Council meeting on November 6, while Blackburn, Manor, and Simons were in Vietnam briefing General Abrams. According to a "Secret, Sensitive" memorandum for the record that Laird dictated afterward,

> . . . while I would take full and complete responsibility for the promulgation of the action and particularly any adverse outcomes, I wanted the President to have knowledge of the plans and the opportunity to veto my proposed actions. I outlined both the positive and the negative results which I could foresee from the plan which the Chairman of the Joint Chiefs had proposed and strongly recommended. I indicated further that, on balance, the potential positive results justified the obvious and substantial risks involved.
>
> The President did not choose to alter the plans I outlined. Upon my urging, he indicated permission for me to advise the Secretary of State of the operation. The President and I agreed that would be done not more than twenty-four hours before the initiation of the activity.

As soon as Moorer and Bennett left, Laird picked up one of his phones—a direct, secure line to the White House—and asked for the President. He told Nixon of the news that Bennett and Moorer had presented: 17 more POWs had died; the prisoners had been moved from Son Tay; but new SR-71 photos showed that the camp may have been reoccupied by *someone.* He had decided, Laird said, to let the raid "Go" as planned. Nixon agreed. He asked Laird to keep him informed as the operation unfolded.

Nixon was not the cold, uncaring political robot many thought him to be. He sat down and wrote Laird a handwritten, unsigned note on buff stationery without the presidential seal, imprinted simply "THE WHITE HOUSE" in block letters. Characteristically, he used dashes instead of periods at the end of each sentence:

11/19

Mel

As I told Moorer after our meeting yesterday—<u>regardless</u> of results the men on this project have my complete backing and there will be no second guessing if the plan fails—

It is worth the risk and the planning is superb—

I will be at Camp David Saturday—I would like for you to call me as soon as you have anything to report—

There was nothing more that Blackburn and Mayer could do. They drove home. They had barely fallen asleep when their phones rang shortly after 4:00 A.M. A message had been received from Manor at 3:56 A.M.; the raid would be *advanced* 24 hours. Manor had given a "final go" to Simons and Task Force 77, and advised CINCPAC headquarters. In the dark of that Friday morning, November 20, Blackburn and Mayer rushed back to the Pentagon, bleary-eyed from a week of nightmares that might soon come true.

"God Almighty," Blackburn worried on the drive down the George Washington Parkway, "the spooks are going to convince Moorer to call the whole thing off." To him, a successful raid into a "dry hole" would be better than no raid at all.

Mayer had the opposite concern. Heading for the Pentagon, he thought: "That crazy Blackburn is going to invade North Vietnam so Bull Simons can land in an empty prison camp."

Mel 11/19

As I told Moore
after our meeting yesterday —
regardless of results.
The men in that project
have my complete ?to
backing and their
will be no secret.
... if the plan fails —
... it is worth the risk —
and the planning is superb —

I will be at
Camp David Saturday —
I would like for
you to call me
as soon as you have
anything to report —

But he had other problems to worry about. *If* the raid was going to go, he had only a few hours to get the Pentagon Command Center ready. And Moorer, Laird, and all the "brass" would have to have briefing books before them as the operation unfolded. He had left the Pentagon a few hours ago thinking that they could be made up on Friday, for a raid that wasn't scheduled until Saturday.

As soon as he reached the Pentagon, Mayer got on the phone to call in his command center duty officers and alert the service DCSOPS that Kingpin would launch that day. Meanwhile, Blackburn met again with Harris and his DIA experts for a last-minute intelligence take so Moorer and Laird could decide whether or not to abort the mission or recall the raiders. It was five o'clock in the morning when he asked them calmly, "Yes or no?" They began to hedge: "Yes, but . . ." Blackburn cut them off. "Don't give me any buts. All I want is, 'Are they there or not?' That's what I'm telling the chairman, that's what your boss has to tell the chairman. If the chairman asks any questions, you can answer them then. But *first* you tell them 'They're there' or 'They're not.' He needs answers, not questions."

Admittedly, results of the latest photo reconnaissance flights were inconclusive. The Buffalo Hunter failures and the lack of recent low-level coverage made interpretation difficult. The weather made it impossible. The November 6 mission, for instance, had produced a perfect photo—of the only cloud within a mile or so of the camp. It was directly over the compound. On November 13, there had been wisps of clouds directly over the compound, and so many shadows that the large-scale photos were of only marginal quality. The rest of the objective area appeared "normal." The last chance for photographic "prisoner verification" had been with the mission flown on Wednesday, November 18. But that SR-71 had an airborne emergency ("equipment problems") and had to land in Thailand. Because there was no special equipment there to "download" the sensor payload, or personnel cleared even to see what the working guts of the plane looked like, the film would not arrive back at Yokota where it could be processed and "read" until Friday evening, the 20th. By then, the raid would be under way.

When Bennett got word that the November 18 "shot" had gone awry, he immediately arranged to "lay on" another mission very early on the morning of the 20th. Two passes would be made over the objective. SAC's crews and DIA's interpreters would work quickly to see what the photos looked like, and the information would be relayed from Yokota to Manor at Monkey Mountain near Da Nang by "Autovon" telephone "in coded form" at eight in the evening, three and a half hours before Simons's men would take off from Udorn into North Vietnam.

If the news was bad, the raid could still be recalled by RED ROCKET message, Moorer had told Laird the evening before. But, he had made clear, he wanted to "go" even if there was only a "10 percent chance." News of those 17 dead POWs weighed heavily on his mind.

Still, Moorer was torn. "Nothing is ever black or white," he would explain later. With cruel irony, on the same day he had learned from one source that the raid at Son Tay would be too late, he also learned from another that it was all the more urgent to launch one.

Moorer and Bennett conferred with Blackburn one last time. All agreed the raid should go forward.

In room 3E880, long before most Pentagon employees had even arrived at work, Laird was about to make a quick trip to Capitol Hill when a Navy captain from DIA told Pursley he had to see the Secretary right away. It was "urgent," he said. (It was probably Spots Harris, although years later no one could recall for certain.) He caught Laird in the vestibule of his private elevator and gave him the latest news, that the probability of anyone being in Son Tay was now extremely remote, very remote. While the news hardly differed from the night before, the captain proffered it as if to ask, "What the hell do we do now? Did Laird still want the mission to go?" Again, Pursley would recall, Laird didn't hesitate one scintilla: he told the captain emphatically, "Of course it's a Go!"

"It was a gutsy call," Pursley would remember over thirty years later. "It impresses me to this day."

Laird would only say of the encounter, "I knew it was not a sure thing. But they were spring-loaded, ready to go. There was not going to be any looking back, no second-guessing. I wouldn't permit it. These men were all volunteers. You just don't do that."

Soon after Laird returned from the Hill, Richard Helms, the CIA's director, called him on their private line to ask if he could come to the Pentagon and sit with Laird while they monitored whatever news of the operation might come from the National Military Command Center. Laird was deeply moved by the gesture. Helms came over late that morning and the two had coffee with Moorer. From time to time they went down to the Command Center. Laird went over the Gamma intercepts and conflicting intelligence reports with him, but told Helms he had decided the raid should go as planned. Laird noted, ironically, that Cora Weiss's husband would be in Hanoi as the raid was under way. When Helms left, Laird checked the Southeast Asia weather reports once more: two of the "decision points" spelled out in the Kingpin briefing book before him were a "Final weather 'Go/No Go' " by 9:18 A.M., Washington time, and a final chance to "Abort operation prior to launch" at 10:08.

Just before leaving Washington, Manor had asked for the authority to launch one day early if necessary. He had been assured there was almost a 100 percent chance of clear weather, but he knew that weather in Southeast Asia could be fickle. (Slippage wasn't a problem because plans called for a five-day launch window beginning on the 21st.) Moorer and Laird had agreed instantly that he should have that latitude. Having received execute authority on the 18th, all the tactical details were now left to Manor. "From that moment on," Manor would later note, "I didn't get any instructions. From that point on the decisions were up to me."

Thus, Laird called the President and told him that because of severe weather, the launch date had to be moved up by one day and the raid now would be under way within hours, at four minutes after noon. He told Nixon that he and Helms had just compared notes on the grim news Moorer and Bennett had unloaded about the NSA/CIA Cora Weiss intercepts—the list that showed 11 more dead POWs, making a total of 17 that month. Worse, Laird noted, three men on the latest list had died in 1970, one of them in October and one only 15 days ago. Laird said that had bolstered his determination to do anything possible to help the POWs, and that he had just reaffirmed his decision to launch the rescue mission in spite of the latest information that the camp was probably empty. Nixon agreed that the operation should go, just as Laird had called it.

FOUR

"Kingpin"

Takhli Royal Thai Air Force Base

The Son Tay raiders landed under cover of darkness at Takhli, Thailand, after a grueling 9,500-mile, 28-hour flight from Eglin Air Force Base via California, Hawaii, Guam, and the Philippines. Manor and Simons were on hand to greet them when they stepped off the plane. It was 3:00 A.M. Wednesday, November 18, in Thailand—12 hours ahead of Washington time.

Even at this late date, only four men in the ground force—Simons, Sydnor, Cataldo, and Meadows—knew what the target was or how soon the raid would be launched. But everyone sensed that the real show was imminent. Security was intense. Aboard the plane from the States, for instance, none of the men wore any insignia of rank or any U.S. Army identification on their uniforms. Even their green berets had been collected at Eglin and flown to Thailand ahead of time on a C-141 which also carried their specially rigged satchel charges and other explosives. When they stepped down the C-141's rear loading ramps at Takhli, they were quickly boarded into closed vans, not buses, for the short ride to their billets in the former CIA compound on a remote corner of the sprawling base.

Simons's men were given only six hours to sleep and recover from the "jet lag" of the monotonous, fatiguing trip. At two that afternoon, Manor and Simons briefed them for half an hour. But still they were not told the target, or even where they were. They knew they were somewhere in Southeast Asia, but that could cover a tract of land from Taiwan to Indonesia; for all they knew, the C-141s could have been flying in wide circles for half the trip across the Pacific. Manor and Simons simply said they were now "ready," gave them a rough schedule for the next two days, told them there wouldn't be any time to waste, went through the general air and ground plans they had been rehearsing for weeks, and said they would learn the target as soon as—and "if"—final approval for the mission arrived from Washington.

After a half hour break, while Sydnor briefed the platoon leaders, the assault teams went through their detailed plans once again. Then they began unpacking their personal gear and web equipment. Chow was served from five to six. For those who wanted to attend, a movie was shown at 8:30 P.M.; some recall that it was the Burt Lancaster prison film, *Birdman of Alcatraz*. Whatever it was, most of the men thought it was lousy.

At 3:30 A.M. the next morning, November 19, Leroy Manor was awakened and handed a coded RED ROCKET message. It was the one Mayer had had so much trouble getting Vogt to approve. In just three words, it told Manor that the President had given his approval to execute. He had a "final go." Manor was now faced with his toughest decision of the entire operation: when to launch the raid.

It involved the weather. As the Son Tay raiders flew to Southeast Asia, Typhoon Patsy was forming east of the Philippines. By Thursday, the 19th, the typhoon had hit the Philippines and begun moving west, bringing with it some of the foulest weather Southeast Asia had seen in a decade. To make matters worse, a front was moving down from China, and the two were forecast to converge over Hanoi on Saturday, November 21, the primary launch date.

The only thing that could save the day, Manor's weather experts told him on the 18th, was that a high pressure ridge might form over Hanoi. If that happened, the clouds might move out of the Hanoi area for a few hours, giving the aircraft just enough of a weather window to get Simons into the target with the quarter-moon visibility on which the entire ground operation would depend.

Manor knew that for the raid to succeed, a rare and precise combination of weather and light conditions had to exist over a distance that spanned 500 miles. A one-quarter to three-quarter moon, 15 to 45 degrees above the eastern horizon, would give them 64 percent of the total light of a full moon and was required for navigation to the target, to reduce detection, and to give Simons's men adequate light on the ground. The aircraft could take off from Thailand under instrument conditions, but good visibility was needed between 5,000 and 10,000 feet en route so the A-1s, C-130s, and assault helicopters could join up in close formation. Only light turbulence aloft could be tolerated or the helicopters would not be able to refuel. As the planes crossed over Laos into North Vietnam's Red River Valley, there could be no more than scattered low- and middle-altitude clouds or the assault helicopters would not be able to navigate into the target, since they needed reflections from lakes and rivers for their checkpoints. Only scattered clouds could exist below 3,500 feet or the A-1s could not deliver the cannon fire, fire the rockets, or drop the bombs that might be needed to seal the target off from North Vietnamese reaction forces. Visibility had to be good on the ground and surface winds light for the helicopters to land. For the Navy diversion, seas in the Tonkin Gulf could be no worse than light to moderate; visibility had to be good. Over North Vietnam's coast, ceilings had to be high enough for the Navy attack aircraft to operate all the way up to 17,000 feet.

After six months of planning and three months of rehearsals, everything now hinged on the weather. Manor needed hourly, around-the-clock updates of precise weather information at specific locations all the way from Takhli in Thailand, to Son Tay and Haiphong in North Vietnam, and Yankee Station in the Gulf of Tonkin. But when he settled down in the electronic marvel that was the Takhli Royal Thai Air Force Base operations center, he discovered that he might not be able to get that information. The Air Weather Service had its own rigid set of security restrictions and release authority for access to its classified weather data. Manor, the mission commander of the most sensitive operation of the Vietnam War, found out that his Staff Weather Officer did not have the right clearance.

First Weather Group's forecast center, a controlled-access facility on Tan Son Nhut AB, had the best sources of weather data in SEA. Manor's Staff Weather Officer (SWO) knew this. As a member of the JCTG planning staff, he had a clearance that should have opened all doors. He arrived on the 11th to contact the 1stWeaGp commander, Lieutenant Colonel Leonard E. Zapinski, under the impression that Zapinski had been personally briefed in advance on the SWO's clearance by General Clay, the 7th Air Force Commander. Zapinski would later deny getting any advance notice (and convincingly supports his denial in a copyrighted account of his part in Manor's support). Manor's first problem: an impasse between his SWO's need to withhold mission details using only a "trust me" approach and the weather commander's need to follow Air Weather Service guidance. Access was granted by the 13th when the SWO's Top Secret clearance was confirmed, but with a catch: Zapinski was told Manor's SWO had no "special tickets" for any backroom data, some of it comparable in sensitivity to Operation Popeye. Zapinski told his forecast center supervisors to help Manor's SWO using the special data "subliminally" in their discussions with him.

Manor's planners had "made detailed studies, climatalogical studies back five years," and "indications were . . . that we would have a 97 percent chance of having clear weather if we" did the operation during October or November. "It didn't turn out to be quite that simple," he would acknowledge wryly; typhoons happened that time of year only about "once in every ten years."

It was soon apparent that Manor's operating base was not in the Saigon area, but at Takhli, so Zapinski offered the services of his two best forecasters, Senior Master Sergeant Dennis H. Van Houdt and Master Sergeant Loyal E. Ralston, to help the SWO with briefings there. Manor approved their involvement. Ralston made the first trip to Takhli on the 18th. He saw and heard enough to tell his boss upon return that there was an Air Force general running a big show for North Vietnam with presidential interest. The scheduled launch was less than 72 hours away, with an option to go 24 hours early. That meant Manor's decision would be made during Ralston's next trip. To give Manor an added confidence factor in a possible difficult go-early decision, Zapinski took the authority to have Ralston take his most sensitive data and brief Manor privately on the night of the 19th. In the wee hours of Friday morning, Manor made his decision based on Ralston's briefing.

Upon arrival at Takhli and prior to the involvement of Ralston and Van Houdt, Manor found that Takhli no longer had the right communications net in Thailand to handle the classified weather data. Nor was there a secure voice circuit from Takhli to Monkey Mountain, the elaborate electronics command post north of Da Nang where Manor would coordinate the raid's air, sea, and ground elements and monitor its progress. There would be no way that he could discuss the weather with Bull Simons and the Air Force flight leaders.

Moreover, the security people were now nervous about all the curiosity being stirred up by last-minute requests to reinstall the weather facsimile display and map plots which long ago had been stored or shipped out as air units redeployed from Thailand in the first three increments of Nixon's withdrawal from Southeast Asia. It was almost the last straw. Manor told his security people to concoct any kind of cover story they wanted to, but get the maps and weather facsimiles released, installed, and operating—fast.

That problem was solved, but the communications problem remained, and needed a quick solution. Manor's communicators at Monkey Mountain and their counterparts at Takhli got to work jury-rigging a workable setup. Without time to fine-tune a secure voice circuit, they settled for clear voice hookups backed up by the slower radioteletype. Through double-talk and verbal codes concocted as they conversed, the communications men would be able to convey the essentials of weather information without compromise; that is, if conditions permitted the raid to be launched at all. As it developed, Manor tasked Sergeant Ralston to monitor weather during the assault from Tan Son Nhut and to advise him at Monkey Mountain of any forecast changes. Ralston didn't have to call.

The weather wasn't cooperating. When Manor was finally able to get the information he needed, he learned that Typhoon Patsy was forecast to bring high winds, low clouds, rain, and poor visibility to the northern half of South Vietnam, the panhandle of North Vietnam, and the southern Gulf of Tonkin by the evening of Saturday, the 21st. By Sunday, a cold front was expected to enter the Red River Valley; at least four days of very poor weather would follow.

But the high pressure ridge was building as forecast; the weather was clearing in southeast China and was just beginning to enter North Vietnam. Manor might have a launch window after all, but it would be marginal, much shorter in duration— hours, not days—and earlier than planned.

It was clear that by Saturday, November 21, Typhoon Patsy would force the raid to be canceled. Within 48 hours, Manor knew, Task Force 77 would be hit by the typhoon itself. The seas were already getting rough. Thus, Manor had two choices: delay for at least five to seven days, hoping for improved weather but marginal light conditions at best; or launch early on the 20th under marginal conditions en route to the target. At 4:11 Thursday afternoon, November 19, he advised the JCS and CINCPAC that a delay due to weather was possible. But by the next morning, November 20, an early launch that night looked like a better bet. Manor sent a message to Admiral Bardshar at 10:10 A.M. It advised him of a "preliminary go."

Manor went to Udorn to line up a weather recce mission with the 1stWeaGp's WC-130 unit commander, Lieutenant Colonel Franklin A. Ross. He wanted a look at the Laos–North Vietnam border area, asking Ross to land at Takhli by 5:00 P.M., before the final assault team briefing. Ross, also qualified in the RF-4's at Udorn, persuaded Manor that the RF-4 would be more effective and volunteered to fly as the weather observer. After takeoff, the inertial navigation system went out. Ross persuaded the pilot in front to disregard unit policy and continue the mission. They landed at Takhli with data that confirmed Van Houdt's Friday afternoon private briefing forecast to Manor for "Go!" weather on the night of the 20th.

At 3:56 A.M. on Friday, Manor sent a message to CINCPAC and the National Military Command Center at the Pentagon advising them of his early launch decision. Thirty minutes later, Fred Bardshar got a similar message. Then Manor took off for the Monkey Mountain command post. His decision would prove to be the right one. By Saturday night, the 21st, Typhoon Patsy was less than 100 miles off North Vietnam. The Navy diversion would have been impossible; and the raid itself would have been halted by the high winds and poor weather that would cover the North Vietnam panhandle into the following week. The night of November 20/21 was the only date within weeks when the Son Tay raid would have been possible. General Dwight D. Eisenhower had been faced with a similar decision on June 5, 1944—the day before D-Day. In 1970, Manor didn't think back to the invasion of Normandy as he grappled with his own weather decision; he too had been able to make a correct but narrow call.

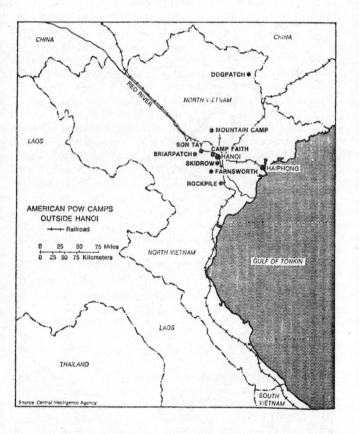

AMERICAN POW CAMPS
OUTSIDE HANOI
—+— Railroad

0   25   50   75 Miles
0 25 50 75 Kilometers

Source: Central Intelligence Agency

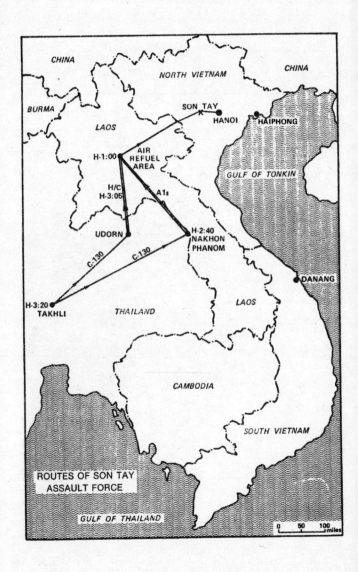

ROUTES OF SON TAY
ASSAULT FORCE

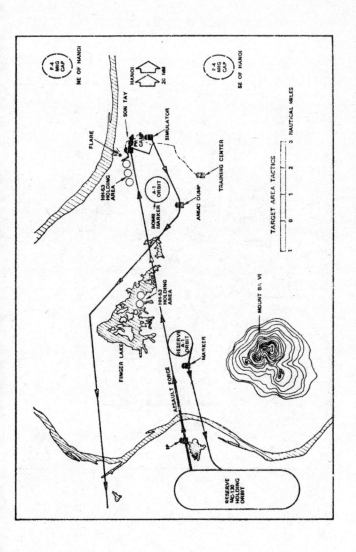

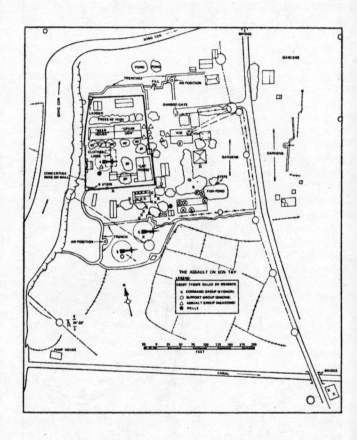

Udorn Royal Thai Air Force Base

Breakfast on the morning of Thursday, November 19, was served to Simons's men at six. By nine, they were drawing their ammunition and satchel charges. After an early, light lunch, the local Air Force search and rescue commander gave a one-hour briefing. He showed them how to operate their survival radios, gave them call signs for the rescue aircraft, and told them, "Here's how we run a search and rescue mission in *this* theater." He didn't have to tell them that if the SAR effort failed, they could use their pen-sized signal flare as a point-blank pencil—either to kill an approaching enemy, or to commit suicide.

Early that afternoon, the three assault teams each spent 45 minutes on the range under Dick Meadows's supervision, test-firing their weapons. Again, the men and their weapons were transported by closed van. The firing was not extensive, just enough for each man to check his weapon and be sure that it would function properly. Back in the billets, the men cleaned their weapons quickly. None were disassembled; the men just cleared the barrels with a cleaning patch and solvent. Then they began unpacking and checking their satchel and demolition charges.

There was no movie after dinner that night. Instead, the CIA's operations chief from Udorn, George Morton, gave a one-hour escape and evasion briefing. A specialist in CAS operations, he talked about Laos, not North Vietnam. Most of his briefing was on special code signals that the men could use to alert reconnaissance aircraft when a clandestine pickup might be made. Finally, Morton gave each man a small, plastic escape and evasion map and his personal "blood chit." This was a small piece of silk with a map on one side and an almost invisible, microthin compass sewn into one corner; the other side had such phrases spelled out phonetically, in Lao and Vietnamese, as "Which way is north?"—"I need water"—"Can you find me a doctor?"—or "I am an American." By nine, Simons's men were bunked down, lights out.

On Friday, November 20, the pace quickened. After breakfast, night-vision and infrared viewing devices were issued, fitted, checked, and stowed carefully in each man's web harness. After an early lunch, Doc Cataldo surprised everyone by issuing sleeping pills—and then checking personally to make sure that every man swallowed one, even Simons. Manor issued the "final go" order at 3:56 that afternoon, while Simons and his men were asleep. They were awakened at five for chow. Cataldo told them to eat hearty. They would take off in 5 hours; this would be their last meal in 12 hours.

Simons and Sydnor held the final briefing at six o'clock. It lasted 45 minutes. Simons spoke first, for less than three minutes. Right off, he told the men, "We are going to rescue 70 American prisoners of war, maybe more, from a camp called Son Tay. This is something American prisoners have a right to expect from their fellow soldiers. The target is 23 miles west of Hanoi."

For a second or two there was absolute silence. "You could hear a pin drop," Simons recalled. "I want to tell you it got pretty quiet. Very quiet."

A few men let out low whistles. Then, spontaneously, they stood up and began applauding. Reports would conflict. Some would say "Cheers went up"; but Simons would remember, "No, no, there was no cheering. They just applauded." But their response told him they were ready. "They made me feel good; they wanted to do it, that was obvious—and God damn it, I thought, they ought to want to do it."

Simons had one other thing to say: "You are to let nothing, nothing interfere with the operation. Our mission is to rescue prisoners, not take prisoners. And if we walk into a trap, if it turns out that they know we're coming, don't dream about walking out of North Vietnam—unless you've got wings on your feet. We'll be 100 miles from Laos; it's the wrong part of the world for a big retrograde movement. If there's been a leak, we'll know it as soon as the second or third chopper sets down; that's when they'll cream us. If that happens, I want to keep this force together. We will back up to the Song Con River and, by Christ, let them come across that God damn open ground. We'll make them pay for every foot across the sonovabitch."

Simons turned the briefing over to Sydnor and strode down the aisle. The men stood up again and applauded. As he left the theater, he heard one man say, "Jesus, I'd hate to have this thing come off and find out tomorrow I hadn't been there." Simons told Blackburn later that for the first time in his life, tears came to his eyes.

After Simons's men had "harnessed up" in their barracks

and stowed their personal effects—family photos, letters, money, anything that should be returned to their next of kin—they took another ride in the closed vans, this time to the base's biggest hangar. There, a four-engine C-130 waited to take them on board. They made a final equipment check that lasted one hour and 45 minutes. Every weapon was checked, every bandolier of ammunition opened and inspected. It was quite an arsenal for 56 men, 111 weapons in all: two M-16 automatic rifles (1,200 rounds of ammunition), 48 CAR-15 assault rifles (with 18,437 rounds), 51 .45-caliber pistols (1,162 rounds), four M-79 40mm grenade launchers (219 rounds), four M-60 machine guns (4,300 rounds), and two 12-gauge shotguns (100 shells); in addition, they carried 15 claymore mines, 11 special demolition charges, and 213 hand grenades. Finally, each man strapped a specially made six-inch knife to his thigh.

Next came a careful check of the special rescue equipment: 11 axes, 12 pairs of wire cutters, 11 bolt cutters, seven coils of rope, two oxyacetylene cutting torches, two chain saws, five crowbars, 17 machetes, 34 miners' lamps, six pairs of handcuffs, one 14-foot ladder, two crash hatchets, four fire extinguishers, one set of hammer and nails, five bullhorns, six infrared flashlights, six strobe lights, six night-vision devices, six baton lights, 14 "beanbag" lights, and two cameras.

Lastly, the platoon leaders carefully went over each man's personal gear: goggles, AN/PRC-90 survival radio, pen flare, pen light, survival kit, strobe light, aviators' gloves, compass, and earplugs. By about ten o'clock the plane was loaded. The last detail was for each man to camouflage or darken his face and pin his insignia of rank on his collar. The deception was over.

The C-130 taxied to its marshaling apron. It took off at 10:32, Southeast Asia time, 10:32 Friday morning at the White House. From Monkey Mountain, Manor signaled to the Pentagon Command Center at 10:45: Simons's men had departed the Takhli staging base for Udorn.

When they arrived at Udorn, the men transferred quickly from the C-130 to three of the five helicopters waiting at a heavily guarded parking apron. Next to them were two C-141 aeromedical evacuation planes, waiting to fly the prisoners home. In silence, Simons and his troops made a final check of the special medical supplies preloaded on the helicopters,

2,690 pounds in all. They included 150 cans of water, 100 cans of survival food, the special sneakers and lined "poncho-blankets" to keep the prisoners warm—and lots of Doc Cataldo's Heinz baby food. There were also earplugs for every prisoner, to protect him from the roar of the helicopter after years of silence in a prison cell.

Many of the raiders were surprised when Doc Cataldo climbed aboard Apple 2, the helicopter carrying Bud Sydnor and the Command and Security Group, the team known as "Redwine" and headed by Captain Dan Turner. They had assumed Cataldo's role would be to check the POWs after their return to Udorn and treat them there as well as any battle casualties. Others were even more surprised when Simons climbed aboard Apple 1 as a command backup (without diminishing Sydnor's role as the overall ground commander during the mission), thus joining Captain Udo Walther's "Greenleaf" support group.

At 11:25 P.M., Manor sent another message from Monkey Mountain: the last HH-53 had taken off from the launch base at Udorn with the assault force at 11:18, led by the tanker C-130. But as those helicopters lifted off and began to marry up, an unidentified aircraft flew through the formation on the opposite heading, causing them to disperse. They quickly rejoined, however, and aboard his helicopter, "Apple One," Bull Simons decided to get some more sleep. In exactly three hours, he should land at Son Tay; Simons told his men to wake him up when they were 20 minutes away from the objective.

One of the planes almost didn't make it. The Combat Talon C-130, which was to guide Dick Meadows's "Blue Boy" assault group and the rest of the ground force after the tanker refueled the helicopters, couldn't get its number-three, right inboard engine started. Maintenance crews were unable to find anything wrong. Manor ordered the plane to take off with three engines. But as he prepared to take off, Major Irl Franklin, the pilot, made one more try; inexplicably, the engine started, but Franklin was 23 minutes behind schedule.

Anxious to make up lost time, instead of following the base's prescribed takeoff pattern, which first called for a turn to the south, Franklin turned directly north as he was retracting the landing gear. Strict radio silence was being observed and his plane had no lights on; just a faint blue hue could be seen through its open loading ramp from 15 or 20 meters away. Suddenly his radios came alive. It was the airfield tower ordering him to reverse course: "Turn south. Head *south!* You are not authorized to fly north." It repeated that over and over, as if oblivious to any instructions about electronic transmissions. Franklin ignored the frantic messages and applied more power.

At four minutes after midnight, another Combat Talon and the A-1s took off from Nakon Phanom to rendezvous with the helicopters and Franklin over Laos.

The Nakon Phanom tower was empty when a C-130 from Takhli landed without any lights, taxied to the ramp, and barely stopped before lowering its rear ramp to disgorge ten A-1 crew members. It then pulled up its ramp, taxied quickly, and took off to deliver other people to other locations. Only one other person was on the Nakon Phanom ramp with the A-1 crew chiefs and the planes' crewmen, who picked up their flight gear and headed straight for their birds. It was the base commander, who followed the airmen around "like a puppy dog, asking question after question, none of which I could answer," Major John C. Waresh, the co-pilot of Peach One, would later write. "He got rather pissed, as I recall."

The A-1s started their engines and taxied out.

No taxi, runway, or aircraft lights were used and no radio either, total silence. (The radio was not to be used until [we were] over the camp.) Taking off at the exact second we did a 360 over the base to join up. An MC-130 Talon was to rendezvous with us there and lead us on. Timing was everything. It wasn't there. We did two more 360s and couldn't wait any longer. We were, by that time, about ten minutes behind schedule.

The backup plan was to navigate ourselves to Son Tay, following the planned route and arriving at the appointed time, 0200 local Saturday, 21 November. No way, Jose! We had agreed earlier that that was not a viable plan. We would fly the course until we got lost and then head straight for Hanoi, hold just south of the IP [initial point], which was the Black River straight west of the camp, and do our thing at the TOT (Time Over Target).

The raid was under way.

Only then was one final requirement made known to U.S. personnel at Udorn. Major Richard Peshkin, who had joined SACSA's planning group in August and been in charge of all airlift planning at Eglin, had arrived in Thailand with Manor's security and maintenance teams aboard one of the two MC-130s that would fly the mission. Once at Udorn, he went to the base hospital and told its commander that his hospital should prepare to receive what might be a large number of patients. Some might have combat injuries; others might have unspecified medical problems that would require immediate attention. There was nothing else Peshkin could tell him—except that the emergency medical care would be needed for only a short duration because two Military Airlift Command C-141 medical evacuation aircraft would soon be landing from Clark Air Force Base in the Philippines to take the patients away. As John Gargus would note later, the hospital commander probably didn't believe a word about the two C-141s until the planes landed—within an hour or so of Peshkin's request.

By then, the College Eye EC-121Ts had somehow been rewired, undergone five shakedown flight tests, and launched for their mission over hostile territory. Their crew members had been briefed on their general mission only at the last minute; but they still knew nothing of the specific mission objective.

By now the A-1s, Peach 1 through 5, were almost as much in the dark: they were able to make up only some of their lost time and missed by five minutes or so a backup rendezvous with the MC-130 near Vientiane, Laos, where they were to have dropped to low level and weave their way through the karst and valleys to Son Tay. That was impossible at night for the A-1s on their own. Nevertheless, they turned north again and pressed on, "no lights anywhere, ink black," as Waresh, who was flying in the lead plane, would describe their plight. "And then our worst nightmare loomed up. A cloud bank." The planes scattered "like a covey of quail, everyone in God knows what direction." Waresh's pilot, Major James R. Gochnauer, climbed straight up and soon popped out above the cloud cover: "Not an A-1 in sight and no hope of joining up again without lights or radio. We were all on our own." But soon Waresh saw a speck of light ahead, too low to be a star, and he headed straight for it.

It took some time to catch up. A fully loaded A-1 is no speed demon. Sure enough, there was our Talon with a teeny-weeny white light on top of the fuselage and a dim bluish glow coming from the open ramp in the rear. . . . There were already two A-1s there, one on each wing. . . . A few minutes later the other two A-1s slowly pulled up, . . . the little white light went out, the bluish glow went out, and the Talon descended into the black. From there on it was hold on tight as it bobbed and weaved through the hills and valleys.

The Talon driver was top notch. His power applications during climbs and ascents and gentle banking allowed our heavy A-1 to hang right in there. The three-day "moon window" we had for this operation provided good night vision, with one exception. Several valleys we drove through were so deep that mountains, karst, trees, or whatever eclipsed the moon. When that happened it was diving into an inkwell. . . . As we emerged from the backcountry out over the Red River Valley it was almost like being over farm country with Omaha/Council Bluffs—Hanoi—up ahead. Lights everywhere.

Yankee Station

In the Tonkin Gulf aboard the aircraft carrier *Oriskany,* Admiral Bardshar was handed a top-priority, specially coded message at 6:25 on the morning of Thursday, November 19—about the time Simons's men were making a final check-out of their personal gear. The cryptic message was from Manor: "NCA approval received." It meant that the raid would go; the only question now was when. Bardshar set things in motion to launch the Navy diversionary strikes. The weather from Typhoon Patsy was closing in, however, and his carriers were tossing "moderately" in gale-force seas. Two of the carriers would be conducting their first night operations on the eve of their deployment. Bardshar knew he could probably *launch* the planes—his pilots would be glad to be off the heaving, rolling ships—but recovering them in this weather would be a "sporty proposition."

Bardshar had one other problem. His pilots were about to fly one of the largest and most concentrated Navy air operations ever made over North Vietnam—but there was "no authorization for the Navy forces to drop bombs." How the hell, Bardshar wondered, do you send pilots into the North Vietnamese air defense network with no bombs? What do you tell them? There wasn't much he *could* tell them.

Thus, when his carrier and air wing commanders got their preliminary planning briefing, they were read what was probably the oddest operational order ever given to a Navy strike force. They would be flying over Haiphong in the dark, both literally and figuratively. All they could tell their aircrews about the purpose of their mission was this:

A special operation will be conducted by a Joint Contingency Task Group in the near future. It will be supported by elements of Task Force 77 whose function will be to create a diversion in order to assist in the successful execution of the basic mission. Security considerations prohibit full disclosure of the exact nature and timing of the operation. . . . Should any questions arise concerning the conduct of this operation, they will be directed to me [Bardshar personally signed the order] personally, by courier whenever possible.

Bardshar had not even permitted the operations order to be transmitted electrically: couriers flew it to the other two carriers, whose commanders were told that they would be waging war with blank ammunition. Bardshar's order read: "It is doubtful that political considerations will permit the expenditure of air-to-ground ordnance other than flares. Within these limits, the objective is to create as much confusion in the NVN command and control system as possible."

No Navy strikes had been flown over North Vietnam for more than two years, since October 31, 1968. Yet Navy carriers had remained on station in the Tonkin Gulf, ready to launch them any day. Finally, the aircrews were to be sent back north—but in planes dropping *flares* over the heaviest air defenses in the world. Without being told why. It was bizarre, an archetypical moment of the Vietnam War.

Commander Douglas F. Mow, the skipper of Combat Air

Group 19 aboard *Oriskany,* Captain J. E. McKnight, commanding Combat Air Wing 2 aboard *Ranger,* and Captain G. H. Palmer, leading Combat Air Wing 21 from *Hancock,* opened their operations orders. With them were the three carriers' commanders, Captains Frank S. Haak, J. L. Coleman, and T. C. Johnson. The detailed plan which Commander P. D. Hoskins had drawn up in less than ten days told them which planes would launch when and from what carrier, how they would rendezvous, what radio frequencies they would monitor, which call signs would be used, where the planes would orbit and refuel, what navigation tracks would be flown, and precisely when and where the pilots would "attack" Haiphong with naval aviation "lightbulbs." One of the skippers quipped, "We've flown 300,000 sorties over the north and we're finally going to make them see the light."

Bardshar's operations order wasn't all bad news, however. "Search and Air Rescue efforts over land in NVN are authorized," it read. And if someone was shot down, four A-7 attack aircraft would be "authorized to expend" Rockeye cluster munitions and 20mm cannon fire "in support of SAR efforts." But Bardshar had to remind his crews again: "No air-to-ground ordnance is authorized with the exception of the flares carried by Strike aircraft and the Rockeyes and guns carried aboard the Rescue Combat Air Patrol." Bardshar would be able to ease those restrictions at the last minute, however; a few planes could carry "Shrike" radar-homing missiles to suppress North Vietnamese air defense SAMs and radar-directed antiaircraft batteries.

Bardshar's operations order closed with some "special instructions" that clamped a tight lid of security over the naval division:

(1) Once this plan is opened by the designated addressees, disclosure of such portions as necessary to accomplish your assigned mission is authorized. Such disclosure will be restricted to those with an absolute need to know and will be accomplished as late as possible in order to minimize the chances of compromise. Once this plan has been opened, no personal mail will leave your unit and personnel will be transferred only in emergency cases until the operation has been terminated or canceled.

(2) Scheduled D-Day and H-Hour are————at———— [the exact times would be filled in when Bardshar got Manor's "final go"]. These will never be transmitted electrically. . . .

(5) No public statements regarding this operation are permitted even after its completion, unless specifically authorized by [the Commander of Task Force 77]. . . . Additionally, press and other visits to units involved in this operation are to be discouraged whenever possible, provided that such incidents will not lead to unnecessary speculation. Refer all decisions on these matters to [the Commander of Task Force 77]. . . .

(8) Upon termination of this operation, this [operations order] will be destroyed. Message report to originator stating that destruction has been accomplished is required.

Late the next morning, on November 20 at 11:10 A.M. Tonkin Gulf time, Bardshar received another message from Manor; it advised of a "preliminary go." At 4:56 that afternoon, a new message advised of a "final go." Boot Hill and Hoskins both flew from carrier to carrier to brief Task Force 77's air wing and squadron commanders personally. They explained that "D-Day" would be early the next day: the first planes would launch at 2:23 A.M. Tonkin Gulf time (1:23 A.M. over Son Tay). Still they could not divulge the purpose of the mission, although Hill said cryptically that when they learned the real objective, they would approve of it heartily. Hill had the commanders instruct their armament crews to break out a few Shrike missiles, some 20mm gun ammunition, and all the flares *Oriskany, Ranger,* and *Hancock* carried. The largest night air operation ever flown over North Vietnam would launch exactly 55 minutes before Bull Simons and his men were to land in Son Tay Prison. Their helicopters would have finished refueling over Laos four minutes after the first A-7 was catapulted off *Ranger's* pitching flight deck.

A few minutes after 2:00 A.M. on November 21, a newly married Navy lieutenant climbed up to the 1,039-foot-long flight deck of the 78,000-ton U.S.S. *Ranger*. Making the usual walk-around inspection of his A-7 attack plane, he noticed that, just as he'd been briefed, every bomb rack was loaded with *flares*. He decided to resign his commission from naval aviation as soon as his tour in the western Pacific was over. His father was the Commander, Naval Air Forces, Pacific. The young aviator knew that his father probably wouldn't understand. In fact, the admiral had no idea that his son—or any other Navy pilots—would be flying over Haiphong Harbor that night, armed only with flares and Shrike antiradiation missiles.

The three carriers launched fifty-nine aircraft—twenty-seven A-7 light attack planes and ten A-6 medium attack aircraft flying two waves in three tracks, each about three minutes apart, the A-6s coming in at low altitude as if headed for Haiphong Harbor and the A-7s at 18,000 to 20,000 feet. Some of the A-7s made deep penetrations toward the northeast of Hanoi to activate and saturate the China/North Vietnamese cross border air defense system; others dropped their flares along the coast. Six F-4 fighters and six F-8s flew top cover against enemy fighters while two E-1Bs and seven EKA-3Bs handled electronic countermeasures. One P-3 Orion surveillance aircraft was launched to check against seaborne threats. In addition, ten F-4s were overhead flying "Bar Cap" missions, barrier combat air patrols to protect five Air Force support aircraft that were orbiting over the Gulf of Tonkin—EC-121T College Eye airborne early warning and control aircraft, two RC-135M Combat Apples for communications support, and one KC-135 radio relay plane.

The Navy diversion worked so well that the North Vietnamese fired an estimated 20 surface-to-air missiles at the strike force. All were ineffective. The Navy planes responded with three Shrike missiles fired at the SAMs' radar sites. No MIGs reached the diversionary force.

As *Oriskany*'s deck crews watched the engine plumes of the A-7s and F-8s fade into the night toward Haiphong Harbor, Bardshar made his way below. His brow was furrowed. He had two concerns: would the diversionary raid create enough confusion to prevent air action against the helicopters; and would North Vietnamese MIGs come up to oppose Task Force 77's aircraft? In the carrier's sealed-off Combat Information Center, he put on a set of earphones. Through one part of a "split phone," he would be able to listen to conversations between the strike aircraft, and between them and their carriers; through the other earphone, he would listen to a translation of every intercept from North Vietnam's fighter control net. Thus, he would know on a second-by-second basis what instructions the North Vietnamese air controllers were giving their MIGs. The North

Vietnamese were slow to react. For 30 to 35 minutes, that ear-phone was silent.

It came alive at 2:17 A.M., Son Tay time, exactly one minute before Simons's helicopters were to land at Son Tay. Bardshar heard an excited North Vietnamese MIG pilot asking the control tower at Phuc Yen airfield to "give me a vector, give me a vector." He wanted to know what compass heading to fly, "where the action was." The controller told him to wait. For a moment, Bardshar grew apprehensive. One of the runways at Phuc Yen took off right over the camp at Son Tay, only 22 miles to the southwest; there was now at least one "hot" MIG ready to launch while the raid was under way. But Phuc Yen's control tower remained silent as more pleas came from the pilot—"Give me a vector, give me a vector," he called.

Four long minutes passed. Finally, at 2:21 A.M., Son Tay time, Bardshar heard Phuc Yen's controller tell the MIG pilot. "It doesn't make any difference, they're *all over!*" When the pilot asked him to clarify those instructions, Bardshar heard the controller tell him in desperation, "I don't care what you do. Go to China if you want to."

Bardshar relaxed. The Navy diversion was working. The North Vietnamese were thoroughly confused, and he knew that Simons's force would get in and out of Son Tay without any interference from the air. But there was one thing he didn't know. Bull Simons had just added to North Vietnam's confusion by blowing up the wrong camp.

Son Tay

Nearing Son Tay, Marty Donohue banked his HH-53, "Apple Three," into a tight downward left turn to break off from the rest of the formation. Manor's task force had finished its training over the southeastern United States with a total of 13 Air Force assault and strike aircraft—one HH-3 ("Banana" One), five HH-53s ("Apple" One through Five), two MC-130s ("Cherry" One and Two), and five A-1Es ("Peach" One through Five). Crew members and planners had nicknamed their mini-wing or little air force "Fruit Salad." But Donohue's helicopter was now only one of 116 American aircraft flying over North Vietnam, Laos, and the Tonkin Gulf for the raid on Son Tay.

In all, Manor and John Gargus would later count 44 Air Force aircraft that had been added to cover or support the rescue attempt and put under Manor's control. They included ten F-4s for MIG Cap ("Falcon" One through Ten); five F-105 Wild Weasels for decoys and SAM suppression ("Firebird" One through Five); two HC-130P tankers ("Lime" One and Two); ten KC-135 tankers (eight flying over Laos and two over the Tonkin Gulf); and 17 other planes over the Tonkin Gulf—the two RC-135M Combat Apples, the EC-135 for radio relay; the two C-121T College Eye radar platforms, the ten F-4s flying Bar Cap, and two KC-135 tankers in case any of them or the Navy aircraft needed refueling.

Collectively, then, Manor's final task force consisted of 57 Air Force aircraft supported by 59 Navy planes—48 attack and 11 support aircraft. The 116-plane armada had launched from ten different bases—five in Thailand, one in South Vietnam, and one in Japan, plus the Navy's three carriers.*

One way or another, 81 planes were in the air providing direct support or creating a diversion for the 13-plane strike force heading directly for Son Tay. All were now converging on their targets or orbiting on station. It was the largest concentration of airpower yet focused on North Vietnam; the first time in almost three years that the enemy had been threatened near its capital; by far the most extensive night operation of the Southeast Asia conflict; and the first time the Navy had launched an attack from three aircraft carriers simultaneously.

Donohue and the assault helicopters behind him descended quickly through the thin layer of scattered clouds hanging 2,000 feet over the Red River Valley. On the ground 500 feet below, his checkpoints came up rapidly, just as advertised—the Black River ten miles west of the target, Finger Lake seven miles out, finally the Song Con River as it turned sharply north two miles south of Son Tay. Donohue slowed to 80 knots as the Combat Talon C-130 pulled up and away from the helicopters.

---

*Other USAF aircraft supported the mission but never came under Manor's control: the two C-141 medevac planes, an SR-71 for postassault reconnaissance, the three C-130s flying intratheater lift, and one weather recon F-4. At least eight aircraft were on standby alert. Among them were one HH-3, two HH-53s, and two A-1Es, all in case others had to abort; two Navy KA-6B tankers were also on standby alert in case in-flight refueling would be needed.

The last two helicopters, "Apple Four" and "Apple Five," climbed to 1,500 feet to perform their role as spare flare-ships in case flares and firefight simulators dropped by the C-130 failed to ignite or were off mark.

The Combat Talon pilots had timed the 337.7-mile flight from Udorn perfectly. Irl Franklin had made up his 23-minute delay in departure by eliminating doglegs planned for just such a contingency. After three hours and 23 minutes of twisting, turning, terrain-hugging flight over Laos and down into the Red River Valley, they were less than one minute ahead of schedule. The timing was important. The guards at Son Tay changed on the hour or half hour, and the raiders wanted to land as close as possible to the quarter hour. That would give the guards who had just come off duty time to fall asleep, and those who had just gone on duty time enough to "settle down."

Donohue wracked the lumbering bird into a hard right 270-degree turn and slowed his chopper to 70 knots. Two and a half months of intensive training, 40 night training flights, and 15 "live-fire" rehearsals were behind him, but only two of those flights involved what he had to do now. Ahead of him, "the lights of Hanoi were beautiful," Donohue recalled later. Suddenly, "just beyond them, the Navy planes had the sky over Haiphong Harbor lit up like the Fourth of July with flares."

Donohue was now two miles from Son Tay.

It was 2:18 Saturday morning, November 21, Hanoi time. The most important five seconds of Marty Donohue's life were coming up, after 16 years and 6,300 hours in the cockpit of a helicopter.

He would be the first man over Son Tay Prison. At treetop level, moving at only a few knots' forward airspeed, Apple Three would fly between the two guard towers on Son Tay's west wall. Two Gatling gun–like cannons, one mounted in each side door, would open fire and spew out a cone of converging tracer bullets at 4,000 rounds a minute to knock out the guard towers and then a guard barracks just outside the gate on the east wall.

Just as the prison came into sight, the sky above Son Tay exploded in brilliant light. The C-130 flare-ship had timed its job perfectly. Donohue and his crew would have been blinded for two or three minutes if they looked directly at the bright flares. Two miles east of Son Tay city and to its south, Donohue could see the firefight simulators exploding, as if a ground battle was raging there.

Suddenly the yellow warning light on his instrument panel started flashing: "Transmission," "Transmission." Donohue's copilot, Captain Tom Waldron, pointed to it excitedly, jabbing at it with his finger. Donohue pushed the intercom button and told his crew, "Hold, hold," meaning not to fire. On any other mission, the "chip light" would have been tantamount to an order for an emergency landing, even over water, and to declare that emergency to any aircraft nearby. Transmission trouble in a helicopter is not something to fool around with: too many transmissions had disintegrated catastrophically when pilots failed to land quickly enough. This time, however, Donohue quietly told his copilot, "Ignore the sonovabitch." He decided not to declare the emergency, knowing that it could cause confusion and concern.

In the last seconds of their approach to Son Tay, there was another tense moment—a "near-miss." As they set up their firing pass, amid the distractions of the ominous flashing of the transmission warning light and the exploding C-130 flares, Donohue and Waldron were unaware that wind changes and lack of reference had caused them to drift slightly to the south, less than 200 yards, of their planned approach. Donohue saw an installation very similar to the Son Tay compound still farther to the south, another 200 yards or so. He turned there momentarily, realized it wasn't the right place—there was no river outside its nearest wall—and quickly corrected course 400 yards to the north. Then he saw the towers on the west wall of Son Tay Prison—but the trees inside the compound just beyond it were higher than he had expected, much higher. Everyone had forgotten how much those 40- or 50-foot trees, photographed so carefully in June and August, would grow in the heavy rains and sweltering summer heat by the time the raid was launched. Some were close to ten feet taller than they had appeared in the last clear overhead photos of the camp. Moreover, five months had passed since the CIA had so meticulously constructed Barbara, the model of the prison that Captain James A. Jacobs and Major Art Andraitis had measured every which way from Sunday to see how a helicopter might squeeze in.

Instantly, Donohue pulled up on his collective stick to give the helicopter blades more bite, eased off on the throttle to slow down while he gained precious feet of altitude, and told his crew calmly, "Okay, ten seconds and open fire." Then he eased the helicopter over the trees in the prison courtyard, pushed the intercom button again, and ordered, "Ready—Fire!"

Donohue was too busy flying to see it, but the northwest tower came crashing to the ground within seconds, its four-by-four-inch support posts chewed to sawdust by an almost solid hail of machine-gun bullets. The southwest tower and a guard barracks beyond the camp were chewed to shreds by subsequent bursts. Donohue's gunners, Staff Sergeants James J. Rogers and Angus Sowell, came on the intercom: "We got 'em, we got 'em. They're out." Donohue applied full throttle, turned to the north as he picked up some altitude, and searched for a small rice paddy east of Finger Lake. There, he set the helicopter down in a "holding area" about one and a half miles west of the objective. All he could do now was sit and wait until Bull Simons's men and the rescued prisoners were ready to be extracted from the target. Donohue and Waldron turned up the volume on their radio sets. For the next 27 minutes, they would monitor a bank of electronics gear as Simons and his men raided the Son Tay compound. Suddenly three hours of radio silence was finally broken. Their cockpit echoed with a cacophony of harsh, discordant FM, UHF, and VHF transmissions. Donohue tried to monitor them all.

The crash landing inside the Son Tay compound was harder, much harder, than Dick Meadows had expected, even lying flat, pressed against a mattress on the HH-3's floor to let his whole body absorb the impact. Meadows did not know it at the time, but his pilot, Herb Kalen, almost lost control of Banana One at the last second when it skimmed the trees and then hit a clothesline strung across the middle of the small compound, hardly as big as a volleyball court. One tree, Herb Zehnder, Kalen's copilot, would recall, "must have been 150 feet tall, much higher than we thought. We tore into it like a big lawn mower. There were limbs, brush, branches, and leaves everywhere. There was a tremendous vibration, the rotor system was damaged and we were down." As the helicopter's rotor blades chopped through the tree branches, its tail rotor struck a ten-inch tree trunk, almost embedded itself there, and whipped the helicopter violently 30 or 40 degrees to the right.

The impact was so hard that a fire extinguisher tore loose from its bracket and hit Kalen's flight engineer, Technical Sergeant Leroy Wright, with such force that it broke his ankle. First Lieutenant George L. Petrie, a blond, thirty-one-year-old Green Beret, wasn't supposed to be the first man to exit the helicopter, but he was. Riding in the left-side gunner's door, he wasn't braced right for the impact. "The crash landing threw me out," he explained later. Staff Sergeant Kenneth E. McMullin, one of the "shooters" in Meadows's assault group who was to be the second man out of the helicopter, off the rear ramp, would describe it somewhat differently: "When the rotor blade hit the tree, George *launched* out the door and ended up being the first man on the ground. That was supposed to have been Tom" [Master Sergeant Thomas J. Kemmer, a left-handed shooter]. Petrie landed 15 or 20 yards away in the courtyard.

Dick Meadows got to his feet quickly and ran down the rear ramp clutching his bullhorn. At that moment, it was more important than any weapon he had ever carried; the CAR-15 assault rifle in his other hand and the .45-caliber pistol in his shoulder holster were almost incidental to the job ahead. Fifteen yards from the helicopter, Meadows crouched in a kneeling position, pressed the bullhorn's "trigger," and gasped for his breath to come back. He announced in a calm voice: "We're Americans. Keep your heads down. We're Americans. This is a rescue. We're here to get you out. Keep your heads down. Get on the floor. We'll be in your cells in a minute."

His voice reverberated over the compound.

There were no answering cries.

The thirteen other men in Meadows's assault team streaked for the cellblocks and front gate. Staff Sergeant Ken McMullin would relate later that the guards "ran all around the outside of the building instead of heading for the gate. That was a big mistake." As the whine of the HH-3's engines died, Son Tay Prison came alive, crackling with automatic weapons fire. Meadows stayed crouched on one knee and announced once more: "We're Americans. We're here to get you out." His radio operator called Sydnor on the command net, "Wildroot, this is Blueboy. We're in."

So thoroughly had the assault been planned that Captain Dan H. McKinney rushed for the guard shack by the gate, since "the word was that there might be one POW in a dungeon under there," Sergeant McMullin would recall.

Three minutes into the raid, a blast from the south wall knocked Meadows to the ground, but he was relieved when he saw the gaping hole there. It meant that Bull Simons's support group and Bud Sydnor's command team had landed safely outside the compound and the satchel charges had worked. Now they had a way to get the prisoners out quickly. Meadows saw a group of men rush through the breached wall and run to their covering positions inside the compound.

But Meadows was wrong. They weren't Simons's men; they were all Sydnor's.

Bull Simons had landed at the wrong camp. He and 21 other men, the biggest part of the Son Tay raiding force, were 400 meters south of the target, plunked down by mistake outside the compound that the spooks had labeled "Secondary School" on all their maps.

Three days before the raid, ironically, intelligence men had warned Simons and the helicopter pilots that the "Secondary School" might be mistaken for the real target. Its compound was about the same size; the canal north of the school could easily be mistaken for the Song Con River as it turned east just to the north of Son Tay; and if there were moderate winds in the Red River Valley, the helicopter formation could easily drift a few hundred yards south during its final run into Son Tay. Donohue had drifted south, and trailing Donohue in his HH-3, Herb Kalen had also turned toward the installation to the south, but both men caught the mistake and corrected course to the Son Tay compound. Donohue almost broke radio silence to warn the helicopters behind him of the error, but decided against it. Every second of surprise counted. Behind him, however, Warner Britton was too far atrail and too busy concentrating on his landing zone outside the south compound wall to see Kalen change course in the last few seconds.

Piloting Sydnor's chopper, John Allison was far enough above the first three helicopters to see Kalen turn away from the southern complex; he set Sydnor's command group down outside the walls of Son Tay "right on the money." But as Apple

Two, Sydnor's chopper, approached its landing point a few yards south of the Son Tay compound, Captain Dan Turner, whose job then was to look out the window and tell Sydnor when Simons's helicopter had landed, heard Lieutenant Colonel John Allison, piloting Apple Two, announce over his helicopter's intercom, "Apple One is missing!" and realized that Simons had landed at the wrong target. He told Sydnor, who wondered, "What's that crazy sonovabitch doing over there?" At H-Hour plus two minutes and 45 seconds,* Sydnor told Turner to radio everyone that Plan Green was in effect. It was the alternate plan they had rehearsed over and over again in Florida in case Simons's support group helicopter aborted or was shot down en route to Son Tay. Turner yelled into his radio, "Plan Green. We're into Plan Green." But there was so much other traffic on the air that later he would recall telling Sydnor, "I don't think anyone's listening." But just as they had rehearsed endlessly, Redwine's elements went into Plan Green's actions immediately. Sydnor and his small command group stepped off the helicopter and moved toward the drainage ditch and a small building near the south wall of the compound. An armed soldier in shorts appeared, but Sydnor had both hands full of microphones, was carrying almost a hundred pounds of assault gear, and couldn't disentangle himself immediately. He calmly told his radio operator, Staff Sergeant Paul Poole, to shoot the man. Sydnor realized that he'd have to pull off the raid with 22 fewer men than planned because the largest part of the raiding force was visiting the wrong part of North Vietnam. The thought didn't bother him very much. He knew exactly what had to be done. Men who had served with him described his reaction to crises this way: "Bud Sydnor has ice water in his veins." John Allison slowed Apple Two to set Sydnor and his men down.

At the "Secondary School" south of Son Tay, it took Simons only a second or two, after his helicopter landed, to realize that he was in trouble. The school's walls were ringed with barbed wire. Otherwise, the compound and ground outside it looked

---

*Times given in this chapter are based on actual tapes of the UHF and FM radio transmissions made during the raid by one of the EC-121 radio relay aircraft.

like what he expected at Son Tay, and the small-arms fire that cracked and thumped all around him sounded like what he expected. But Captain Udo H. Walther knew something was wrong the moment his team breached the compound's wall and rushed inside: there was a two-story building across the courtyard, and Son Tay didn't have any two-story buildings. Simons, outside the helicopter, knew something was wrong when he failed to hear Meadows bellowing over his bullhorn. That told Simons he was at the wrong compound. Inside it, Walther and his six men were very busy improvising a field of fire, three men on one side of the building, four on the other, trying to keep "a whole slew of people" from getting to their arms room while Walther's team tried to get back to their helicopter. As Walther would describe it later, "I was scared shitless . . . there were so many of them." About the time he ran out of ammunition, "My frigging belt broke." Walther stripped a belt from a nearby body: "I just wanted to hold my pants up. It was hard to do that. I went and got one and put it on." Bull Simons would later recall his main concern—to get back to the right landing zone before it was all over. He wasn't worried about screwing up the mission: that's why he had picked Sydnor and Meadows; he was confident they would pull it all off without him. But, he lamented later, "I hated to be left out, and I knew it would all be over in 26 minutes."

Simons soon had a more immediate concern, however. A firefight was exploding all around him, and he saw a startled North Vietnamese stand up from a foxhole near the compound's southwest corner. He was clad only in skivvies, naked from the waist up in the warm night air, but he was armed—and only a few feet away.

"He was frightened, I mean really frightened, dumbfounded," Simons would recall. "The guy was looking at me like I was made out of green cheese. I don't blame him; we landed out of nowhere. I remember thinking, 'This is a lousy time of night for introductions.' I shot him through the chest."

Simons turned to his radio operator, Staff Sergeant Walter L. Miller, who was calmly taking the brunt of everything that was going wrong. He'd worked with Simons before in Laos and for three years at the Special Warfare Center. "Get that fucking chopper back in here," Simons bellowed at him. "Tell Sydnor to go into Plan Green." Then he turned to his other signal specialist, Staff Sergeant David S. Nickerson. "Turn that strobe light on fast; mark the landing zone."

Overhead, Warner Britton saw the explosions and firing 400 meters north of where he'd set Simons down and realized the mistake he made. It was, he thought, "an incredible blunder." Before Nickerson's strobe light even began flashing, Britton wracked Apple One into another tight turn and headed back down to pick up Simons and his men.

Three violent ground battles were now raging within two miles of Son Tay: the fake one to the south and east, Meadows's and Sydnor's assault on the prison, and Bull Simons's accidental exposure to North Vietnam's secondary education system.

While Britton maneuvered his chopper down into the thick of the firefight, Simons's support group was turning the "Secondary School" into a blazing ruin. Simons would say that he simply launched a "preemptive strike." "There was a hell of a firefight going on and suddenly the place lit up like a damn Christmas tree." He speculated later that "perhaps some tracer rounds ignited some gasoline barrels."

Warner Britton's "mistake" may have saved the lives of half the Son Tay raiders. The "Secondary School" was bristling with hostile troops—but only the guards were North Vietnamese. Simons's men noted as they took the others under fire that they were *much* taller—"5 feet 10 inches to 6 feet, Oriental, not wearing the normal NVA dress, but instead . . . T-shirts and fitted dark undershorts." All of them were "much better equipped" than the guards at Son Tay. Some raiders reported they were not only "larger" but had "lighter skins." "Ground forces personnel," Manor wrote later, "were unable to determine [their] nationality."

Sergeant First Class John "Jake" Jakovenko, carrying an M-60 machine gun with 900 rounds and firing solid tracers, would recall later that one of his targets "was a lot larger than a Vietnamese." Staff Sergeant John E. Rodriguez, who was with him, spoke Vietnamese. He told Jakovenko, "He ain't Vietnamese!"

Were they Russians . . . or Chinese?

In seven minutes, the task force afteraction report would note, Simons's 22 men killed 16 of them. Walther noted as his men took those inside the compound under fire that "the majority of them were *not* North Vietnamese." And, he would add, "One thing it was *not:* it was *not* a 'Secondary School.' "

Bull Simons had eliminated "the primary external ground threat" to his 56-man force—and it was only 400 yards, not several miles, from the objective. Warner Britton's "blunder" may have proved to be the most fortuitous break of the Son Tay raid. Early in November, photo reconnaissance had revealed that the "Secondary School" had been "reactivated," but only later was it learned that the heavily guarded compound might have housed Russian, North Korean, or Chinese troops who were training North Vietnamese air defense technicians on "early warning/ground control interceptor equipment" that had been moved into the "light industrial complex" about 300 yards east of the "school." Manor's after-action report, in the classic understatement of the entire operation, would recommend that the "Secondary School" be "reclassified as a 'military installation' as numerous armed personnel were encountered at this location."

Britton landed his helicopter to extract Simons's force—it was like flying into the middle of a burning ammunition dump—and put them down outside Son Tay. His men were still under fire as they broke contact with the enemy and re-boarded Britton's HH-53. The Son Tay raid was now eight minutes old.

Nine minutes into the raid, Sydnor radioed Meadows to "revert back to the basic plan." Thirty seconds later, Britton landed Simons and his men outside the walls of Son Tay, without any warning to Sydnor. He may have set a new record: three combat assault sorties in nine and a half minutes. Britton took off immediately, as planned, and flew to the holding area.

Without delay, Redwine and Greenleaf conducted an informal passage of lines, with each group reverting to their original plans. Sydnor would later reflect on how seamlessly the complex changes took place: "God must watch over those who conduct many rehearsals!"

Simons's demolition team raced into position to knock out the bridge north of the prison. SFC Jake Jakovenko almost didn't make it back to the fight. Britton's helicopter had landed just south of what had been labeled a "small drainage ditch," and Jakovenko had to jump across it lugging his M-60: "It was about six feet deep and wider than I could jump." Sydnor's men executed the few elements of the basic plan not yet carried out: destroying the power station and power poles outside the compound, and clearing the pumphouse on the canal southwest of the camp.

Inside Son Tay, Dick Meadows and his men—unaffected by the change of plans—were still clearing and searching the prison. They were taking sporadic fire, but they had landed with devastating surprise. The heaviest fire came from an AK-47 machine gun near a well inside the compound as guards rushed through the front gate. Sydnor's team came under heavy fire from a building just south of the compound's west wall. As many as 22 North Vietnamese were killed or wounded south of the compound. By the time Simons landed, there was little resistance left, but his men stirred up a hornet's nest when they cleared the headquarters or command building outside the front gate and a large guard barracks south of it. They accounted for another ten dead North Vietnamese.

Most of the North Vietnamese guards at Son Tay Prison, about 55 of them, were dead or wounded before their eyes could focus on the crazy Americans who were shooting up an empty prison. For by now, Meadows's men were reporting "Negative items" (no prisoners) as they broke into one cell after another. Ten minutes into the raid, Meadows radioed over the command net: "Wildroot, this is Blueboy: Negative items at this time." He ran into the cellblocks to check for himself. One minute later he radioed again: "Search complete: Negative items." Son Tay Prison was a dry hole.

Sydnor reacted instantly: "Prepare to withdraw as normal to LZ [the landing zone] for extraction. Blueboy and Redwine exit on first extraction helicopter. Set up LZ security: Redwine to west, Greenleaf to east."

Sydnor sent one of his photographers racing through the breached walls to photograph the empty cells. Then he called for an A-1 to strafe the bridge to the north. Fourteen minutes into the raid, he ordered one of the HH-53s to take off from the holding area and land back at Son Tay. He told Nickerson to fire off a flare as a directional aid. Eighteen minutes and 50 seconds into the raid, Warner Britton's HH-53 was back at Son Tay, in the rice paddies 150 feet southeast of the compound. Sydnor told Meadows to get his 13 men aboard, plus the three Air Force crewmen—Kalen, Zehnder, and Wright—

from Banana One. Sydnor directed his men to board as well, with the exception of a security group, his pathfinders and his "Marshaling Area Control Officer" (MACO).

The MACO's job was to count every man boarding the departing helicopters; Simons was going to leave Son Tay with exactly as many men as had flown in there with him. The MACO reported, "Count 26: count correct." Sydnor signaled the helicopter to get the hell out of North Vietnam. Britton lifted Apple One off and headed west.

(Simons had told Sydnor at their first planning meeting that he would not interfere with the ground force commander's conduct of the operation, and he did not—ever.)

Twenty-two minutes into the raid, Sydnor's actions and commands called for the second HH-53 to land. There were now 33 men left at Son Tay: Simons's team, part of Sydnor's and Dick Meadows. Just before Simons's men "readjusted the landing zone security" Redwine had M-79 grenade launchers fire at four small vehicles racing up from the light industrial complex 600 meters southeast of the objective and about to cross the footbridge south of the compound. Dick Meadows initiated the ten-minute delay to explode the demolition charges inside Herb Kalen's badly bent-up, million-dollar HH-3.

During those 22 minutes, most of the 20 aircraft—A-1s, F-4s, and F-105s—flying cover over Son Tay for or in direct support of the Combat Talons, helicopters, and ground troops, had been as busy as Simons's 54 raiders. Only the ten F-4s flying MIG Cap, Falcon One through Five and Eleven through Fifteen, all orbiting high overhead, were not heavily engaged. Confused by the Navy diversion, no MIGs headed for Son Tay and apparently there was nothing for them to intercept.

The two MC-130 Combat Talons, Cherry One and Two, were dropping flares, firefight simulators, and napalm markers in a carefully choreographed but fake air-ground war. Cherry One preceded Cherry Two over the Initial Point by two minutes, flying at 800 feet. It climbed to 1,500 feet over the objective to drop its ordnance. Because each MC-130 would have only one pass over Son Tay and because the desired impact points were so close together and not in a straight line, some of the battle simulators and flares had to be dropped while the planes were in tight turns. This required shallow, precision maneuvers that had been laboriously plotted and replotted so the ordnance could be dropped at precisely timed intervals; airmen in the back who were dropping the Mark 6 log flares by hand had to be extra careful maintaining their balance. Once its ordnance was expended, Cherry One climbed to 3,000 feet and turned west to orbit over Laos, clear and well north of the still eastbound strike force led by Cherry Two.

At the IP, three and a half miles short of Son Tay, Cherry Two also dropped to 1,500 feet (while the A-1Es proceeded four miles to Son Tay), turned, and dropped its first napalm firebomb to establish a reference point for the A-1s providing close air support. (Because of the bombing halt, U.S. planes were still not allowed to "bomb" North Vietnam; instead, the napalm "created huge fireballs," John Gargus would note later. The fireballs may have made an unusually strong impression on him because the napalm was "dropped in an ammunition depot area to avoid civilian casualties," Bud Sydnor would recall later.) Cherry Two turned right on a reciprocal heading and dropped its log flares, battle simulators, and second napalm marker. One of Cherry One's napalm bombs landed within a mile of a missile site that was well defended by antiaircraft guns. Although their low altitudes made them unlikely missile targets, the C-130s were subjected to considerable antiaircraft and small-arms fire. Cherry Two then flew a preplanned orbit within sight of Son Tay to monitor all radio transmissions of the ground force. It was also on standby to use its nose-mounted, yoke-shaped Fulton recovery system to pluck a man from the ground (in a reverse form of bungeejumping) in case someone got shot down and required rescue that could not be provided by helicopters in the area. As John Gargus would note later, the aircrews were mindful that the primary mission of the HH-53s "was to bring home the prisoners. Helicopters with freed POWs would not be diverted to a rescue effort that would jeopardize their expeditious extraction from Vietnam."

The Peach crews had equally busy times. From Peach One, Major John Waresh would later recall proudly that the A-1s had crossed the IP only two seconds off schedule, a tribute to their C-130 guide dog, Cherry Two, as well as to their own airmanship, flying S-turns for almost three and a half hours all 337.7 miles to Son Tay while staying within a six-mile-wide corridor, just to maintain speed with the Combat Talon. Peach Five peeled off to the right to orbit around a hill south of the objective until called in. The hill turned out to be an artillery practice range; in short order the plane found itself being shot at and decided to stand by elsewhere. Peach Three and Four peeled off to the left to hold just short of the camp until called in. The plan was to call in the backup planes when the two that were on target had expended half their ordnance. That way, if an aircraft were to be shot down, there would always be someone in the air with ordnance left. Then Two dropped behind Peach One so the two aircraft could set up a Daisy Chain around the prison, "a precision ballet," according to Waresh, who noted that "a computer simulation could not have timed it better."

Soon after Bull Simons called Apple One to extract him from the firefight at the Secondary School, Waresh launched a pre-planned air strike on a footbridge to "the Citadel," their code name for a group of buildings surrounded by a small moat that lay a few hundred meters southeast of the camp. Intelligence analysts had deemed it a military cadet training facility and Simons didn't want anyone from it getting within rifle range of the prison. Major James R. Gochnauer, flying in Peach Two, hit it with white phosphorous bombs, which also set afire "a few blocks of buildings between the camp and the Citadel. WP does a real number on wooden structures," Waresh would relate later. Events got "all jumbled up" about the time Simons's and Turner's troops were landed back at Son Tay, Waresh would recall:

> I had no idea what happened first, second and so forth . . . The first SAM took off. You cannot miss a SAM launch at night. It's like a mini-Shuttle launch, lights up an area for miles in all directions. The first few were called, "SAM, SAM! DIVE, DIVE!" but that soon became silly. There were so many launches you couldn't call them. There seemed to be about four launch sites within a few miles of the camp west of Hanoi. The rest were farther east and we didn't think they were a threat to us. Most of the SAMs went high, after the MIG Cap, Weasels, and the Navy's two-hundred-plane feint coming in from the East.

Waresh heard the North Vietnamese air defense commander order his antiaircraft and missile crews to "Fire at will," shut down his net, and go off the air. They decided to quit flying at 3,000 feet when they saw the SAMs coming their way and hit the deck. A SAM fired from the site closest to them, trying to bag one of their planes to the west, rose, leveled off, and stopped moving on their windscreen. "You know what that means: collision course." They dove toward the Red River as Waresh turned around and "kept an eye on the damned thing as it charged at us over my right shoulder." He kept moving the stick forward—"Lower, lower!"—while Major Jerry Rhein, his pilot, "kept bumping the stick back saying, 'We're going to hit the water.' " When the rocket plume seemed about as big as his A-1, Waresh called "Break left!" They cleared the riverbank by 50 feet and headed straight south at the height of a phone pole. They never saw the missile again. But "For about a thirty-minute period, there were no less than three SAMs airborne at any one time and other times so many you couldn't count them."

From the ground, SFC Jake Jakovenko, who had landed at the Secondary School with Simons, saw the North Vietnamese launch nine SAMs. He would recall turning to Staff Sergeant Robert L. Nelson and joking, "Damn, I think they know we're here. I didn't know what a SAM was. All I can say is they looked like fireballs launched from a Roman ballista."

As he was ready to extract the ground force, Sydnor radioed the code words "Free Swing," thus signaling pilots could take whatever actions they deemed necessary. That let the A-1s take out the "big bridge" north of Son Tay, but they had no hard ordnance for the job, just white phosphorous. Down to half their ordnance, Peach Three and Four switched roles with Peach One and Two, which dumped CBU-24 Rockeye cluster bombs, "not very good for bridges"; but their small, shaped-charge bomblets presumably "put a lot of holes in it." Then they strafed it.

Jakovenko was about 75 yards from the bridge at the time and would later relate, "I saw this A-1E go north on the road about ten feet above the ground. I thought, 'Now that is one brave pilot.' "

The bridge was to have been one of Redwine's objectives, blowing it with satchel charges, but they never made it there because of their late start and the Kabuki dance that unfolded when Simons called for a change from Plan Red to Plan Green and then back to Red while his men and Sydnor's—or, more precisely, Walther's and Turner's—were scurrying to avoid each other's line of fire. "The radios went bananas again," Waresh would relate later: "There's part of Redwine's team in Greenleaf's area of responsibility and part of Greenleaf's team in Redwine's area." Men were yelling over and over again, "Do not fire without identification."

By then, Waresh would remember vividly, ". . . we started picking up MIG calls," even though the strike force had been told North Vietnam had no night-qualified MIG pilots, so they "would have no trouble with MIGs. Right! There was one call of an air-to-air missile firing. [Someone] said it zoomed right past his plane. . . . But the MIG-warning calls from College Eye or whoever makes those things were coming regularly."

The five F-105 Wild Weasels, Firebird One through Five, had arrived in the Hanoi area shortly before the strike force got to Son Tay, ready to suppress air defenses that threatened the lower and slower-flying helicopters and C-130s, which would have been sitting ducks. The two pilots in each aircraft knew they were bait, there to divert attention from the strike force and put enemy radar sites off the air while the ground force was assaulting the prison. Their mission was an aerial form of Russian roulette, diverting SA-2 missiles away from the assault force and the F-4s flying combat air patrol against MIGs, dodging the missiles as they streaked skyward for a kill, locking on to jam their Fan Song radars, and diving to fire Shrike radar-homing missiles even as more SAMs were launched toward them. They used a standard tactic: four aircraft flew in two opposing orbits at about 13,000 feet, well within the SA-2's lethal range, while the fifth plane was pointing toward and attacking a known threat at all times.

(Because of the bombing halt, none of the Wild Weasel crews had even seen an SA-2 before, and only two of the crews had ever been fired upon. One of their planes had been hit by a SAM and shot down the previous March. All ten men flying that night had volunteered for the mission. They had been told of it only two days beforehand, but only that it was a "special mission." Even as they had taken off from Korat, they did not know the purpose of the mission, just that they would be supporting American soldiers and airmen on a dangerous mission near Hanoi.)

Only minutes after Marty Donohue flew over Son Tay prison, the first SAMs went off, right after the F-105s arrived. They came very close to Firebird Three, flown by Major William J. Starkey with Major Everett D. Fansler as his electronic warfare officer in the backseat. When the missiles were about a mile away, Starkey rolled over and dived to 5,000 feet. As the two missiles arched down to follow his aircraft, Starkey forced the plane into a hard pull-up. The first SAM passed over him and detonated behind the plane. The second passed under him and exploded below and slightly behind his left wing. A lot of shrapnel hit the plane, and for twelve to fifteen seconds it looked like Starkey's wing was on fire. Major Donald W. Kilgus and Captain Clarence T. Lowry were flying Firebird Five in orbit west of the target area, and to them it looked like the plane had blown up. They were watching closely because their job was "to replace the first airplane we lost." Starkey called a Mayday, but the fire quickly went out and he said he was okay.

Almost immediately, Lowry and Kilgus locked onto a SAM site directly ahead and attacked it with a Shrike missile—about the same time it fired at them. Kilgus made the SAM miss, as well as one fired right after it, and then he evaded a third one. As Lowry would recall later, "The sky was alive with missiles." The plume or fireball of a fourth missile headed toward them. They thought they had evaded it when its 450-pound warhead exploded close to their plane, filling it with holes and badly damaging the stability augmentation system. In an F-105, that was bad news. Kilgus could not get the system to reengage, but he didn't bother telling other members of the flight that they'd been hit. Lowry "indicated my desire that we leave the area," he would joke later. Kilgus told him their airplane was still flying and "we still have guys on the ground down there, so we're staying." Shortly after being hit, they engaged another SAM site and fired their last Shrike missile at it.

By now, surface-to-air missiles were exploding all around them after their boosters burned out and the missiles impacted the ground. In all, 16 of the 18 missiles fired near Son Tay were directed at the F-105s. As the "flying telephone poles" streaked through the skies of North Vietnam, someone joked that Simons's men would be the first Americans to describe what a fiery Russian SA-2 looked like from the ground.

Twenty-seven minutes into the raid, the last 30 raiders and

Simons, Sydnor, and Meadows were aboard the second HH-53. Simons told the pilot of Apple Two, John Allison, "Count 33, count correct," and the plane lifted off. As it streaked for the Laotian border, zigzagging to avoid potential ground fire or missiles, Simons learned with relief that only one man had been wounded, a sergeant with a flesh wound in the inner thigh.

Apple Two was six minutes out of Son Tay when there was a huge explosion in the target area. Through the open ramps of their departing helicopter, Sydnor and his men could see that the HH-3 demolitions had worked as scheduled, detonating after the ten-minute delay that Meadows had set.

The A-1 crews had headed west as soon as the HH-53s bugged out for their flights home, but heard "the MIG calls . . . [still] coming every few minutes." John Waresh was sweating profusely: "The A-1s were spread out, who knew where, but still in radio contact." Waresh listened to the HH-53s relaying Army head counts back and forth of how many people they had aboard and would recall, ". . . there was some confusion." He would recall that, "The high-orbiting EC-135 must have been relaying all that back to Udorn, and it was interpreted by the Intel people as a prisoner count. They all thought we had rescued some thirty prisoners."

By then, Kilgus's and Lowry's F-105 had been leaking fuel for some minutes faster than it was burning it. One of the A-1 crews saw its afterburner igniting the fuel in dashes across the sky as Kilgus and Lowry headed west for Laos, hoping to coax the aircraft back to Udorn. Kilgus called out "Mayday!" but the plane flamed out at 32,000 feet over high mountains about 100 miles short of their destination, only three minutes and eight miles away from a KC-135 tanker, dead ahead at 24,000 feet, that had started racing north to rendezvous with them. Kilgus radioed that even if they could reach the tanker, he doubted he had enough hydraulic power left to open the refueling bay door. Lowry would write of him later, "He was probably calmer at that moment than most people are in their daily lives." They glided another 20 miles until they reached about 12,000 feet and ejected 4,000 feet above the terrain.

Simons's assault teams and Britton's pilots had performed flawlessly. The landing had been fast and violent. Surprise was total. The search had been swift, fire precise, reactions unflappable, the withdrawal smooth. It was "beautiful."

There was only one thing wrong. Not a single prisoner was with them as they headed back to marry up with refueling tankers over Laos.

The flight back to Thailand was quiet but not uneventful. Simons's men were "very let down, very quiet." They knew they had done their job, and done it well—but it was not the job they had wanted to do. Forty-five minutes out of Son Tay, when he was supposed to report on the condition of the rescued prisoners, Simons pulled out a codebook and composed a message for Manor. He looked up the word for "prisoners," put the word "Negative" in front of it. He looked up the word "moved," put "Previously" in front of it. Then he asked Allison to relay the message to Monkey Mountain.

It was now 3:35 A.M. at Manor's command post near Da Nang, 1 hour and 17 minutes since Meadows had landed in Son Tay. Manor received Simons's message. There were no prisoners at Son Tay. They had been previously moved. Simons thought Manor already knew that by monitoring Meadows's transmissions while the assault force was still on the ground. But the "dry hole" was news to Manor. He read the message again: "Negative prisoners. Previously moved." He asked for the message to be repeated, but got back only a "garbled" transmission. Within seconds, he sent a flash message that would reach the Pentagon Command Center ten minutes later: "Possibly negative POWs. Leaving TACC-NS for Udorn." It meant that he was taking off from Da Nang to be on hand personally to clarify the situation when Simons landed at Udorn.

Because technology had failed him again, Manor had been able to pick up only a hazy picture of what had happened at Son Tay. Two EC-121 "College Eye" airborne radar platforms had taken off from Korat Royal Thai Air Force Base in Thailand as scheduled to orbit over the Tonkin Gulf and let Manor monitor, as it happened, every radio transmission of the Son Tay raid. But one of the planes had broken an oil line, lost an engine, and had to abort, landing at Da Nang. The backup plane reached its orbit point over the Gulf of Tonkin, but then "experienced IFF/SIF equipment failure and was unable to receive IFF/SIF returns at extended ranges." This meant that it could no longer maintain voice contact with some of the friendly planes over Son Tay. A spare unit was installed—"with negative results." Moreover, there was so much interference on the key frequencies that Manor, sitting in front of three of the six huge display consoles in Monkey Mountain's electronic brain, had at best a confused idea of events at Son Tay. Beyond 30 or 40 miles range, the signals weren't reliable. He said later, "There is no adequate explanation for the interference or lack of IFF/SIF returns," but then added, "It must be noted, however, that the Navy was jamming NVN radars at this time."

To add to the confusion, a "computer-buffer" operated by the Marine Corps to link the Air Force and Navy's "automated systems" had also failed. This deprived Manor of the display he was supposed to have before him of what the Navy planes were doing. A backup, automated teletype was finally hooked up, but it gave him the information only "after the fact."

All of this, however, should not have prevented Manor from monitoring the raid's key radio traffic "in real time." Something else did. Before leaving the States, he had arranged with SAC to have an RC-135 "Combat Apple" radio relay aircraft orbit over the Tonkin Gulf. It normally operated with four UHF channels; but to monitor "all of the discrete frequencies" that would be used by the assault force, Manor asked SAC to have four additional channels installed. The necessary equipment, he was told, was already in Southeast Asia. But after he arrived there, "the in-country personnel had no knowledge of their location." As a result of these unexpected "cavities," Combat Apple could relay ground force transmissions to Manor only when simultaneous FM and UHF contact was possible. He had not heard Meadows's FM radio message to Simons, "Count complete. Negative items."

The communications plan for Kingpin was perhaps more complex and sophisticated than for any other operation in the Vietnam War. It had failed Manor at the crucial moment. The commander of the raid on Son Tay had been without his "eyes and ears." It was a situation that could have resulted in serious trouble. What if some last-minute event had necessitated canceling the raid? Could Manor have recalled the assault force after the raid had been launched, as the President had been assured? It probably would have been possible through the many permutations and combinations of radios and frequencies that were available. But Manor would have had to act swiftly, "jury-rigging" the same kind of communications patch that it had taken to get the weather information he needed. But what if something had gone wrong at Son Tay? When would Manor have learned of it? And in a crisis, when every second counted, what action could he have taken?

About ten minutes out of Son Tay, Simons was a very troubled man. He couldn't believe it: there were only 25 men, not 26, aboard the first helicopter. "Oh, my God," he thought, "we blew it!" They'd left someone behind. Simons requested a recount. Without the aid of cabin lights, several counts and recounts were taken aboard two "very, very crowded aircraft." The Marshaling Area Control Officer, Captain James W. Mc-Clam, had not made a miscount during one of the more than 170 rehearsals the ground force had made at Eglin Air Force Base; but Simons had decided to withdraw his men on two instead of three HH-53s, as had long been planned, and that confused the issue of an accurate count. (Donohue's helicopter, empty except for its crew, was to stand by to pick up raiders if Apple One and Two didn't have room for them because they might be full of POWs. If there were no POWs, he was to wait until Apple One and Two confirmed the count was correct. If any men were missing he was to return to Son Tay.) It took repeated efforts to finally confirm that the second helicopter had the raider who was missing from the first aircraft. Throughout these otherwise tense moments, Simons never interjected or commented, but simply let Sydnor and his men do and redo their laborious head counts. Sydnor would later comment of that, "What a great boss!" What seemed like an eternity passed before Simons was reassured that all 59 men of his assault force were airborne on their way back to Thailand. There were only 25 men aboard the first helicopter, but there were 34, not 33, in his.

As the first extraction helicopter had been about to take off, one of Sydnor's men—who should have boarded it, and did—noticed there were "hot wires" on the ground from a power-transmission tower he had blown. He knew another chopper would land there soon and jumped back out the rear ramp to cut the wires. Then he had scampered aboard the second aircraft, before the marshaling officer could begin his count for the final extraction.

On the long ride back to Udorn, Bull Simons wondered, half chuckling to himself, what the North Vietnamese would make of it all. Someone—they could not be sure who, because there wouldn't be any bodies to examine or prisoners to interrogate—had assaulted an empty compound 23 miles from Hanoi; blown up a remote command center nearby and killed a "shit pot full" of Chinese or Russians; apparently landed a few miles to the south and east and had "one helluva firefight, without even engaging North Vietnamese troops; and had 'raided' Haiphong, would you believe it, with a flock of *flares*." It was "good stuff," he thought, "going in and twisting the tails of those sonsovbitches 20 miles from Hanoi."

And they were all on the way back home, so far as Simons knew, without losing one man or one plane. He was unaware that Marty Donohue was still on the ground in Apple Three, waiting about 15 minutes for confirmation that the count was correct and that another plane which had taken part in the raid had been shot down.

East of Finger Lake, on the ground in the holding area a few miles west of Son Tay, Marty Donohue and Tom Waldron couldn't believe what they had been hearing on the radio. First it sounded like Simons's chopper had been shot down; why else had Sydnor called for Plan Green? Soon they saw missiles going off all around them. They counted 18 of them, four close enough to be of concern. "They lit up the sky," Donohue later said, "just like a launch at Cape Kennedy."

Then Donohue and Waldron heard Meadows report, "Negative items at this time," followed only a minute later by: "Search complete: Negative items." Their reaction was one of "complete disbelief. Everything had gone so well," Donohue later remarked. "There was less confusion than any mission I had been on. But I just couldn't believe it. It didn't really come through. We just sat there." He turned to Waldron: "Did you hear that?" "I heard it," Waldron replied, "but I don't believe it. Let's wait." They agreed: "Let's make sure. It *can't* be right."

They were on the ground in a rice paddy surrounded on three sides by a crook in the winding Song Con River where it was about 20 feet wide. A minigun on the rear ramp covered the ground behind them. They sat there waiting. In the dark of night, they could see people, 20, maybe 30 of them, in fields across the water. They were obviously looking for something— the noisy helicopters that had landed nearby. Donohue and the four other men in Apple Three couldn't tell if they were soldiers or civilians. They were less than 50 yards away.

Donohue waited there for clearance to depart. He heard Simons's code-word messages calling in Apple One and Apple Two to extract the ground force. Then he heard "more traffic" and saw Apple Four and Five lift off and head west. That left him, Apple Three. More SAMs were going off; "it was pretty busy." Still he waited.

Donohue was listening on his UHF channel for the code word telling him to "bug out" when he overheard Allison relay Simons's report on the long-range HF net to Manor: "Negative items." But there was a "lot of interference." The HF signal was "bouncing" and not that clear; nor could Donohue hear the acknowledgment from Manor. Several transmissions followed, however, reconfirming the bad news. There were no prisoners.

Soon it got very quiet. Donohue's helicopter was to be the "clean-up ship," the last one out. The "SAMs were all over [finished firing] by then," Donohue remembered. He and Waldron had been on the ground longer than they had expected, but still there was no signal releasing them. They didn't want to spend the winter in North Vietnam. "Somebody," they joked apprehensively, "may have forgotten us for a while." Had someone forgotten to send the final bug-out message to the last five men who would leave North Vietnam that night? Or was something else wrong?

Suddenly the radios came alive again. Donohue listened with mounting concern as Apple One and Two discovered their "head counts" were wrong, wondering if a man had been left behind at Son Tay. To keep North Vietnamese signal intercept centers from sending out word that an immediate, thorough search at Son Tay might produce a new prisoner for the empty cells there, the two helicopters were communicating on their FM net, whose range was limited to about 15 miles.

But this meant that as the helicopters continued their flights toward Laos, the signals Donohue was trying to monitor were getting weaker and weaker. He and Waldron strained to hear what was going on as Apple One and Two passed their count back and forth two or three times, but the outcome wasn't clear to either of them. Donohue radioed on his longer range UHF set, asking if they had "figured it out."

He was about to ask them to let him fly back to Son Tay and

try to "police up the stray" when he heard another FM transmission. It sounded like Apple One was telling Apple Two, "Count Correct." The signal was much too faint for him to be sure, however. Almost in desperation, Donohue radioed one of the A-1 pilots "in the clear": "Did I 'read' that right, 'Count Correct'?" The "Sandy driver" confirmed the good news. He told Donohue he was "clear"; there was nothing left to clean up. Apple Three was finally released. Donohue should "get the hell out of there." Even at full throttle, it took him almost half an hour to catch up with the other helicopters.

Donohue would swear that, in their frustration, none of his men goosed a baby water buffalo up the rear ramp of his helicopter and flew a "prisoner" out of North Vietnam. A few days later, Henry Kissinger was convinced that *someone* had.

The National Military Command Center

In the Pentagon, Ed Mayer barely had everything ready when the Joint Chiefs of Staff began assembling just after noon on November 20, Washington time, in the National Military Command Center. By then, Simons's assault force had taken off from Udorn and was headed north over Laos. The complex routes, intricate time schedules, and target area tactics were mapped out on four huge, backlit, Plexiglas display panels hanging overhead.

As progress reports came in from General Manor at Monkey Mountain, they were posted for all to see. The raid seemed to be unfolding on schedule:

12:04 P.M.	"HC-130s and A-1Es off on time."
12:43 P.M.	"Situation satisfactory."
1:23 P.M.	"Navy diversion launched."
1:27 P.M.	"Refueling complete."
1:40 P.M.	"Task group crossed NVN border."

Tension began to build. Then Blackburn and Mayer realized that General William C. Westmoreland had shown up. He had been the Army's Chief of Staff for more than two years, but had left the operational side of the Army up to his Vice Chief, General Bruce Palmer. To the best of most people's recollection, this was Westy's first presence at a working meeting of the Joint Chiefs. He had been very busy—traveling around the nation and the world, trying to rebuild his image and bolster the Army's. And it was the first time the Joint Chiefs had ever used the command center to monitor, or "command," a real operation.

Blackburn and Mayer had drawn up a precise roster, approved by Vogt, of those who were authorized entry to the command center to watch the raid's progress. Aside from SACSA personnel, the command center duty officers on watch at the time, the Joint Chiefs and their deputies for operations, there were only 19 other names on the list. Mayer was "stunned," therefore, when Defense Secretary Laird walked into the room around 1:30 P.M., followed by an entourage of about 15 people, mostly civilians. Laird's military assistant, Pursley, shrugged his shoulders, raised his eyebrows discreetly, and thus "told" Mayer to let everyone in.

Laird's entourage and most of the others present sat in a low balcony at the back of the command center, the Service Deputy Chiefs of Staff for Operations in the front row with elaborate communications consoles before them. Laird, Moorer, and Vogt sat with Mayer in a soundproofed, glass-enclosed room to their right—the "National Command Authority" room. The Joint Chiefs sat at a conference table below the balcony, looking up at the display consoles. With them was General Bennett of the DIA, the man who—unbeknownst to all but a few of those present—had "blown the whistle" about 20 hours earlier, signaling that Son Tay might be empty. But instead of his usual seat on the far left of the Joint Chiefs, Bennett was sitting at the end of the table, facing them and in front of a podium from which Blackburn and Spots Harris would "brief" those present on the raid's progress.

"Sitting there, doing what?" Bennett was asked later.

"Sitting there, dying!" he answered.

Suddenly the reports began to accelerate. At 2:29, Manor signaled, "MIG threat"; one minute later, "Landed in objective area safely." Blackburn checked the Kingpin timetable on the huge screen above them. The assault was 11 minutes behind schedule, but there was no explanation. He did not know that the raiders were "right on the button" but that Manor's communications system was way off its mark. Another three minutes passed, then "MIG threat all clear"; three more minutes, "Situation satisfactory."

There were no more reports for a quarter of an hour, then: "All aircraft departed objective area."

Periodically, Vogt would call the White House situation room, or Al Haig, with a crisp progress report on the raid. Everyone was waiting to hear one thing: had Simons rescued any POWs? There was no word about the prisoners at Son Tay.

Twenty-five minutes later, at 3:15 P.M., there was another signal from Manor: "Task Group crossed Laos border." Still no word on the prisoners, or about casualties among Simons's force. Forty-six minutes had passed since the planes had landed "safely."

Twelve more minutes passed before the next message: "SAR effort required. F-105 down."

Vogt almost leapt out of his chair: "F-105! What the hell's an F-105 doing up there?" He turned to Mayer. "Where did *it* come from? What's going on?"

Mayer didn't have the foggiest notion, nor did Blackburn. Nowhere in planning or training for the Son Tay mission had the use of F-105s been mentioned. Every aircraft employed in the raid was spelled out in the black, three-ring binder Kingpin briefing book, before the senior officers in the room. No one could find any F-105s listed.

Everyone had different thoughts. It was the only "glitch" so far, at least as far as anyone in the command center could tell. But it *could* be a big one. Blackburn wondered if "some crazy, frustrated bastard" had taken off from Thailand to renew the air war or challenge the North Vietnamese air force all by himself. Or was it part of that "other operation" he had heard of, but wasn't cleared to know about? If so, why was Manor sending the message?

The F-105s were Manor's idea. At the last minute, in Thailand, he had decided to have the raiding force escorted by a flight of five F-105 "Wild Weasel" aircraft from the 388th Tactical Fighter Squadron at Korat. They would work as "decoys" to jam North Vietnam's "Fan Song" radars, direct SA-2 missiles away from the assault force, knock out the "hot" SAM batteries with Shrike radar-homing missiles, and help protect the ten F-4s flying combat air patrol against MIGs.

They were, to put it bluntly, "bait."

In the crush of all the problems they had to wrestle with between November 17 and 20, Manor and his staff simply forgot to tell Washington that the F-105s had been added to the Son Tay strike force.

About this time, Marty Donohue finally took off in Apple Three from his holding position near the Son Tay compound. Apple Five, piloted by Major Kenneth Murphy, had just intercepted him, to escort Donohue home, when the radio crackled that an F-105 was down. Donohue picked up "trail" on John Allison in Apple Two, while Murphy in Apple Five and Lieutenant Colonel Royal C. Brown in Apple Four stood by in the area to refuel and rescue the downed pilots. Soon a C-123 dropped flares where the survivors were thought to be. Murphy located both men, but started taking ground fire. Another refueling followed, and then several A-1 strike planes arrived to protect the helicopters. Everyone decided to wait for "first light" to make the "pickup." Finally, Brown swooped down and rescued Kilgus, while Murphy went in half a mile away and hoisted his back-seater, Lowry, out of the jungle.

By then, Murphy and Brown had been flying their HH-53s for more than nine hours, almost all of it over hostile terrain and at night. But they brought the last two Son Tay raiders home alive.

As Simons's helicopters flew the last leg of their lonely, long flight back to Udorn, Manor's cryptic message "Possibly negative PWs" arrived at the Pentagon Command Center. It was 3:35, Friday afternoon, November 21.

The message was in code, of course. When it was deciphered, an Army brigadier general who was the senior command center "watch officer" that afternoon grabbed it and rushed to the Command Authority room. He was supposed to hand all incoming messages to Mayer or Vogt and a copy to Blackburn. Instead, he strode through the door waving the message and announced over and over, idiotically, "There are no prisoners in Son Tay! There are no prisoners in Son Tay!"

That was not the news the men in the command center had been waiting for; their reactions were a combination of disbelief, disappointment, anger.

Vogt called Haig: "Looks like a bust, Al. No prisoners. Manor said 'Possibly,' but we'd better expect the worst." Within minutes, the President was on the phone to Laird and Moorer. He asked them to convey his personal thanks to everyone concerned for a "courageous" effort.

Laird got up and left without much comment, not abruptly, not in disgust or anger, but obviously disappointed. "Well," he said, "these things happen. At least we tried." Moorer left the room with him. With Laird gone, the room "erupted," as Mayer would describe it, in a cross fire of recriminations. The comments, Mayer recalled, were "*very* critical."

Westmoreland was livid; "*Another* intelligence failure," he said, shaking his head. Others among the Joint Chiefs made critical and sometimes bitter comments. John Vogt finally interrupted to say very quietly, "Gentlemen, before we come to any conclusions, we're going to go back and examine what *did* go wrong."

As the meeting broke up, the JCS J-3, Lieutenant General Melvin R. Zais, injected a note of humor: "Well, I guess we'll have to fire Blackburn." He was trying to make light of things, but no one thought it was very funny.

That Friday afternoon and evening, a lot of men spent some very rough hours. At Fort Belvoir, Claude Watkins was told of Manor's 3:35 message, "Possibly negative PWs," and went to the latrine and puked. After he and others from the 1127th Field Activities Group were pulled off the planning group, he never knew when, or even if, the raid would be launched. "It went so fucking long I decided they weren't going to have it. But I woke up every morning," he would recall, "wondering if it had taken place." Six and a half months after he had prepared briefing charts for an "urgent rescue," the Pentagon had drilled a dry well.

Don Bennett drove to his quarters at Fort Myer, Virginia, went to his study, and just buried his head in his hands. His wife, Bets, a sensitive, supportive woman, knew it was no time to ask why. Ed Mayer cried in front of his wife, Claire, for the first time in his Army career. Don Blackburn drove home to

McLean, Virginia, and in typical humor told his wife, "Well, Ann, I really blew it." She understood. For months, she had listened to his nightmares about a "dry hole," but never told him.

It was 4:28 in the morning by the time Bull Simons and his force landed at Udorn Royal Thai Air Force Base. Manor was there, waiting. Simons strode out of the helicopter, shrugged his shoulders, and told him, "No prisoners."

Manor couldn't believe it. "For *real?*" He had received Simons's message, but the transmission had been garbled.

"Yeah, it's real; you're damned right," replied Simons, then raised his eyebrows and pursed his lips as if to add, "So what else is there to say?"

He told Manor that Meadows and his men were sure the camp had been empty for a long time; one of the cells had a bunch of cement bags in it. There weren't even leg irons or shackles left in the others.

While Simons watched his men debark from the second helicopter and assured himself that everyone was accounted for, Manor headed for the operations center to call the Pentagon Command Center. When Simons entered a few minutes later, Manor and Laird were talking on the phone. It was a nonsecure voice line, so Manor's report was very brief. He would cable a coded, more complete report in a few hours. Manor asked Simons if he wanted to speak with Laird. Simons told him, "What the hell for? I don't have anything to say to him."

Simons's men and the aircrews were bushed, but it would be a long time before they could get some sleep. They sat down on the cement ramp, joined by some of the A-1 crews sitting cross-legged, Indian style, in circles of about ten, "Us in our reeking, sweat-soaked flight suits and the grunts with their blackened faces, guns, grenades, and what-have-you hanging off them," as Waresh would describe the scene years later. "They were bleeding from every square inch of exposed skin from dozens of cuts, scrapes, and bruises. We all just sat mumbling at each other. No stories were being told. . . . Then someone came out and handed a bottle to each one of the circles. Everyone took a sip and passed it around and around and around, 'til it was empty. All of us still just mumbling to ourselves. I can't attest to what was going on at the other circles, but there wasn't a dry eye at ours. A tear running down every cheek. A gallant effort with nothing to show. To hell and back for naught."

After their rescue from Laos, Firebird Three's Kilgus and Lowry were taken to the hospital at Udorn, where no one yet knew that a POW rescue mission had been launched from their base the day before. The two airmen would find out only from a *Stars & Stripes* article the next day that they had been shot down in the Son Tay rescue attempt.

North Vietnamese newspapers would soon report that American planes had "bombed" a prisoner-of-war camp. Manor would note later, "That was not correct. We did not bomb a POW camp; we leveled one." Intelligence teams were standing by for debriefings that would last for hours. Marty Donohue was one of the luckier ones; he was debriefed by a very pretty girl.

Before they could turn in for some rest, the senior officers had to write out a detailed "Summary of Operations." It was put on the teletype at 9:15 that morning, directed to Moorer.

It got lost.

As the report was being completed, Manor and Simons got word that they were to fly back to Washington immediately. Simons asked Sydnor to assemble the men. He wanted them to know how he felt, and he felt "very strongly." He told them, "I know you are disappointed. We had the place right by the ass. But you have nothing to feel bad about, nothing to be ashamed of. You did your job and you did it as well as any combat commander could ask of you. We don't have a thing to be ashamed of. The operation, as far as what *you* did, was successful. You could not have done it better."

Simons would not recall their reactions. "Hell, I wasn't looking for any reaction. It was just something I wanted to say. I didn't give a God damn what their reaction was."

Manor and Simons climbed aboard a small courier plane, flew to Saigon, and there boarded another plane for the flight home. It was their fourth trip across the Pacific in three weeks. Admiral McCain met them in Hawaii and took them aboard one of CINCPAC's flying command posts, a modified KC-135 tanker called "Looking Glass." Simons would remember the plane vividly: "Jesus, it was unrecognizable. It was crammed solid with radios and electronic equipment, the whole damn thing. I mean from asshole to appetite. *Solid!* An electronic *jungle.*" McCain took them to the rear of the plane; he showed them a small compartment where they could sleep, "which," Simons said, "I promptly did."

Sydnor and the rest of the ground force, meanwhile, had been flown from Udorn back to their staging base at Takhli, packed up for the long flight to the U.S., and were airborne by six o'clock that evening, roughly fifteen hours after the raid was over. Sydnor would later describe the trip: "It was probably the quietest group of NCOs and officers I had ever been around. Why? Maybe exhaustion, disappointment, adrenaline depletion, or all of the above."

Manor and Simons arrived at Andrews Air Force Base at about three o'clock in the morning, Monday, November 23. Blackburn met the plane, said they were to have breakfast with Laird and Moorer, and took them to the Visiting Officers Quarters so they could freshen up and get some more sleep.

Simons told him about landing in the wrong camp. He thought that was "pretty funny. I bet we really shook those bastards up." But everything else had gone like clockwork, he said, "a real smooth operation." Blackburn remarked that the Joint Chiefs were probably more shook up than the North Vietnamese.

That bothered Simons. "What are you telling me, Don, that we got a black eye? *I'm* not mad at anybody. I thought the thing was *great.* Okay, so we didn't get 'em. Christ, the thing was worth doing *without* getting them."

FIVE

Disarray

The Pentagon Press Room

Manor and Simons caught only a few hours' sleep before they were escorted to Laird's office in Room 3E880 of the Pentagon. Moorer was there and greeted them warmly. Laird apologized for having to recall them so quickly; there had been a change in plans, he said. He would explain over breakfast.

Laird led them next door into his private dining room, where Pentagon spokesman Dan Henkin joined them. The five men sat down at a conference table in the middle of a room big enough to comfortably host a cocktail party for 120 people. The room, in fact, was often used for that purpose, after a major award ceremony or whenever a new presidential appointee was sworn in to the Pentagon hierarchy. Out its windows, across the Potomac, the Jefferson Memorial, the Washington Monument, and the White House were in clear view.

Filipino stewards in short, powder blue mess jackets served orange juice and poured coffee as Laird explained what was up. The White House had called him "almost immediately" after being notified that Son Tay was empty, but that everyone had been recovered safely. Laird was ordered to bring back the two commanders "immediately"; the President wanted to decorate them personally. And Laird had been advised that two enlisted men were to be decorated as well. One of them, the White House insisted, had to be black.

Manor and Simons were asked to recommend the two enlisted men—with the proviso laid down by 1600 Pennsylvania Avenue—but their reaction was "not enthusiastic." Everyone who had crash-landed inside Son Tay Prison, they felt strongly, should be treated equally. Laird and Moorer acknowledged their feeling, but explained that it "wouldn't sell." Ed Mayer had already been given instructions to draft the appropriate citations—"fast." Manor and Simons could pick the men, of course, and "fine-tune" the proposed citations. The White House's flair for public relations won out over Manor and Simons's concept of fairness.

The awards ceremony, moreover, would be public. That meant, Laird noted, that the Pentagon would have to reveal a lot more about the Son Tay raid than had ever been intended. Until that call from the White House, the cover plans had one purpose: never to reveal that the operation was unsuccessful, if that's the way it should turn out.

Laird and Henkin wondered now whether that would have been feasible. Given the number of people involved, they asked, could the raid really be kept secret on a long-term basis, or could they keep only a "short lid" on it? Should the Pentagon "break" the story now or try to "hold it," at least until the White House awards ceremony? How much of what really happened would get out anyway? What was the *least* that could be said? What was the most that *should* be said? How should the press be told, although Laird didn't phrase the question quite this way, that the Pentagon had sent 56 men deep into North Vietnam, only to plunk them down in a "dry hole"?

Laird interrupted the discussion to admonish everyone, "This is *not* a failure. This is a *complete success*."

It was an odd meeting, Simons would recall. At the very seat of American military power, "They were mainly concerned about a press release, and we haggled back and forth over eggs and bacon."

Laird finally asked Simons what he felt should be done. By then, Simons had decided to give Laird a recommendation "anyway," whether he asked for one or not. He told Laird to have the press conference "now." The only question, in Simons's view, was a choice of a "fist fight" over "their" story—as the press would write it, if it broke without the Pentagon's initiative—or whether, he told Laird, it would come out as "your story." "This is a perfectly legitimate operation," he said. "These are American prisoners. This is something that Americans traditionally do for Americans. For Christ's sake, what is it we're afraid of here?"

Simons would not recall if anyone else agreed with him, "but Mr. Laird did and he was the only guy I was talking to. I really didn't give a God damn whether anybody else agreed with me or not." Nor would he remember how Laird voiced his opinion, but "Five minutes later we were planning the press briefing."

The raid on Son Tay had been planned and executed in the strictest secrecy. Now, the final act was about to unfold in a glare of publicity and public relations. The five men at Laird's conference table focused all their attention on how to put the raid in the best possible light. There was almost no discussion of what had gone wrong, or right. Asked later if he told Laird that he had landed in the wrong compound, Simons replied: "No, no." It wasn't the kind of conversation, he pointed out, that got into "tactical details." Both Manor and Simons, however, assumed that Laird and Moorer knew of the fortuitous "blunder" that landed the biggest part of the raiding force in a hornet's nest at the "Secondary School." Manor had spelled it all out in the short after-action summary cabled to the Pentagon Command Center just before he and Simons left Udorn. They did not know that the message had gotten lost. It wasn't to reach Washington until almost a week after the raid—and then columnist Jack Anderson would get part of it before Laird saw any of it.

As the public relations conference went into the "fine details" of how the Son Tay press release would be phrased, it became obvious that there was "no way" it could be ready in time for the usual daily press briefing. Henkin ordered the "eleven o'clock follies" postponed until mid-afternoon. No one was to tell the 55 newsmen and radio/TV commentators accredited to the building why.

Laird strode into the Pentagon newsroom at 3:30 P.M. that afternoon, accompanied by Moorer, Manor, and Simons. As he stepped onto a low platform and adjusted the microphones, high-intensity lights came on to illuminate the four men for the TV cameras. There was an air of expectancy among the reporters; they knew a big story was about to unfold. Laird cleared his throat and told the reporters that he wanted to give them details of an "operation that took place north of the 19th parallel this past weekend."

Notebooks snapped open; pencils moved quickly. The reporters were well aware that until the preceding weekend,

North Vietnam had not been bombed for more than two years. But this story would obviously be about something more than a bombing; in the glare of the klieg lights before them was not only an Air Force general, but also a very well decorated soldier who clearly was not from some headquarters staff.

Laird spoke of North Vietnam's "adamant refusal" to exchange prisoners of war or abide by the Geneva Convention. He said that "some months ago" he had prepared a contingency plan to rescue "as many of our prisoners as possible." The pencils and pens were literally flying now across the reporters' notepads. A special Army–Air Force task force had been assembled for a rescue mission, Laird continued; its training had been "meticulous, intensive, often around the clock." A "key factor" in his final decision to launch "this search and rescue mission" was "new information that we received this month that some of our men were dying in the prisoner-of-war camps" of North Vietnam. Flashbulbs began popping.

A raid, Laird announced, had been made on a prisoner-of-war compound "approximately 20 miles west of Hanoi" at about 2:00 A.M., Hanoi time, the previous weekend. TV crews checked to see if their recorders were getting it all down; cameramen and photographers jostled each other to get closer to the podium.

Laird said that the two distinguished officers beside him—Manor and Simons—had led the operation. Brigadier General Leroy J. Manor was in overall command, and Colonel Arthur D. Simons led the team in the search and rescue attempt. Simons and his men, Laird clarified, "landed, entered, and searched the compound." Laird spoke for over three minutes before he admitted: "Regrettably, the rescue team discovered that the camp had recently been vacated. No prisoners were found."

There was a murmur of surprise among the newsmen. Laird went on to give them some of the more general details of the raid, then opened the news conference to questions. The newsmen were ready. But they wanted more information about how the raid was executed—and why it was launched against an empty POW compound—than the Pentagon was willing to give them.

"Was this the first time that American forces had been used in North Vietnam?" Laird: "We have carried on search and rescue missions in North Vietnam quite regularly." "How many men were in the mission?" Simons: "I cannot tell you." Would Simons give them a "narrative dispatch right straight through what happened?" "No, sir, I can't do that." "Did the mission have a code name?" "I can't answer that question." "Did you fly from an aircraft carrier?" "I can't answer that." "What kind of a helicopter was it?" "I can't answer that." "How many men did you hope to free?" "I can't answer the question." "Did you have an alternate target that you might hit?" Manor: "I can't answer that." He wasn't about to reveal that they *had* hit an "alternate target"—by mistake. "Did you take any prisoners?" "I can't answer that." "Did you fire your weapons?" "Yes, we did fire our weapons." "Did you kill anybody?" Simons: "Yes, I would imagine so."

One question caused Simons to gulp noticeably: "Did you land right in the prison?" It was awfully close to: "Did you land in the right prison?" He hesitated, then answered "Yes."

Laird fielded 10 of the reporters' 35 questions himself. The smooth-talking defense chief offered a stark contrast to the gruff, matter-of-fact Simons, who at times could barely get a word in edgewise. Because of "security," Manor and Simons would reply, "I can't answer that," or "I can't comment," or "I cannot tell you," to 40 percent of the questions they "answered."

Manor and Simons were relieved by the interference that Laird was running for them. But some of Laird's answers were later to cause a credibility problem. He told the reporters that "There was no ordnance involved [in the air part of the operation]." Only four days later, President Nixon would tell White House visitors that "an air raid was carried out on a military installation next to Son Tay to keep North Vietnamese troops pinned down before the helicopters landed." Dan Henkin was forced to "clarify" the discrepancy the following day.

Laird was also asked if the raid was the first search and rescue mission that had "ever been run" of "approximately this scope," not involving SAR attempts immediately after a shootdown. Laird wasn't about to open Pandora's box, or dilute the impact of this briefing, by telling the press that there had been more than 60 POW raids in South Vietnam and Cambodia—the net result of which had been to recover exactly one American POW, who died two weeks later of wounds inflicted by his captors as the rescue was under way. So he told the press: "This is the first SAR mission conducted in North Vietnam on prisoners of war during this war."

At 4:12, Laird cut off any further questions with, "Thank you very much, gentlemen." The reporters rushed out of the pressroom to write up a story that was to dominate the news media for weeks. But what did they really know about the raid? They had been given a hard news story full of drama, yet empty of detail. They knew only that a raid had been launched into the heart of North Vietnam to rescue American prisoners of war. The raid was a success in that no American lives were lost. But the Son Tay compound was empty, and had been for "several weeks." To the newsmen the implications were clear; there had been an "intelligence failure." But when asked on whom he blamed the intelligence failure, Simons had replied: "I can't answer the question at all. I am not sure what you mean by 'intelligence failure.' "

The Pentagon had told the story its way, but to the reporters present at the briefing, it was obvious that they had not been told the whole story. The news dominated that evening's newscasts.

Home at Eglin Air Force Base by then, Simons's men had been alerted to watch the Pentagon press conference on TV and to call their families to watch it as well, but to tell them nothing more. Later they were given transcripts of the press conference and told that that "constituted their official debrief. If it was not in the [press conference] notes, we were not to talk about it." Twenty-seven years later, Bud Sydnor would add, "We have not yet been relieved of that situation." He said that five years later, *The Raid* "became an unclassified source for us all" and allowed his men to talk for the first time about their mission into the heart of North Vietnam.

Most of the next day's front-page headlines reflected the only conclusion the reporters had been able to draw from the briefing: Son Tay was a failure. Nixon was once again blamed for undertaking a perilous new policy. The North Vietnamese canceled the upcoming session of the Paris peace talks in protest. On Capitol Hill, the reaction was far from favorable. Senator J. William Fulbright, Chairman of the Senate Foreign Relations Committee, called the raid "a major escalation of the war . . . a very provocative act to mount a physical invasion. . . ." Fulbright's committee agreed unanimously on new hearings on the political implications of the raid.

The "fist fight" that Bull Simons had predicted was going to be a tough one.

The Halls of Congress

Less than 24 hours after Laird's dramatic announcement to the Pentagon press corps, both floors of Congress locked in acrimonious debate over the raid. Senator Henry Jackson said the rescue attempt was "fully warranted." Senator Edward M. Kennedy said of the raiders, "I admire their courage. I just deplore the policy that permitted them to go." Senator Birch Bayh told newsmen he feared such raids might "result in . . . POWs being executed." He called the raid a "John Wayne approach." Senator Robert Dole introduced a resolution praising the men who had risked their lives in the abortive mission. He said the raid was successful in "demonstrating American concern. Some of these men have been languishing in prison for five years." Senator Kennedy snapped back, "And they're still there."

In the House, emotions ran equally strong and were just as divided. Congressman Charles Vanik said it was "incredible that our military intelligence should have risked the lives of brave men in raiding a prison which was unused for weeks. This vain action jeopardizes the life of prisoners of war who still survive in North Vietnam." Minority leader Gerald R. Ford said he hoped America would launch "other operations of a similar nature which will be successful." Representative Robert Leggett said the raid "must have been planned by the Saigon army or perhaps by the script-writer of a grade 'C' war movie." It was, he charged, a "first magnitude blunder" and the only thing "that kept it from being an even greater blunder was the fact that there were no POWs in the camp." The North Vietnamese, he was sure, would have shot them all. Moreover, he predicted, the operation had "radically decreased our chances of negotiating better treatment" for the POWs.

Later that same day, Defense Secretary Laird met with a hostile Senate Foreign Relations Committee. The hearing, open to the public, had been called under the guise of getting Department of Defense testimony on a $255 million supplemental foreign aid request for Cambodia. But by the time it adjourned at 6:25 that evening, not one question had been asked about the Cambodian appropriation.

Laird had notified the committee at noon that he could appear later that day. It was 4:05 P.M. when the hearing opened, a time when congressional offices were usually closing so everyone could get a head start on Washington's rush-hour traffic. Notwithstanding the hour and last-minute scheduling, 10 of the committee's 15 members were present as Laird began his prepared statement. Its chairman, Senator Fulbright, had agreed in advance to let the Secretary of Defense speak "uninterrupted" for 15 minutes.

Laird spoke for only a third of that time. He added few new specifics to what he had already given the press about the Son Tay raid. There wasn't much he *could* add. For one thing, he still hadn't received the after-action operations summary which Manor had cabled from Thailand. "I didn't get that darned thing for *days*," he would note later, "and I was really there 'naked' for a while." But after 22 months as Secretary of Defense, Laird suspected he didn't really have the full story. "I learned one thing," he would explain: "You don't accept the first report, you don't accept the second report, you don't accept the third report; maybe by about the fourth time, you get the straight information." There were, he told the committee, reports from "unofficial sources" that "even more Americans, in addition to the six reported earlier this month, have died in captivity in North Vietnam." On a human interest level, he noted that Colonel Simons was a journalism graduate from the University of Missouri. A former Congressman himself, Laird was skillful in handling the legislative critics. One of the Senate Foreign Relations Committee's most vocal members, Senator Stuart Symington, represented that same state of Missouri.

Laird closed by telling the committee of the Son Tay raid: "I have not faced a more challenging decision since I have been Secretary of Defense." And he added, "It is my firm belief that if there had been prisoners of war at Son Tay they would be free men today." The rest of his remarks expressed his respect for and gratitude to the soldiers and airmen who had "performed heroically."

For the next two and a third hours, Fulbright and the other members of the committee questioned Laird intensively. Joint Staff Director John Vogt, not Moorer, sat beside him, but Laird handled every single question himself. He knew the hearing would be a "no win" proposition and had decided to "take the heat" himself. Vogt never got to say a word.

The issue Fulbright focused on early in the hearing was "not whether this was a brave or a valorous attack, but whether it was a wise attack." He granted that "There is certainly no question . . . about the valor and heroism of the men who conducted it. The men performed perfectly." But when he added that "whoever directed it, did not," laughter broke out. "There was something wrong with the intelligence," Fulbright said bluntly.

"It was not a failure, Mr. Chairman," Laird said.

In that case, Fulbright replied, "There was something wrong with the plan."

"These men knew full well the chance that there might not be POWs present," Laird insisted.

By "these men," Laird must have been referring to the raiders. But Manor and Simons certainly did not know. When Simons was later asked if he had been told before launching for Son Tay that the prisoners had been moved, he said vehemently, "Absolutely not." Asked if he had been told that the prisoners had been moved "but that the camp might have become active again," Simons replied, "I don't remember *any*body ever saying that to me." Asked to what extent, before he launched from Udorn, it was ever suggested to him that the camp "*might* be empty," Simons said categorically, "Nobody *ever* suggested it to me." He would add, however: "I suggested it to myself. I considered that it *was* a possibility." But the first time he *ever* heard that the prisoners might have been moved in July, Simons said, was when he talked with some of the POWs he had tried to rescue after they came home in 1973.

Laird continued trying to deflect Fulbright's concern about an intelligence failure. "I would like to tell you, Mr. Chairman," he said, "we have made tremendous progress as far as intelligence is concerned." The hearing again broke out in laughter. Laird's next statement was interrupted, but he made a telling point, which became probably the most widely quoted single comment on the entire raid: "We have not been able to develop a camera that sees through the roofs of buildings."

Except for that, he said, "The intelligence for their mission was excellent." Laird tried to tell, and show, the hearing how much *was* known about the camp and North Vietnamese air defenses, but Fulbright cut off each of his next four sentences with another question. "I do not think this is relevant," he said finally. "There weren't any prisoners there. What difference does it make?"

The committee then began to zero in on the question that clearly troubled its members: *When* was the mission authorized, and *why* was it authorized if there were no prisoners at Son Tay? Laird was evasive.

He testified that his recommendation to President Nixon to proceed ["execute the mission," he clarified in the next sentence] "was made very early Friday morning." He did not go into detail, or reveal that the RED ROCKET message telling Manor to execute Kingpin was sent precisely at 5:30 P.M. on *Wednesday* afternoon, but that he had consulted with the President again before the actual launch on Friday.

Laird was pressed on his announcement about "even more" POW deaths than the six reported earlier in the month. "When did you receive these reports?" one Senator wanted to know. "Well," Laird hedged, not wanting to be pinned down, "those reports were received earlier this month. But since that time we have had further reports within this past week—these have been confirmed, of course—but these reports had come through channels that have contacts in Hanoi." Asked next if his recommendation to proceed with the raid had followed or preceded "these reports [of the POW deaths]," Laird was very specific: "It followed those reports."

No one asked him how he had learned on Friday, the 20th, of information Cora Weiss had not released to the State Department until Tuesday, November 23. But Laird's testimony would cause near-panic in the intelligence community; although the Gamma intercepts were one of the few sources of "hard intelligence" on the POWs, some of them were highly illegal. Moreover, peace activists like Cora Weiss weren't the only targets of those intercepts. It was a massive operation, and one of the targets was none other than Senator Fulbright himself. Laird had come close to compromising one of the nation's most carefully guarded secrets in a public hearing. Yet not one member of the committee or its staff would catch the significance of his statement, and in the weeks that followed, only one Washington journalist would pursue its implications.

Laird had problems with other questions that afternoon. Again defending the quality of the Pentagon's intelligence, he said to the committee, "Everything was exactly as [the raiders] had been told. . . . Every bit of intelligence proved to be correct." He still had not been told, of course, that the compound the intelligence experts had dubbed a "Secondary School" was, in fact, a military installation bristling with hostile troops.

Senator Frank Church, who five years later would head the Senate's special committee investigating the American intelligence community, asked Laird what could have been the most probing question of the entire hearing: "Was there any evidence that the prisoners had been evacuated just before the mission or within a day or two?"

"No, there was no evidence of that," Laird replied truthfully. There was evidence, of course, that the prisoners had been evacuated *months* before the raid. Had Church's question been rephrased only slightly—"Was there any evidence, just before the mission or within a day or two, that the prisoners had been evacuated?"—Laird would have had to answer "Yes," or to hedge, lest he reveal the Gamma intercepts. But no one asked that question.

Senator Albert Gore asked Laird an intriguing question: "Was the decision on the final execution postponed at any time before that final date?" This time Laird's reply was less than precise: "No. The decision had not been postponed. As a matter of fact, there was no postponement as far as the plan was concerned."

The committee soon turned its attention to another matter. Laird was badgered at length about the "limited duration, protective reaction strikes" flown south of the 19th parallel only hours after the Son Tay raid. Had the Department of Defense resumed large-scale bombing of the north? No, Laird said; the strikes were flown to retaliate for an unarmed RF-4 reconnaissance plane shot down ten days earlier, on November 13. Both crew members were lost. No parachutes were sighted.

The shootdown, Laird contended, violated "an understanding" made with the North Vietnamese when the bombing halt was called in 1968, that U.S. reconnaissance flights could continue to be flown over North Vietnam. A further part of the "understanding" was that the North Vietnamese would no longer shell major population centers in South Vietnam. Yet, he said, North Vietnam had shot down nine other reconnaissance planes or their escorts since the bombing halt, and had indiscriminately shelled Saigon and Hue earlier in the month. The strikes, which involved 225 strike aircraft and lasted over a period of "only seven hours," were flown in retaliation.

Laird did not mention, however, that the strikes—one of the most concentrated aerial missions of the entire war—had been planned for almost a month *before* the shootdown of the reconnaissance plane. Moorer had asked Blackburn's opinion about the possible consequences of such a strike early in November.

Again Laird, a 17-year veteran of the Congress himself before he had been appointed Secretary of Defense, had to be less than candid before the branch of government he had served so well. The committee was frankly skeptical of his explanation of the air strike, and newsmen, with only a few exceptions, gave Laird's testimony the worst possible interpretation. The humanitarian aspects of the Son Tay raid were ignored by many editors and television commentators decrying the resumption of large-scale bombing over North Vietnam.

Blackburn's and Mayer's worst fears had come true. Asked weeks before to comment on the possible impact of such strikes, they had warned, in writing, that it would be devastating. The reasons were obvious. "Rescue" and "retaliation" were two pages apart in *Webster's Dictionary* and two light-years apart in public opinion. But even more critical, in their opinion, was the fact that retaliatory strikes might provoke actions against the remaining prisoners that, they hoped, the raid itself would not.

Blackburn and Mayer had been told that Kissinger had agreed to "no bombing." But then came those odd, last-minute hints that a 24-hour delay in the Son Tay raid might "interfere with other operations" they were no longer privy to. The two missions had been launched almost simultaneously—105 planes supporting the rescue of prisoners of war near Hanoi meshed with 225 strikes in the south of North Vietnam retaliating for one RF-4 shot down ten days earlier. The timing of those retaliatory raids on Saturday, November 21, only hours after the abortive rescue attempt, was "to haunt us for months," Mayer would recall. Around the world, newspapers which lauded the rescue attempt in one sentence deplored resumption of the bombing in the next. The whole purpose of the Son Tay mission was getting lost in the flak.

Having been equally evasive before the Foreign Relations Committee about both the retaliatory strikes and the Son Tay rescue, Laird tripped on one crucial fact that day. Asked by Senator Stuart Symington about losses on both missions, Laird said, "We had no losses of any planes in the protective reaction attacks south of the 19th parallel this weekend and we had only two casualties in the operation to rescue the POWs." The statement was true. But it didn't sound that way a few days later when word leaked to the press that an F-105 on the Son Tay raid had been shot down and lost over Laos. Some newspaper editorials suggested that Laird was "quibbling"—and wondered what else had happened on the raid that the administration was not making public.

Members of the committee felt Laird was also quibbling on other matters. One of his biggest supporters, Senator Jacob Javits of New York, obviously didn't like the retaliatory strikes, but that, he said, was "separate" from the Son Tay raid. "War is not a pink tea business," he acknowledged in one of the hearing's most friendly remarks. But when Javits asked Laird if this was the first such POW rescue attempt, Laird told him, "It was the first time in Southeast Asia in this conflict. I apologize if I gave the impression that I was referring to the history of our country."

Javits would remember that answer when newspapers revealed, in the next three weeks, sketchy accounts of three or four other rescue attempts. They had occurred in South Vietnam and in Cambodia, and they, too, had been "dry holes." Members of Javits's staff were piqued that Laird hadn't spelled them out. When they asked the Pentagon about those other rescue attempts, they became even more miffed when they learned that the news accounts touched only the tip of an iceberg. Its full dimensions, however, would remain hidden for five years.

Son Tay was not only *not* the first rescue attempt "in Southeast Asia in this conflict": it was, in fact, the 71st "dry hole." In South Vietnam, Cambodia, and Laos, 91 such rescue operations were mounted between 1966 and 1970. At least 45 of them, probably closer to 50, were triggered by reports of U.S. POWs. Seventy-nine of the operations involved outright "raids." Of the 91 rescue operations, 20 succeeded—in rescuing 318 South Vietnamese soldiers and 60 civilians. But of 45 raids mounted to rescue American prisoners, only one succeeded. Army Specialist Fourth Class Larry D. Aiken was rescued on July 10, 1969, from a Viet Cong POW camp, but he died in an American hospital 15 days later of wounds inflicted by his captors just before his rescue. The raid, apparently, had been compromised at the last minute.

All of the rescue missions before Son Tay had been handled within the Joint Personnel Recovery Center (JPRC), a separate staff section within MACV Headquarters in Saigon. The results of the JPRC's efforts were no less heartbreaking than the raid on Son Tay. In December of 1966, for instance, a confidential informant passed word of American prisoners being held by the Viet Cong. The JPRC found his information credible and launched a raid. There was a heavy firefight in which 35 Viet Cong were killed and 34 others detained. During interrogation, they confirmed that Americans had been held in the camp. The prisoners had been moved just before the raid.

Some of the JPRC's raids failed because intelligence was compromised, others because the rescues weren't launched quickly enough. This happened on one raid in 1967 when a South Vietnamese escapee from a Viet Cong POW camp reported the location of two camps containing American prisoners. His report was challenged at first, then finally verified. A raid was launched, and at one camp, 21 South Vietnamese prisoners were recovered. The other camp was empty. Yet evidence showed that American POWs had been there. The released South Vietnamese POWs said that the Americans had been moved about 30 days before the raid, after the escapee first reported the presence of American prisoners there.

After Aiken's 1969 rescue, efforts to find POW camps and free prisoners in South Vietnam and Cambodia intensified. In 1970 alone, 24 separate rescue operations were conducted in the south. They failed to unearth even the remains of a single U.S. prisoner. The rescue missions continued even after the failure of the Son Tay raid. By 1973 such missions would total 119, including 98 raids. Aiken would remain the only American ever to be recovered.

Against that backdrop, the Son Tay raid was not the spectacular failure, or at least not the unique failure, that it seemed to be to the hostile senators who had questioned Laird. By denying that other similar rescue missions had been attempted, Laird missed an excellent opportunity to put the Son Tay "failure" in better perspective. Yet he may not have known the tragic history of those earlier rescue missions. Ed Mayer knew of them, for instance, but Blackburn, his immediate boss, would insist that *he* never did. Had the Congress and the American people been informed, they might have better understood the motives behind the Son Tay raid—and the slim chance for its success.

Laird had not sounded candid with the Congress or the American people. Perhaps it was because the Pentagon is reluctant to admit its failures; perhaps because the committee's pejorative questions and comments ridiculed a mission in which Laird believed deeply; or perhaps because Senator Fulbright was viewed as a public enemy only a shade less dangerous than North Vietnam's General Vo Nguyen Giap by an administration that felt that any information given to him was too much.

Whatever the reason, Laird's testimony shed little light on the Son Tay rescue and contributed so much misinformation that it only added to the controversy. Soon after he became Secretary of Defense, a small restaurant/bar on Connecticut Avenue nine blocks from the White House had paid Laird a special tribute by naming one of its sandwiches after him: "The Melvin R. Laird: provolone and baloney, $1.85." But Laird had offered one comment at the Fulbright hearing that would prove to be anything but baloney. Senator Javits asked him, "What signal do you want Hanoi to get on our commando raid on the POW camps?" Laird told him, "That we will take rather unusual means to see that these men are returned as free Americans." And when Senator Claiborne Pell asked him what he thought North Vietnam would do about the POWs "as a result of the raids," Laird's response was prophetic:

"I would assume that they might be guarded more closely."

Public Relations

At the White House on Wednesday, November 25, President Nixon personally decorated four of the Son Tay raiders.

Some time before the ceremony, Laird ushered Manor and Simons into the Oval Office. Nixon had asked to meet with them privately, to express his thanks—and ask what had happened. The President was "very cordial," but he didn't find out much.

Stewards from the White House mess offered drinks or coffee as the men "relaxed" with their Commander-in-Chief in deeply upholstered chairs arranged around a rug with a huge seal, "President of the United States," woven into it. Asked later what he and the President had talked about, Bull Simons would recall, "Not much. He asked me what year I had graduated from West Point. I told him I didn't, that I was a reserve officer commissioned out of ROTC from Missouri. That seemed to faze him. He said, 'Oh!' and turned to Manor. They did the rest of the talking." The meeting was "very thoughtful of the President," Simons said, "but I wouldn't call it a thought-provoking visit. In fact, it was kind of dull and uncomfortable."

The ceremony began at 4:05 P.M. in the White House State Dining Room. Nixon delivered a short, prepared introduction before Laird read each man's citation. Simons was awarded the Distinguished Service Cross for "extraordinary heroism," the nation's second highest award for valor. Army Sergeant First Class Tyrone J. Adderly, the M-79 grenadier and ground guide in Elliott Sydnor's command group who had twice come under heavy automatic weapons fire but "eliminated the threat to the force," received the same award. Air Force Technical Sergeant Leroy M. Wright, his foot in a heavy cast from the fire extinguisher that had torn loose from the wall of Banana One when it crash-landed inside the walls of Son Tay, received its equivalent, the Air Force Cross. Leroy Manor was awarded the Distinguished Service Medal. The President pinned on each man's decoration personally.

The President's remarks and the citations were very general, adding little to what the press had been told about the raid two days earlier. Nixon expressed his pride in the "mission of mercy" to free men held captive "under the most barbaric conditions." The raid, he said, had been carried out not only with "incomparable bravery" but with "incomparable efficiency," as though Senator William Proxmire might otherwise launch an investigation into what it had cost. (The best estimate was about $7 million, but some would suggest an estimate closer to $70 million.)

Nixon then told those present, "Before I gave the final order, I asked some very searching questions." He discovered, he said, that "each man who participated in this mission was a volunteer." That was true enough. But the President's next remarks, which may have been provided by his speechwriters or may have been made up on the spot, certainly came as news to the men who were being decorated. "I [also] found out," he said, "that each man who participated in this mission knew before he went that there was a 50 percent chance the mission might not succeed." Then he added, "And I found out that each man who participated in this mission knew there was a 50 percent chance that he might lose his life."

Nixon invited Laird, Moorer, Admiral McCain, several POW wives, and the gaggle of congressmen and reporters present to congratulate the four men "personally." At 4:18, the President left the room. The ceremony had lasted 13 minutes—half as long as the raid.

All three TV networks carried clips of the scene that evening. But if the White House thought the ceremony would quell the storm of controversy about the raid, it was mistaken. CBS commentator Eric Sevareid noted caustically that although "Everyone admires the brave men who tried it, a great many cannot help feeling there was something harebrained about the concept." ABC's John Scali noted that "Outdated, inadequate intelligence is being blamed for the failure of the mission. And the finger is being pointed at the Pentagon's Defense Intelligence Agency, not the government's Central Intelligence Agency which was not involved." Scali did not say who had "pointed" the finger, or on what basis he could report that the CIA had not been "involved."

It was the opening shot of another behind-the-scenes CYA—cover your ass—effort launched from CIA headquarters in Langley. Newsmen with a "good pipeline" to CIA headquarters would later report that the raid had been planned and executed without consulting the CIA. The DIA, which had provided the intelligence for the mission, was criticized for giving the Son Tay planners POW information that was "at least six months old." Vice President Spiro T. Agnew exacerbated the situation by decrying the "faulty intelligence"—although his assistant for military and foreign affairs would admit later that Agnew had never been briefed on the raid, before it *or* after.

This new controversy further obscured the humanitarian motives for the raid, and led to another bitter clash between

Laird and Fulbright. Called once again to testify before the Senate Foreign Relations Committee, Laird denied Fulbright's assertion that the CIA had not been consulted about the raid. "All agencies were consulted," he said, and "information taken from all of them."

Fulbright interrupted with a statement that came close to accusing Laird of being a liar: "That is not very accurate," he said. "I personally asked the Director of the Intelligence Board if he was consulted and he said 'No.' "

"I don't think that can quite be the case," Laird said, seething, "he was consulted and advised."

Fulbright remained unconvinced. At Langley, where the words "And Ye Shall Know The Truth, And The Truth Shall Make You Free" are carved in 7-inch letters on the marble wall of the entrance lobby, a CIA spokesman declined to comment on the Laird-Fulbright exchange. The buck was skillfully being passed to the DIA for the Son Tay "snafu," further straining relations within America's already fractionalized intelligence community.

On Thanksgiving Day, Thursday, November 26, President Nixon shared his Thanksgiving dinner with 106 servicemen wounded in Vietnam and made a promise to "free the prisoners of war at any cost." Hanoi's delegation to the Paris peace talks called a press conference. North Vietnam's spokesman condemned the "protective reaction strikes" launched the previous Saturday, claiming they had killed 49 civilians and wounded 40 others. He refused to acknowledge that a raid had been made to free prisoners from a camp near Hanoi, referring only in general terms to "acts of war."

That same day in North Vietnam, which was usually quick to charge the United States with aggressive acts but obviously embarrassed that American helicopters had been able to land undetected within 23 miles of its capital, Hanoi finally informed its population of the raid on Son Tay. North Vietnam claimed that the futile, inept effort had cost frightful casualties among the American raiders and that a "number" of POWs had been "wounded" in the raid. In Moscow, *Pravda* charged that the raid was the first step toward "spreading the land war into the territory of North Vietnam."

North Vietnam's claim that there were casualties among the Son Tay raiders and the POWs they were attempting to rescue spawned a new controversy about how much—or how little—the Pentagon had revealed about the raid. In the absence of hard facts, "inside" reports abounded, one of them claiming that the raiders had seized "a few" North Vietnamese prisoners at the empty compound and taken them to an undisclosed location in Southeast Asia for interrogation. The report was wrong. Blackburn and Simons had flatly ruled out the advisability of taking enemy prisoners long before the training at Eglin began. Simons would later explain why: "I wanted *nothing* to distract us from the real mission. Moreover, a helicopter is a very fragile machine. In the rush of boarding to get out of there in the dark, what do you do? Flash a guy down, turn up nothing, and then find out he's got a grenade in his jockstrap? You'd lose the plane. So I scratched that idea off my list. We didn't do it."

But Henry Kissinger was convinced that Simons's men had taken one prisoner—a baby water buffalo. Just where the rumor started is uncertain, but one of Kissinger's key deputies asked a reporter to check it out "off the record." Kissinger, he said, was livid. If word leaked out, the operation would look even more ludicrous, and there was already more egg on everyone's face than the White House could stomach. Asked on what basis Kissinger concluded that a water buffalo had been kidnapped, the deputy explained that there had been rumors of a prisoner being seized. The raiders denied it, but when the White House ordered the helicopters to be searched with a fine-tooth comb, there were unmistakable traces of water buffalo dung beneath the floorboards. Since the White House would look kind of silly asking too many questions about water buffalo dung, could the reporter make a few quiet inquiries and report back? Concern for the POWs in North Vietnam that had motivated the raid on Son Tay had deteriorated into a White House flap over a baby water buffalo.

When the reporter queried Blackburn about the rumor, he laughed, incredulous. "You're out of your raving mind!" he said. "May be," the reporter replied, "but why don't you check quietly? Maybe your Special Forces group on Okinawa is babysitting the tike until it's safe to bring him into the country." Later that afternoon, Bull Simons thought Blackburn had lost his marbles. "A *water* buffalo, for Christ's sake? No, my God, we don't have a water buffalo!" Blackburn asked him to check anyway. A few days later Kissinger learned with relief that the water buffalo either didn't exist or was hidden in impenetrable cover.

Five years later, Simons would not be amused when he was asked again about the mascot. "There is no mistake about it," he insisted. "Can you imagine running out in the dark and grabbing a water buffalo by the ass in the middle of all that? The idea is ridiculous." He denied categorically that his men had kidnapped a water buffalo. "I know God damn well it did not come back with the ground force," he said, "because I watched them load the planes." But what about the helicopters that landed near Finger Lake? "Oh," Simons replied carefully, "I don't know about that."

Marty Donohue was the pilot of one of the helicopters that landed about one and a half miles from Son Tay, the only one that remained on the ground long enough to wrestle a baby water buffalo aboard. "It was a lonely time," Donohue would recall. "Three SAMs were launched toward us as we egressed." Donohue swore that he didn't kidnap the beast either.

Henry Kissinger apparently got some very strange intelligence briefings.

Early in December, as he was mulling over the 30 days' leave he would soon be taking, Bull Simons got a call from the Pentagon. Defense Secretary Laird, he was told, would fly to Fort Bragg in a few days with a plane full of congressmen and other dignitaries, plus some members of the Pentagon press corps. The secretary of defense, on behalf of the President, would personally decorate each of the Son Tay raiders for heroism and meritorious service. Because so many details of the individual citations which Simons had submitted soon after the raid were "rather sensitive," the Army had decided Laird would read just one citation covering all of the raiders. The individual citations would be processed later and put into each man's personnel file. The call was to "clear" the wording of Laird's citation with Simons. Simons asked a few questions and then slammed down the phone.

Of the 56 men he'd led into North Vietnam, he had just been told, only two others would receive the Distinguished Service Cross which President Nixon had pinned on him and Sergeant Adderly at the White House. Two of Simons's men would receive the Silver Star; 22 would get the Bronze Star with "V" device (for valor); the remaining 30, over half of his men, would get the Army Commendation Ribbon with "V" device. Soldiers called it the "Green Weenie." As a medal, it ranked one notch above the Good Conduct Ribbon, which soldiers could earn for staying in uniform three years without catching VD.

It was clear to Simons that the Army's decorations and awards branch had decided on a "standard G.I. issue" of medals to his men. He could just picture what had happened. Some chair-borne colonel looked at the stack of citations which Simons had worked hard to draft and submit for fast approval—and then shoved them aside. He flipped through Army Field Manual 101-10-1, issued in September of 1969, which cited as a "guide for commanders" the rates at which medals are "normally" awarded. Then flicking on a desk calculator, he said: "Let's see: that'll mean two Silver Stars or better, twenty-two Bronze Stars and thirty Commendation Ribbons." Having figured out the formula, he handed some major the stack of Simons's citations: "Have these rewritten accordingly, will you?"

Disgusted by his call from the Pentagon, Simons walked out of his office and said to one of his sergeants, "You lucky sonovabitch, you're going to get the 'Green Weenie.' "

"I don't understand, sir," the sergeant said.

"It's simple, you dumb shit; the Pentagon thinks you went to a North Vietnamese tea dance. Some dumb bastard in the awards section up there flunked his map reading course: he couldn't find Son Tay if it was inside the Kremlin. He thinks you went to a tea dance in an enemy brothel."

That evening, Bull Simons decided to lay it on the line. He picked up the telephone, dialed Fort Bragg's command center, and told the operator simply, "This is Colonel Simons. Priority call. Get me the Army Chief of Staff."

Within a minute, the Army operations center in the basement of the Pentagon had Simons back on the phone; General Westmoreland was en route from Iran and would arrive at Andrews Air Force Base about seven the next morning. General Palmer was the acting Chief. "Did Colonel Simons want to talk with General Palmer or wait for General Westmoreland?"

Simons refrained from swearing and asked for Palmer.

In seconds, the Army Vice Chief of Staff was on the line: "Bull, this is Bruce Palmer. What's up?"

"General," Simons told him very calmly, "some dumb

sonovabitch is sending the secretary of defense here in a day or two with a box full of Green Weenies. It might be best if he didn't come; I'd hate to see some of the men turn those decorations down in front of a flock of reporters."

"Turn them down? What do you mean, Bull?"

Simons told him, "General, I don't want to embarrass the Army, but one of my men is just likely to shove an Army Commendation Ribbon straight up Mr. Laird's ass. These men risked their lives outside Hanoi; they weren't on a Boy Scout patrol in the suburbs of Saigon. Your awards section is handling these decorations as though it were business-as-usual and we were holding up their Friday afternoon golf outing. This wasn't business as usual. These guys laid it all out; every one of them earned at least a Silver Star. For what they did, Green Weenies are an insult, not a decoration."

"I understand how you feel, Bull," Palmer said. "I'll look into it."

On Wednesday, December 9, 1970, Defense Secretary Melvin Laird arrived at Fort Bragg aboard Air Force Two. He awarded 54 medals to the Army Son Tay raiders. Four of them were Distinguished Service Crosses; 50 were Silver Stars. There were no Green Weenies in Laird's box of medals.

Forty-three of the raid's Air Force participants were decorated in the same ceremony. John Allison, Warner Britton, Marty Donohue, and Herb Kalen were awarded the Air Force Cross, their service's counterpart of the Distinguished Service Cross. Laird pinned the DSC on the blouses of Elliott Sydnor and Dick Meadows.

Doc Cataldo got a Silver Star. Only a few days after the raid, he had gone to see Ed Mayer. He volunteered to go back to North Vietnam—as a prisoner.

Cataldo knew the POWs needed a doctor. Why not "send" them one? He told Mayer he was willing to have any kind of device implanted anywhere in his body to keep track of him—and to help him, in turn, report back on the prisoners or perhaps call in another raid. Mayer could arrange to have him shot down, if that's what was needed to make his capture plausible. Cataldo didn't know how to fly, but he was willing to take off in the backseat of an RF-4, have the pilot put the plane on autopilot, and eject over friendly territory while Cataldo "flew" into Hanoi. Once he saw or heard the North Vietnamese air defense batteries open fire, he would set off a time-delay destruct mechanism to shoot *himself* down—and bail out just before it was due to go off.

The Silver Star Laird pinned on him cost the American taxpayer $1.70.

Until that ceremony, Cataldo's family was skeptical that he had really been on the raid. Before the operation was launched, Simons, Manor, and Mayer had polled their men to ask who wanted his participation to be made public or was willing to be interviewed, within *very* tight restraints about any operational details. Most of the men asked for their names not even to be made public. That fell through, however, when Nixon and Laird decided to decorate the men in a public ceremony. It was an attempt to quell the controversy that surrounded their mission. But the detailed citations that Simons had drawn up for his men would *not* be made public. There were still a lot of questions about the raid that the administration didn't want to answer.

One award for the Son Tay raid was never made. It was an Army Commendation Medal for a sergeant first class from Company A, 7th Special Forces Group. Until a few days before the raid, he was on Simons's assault force. But "Blue Max" got wind that the man was having some serious family problems and, although a "fantastic, damned brave soldier," had developed serious doubts about the war in Vietnam. Simons "amputated" him and put the soldier in the 36-man Support Group. He was gravely disappointed. He wanted more than anything to be on the raid. After the assault force had left for Thailand, Blue Max learned that the sergeant was thinking about defecting. But he worked hard and when Simons returned, he wrote him up for an Army Commendation Medal. A few days later, the soldier deserted. He fled to Denmark, then Sweden, and became a war protester. Ed Mayer "yanked" his medal. To his great credit, however, the sergeant turned himself in to the U.S. military attaché in Sweden within weeks, and asked to return to the United States to "face the music" for deserting. To the Army's credit, it did not press court-martial charges against him, but gave him a general discharge.

Another of the most important Son Tay "awards" had already been made—in an unofficial ceremony at a cocktail party in the Virginia suburbs.

A few hours after the raiders returned to Udorn, one of

Simons's noncommissioned officers snuck off base and entered a small tailor shop frequented by American GIs just outside the main gate. He asked the proprietor if he could make up about 100 embroidered shoulder patches in the next three hours. He showed the merchant a sketch. The patch was about three inches round. In its center against a black background was a steaming white mushroom with two beady eyes peering out from under it. On a small tab just below were the initials KITD/FOHS in black letters against a white background.

It was mid-afternoon on November 21. The sergeant's eyes were bloodshot, his face was tired; he'd been back from the Son Tay raid less than eight hours and he had not slept in two days. He was also risking a court-martial. In a flagrant breach of security, he'd left the intelligence debriefing compound to sneak off base and get these patches made up. Time was a problem. Instead of resting at Udorn for a few days, the raiders had learned, they would load aboard one of the medical evacuation C-141s which had been standing by for the rescued POWs; right after dinner, they would be flown out of Thailand directly back to Fort Bragg and Eglin. The sergeant was determined not to leave without those patches.

The tailor checked with one of the seamstresses in the crowded back room of his shop and returned to the front counter. The patches could be made, he said, but they would cost $2, American, apiece. "Can you have them ready by five o'clock?" the sergeant asked.

When the Son Tay raiders returned home and could finally tell their families what they had been up to over the months past, a few of them held cocktail parties. After the JCS after-action report had been submitted, thank-you letters written, and recommendations for awards and decorations made, the men on the planning and support staffs could also relax; and early in December, Air Force Lieutenant Colonel Benjamin N. Kraljev, Jr., invited Blackburn to a party at his home in suburban Virginia. Kraljev had been one of Manor's key operational planners. Midway in the party, he called for silence and turned to Blackburn. "General, the men have made up their own patch. We'd like you to wear one. You earned it too." He gave Blackburn the round black patch. Blackburn looked at the quizzical eyes peering out from beneath the mushroom, smiled, and asked, "What does this stand for: KITD/FOHS?"

Kraljev answered quietly, "Sir, that's us: Kept In Total Darkness/Fed Only Horse Shit."

Postmortem

Whatever its public stance, the Pentagon was badly shaken by the reaction to the Son Tay raid. Shortly before Laird had flown to Fort Bragg to decorate the raiders, Manor's after-action summary finally arrived from Thailand—almost a week after the assault. Part of the report—fortunately, its most innocuous pages—immediately fell into the hands of columnist Jack Anderson. Already unhappy that communications had failed at every key juncture of the raid, Laird viewed the delayed post-operations report and the Anderson leak with even greater annoyance. He and Moorer decided it was time for a shake-up of the military communications network worldwide.

Another shake-up was in the wind. Most of the criticism about the raid was directed at the various intelligence agencies that had supported it. Despite Laird's protests that the raiders had been given "excellent" intelligence, despite attempts by members of the intelligence community to pass the buck or simply retreat behind a wall of official silence, the impression left on the press and public was clear: a well-intentioned military operation had been doomed from the start by faulty intelligence. The message was not lost on the Pentagon and the White House. As a senior member of the National Security Council would later remark: "Son Tay was the last straw." At the time, the NSC viewed the raid as just one more of the snafus that prompted a major reorganization of the intelligence community put into effect one year later.

But in the meantime, the Pentagon undertook another line of investigation to determine if the cause for the raid's failure was faulty intelligence or faulty security. That investigation would turn up some significant facts about the enemy's reaction to Son Tay.

Two months after the raid, Sully Fontaine was on his honeymoon when a "counselor" from the American embassy tracked him down and told him to be on the next flight for Hong Kong.

Someone would meet him there with further instructions. Fontaine had planned to spend almost a week with his bride in Bangkok, one of his favorite cities. But after 28 years in the intelligence business, he was used to getting unexpected orders in strange places at inconvenient times.

Forty-four years old, Belgian-born of French parents, fluent in four languages, Fontaine was a professional spook, an experienced Army clandestine operator. He had joined the British Army in 1943, went through Commando training and airborne school, and parachuted into Europe to work with the American OSS, and the Dutch, Belgian, and French undergrounds. He earned the Croix de Guerre with Palm from both Belgium and France. After the war, he studied philosophy at the Belgian Military School, was posted to the United Nations for three years, and then coaxed into the United States Army for officer training while the Korean War was winding down. There, he commanded the United Nations Honor Guard, a crack, 99-man American unit augmented by special platoons of elite troops from seven other countries. Fontaine had his own private international peacekeeping force. But he was soon back in the "underground" commanding one of the Army's first Special Forces' training teams in Korea.

For the next three years, Fontaine's assignments fluctuated between military intelligence and more Special Forces work. Sent to the 10th Special Forces Group in Germany in 1959, he organized "special missions" in Africa and the Middle East instead. In 1963, he was sent to Vietnam to organize a Special Forces camp where the Mekong River crosses into Cambodia, and to help train South Vietnamese and Cambodian units. He did his job well and ended up in Don Blackburn's Special Operations Group. Blackburn put him in charge organizing agent networks, recruiting Montagnards, and supervising special operations in Cambodia and Laos.

After three tours in Vietnam, Fontaine was put into criminal intelligence work in Europe. One of his duties was to serve as the U.S. military liaison officer to Interpol. Two years later he was back in Southeast Asia, investigating international crime organizations throughout the Far East. At the time his honeymoon was so abruptly interrupted, Fontaine was on leave from a tour as deputy commander of all Army criminal investigatory work in the western United States. He had been looking forward to introducing his bride to life in San Francisco when their honeymoon was over.

Fontaine and his bride flew immediately to Hong Kong. There, another embassy "counselor" met his plane and handed him an envelope. His leave was canceled; he was directed to fly to Washington.

In Washington, Fontaine was escorted to the Pentagon and ended up, he would recall, "in a cellar someplace." There, in a cramped office with a "Special Access Only" sign on the door, he was told: "We have just received an order to investigate a leak on the Son Tay raid. You're in charge." It was not a routine investigation. His orders were signed personally by the acting Army Chief of Staff, General Bruce Palmer, "by direction of the Secretary of the Army."

Fontaine knew only what he had read about the raid. For two days, he examined the Son Tay files: draft after-action reports, counterintelligence assessments, security files, "everything involved." He concluded that investigating a possible leak was ludicrous. With professionals like Simons and Blackburn behind the raid, there couldn't have been any. Moreover, he knew that if there had been a leak, Simons and his men would have been creamed seconds after landing in North Vietnam. Simons had brought all his men back virtually untouched. Fontaine had served with Simons—"the greatest soldier I ever met."

But Fontaine's Pentagon contact was adamant: "No, we had a leak. As you know, there was nobody there when they arrived. Somewhere along the line before the raid, somebody knew that raid was going to be made. We feel that foreign intelligence knew about the raid, told the North [Vietnamese] and that is why they cleared out."

To Fontaine the whole investigation sounded like a "political imbroglio" between different intelligence outfits trying to lay the blame on someone else. But he handpicked a team of investigators, sent one of them to Fort Bragg and another to Eglin Air Force Base, while he flew back to Southeast Asia—without his bride.

In Phnom Penh, Cambodia, Fontaine contacted his "French connections." Given his experience with Britain's Special Operations Executive, the European underground, and American Army special missions in Europe and North Africa, he had some very close French friends. Fontaine had two requests to make of one in particular. First, he wanted to find out what the Chinese knew about the Son Tay raid. That would be "no problem," his friend told him. Second, Fontaine wanted to have dinner with a certain Russian intelligence operative. But it had to be set up through an impeccable, neutral intermediary both could trust. The Frenchman was glad to oblige; he knew Fontaine was in the American Army but suspected he was really working for the French.

That night, Fontaine received a call from a Polish intelligence officer who told him: "I have a Russian I'd like you to meet. You two have many common interests; why don't you have dinner with us?" The Pole and Fontaine, it turned out, had trained together in SOE. Fontaine was elated. "The Poles," he would explain years later, "have the best intelligence in that side of the world. The professional Polish intelligence can run circles around any NKVD, KGB, MI-6, or other agent you want."

At the Café de la Paix the next night, Fontaine knew the Russian was "no flunky" before they'd finished their first drink. The two had known of each other, but only by reputation, word of mouth, and dossiers. The Russian, Fontaine found, was slightly mystified; this odd meeting had been set up through a Pole by a Frenchman who swore that Fontaine was part of *his* team. He asked Fontaine bluntly if he was a double agent. Fontaine disappointed him. No, he just needed some information. What could the Russian tell him about Son Tay?

The question startled the Russian; he told Fontaine that the raid had been a total surprise. But his next remark gave away the Russian reaction to the raid. If the Americans could hit Son Tay, he said, they could " 'hit' anything in North Vietnam," couldn't they?

The next day, Fontaine's French contact met him at the same restaurant. Now, he explained, the Russian had a favor to ask. He wanted to know what the next target was. Was it the Lang Chi Dam near Son Tay?

Fontaine didn't have to lie. He said he didn't know. The Russian, Fontaine's French friend exhorted, wanted to know what Fontaine *thought,* not just what he knew. "You can go back and say, 'I don't know nothing about it,' " Fontaine said, "not a thing!"

The question about the Lang Chi Dam left Fontaine "flabbergasted." It was such an obvious target. The Russians had to be intensely worried about it to have probed him, through a cutout, on *future* operations. "One thing came out loud and clear" from his visit to Phnom Penh; the Russians were worried about the dam near Sòn Tay.

The Chinese reaction, Fontaine found, was different. The raid had caught them by surprise too, but it made them mad. "Something was wrong someplace," Fontaine was told, if North Vietnam couldn't handle a small military force operating close to its own capital. The Chinese didn't ask about the dam. What they wanted to know was, did Fontaine have any ideas for infiltrating the North Vietnamese—so China could find out how badly screwed up things really were in Hanoi? The Chinese, he would report to Washington, "were really shook" by the raid. "They thought the whole God damn country [North Vietnam] was about to be overrun by a platoon of American hippies."

From other sources, Fontaine became convinced that there had been no leak about the raid through friendly intelligence channels. His British contacts were one such tip-off. "If you want to know what's going to happen next week in Washington," Fontaine had always thought, "don't go to Washington, go to London." And one British contact, the head of British military intelligence in North America at the time, told him admiringly, "We were shocked. For once, none of you big mouths even talked."

As good as he was, there *was* a security leak about the raid that Fontaine was not to uncover. It happened in Hawaii, where only three officers knew of the operation beforehand. One was Admiral John S. McCain, Jr., Commander-in-Chief, Pacific. The second was Army Lieutenant General Charles A. Corcoran, his Chief of Staff. And the third was an Air Force officer seven ranks junior to them, Andrew Porth. Porth, however, wasn't "cleared" to know of the raid. In the parlance of military intelligence, he simply "G-2'd it," or figured it out on his own.

Porth was a young intelligence captain in the Escape and Evasion Branch of Headquarters, Pacific Air Force (PACAF), at Hickam Air Force Base. The 5-foot 11-inch, blond, wavy-haired officer was responsible for all POW information and planning for "Egress Recap," the processing of returned POWs. He made sure that every fighter group in PACAF had its own display board of North Vietnam showing photos of the known POW camps. All of the "traffic" on prisoners of war—messages, reconnaissance photos, and intelligence analyses—crossed his desk. He worked closely with the 548th Reconnaissance Technical Group, which compiled the so-called PACAF Index. This was almost a bible for those concerned with POW intelligence; it contained every POW's and MIA's picture, and statements from key witnesses about the circumstances of his shootdown or disappearance. The book was widely used in interrogating defectors or captured Viet Cong or North Vietnamese. Porth's office was literally a vault which he shared with reconnaissance specialists who controlled the "air assets" for certain intelligence missions.

In September and October of 1970, Porth began to notice that routine traffic once classified only "Confidential" was being upgraded to "Secret." And that what used to be "Secret," in turn, soon became "Top Secret." This was particularly true of reconnaissance missions flown over North Vietnam. Photos he used to see regularly no longer crossed his desk; he had no "need-to-know." He sensed that "something was up." Yet, due to a quirk in counterintelligence planning as the Son Tay operation was being "tightened up," he still saw regular data on the "tracks" of proposed reconnaissance missions.

There were other indications that something was brewing. Porth received calls from offices that were now "cut out of the loop," asking him what was going on. All over the Pacific, "assets" were being shifted about—airplanes, missions, people, special communications equipment. As weeks went by, it was becoming harder and harder for PACAF officers to do their jobs. They couldn't manage their part of the war very well when the tools they were supposed to control were taken away without explanation for missions they knew nothing about.

On Wednesday, November 11, nine days before the Son Tay raid, a medical service major in PACAF's Surgeon General's Office called Porth, perplexed. He wanted to know if Porth could tell him anything about a medical evacuation C-141 that had been pulled off regular Vietnam flights and put on alert at Clark Air Force Base in the Philippines. It was specially configured to handle 55 ambulatory or litter patients. It was now standing by on "moment's notice," the officer told Porth, to "launch." The major couldn't figure out what for, and he felt the plane might be needed for regular medical-evacuation missions. (There was still a very real war under way in South Vietnam—312 Americans were killed and 1,940 wounded in October of 1970.)

Porth told the major he had no idea. Then, the number 55 hit him—an airplane specially configured for 55 patients? That was the number of prisoners, according to the latest DIA estimate Porth had seen, of POWs still held in Son Tay. He rechecked the map coordinates of reconnaissance tracks whose photographs he was no longer cleared to see. They were over Son Tay. Porth was suddenly very sure that someone was going to raid Son Tay.

He also knew it was an operation he wasn't cleared for, something he shouldn't discuss with anyone. Still, the idea haunted him. The following Monday, November 16, he put together an intelligence briefing board—a chart on which photographs and maps could be stuck as the briefing progressed, yet quickly removed, put into an envelope, and secured in a vault or locked file drawer. His briefing board spelled out the "indicators" that told him a raid on Son Tay was imminent. Porth put it away, but that Wednesday he told the watch officer on duty in PACAF's intelligence warning center to call him immediately if he came across *any* new mention of POWs—whether on radio news bulletins, the wire services, foreign newspapers, or wherever.

Two days later, on the night of November 20, Porth received a sudden summons to report to PACAF's headquarters building. There he found a "big gaggle" of people. "Something" was going on in North Vietnam. They were "really agitated," stirred up—the air defense system was "hot," missiles were going off like a string of Chinese firecrackers, radio traffic was at a level PACAF hadn't seen in years—and no one knew why.

Porth watched his boss, Colonel Pat E. Goforth, PACAF's Deputy Director of Intelligence, survey all this confusion. PACAF's Vice Commander, Lieutenant General John P. Lavelle, joined the group. Everyone stood around, explaining to Lavelle what the North Vietnamese were doing—but no one could explain *why* they were doing it. Porth went to his office, took his briefing board out of the vault, pasted it all together, shrouded it with a cloth, and carried it back to the headquarters building. He approached the watch director, a full colonel named Walter Stevens. "I think I know what's going on, sir," he reported.

By now, it was close to 9:30 P.M. Still no one had been able to tell the vice commander, Pacific Air Forces, what in hell was stirring up so much action in North Vietnam. Finally, Lavelle was told that a Captain Porth might have something worth hearing. Porth unveiled his briefing board and said: "I believe it's a raid on Son Tay. Here's why I think it adds up."

Lavelle listened to the short briefing, looked Porth in the eye, and told him bluntly, "You're out of your God damn mind, Captain."

Porth quickly retired from the scene. He would recall just one reaction to the encounter: "It was odd. General Lavelle usually doesn't cuss."

Lavelle went to his office, he would relate later, picked up a red phone, his "hot line" direct to CINCPAC headquarters, and asked the officer who answered to speak with Admiral McCain. McCain was in his operations center and could not be disturbed, Lavelle was told. Then he asked to speak with General Corcoran; but Corcoran was with McCain and he could not be interrupted either. Lavelle told the aide to carry a note into them. It explained his concern that something "big" was up in North Vietnam. Within seconds, a rear admiral was on the line: "They know all about it," he said—whatever "it" was—and the situation was under control. Lavelle was asked to have his "guys 'cool it,' lay off, don't speculate."

Three days later, November 23, Lavelle was listening to Secretary of Defense Laird brief the Pentagon press corps about a raid on a POW compound at a place called Son Tay. One of the little-known wonders of military communications is that the Pentagon's daily press briefing can be heard as it is under way in every major headquarters around the world. Few members of the Pentagon press corps were ever aware that their impertinent questions about the Vietnam War were sometimes listened to "live" everywhere from Tehran to Saigon.

At work in his vault that same day, Porth got a call to report to the "vice commander's office, fast." When he entered, Lavelle was still listening to the Laird briefing. "Sit down, Captain," Lavelle said. "I thought you'd enjoy listening to this with me." It was one of the most effective, unspoken tributes of the entire Son Tay episode. When the press conference ended, Lavelle asked Porth, "Are you *sure* you weren't told beforehand that this was going to come off?" Porth told him, "No, sir, I just guessed."

Blackburn and Mayer would not hear of the Porth incident for five years. "This could not have happened," one of them would protest; it meant something had slipped through the elaborate security precautions taken to mask the raid. Nor could they believe that if it had happened, it would not have surfaced sooner; that meant something was wrong with the postraid assessment. But Mayer would also doubt five years later that Fontaine's investigation of Son Tay security had even taken place; he had not heard of it before and would question, if it had, why no one on the team had grilled him.

From his viewpoint, Fontaine would be equally piqued, five years later, to learn from a journalist that Bull Simons had landed at the wrong camp.

There was another, even more disturbing aspect of the raid that remained a mystery for years. Who were those "100 to 200" men killed in Bull Simons's "preemptive strike" at the "Secondary School" south of Son Tay Prison? CIA's George Carver would insist that he had never been told and, when he checked his agency's records, "could not find out." He deferred the question to the DIA, calling it a "military matter." When the DIA checked its records, no entry could be found even indicating that the question had ever been listed as a collection requirement. It might seem, in the aftermath of the Son Tay failure, that the nation's security apparatus went out of its way to avoid learning any more bad news about the operation.

Were those troops at the "Secondary School" Chinese? If so, Bull Simons and his men had slaughtered an entire company of elite Chinese troops and left their billets in North Vietnam "burning like a Roman candle" at the very time when Henry Kissinger and Richard Nixon were massaging every diplomatic channel they could think of to open a dialogue with Peking. Or were they Russians? If they were, they had been killed by American troops almost one year to the day after Moscow and Washington opened their first round of Strategic Arms Limitation Talks. Is it possible that the CIA didn't *want* to know who those troops were—and that the DIA didn't want to report that the Pentagon might have just "blown" Kissinger's secret "game plan" in world power politics?

Almost a decade after Son Tay, the mystery of those Chinese or Russian or North Korean troops at the Secondary School appeared to finally unravel. Captain Udo Walther gave the belt he had "captured" there to hold his pants up to H. Ross Perot, the self-made Dallas millionaire and computer mogul who, after the raid, befriended many of the Son Tay raiders and the POWs they had tried to bring home. Perot proudly accepted the mounted "Thank You" as a "loan" and put it on display in his office. A journalist noticed it late in 1979 and verified that it was a Chinese officer's belt buckle—the only bit of uniform that distinguished Chinese officers from enlisted soldiers. The Defense Department refused to comment on the observation, as did the Chinese embassy in Washington. But Udo Walther would acknowledge late in 1984, "It wasn't a secret that there were Chinese there, and it wasn't a secret that there were a bunch of them. I communicated that and took some photographs. Now, what happened to those, I don't know."

Soon after the raid, it became clear, from sources independent of Fontaine's inquiries, that both Moscow and Peking were shook up by the peculiar events at Son Tay, perhaps because they thought the real purpose of the raid was to give some sort of devious signal that the war was going to get very rough—and on someone else's territory. The Russians reacted almost at once. Soviet armed forces became much more intent about rear-area security; units were reorganized and forces shifted to establish special reaction forces at critical targets all over the world. One of them was the Lang Chi hydroelectric plant, the dam 65 miles northwest of Hanoi whose turbogenerators would soon become operational and more than replenish the North Vietnamese power sources taken out by the American bombing effort that had also put so many prisoners into the cells of North Vietnam.

Ironically, the failure of the Son Tay raid discouraged the Pentagon and the White House from launching similar "pin-prick" operations. Blackburn and Mayer had been planning a raid against the Lang Chi Dam for almost a year before Son Tay. Son Tay had been designed in part to give Blackburn the license to unleash it. But in the glare of publicity that surrounded the Pentagon's failure to rescue any POWs, the military hierarchy forgot that Simons had executed the rest of the mission almost to perfection. And when the new security forces were discovered, the Joint Chiefs would not even formally consider the proposal to knock out the dam. The operation was scrubbed from SACSA's list of "new initiatives."

The dam *was* finally taken out, not in a raid but in a bombing attack. On June 10, 1972, eight Air Force F-4s hit the complex with 15 laser-guided 2,000-pound bombs, one of the first uses of "smart bombs." The strike worked. Generators in the concrete portion of the dam were severely damaged, while the earthen portion was not damaged at all, thus avoiding a flood down the Red River Valley that undoubtedly would have caused a furor of protest around the world. Power available to North Vietnam's national transmission network was once again in such short supply that in Hanoi itself, electricity was rationed.

The Chinese proved equally concerned about rear-area security in North Vietnam. All over the country and in northern Laos, where Chinese "engineers" were not only improving railroads and building roads and bridges but also actually manning air defense batteries, a lot of "construction crews" were soon guarding instead of building. And a week and a half after the raid, it was learned, a Chinese senior delegation traveled from Peking to Hanoi and met with leaders of the Lao Dung Party in a hastily scheduled "review" of the situation in Southeast Asia. Precisely what went on is probably not known, but years later White House sources would admit having learned that Hanoi's leaders were subjected to a "brutal" interrogation. Phrases like, "Have you lost not only the candle, but the hour?" were used. And there were hints, it was reported, that China had reconsidered its generous flow of aid to support North Vietnam's struggle in the south. Perhaps to reinforce that point, a large shipment of Soviet material moving to Hanoi by rail through China was inexplicably held up at the Chinese border. The Chinese would only explain that there were "technical problems" with the Russian shipping documents.

It was, at least in part, the growing enmity between China and Russia that finally enabled the Nixon administration to extricate itself from Vietnam. At last, the three great powers—America, Russia, and China—had had enough of the Vietnamese morass; and the North Vietnamese, fearing Russian and Chinese influence no less than American intervention, were equally eager to be rid of them. Doors that had been locked and bolted for years began to open slowly, and each nation involved in the struggle attempted to extricate itself with some shred of political or military advantage. It was a time-consuming process as North Vietnam, with a skill far beyond its experience in international power politics, played one great nation off against the other to achieve its ultimate goals.

For the Americans, it was an agonizing process. The North Vietnamese still refused to play their trump card: the American POWs. The year 1971 saw American combat deaths in Vietnam fall to 1,380, one-seventh of what they were during Nixon's first year in office; and 177,000 American soldiers returned home safely. But no POWs. At the end of the year, there were 478 known POWs and 1,013 Americans missing in action.

The Joint Staff spent a lot of time that year working on a plan it had sketched out soon after the Son Tay raid. Desperate to get the POWs home, the Pentagon was ready to recommend a replay of the raid on Son Tay, but on a scale of vastly different proportions and with far graver implications. Early in 1972, a "close hold" meeting of the Joint Chiefs of Staff reviewed the plan. Moorer thought well enough of it that he invited Laird to sit in the second time it was presented, early in May.

By then, there were only 62,600 Americans left in Vietnam, but more than 525 POWs and 1,150 MIAs somewhere in Southeast Asia. The President had visited China, but North Vietnam had just unleashed a savage attack in the south. America responded by mining Haiphong Harbor. Bombing of the north was resumed. Yet North Vietnam still refused to budge on the POW issue. America was desperate—and the Joint Chiefs were ready to consider anything to get those men home.

The proposal which JCS planners presented in "the Tank" would show how hopeless the POW situation had become, and how much America cared about those men. It proposed a "raid" by three and a half *divisions* into North Vietnam, an invasion involving 57,500 men to rescue some 500 Americans. The raid would be a simultaneous airborne, amphibious, and airmobile assault to envelope Hanoi and ring it with American troops, cutting every avenue of escape. Small Special Forces teams would seize Hoa Lo Prison, the Plantation, and outlying camps like the Zoo where prisoners were known to be held. To "cover" deployment of airborne forces to within striking distance of

Hanoi, a ruse was devised that joint maneuvers were to be conducted in the western Pacific, in which the entire 82nd Airborne Division would participate for the first time. After "marshaling" on an island en route to those maneuvers, the 82nd would parachute instead on "choke points" outside Hanoi—while Special Forces teams parachuted into the prisons inside the city. The planning was so meticulous—many of the Son Tay planners were involved once again—that detailed maps of the sewer systems from Hoa Lo had been obtained from some of the very French designers and engineers who had laid them out years before.

Such a raid would be an incredible gamble. More raiders would die than POWs could be rescued, its planners knew; and they couldn't be sure of locating every outlying prisoner-of-war camp—the DIA, it would turn out, had confirmed the location of nine of the 13 POW camps North Vietnam had used or was using by then—or of freeing all those in the ones that had been identified. But another element of the plan made them confident Hanoi would release any POWs the raiders would be unable to free.

Some of the Special Forces teams would have a much freer license than Bull Simons's men had been given. Their job was not only to recover as many POWs as possible, but to pick up any hapless, high-ranking North Vietnamese officials they could lay their hands on—the higher the rank, the better—and "extract" them as well. North Vietnam could then be invited to exchange the POWs who hadn't been freed for those members of its high command on whom the tables had been turned.

Although planning reached the point where a Marine division was ready to embark and other forces were "ready to go," the alert order for the raid was never issued. One of the planners would state later that, in his opinion, the raid would have "ended the war." "The God damn country was really that desperate. This is what we were almost forced to do." Had the operation been launched, he felt, the war would have been "all over in two weeks."

The war did not end for another 11 months. Years later, the CIA would profess to know nothing of any proposal to ring Hanoi with three and a half divisions. CIA's memory would prove to be equally bad about a raid that had actually taken place—Son Tay. Its records were "incomplete." "Not that much about Son Tay was ever put in writing," a deputy director would explain. A few "sensitive" records at the Pentagon would turn out to be missing; the files were "cleaned up" in 1973. Memories of some of the men who planned the raid would be more convenient, or protective, than others. A lot more is known today about the raid on Son Tay than was ever made public in 1970. Yet many questions remain.

Contrary to impressions at the time, the intelligence supporting the raid was remarkable. But did it, like the planning and execution of the raid, border on "overkill"? Had the raid been launched soon after the Pentagon learned of the POWs at Son Tay, would they have been rescued? Had the Pentagon forgotten one of General George Patton's favorite dictums: "A good plan violently executed now is better than a perfect plan next week"? Or was the Pentagon right, knowing that the plan had to be not only good but almost perfect if Bull Simons and his men were to get in and out of North Vietnam alive, let alone rescue the POWs at Son Tay?

Yet if the intelligence for the raid was so good, why was it discovered only at the last minute that the prisoners had been moved four and a half months before because of a flood? Or was it known earlier, but never told to those so intimately involved in planning the raid—and those ready to risk their lives executing it?

One senior member of the intelligence community would confirm that the information *was* known well before the raid, but known only to a very few. He would say bluntly, in an interview that he knew was being tape-recorded: "In July of 1970 they had a tremendously harsh typhoon season in North Vietnam. The river outside Son Tay flooded. It stopped flooding when it was two feet from the outer wall. The North Vietnamese were concerned, so they moved out of Son Tay."

Asked if he found out "later" or before the raid that the prisoners had been moved, he replied: "In July. And then *some*body moved back in September. Now, I changed the word right there: *Some*body. We weren't sure who. This is the key part of it right here . . . I am not sure how well known it was, but they moved out because of the rain, the flooding in July."

Were the July floods caused by Operation Popeye? Those cloud-seeding operations, conducted over North Vietnam in

1967 and 1968 and shifted to Laos from 1969 to 1972, entailed some of the most carefully guarded secrets of the Vietnam War. Testimony at a Top Secret briefing of the Senate Foreign Relations Committee in March 1974 would reveal that information about the program was so sensitive that it was denied to the President's closest advisers. So high was Popeye's classification, an Air Force witness explained, that information about the program was even withheld from a National Security Council inter agency panel formed in 1972, while the war was still under way, formed specifically to look into "weather modification and geophysical activities as weapons of war." Another witness, the Deputy Assistant Secretary of Defense for East Asia and Pacific Matters—and the man to whom the Pentagon's Vietnam Task Force reported—would admit that "The first *I* heard of it was as a result of a Jack Anderson column." But he wasn't the only senior defense civilian kept in the dark. The Secretary of Defense himself, Melvin Laird, had told that same committee in 1972 that "We have never engaged in that type of activity over North Vietnam." Two years later, in 1974, he had to write Senator Fulbright that he had "just been informed that such activities were conducted." Without explaining further why the Pentagon's number-one civilian had not been clued in, Laird expressed his "regret that this information was not available to me [earlier]."

Was it possible that, because of the tightly compartmentalized secrecy surrounding Operation Popeye, the Son Tay planners were not told when, or why, the POWs were moved? CIA's George Carver failed to see any connection at all between the flood or their move and Operation Popeye. Recalling, incorrectly, that few Popeye missions were flown over the area west of Son Tay that summer, he would remark: "I think you're all wet about that one." But Carver would admit in 1976 that he hadn't even thought about connecting the "coincidences" before. Another senior intelligence official would confirm, however, that his agency did know in July or early August that the prisoners had been moved. Asked if the planners would have been told, he would reply: "Yes, yes, yes." Would they have been told *before* the raid? "Yes, at the Manor level, that level." Would the Joint Chiefs of Staff have been told? "That's kind of a tough one. They might not have."

The fact is that not one of the Son Tay planners was told.

"I'll castrate anyone who knew that the prisoners had been moved, or thought it, and didn't tell me," Blackburn would remark. Even though the DIA had dramatic photos of the flood as it occurred, Mayer would insist that no one knew until November that the prisoners had been moved: "I would unequivocally, face-to-face, call whoever says otherwise a liar." Moorer would also deny that he was given any such information. It was not until the eve of the raid that the Son Tay planners learned, through Nguyen Van Hoang's pack of cigarettes, that the prisoners had left. And even then it was believed that "someone" had moved back to Son Tay.

The quantity—and quality—of the intelligence made available to the Son Tay planners was indeed remarkable. Otherwise Bull Simons and his men would not have gotten in and out of Son Tay alive, with or without any POWs. But in retrospect, the planning, execution, and aftermath of the raid must be viewed in light of the information that they did *not* have. Not until the last minute did they discover that the POWs they hoped to rescue had been moved. Not until the last minute did Blackburn discover that the CIA had inserted a CAS agent in the vicinity of Son Tay, an agent whose activities might have compromised the security of the raid. Moorer knew, DIA's Don Bennett knew. But Blackburn found out about it only by accident. Not until *after* the raid did the planners realize that the Pentagon and the White House intended to launch massive "protective reaction strikes" over North Vietnam almost simultaneously with the Son Tay rescue.

Yet Blackburn and the other Son Tay planners still knew a lot more than Manor, the man who commanded the raid, and Simons, the man who led it. Should not Manor and Simons have been warned that the camp would probably be empty? In an operation where minutes—seconds—counted, should not Simons have been prepared to touch down, look around, and get the hell out if the prisoners weren't there? It is possible that the planners thought the prospect of attacking a "dry hole" would have an adverse effect upon the morale of the raiders. It is also possible that they were hoping for some last-minute confirmation that "someone" was still at Son Tay. Whatever the reason, the raiders were not told, and with intelligence which indicated that the POWs had, in fact, been moved but that "someone" was still at Son Tay, the raid was launched anyway.

Why? Why was a raid once thought to have a 95 percent chance of success launched at all when the odds looked more like 10 or 20, or at best 50, percent? The Army's Vice Chief of Staff, Bruce Palmer, would insist that "the Joint Chiefs were never made aware, before the raid, that it had only a 50-50 chance." The CIA's George Carver, whose boss would claim soon after the raid that the CIA had not been consulted, would say that the last-minute "traffic" was "fragmentary." It indicated a "possibility" of a "dry hole." "*One* interpretation was that the guys were gone," he said. "There was a conscious last-minute debate," and Carver himself would admit that he had been "back and forth" on the phone with Laird about whether or not to "go."

But Mayer would recall that "the evidence was overwhelming," so much so in his view that "The operation would never have gone had it not been for Don Blackburn." In his own defense, Blackburn would claim that the evidence was not that conclusive. "Had I known, I'd have had to call it off." But he would admit candidly, "I didn't *want* to know. I wanted to *go*. I was looking for any straw I could find to keep that mission alive. I wanted to demonstrate that we could get in there and pull their chain. Sure, I wanted to find POWs; but I didn't *want* to know the truth, I just wanted a shred of evidence to let us hang in there. It was bigger than getting the POWs out. There were too many people who didn't have the perception to understand what this was really about, or could accomplish."

What *did* the raid on Son Tay accomplish? Some of Blackburn's cohorts, years later, would claim that the only thing it proved was how hard it is to call off an operation once military planners set their minds on it, and once the Joint Chiefs and the Pentagon put momentum behind it. The weight of the military bureaucracy. Blackburn's enthusiasm, the possibility that "someone" was still at Son Tay, the desperate plight of the POWs in North Vietnam—all undoubtedly influenced Laird's final decision to "go." Like his advisers, like the President himself, he was willing to risk failure.

Ironically, the Pentagon had avoided one failure when it learned early in the planning that Ap Lo was empty. But the news that Son Tay was empty arrived at the eleventh hour, on the heels of two reports in ten days that 5 percent of the known POWs had died in North Vietnam's prisons. The decision-makers had only hours to grapple with a new conflict, to avoid another failure—or take an even bigger risk.

Was it a risk worth taking? The Son Tay raiders failed to rescue a single POW, and while the Russians, the Chinese, and the North Vietnamese were shaken up by the raid, their subsequent actions made similar rescue attempts, as well as other operations in Blackburn's catalog of clandestine warfare, even more risky. The failure of the raid laid the Pentagon and the White House open to a new barrage of criticism about the conduct of the Vietnam War. But it did demonstrate to the world America's outrage at the treatment of the POWs by North Vietnam, and the determination of the administration to do everything in its power to bring those men home. The North Vietnamese got the message. The raid triggered subtle, but important, changes in their treatment of American POWs. In the final assessment, the raid may not have been a "failure" after all.

SIX

Hoa Lo Prison

From their cells in Camp Faith, Mo Baker and the other prisoners who had been moved there four and a half months earlier from Son Tay saw the raid unfold. There was a large surface-to-air-missile site next to the Camp Faith compound. But they hadn't known it until the battery suddenly opened fire, in salvo, one missile after another, at about 2:30 A.M. that morning of November 21. One "helluva noise" woke them up. It was like sitting on the end of a runway behind a flight of F-105s when they lit their afterburners to take off.

The prisoners leaped off their bunks and pressed their faces to the bars to see what was happening. They could see very little; the walls outside were too high. All they knew was that a "flock" of SAMs had gone out almost underneath their windows. Suddenly from the back side of their cellblock, some prisoners called, "Hey, come look at this." Looking to the west now, they saw flares being dropped, SAMs going off, flashes and explosions, "a lot of action." Immediately they knew: "Damn, they're raiding Son Tay!"

They began cheering and hollering. Some thought other prisoners must have been moved into the camp after they had moved out on July 14. Mo Baker would recall thinking, "Holy cow, there goes my ride home." Elation was mixed with disappointment.

The guards at Camp Faith were upset, frightened, acting as if "they had a riot on hand," one POW would remember. Guards bolted into the cellblocks brandishing rifles and AK-47s. They told the prisoners, "Get away from the windows. Lay down. Back to your bunks."

Mike McGrath would later recall that the guards poking their weapons into his cell were deadly serious: "They knew that we were raiding Son Tay," he would relate, "and they said in no uncertain terms that they would shoot every one of us if anyone came *near* Camp Faith. We were lucky that there wasn't a secondary target—us—or we'd all be dead." Guards in the other quadrants did not react as violently, in part because they (and the POWs) couldn't see that much over the walls, and the explosions were apparently more muffled there. Navy Ensign Gary L. Thornton, who had been held prisoner since February 1967, would insist later that he "slept through the whole thing. Oh, maybe I heard some noise, but I didn't think anything of it, and our guards didn't threaten us that much."

Air Force First Lieutenant Joseph Crecca, Jr., shot down in November 1966, noticed a SAM launch that night and thought he heard afterburners in the distance, but couldn't tell their direction. He would recall that the next morning one POW, First Lieutenant Wayne O. Smith, held prisoner since January 1968, asked an English-speaking guard what had happened. The guard told him, "Not for you to know," no matter how doggedly Smith pressed him. Knowing what would always make a North Vietnamese talk, Crecca asked the guard, "How many planes did you shoot down last night?" Almost jolly and without hesitation, the guard shot back, "One F-4 and one helicopter." Then the guard's countenance changed abruptly from a sneering smile to controlled pensiveness. Crecca disregarded the facial expressions, said "Hah!" and then told Smith, "See that, Wayne? He's full of shit. What the hell would a helicopter be doing up here?" Little did Crecca realize he'd managed to get the guard to divulge something he hadn't wanted to, nor did he attach much significance to the guard's changing expressions. Like everyone else at Camp Faith, he was moved back inside Hanoi's city limits and into Hoa Lo Prison on November 24. Only later did he understand what the odd interrogation had revealed, after he and other POWs read in the *Vietnam Courier* an item that expounded in part, ". . . constituting a dangerous act of unilateral escalation by the White House clique in trying to rescue American criminals, captured in their piratical attacks on the government and people of the democratic Republic of Vietnam."

Within hours, at "very early daylight," the prisoners found out what a "panic move was like." Guards told them to "roll up"—dishes, drinking cups, everything. That afternoon, trucks (not buses this time) drove into the prison. Blindfolded, slapped into manacles, the prisoners were jammed into the trucks and, late that evening, driven to downtown Hanoi. It was dark when they arrived, but they recognized the Hanoi Hilton. This time, however, they were marched in through the back gates. Mo Baker's entire compound from Camp Faith was jammed into one huge room. It was in an old part of the prison Americans had never been held in before. Close to 50 men shared a common "bed" that night, a 15-foot-wide slab of concrete that ran 40 feet down the middle of the room.

The prisoners immediately began to pump several English-speaking guards as well as the officer in charge: "Why were we moved?" No one would tell them. "You will know in the future," was all anyone would say. But the prisoners could figure it out. The North Vietnamese were scared. Even as intelligence officials were debriefing the Son Tay raiders in Thailand, North Vietnam started to round up the POWs from scattered camps all over the north and hustle them into downtown Hanoi. The prediction that Melvin Laird was to make five days after the raid was already being fulfilled.

The roundup continued for weeks. From North Vietnam's view, Hanoi was much better defended. The prisoners wouldn't be vulnerable to another Son Tay. Not even a battalion of madmen could bust open Hoa Lo Prison. From the prisoners' view, the roundup was the best thing that ever happened to them.

Two days after Son Tay, Navy Lieutenant (j.g.) Charles Plumb was suddenly moved to his fifth prison in three years. He had been shot down just south of Hanoi on Ho Chi Minh's birthday, May 19, 1967, on a mission against a military complex called Little Detroit. He was captured in the deadliest month of the air war, only five days before he was due to come home. After weeks of learning how effective North Vietnamese torture was in New Guy Village in the Plantation, Plumb was moved to the Hanoi Hilton with just one cellmate. Four and a half months later he was taken back to the Plantation; this time, he had two cellmates. In July of 1969, he was moved to the Zoo, with three cellmates. In September 1970, he too was moved to Camp Faith, this time with seven cellmates. Two months later, on November 24, 1970, just three days after the raid on Son Tay, he was thrown back into the Hanoi Hilton for what the guards would describe only as "security reasons." There were 57 men in his cell.

It was a dramatic change from the virtual isolation he'd known for almost three and a half years. "Alone," he would recall, "we had no counsel, no power. Alone we despaired." But with 57 cellmates, it was "like walking into the Smithsonian for the first time . . . a brand-new source of information and entertainment." Plumb and his fellow prisoners were crammed into a 25 × 35-foot room with only 14 inches of bed space apiece, but they were "overjoyed to be among comrades."

Other POWs soon joined them at the Hanoi Hilton, and after his release, Plumb would write of the changed circumstances of his captivity:

Approximately 260 POWs became organized into the Fourth Allied POW Wing. We were divided into squadrons, flights and sections. Each subdivision with its own commander attained the same pride we had once known in our flying units. Now we could act as one body—mates in one cell wouldn't be on a hunger strike while fellows in the next cells ate cookies. We had bargaining power . . . SROs now had a unified force to confront the enemy. They also had authority to control the behavior of the prisoners . . . The increasing strength from unity made an impact and our demands were met.*

The POWs reaffirmed their pledge to one another that they would "Return With Honor" and made it the motto of the 4th Allied POW Wing. Their senior officers reminded them frequently of that overriding goal. They were finally allowed to bathe daily. That November of 1970, Plumb would write, "We were happy to be able to discuss, joke, and laugh together in our larger cells, but it was especially rewarding to join for prayer in prison." They decided to rename the Hanoi Hilton "Camp Unity."

Ralph Gaither was also at Camp Faith, only 15 miles away, the night of the raid on Son Tay, his former prison. "The whole sky," he would remember, "lit up" that night. The POWs at Camp Faith heard "tremendous bombing." Some thought that air attacks against the north, at a lull since 1968, had started

I'm No Hero—A P.O.W. Story as Told to Gwen de Werff by Charles Plumb. Independence, Mo.: Independence Press, 1973.

again; others heard the helicopters and wondered if a raid might be under way.

They were washing dishes when the North Vietnamese suddenly told them to load everything—buckets, clotheslines, mops, everything—aboard some trucks. Within two or three hours they, too, were on their way to the Hanoi Hilton where they were crowded 40 to 60 men in each room, some of them only 22 × 45 or 60 feet long. "With so many men, we really got organized," Gaither would recall. "Each room became a squadron. The senior man in the room became its squadron commander, the next man down was executive officer. Other assignments were made: an education officer to correlate subject areas and persons for individual and group study; a recreation officer to correlate games, exercise and other activities; a chaplain . . . a health, welfare and sanitation officer. . . ." Within days, the POWs had made contact with most of the senior officers held elsewhere in the prison. "The new organization, the return to a high level of military efficiency, was very good for our morale." Gaither spent the next year and a half under those dramatically changed conditions. It was "a creative period" for him. He loved to write poetry and his work blossomed.

One of the Hanoi Hilton's last new guests as the Son Tay roundup continued was Navy Lieutenant Commander Edward H. Martin. Shot down on July 9, 1967, while leading a strike against Ninh Binh, he spent the first year of his incarceration in solitary. After months of that he was near death. He lived on one thought: "Six months from now, I'm going home." Every six months, he'd convince himself anew. It was his way of holding on to sanity while they worked him over in the Zoo, finally throwing him into a cell 78 inches long and 60 inches wide with four other men, sleeping on concrete, two of his cellmates in irons, unable to urinate, never getting a shower, not knowing how long they'd be there.

About 2:30 A.M. on November 21, Ed Martin, from his cell in the Zoo, saw the flares over, explosions around, and surface-to-air missiles flying above Son Tay. Instinctively, he knew what was up.

As SAMs arched into the sky almost due west of his prison cell, Martin watched them explode harmlessly only 19 miles away; they were detonating everywhere from 2,000 to 18,000 feet above the terrain. He had seen lots of SAMs—at much closer range. One had finally nailed his F-4 on July 9, 1967. On the morning of November 21, however, Martin realized that not one SAM had hit its target; he knew all too well what the explosion looked like when an SA-2 slammed into a plane in midair. He broke into tears. He knew that Son Tay was empty; but that didn't really matter, he told himself. America cared. He had his best night's sleep in three years.

Thirty-six days later, Martin found himself in relative paradise; he was moved into the Hanoi Hilton the day after Christmas, 1970. In a large room with him were 19 other POWs. Some were old Navy friends, some men he had heard being tortured in the Zoo but had never been able to talk to.

One of them was Air Force Major James H. Kasler, a hero well before he was shot down on August 8, 1966. He broke both legs on bailout and came to be held in virtual awe by his fellow prisoners. Taken to the Zoo, with Martin in a cell only 25 feet away, Kasler was put "on the ropes" one night and worked over unmercifully by a sadistic expert known only as "the Cuban." He was handcuffed, blindfolded, and beaten 700 times with a fan belt—100 strokes a day for seven days. Blindfolded, he couldn't anticipate the blows. There was no way of knowing when to tense up, when to relax; all he could do was wait. Each time he fell mercifully unconscious, the Cuban waited until Kasler came to and then started over.

Finally, Kasler said, "I surrender, I submit." Guards brought pencil and paper so he could sign his "confession." But when they told him to write, Kasler replied calmly, "I've changed my mind." His torture started all over again.

Ed Martin listened to it all. He would say of the Cuban, seven years later, "I'd pay $5,000 right now to find out who that bastard is."

Jim Kasler's fate in North Vietnamese hands wasn't made any easier by a *Time* magazine story about him that hit the newsstands just before his capture. It told of an F-105 pilot who'd become a legend among disgruntled airmen fighting an air war under "rules of engagement" imposed by Washington that made it almost impossible to hit a meaningful target, and which had turned the skies over North Vietnam into a duck-shooting gallery. But, *Time* noted, Major James Kasler somehow always got his target. No one knew how he did it. A week later he was shot down on a strike south of Hanoi. It wasn't long before Hanoi got its copy of *Time* and the North Vietnamese knew they'd nailed a big one. They kept him in solitary for years, determined to break him. Thanks to Son Tay, Jim Kasler finally got a roommate in the Hanoi Hilton.

Another of Martin's cellmates in the Hanoi Hilton was Commander Bill Lawrence, the commanding officer of fighter squadron VF-143 aboard the U.S.S. *Constellation* attack wing commander and former aide whom Tom Moorer had heard shot down on June 28, 1967, a few weeks before he became Chief of Naval Operations. Martin *saw* Bill Lawrence go down; he was leading a strike right behind him. Two weeks later, Martin himself got smoked. Wounded when his plane was hit and beaten to a pulp later, Martin soon became very, very ill. He thought he was going to die. He used the tap code to seek help. Lawrence was the man he contacted. Lawrence told him not to give up. When he didn't hear from Martin, Lawrence tapped out a message asking for *Martin's* help. It forced Martin to "get it together" and not give up. Thanks to Son Tay, Martin and Lawrence finished their "program" in North Vietnam together.

The most senior American POW was Colonel John P. "Jack" Flynn, shot down on October 27, 1967, on his 36th mission over the north, almost all of them on "Route Package Six" near Hanoi, the most heavily defended part of North Vietnam. Held in isolation from the other prisoners at the Hanoi Hilton with a few ranking officers, Flynn was nevertheless able to command the Fourth Allied POW Wing in every sense of the word. As North Vietnam moved more and more prisoners back into the Hanoi Hilton, his secret orders were quietly but quickly passed from cell to cell. Whether the other prisoners understood the reasons for them or not, Flynn's instructions were followed almost to the letter. One of his former officers would say of him, "He led his men through the Hanoi torture chambers when all he had left to lead them with was integrity."

Now a lieutenant general, Flynn would call Son Tay "the most magnificent operation of the war." After they consolidated the prisoners in the Hanoi Hilton, Flynn remembered, "we heard about Son Tay" from POWs who had been in the outlying camps. Some had seen the firing; some had heard it. Some thought it was a commando raid; others felt sure it was to take the POWs out of Son Tay.

"There was a wave of exuberance. Our morale soared,"

Flynn said. "For a while, of course, we didn't have absolute confirmation that there had been a rescue attempt, but we were pretty darned sure. What gave it away, finally, was North Vietnam's own propaganda. We heard them vilifying Vice President Agnew over the squawk box one day. They were complaining about his 'provocative' boast that the U.S. would 'go anywhere, even to the center of Hanoi,' to rescue its prisoners."

For some of the prisoners, however, word of the Son Tay raid was an omen of bad days ahead. Flynn was one of the officers who reacted this way at first. "Among the senior officers," he admitted five years after the raid, "we talked a lot about Son Tay. We reasoned, first, that it was a surprise raid of a type that could not be duplicated again. For one thing, we were all in the Hilton now; it wasn't the kind of place you could bust open very easily. Second, we asked ourselves, why would the U.S. resort to such an extreme? We concluded that the U.S. had lost its leverage at the bargaining table in Paris. Son Tay, we speculated, was a 'court of last resort'—a last chance to get us out, or to get enough of us out to regain some bargaining power, by focusing attention on the prisoner situation and showing the world how badly we were being treated.

"The conclusions discouraged us. Our original estimate had been that the war would last eight years. We said to ourselves, 'Maybe we'd better think of 15 years if we've lost that much bargaining power.' We never transmitted that to our constituents, of course. But for those of us who would have to remain (we weren't sure that there hadn't been some new prisoners in Son Tay by the time they raided it), it signaled that we'd be in North Vietnam a long, long time."

Not all of the prisoners who were moved to the Hanoi Hilton after Son Tay had been shot down over the north. Air Force Lieutenant Colonel Theodore W. "Ted" Guy was shot down over Laos on March 22, 1968. He had been kept in solitary for almost 1,000 days without ever having a roommate. At the Hanoi Hilton, put into an isolated cellblock with the other senior officers near Flynn's, he saw his first American in almost three years. He was still locked up alone, but finally he could "talk" with somebody besides a captor.

Another POW glad to have company was Ernie Brace, one of the earliest shootdowns, a CIA Air America pilot who managed to pass himself off as an Air Force major. He showed up at the Plantation late in 1968, having spent two and a half years held captive in a *cave* near Dien Bien Phu, five miles from the Laotian border. That entire time, over 900 days, he was kept in irons, alone. It was damp, dark, vermin-infested. Finally moved to the Plantation, he was slammed into a closetlike "room." It had a door and a barred window. He had to stand on his "honey bucket" to see out, but the North Vietnamese bolted shutters on the window when they caught him peeking out. When the other prisoners finally established communications with him, they asked how he liked his room. "Gee, this is all right," he told them. "It's a vast improvement over my cave."

Air Force Colonel Norman C. Gaddis, shot down on May 12, 1967, was another man whom the Son Tay raid brought out of hiding. Like Ted Guy, he too had spent over 1,000 days in solitary, most of them in Heartbreak Hotel, the most secure, isolated, and painful part of Hoa Lo Prison. None of the other prisoners had even seen him, but his name was in the "memory bank"; someone had spotted a picture of Gaddis's identification card in a North Vietnamese pictorial magazine. After the Son Tay raid, he was given his first roommate in four and a half years, Air Force Colonel James E. Bean, who also had been in solitary since his capture on January 3, 1968. Both had spent most of their confinement in Heartbreak Hotel, but were finally moved into another remote part of Hoa Lo, "The Mint," the senior officer cellblock where Jack Flynn and Air Force Colonel David W. Winn, another 1968 shootdown, were held separately in nearby cells. Other senior officers were there as well—such as Navy Commanders James B. Stockdale and Jeremiah Denton, Jr., both 1965 shootdowns, and Air Force Lieutenant Colonel Robbie Risner. All had been moved in and out of Heartbreak Hotel to other remote sections, like pawns on a chessboard, making it virtually impossible, the North Vietnamese thought, for them to communicate with the other prisoners.

For Bean and Flynn, the reunion was both joyful and painful. They learned that at least three of their fellow airmen had gone insane while held captive in the north. The three were among a group of 11 POWs called "the Lonely Hearts," men whom the other POWs had identified one way or another as being "in the system" but who were kept isolated even after the Son Tay roundup. The other eight had been shot down over Laos. The

POWs feared that they would be returned to the Pathet Lao and used as separate bargaining chips. When Mo Baker recalled those three men who had gone insane—and never came home—he would note quietly, "The Son Tay raid may have saved the sanity of some others."

One of the POWs everyone was happiest to see was John S. McCain III. Most of them knew how much he had suffered. His spirit amazed them—Jack McCain was the one who cheered *them* up, who had a sense of humor, who uplifted them. He showed them that human decency was not dead: Americans took that spirit to Hanoi, held on to it, and sustained each other with it.

At the Hanoi Hilton, one of McCain's cellmates was Nguyen Quoc Dat, a South Vietnamese pilot nicknamed "Max" as a code name used by the POWs. Born in Hanoi, he fled to South Vietnam with his family in 1954. On May 14, 1966, while flying his four hundred thirtieth combat mission, and twenty-sixth over North Vietnam, he was shot down on an air strike led by Marshal Nguyen Cao Ky. One day Max overheard some guards talking about the raid on Son Tay, the first "positive evidence" the prisoners had of it. Word quickly passed from cell to cell; throughout the Hanoi Hilton, McCain would recall later, there was an atmosphere of "elation."

Dave Sooter, a twenty-two-year-old Army warrant officer, was flying H-23 helicopters for the 1st Cavalry Division when he was shot down over South Vietnam. It was February 17, 1967, less than seven months after he'd finished flying school, when his helicopter was suddenly hit. It exploded 50 feet above the trees. Sooter remembers breathing fire. He passed out before his burning helicopter hit the trees.

When he came to four or five hours later, Sooter was already a prisoner. His captors gave him three days to recover some strength, then marched him to a camp hidden in the jungle about ten miles inside the border of northern Cambodia. He was held there for three years. On November 2, 1967, Sooter tried to escape. He was caught within hours, and his legs and arms were put in stocks while he suffered helplessly as ants and mosquitoes feasted on his festering new wounds. Within a week, he was near death. One night he "saw Jesus' face" and began praying. The next day his captors took off his stocks. That night they put them back on. When morning came, the stocks came off again. Dave Sooter turned into a devout Christian.

As well as he can fix the date, Sooter's long march to North Vietnam began on November 8, 1969. He walked for 43 days. He guesses he walked 600 miles—over jungle-covered mountains, exhausted from the tropical heat, miserable from the frequent rains, weak from malnutrition. When he reached the Demilitarized Zone between North and South Vietnam, he was put on a truck; it drove right up the Ho Chi Minh Trail, at night, and landed him a week or two later in a prison camp near Hanoi. Sooter thinks the miserable, cramped new prison may have been at Ap Lo, near Son Tay. Wherever it was, discipline at the camp was lax; the beatings were sporadic, not regular. He could not recall where he was moved next, but less than a year later, he and his fellow prisoners heard the raid on Son Tay— aircraft overhead, small arms firing, explosions, SAMs screaming through the air. Four days later, with no explanation, the North Vietnamese moved them all into the Plantation in the northern part of downtown Hanoi. Almost every prisoner who had been moved north from South Vietnam, Cambodia, and Laos was soon put into the same camp.

A few days after Sooter arrived at the Plantation, an English-speaking North Vietnamese officer told them about the Son Tay raid. He claimed that North Vietnam had known about it two weeks ahead of time. But when no one paraded newly captured prisoners or American bodies, Sooter knew he was lying. And the camp guards, Sooter noticed with relief and amusement, were too busy digging trenches and foxholes or practicing air raid drills to hassle the prisoners much.

Even before the raid on Son Tay, North Vietnamese treatment of the POWs had begun to ease—"ease" being a relative word. The POWs sensed the change after Ho Chi Minh's death early in September of 1969. Some attributed it to that; others to the massive letter-writing campaigns launched in America urging more humane treatment of the prisoners. Many believe it resulted from the fact that propaganda statements, so often extracted from the prisoners under brutal torture, had backfired. In 1966, for instance, Commander Jeremiah Denton, Jr., had been paraded before a foreign television crew. When U.S. intelligence analysts examined the film clips, they noted that his gaunt eyes were blinking oddly. In Morse code, he had managed to spell out one word: "Torture." American diplomats explained the film quietly to foreign officials around the world.

North Vietnam's campaign to extract military information by torture had also failed miserably. The interrogators spoke little English, the translators were not "hep" on military matters or America's lifestyle, and information extracted in one session or camp was seldom correlated with what had been learned in another. The men held out as long as they could, and when they finally "talked," they came up with some of the most incredible lies fighter pilots have ever concocted. At one time, Mo Baker's compound was put on the racks, one by one; the North Vietnamese wanted to learn the names of every man in their squadrons. Through the tap code, the POWs passed the word on what the new round of torture was designed to wring out of them. The information their captors wanted was ludicrously outdated, but they agreed that each man should hold out for ten days. At that rate, it would take the North Vietnamese a year and a half to extract the dope. By the time the interrogation sessions ended, North Vietnam had pieced together an odd American "air order of battle." Dizzy Dean was Mo Baker's squadron commander, Stan Musial the operations officer, and the rest of the St. Louis Cardinals were his flying mates. Other POWs "broke" as well and named their flying mates: Clark Kent, Bruce Wayne, and Captain Marvel.

Brutal as the sessions were, some questions put to the POWs left them in stitches. One interrogator pressed hard for a working diagram of an aircraft carrier. He became outraged when the POWs wouldn't tell him where its pens for pigs and chickens were located. Word of the interrogation passed quickly among the cells. Morale soared among the battered men. Time was such a horrible waste, but not without humor.

By the time of the Son Tay raid, most of the torture sessions were to extract propaganda statements, but even these had abated dramatically. More and more men were allowed to write, and receive, letters. In the first eight months of 1970, 265 men got to write home, compared with 208 in all of 1969 and only 94 in 1968. POW families received 2,148 letters in those first eight months of 1970; only 699 had come through the year before, only 256 in 1968. Yet a lot of prisoners still went without mail, as did their families. The North Vietnamese were consistent only in their inconsistency—and brutality.

And some men still suffered horribly after Son Tay. Mo Baker was caught building a radio; it was almost complete. He told his interrogators it was to get better reception of the propaganda newscasts which blared over loudspeakers throughout Hoa Lo Prison. He finally told them how it was supposed to work. When the North Vietnamese hooked it up, the loudspeakers went dead: Baker's radio had shorted them out. The North Vietnamese found a special dungeon for him. It was very deep. They kept him there for 90 days. Communicating was hard at first. One day, he finally heard "tap-tap . . ."—"Shave and a haircut, two bits." "Mo, you really pulled their chain," the message told him. Deep down in that solitary dungeon, he felt good that he had given his fellow prisoners something to chuckle about.

By the time Baker got out of solitary, the prisoners were "incredibly well organized." There were regular, communal church services (the starving POWs had forced the issue with a prolonged hunger strike); "movies" (each man reenacted his favorite), plays, and classes. Mo Baker taught college-level math, algebra, trigonometry, differential calculus—15 college credit hours of it. He had never had time to study foreign languages. In the months ahead, he learned to speak Spanish, French, *and* German. Time stopped being such a horrible waste.

In Room 4 of Hoa Lo, Lieutenant Charles D. Stackhouse, a 240-pound officer whose large frame was ill-suited for the small cockpit of the A-4 in which he had been shot down early in 1967, became the "dean" of the ad hoc academic department. Air Force First Lieutenant Joe Crecca would recall that Stackhouse arranged a curriculum starting with informal courses such as Wines (taught by Air Force First Lieutenant Edward J. Mechenbier, another 1967 shootdown), Cuts of Meat (Air Force First Lieutenant Joseph E. Milligan, also a 1967 POW), and Lumber Selection (Air Force Major Wilfred "Will" K. Abbott, held prisoner since September 1966). Future courses became more sophisticated: Crecca was one of five or six serious students learning Russian from Air Force First Lieutenants Ronald G. Bliss (a 1966 shootdown) and James R. "Jim" Shively (1967). They used a Russian text written in English that both recalled having used at the Air Force Academy, and the group learned to carry on conversations using all cases, genders, and plurals. Navy Lieutenant (j.g.) Tom "Bullet" Hall and Crecca even compiled a Russian-English dictionary of several thousand words (which Crecca eventually brought home from North Vietnam). Later, Crecca's Ukrainian friends would often tell him how amazed they were at how well he spoke their language and by his pronunciation. A former Russian army captain later said he didn't have an American accent, but a Latvian one, something Crecca still can't explain. Crecca himself taught classical music from all the masters—Beethoven, Brahms, Tchaikovsky, Mozart, Edvard Grieg, and Mikhail Ippolitov-Ivanov, among others. Among his best students: Joe Milligan, Air Force First Lieutenant Michael T. Burns (shot down in mid-1968), and Charlie Plumb. Crecca would remember little about the movie classes except that First Lieutenant Terry L. Boyer (captured late in 1967) was one of the better movie tellers.

The men were also able to give one another medical care. Some had abscessed teeth. Mo Baker was one of them; he said later that of all he suffered, the fractured thigh hurt, the torture hurt, but his abscessed tooth hurt worst. Finally, he lanced it himself. They made him the room dentist.

Spirits lifted and humor improved among all the POWs after the raid on Son Tay. Still, their release was more than two years away. The Paris peace talks dragged on; the real negotiating was done behind the scenes. By October of 1972, there were over 530 known prisoners in Southeast Asia. One of them, Army Special Forces Captain Floyd S. Thompson, taken prisoner on March 26, 1964, had spent almost ten years in captivity. Some of the POWs, however, felt almost like "outcasts." They were the "new guys" shot down over the north after the October 31, 1968, bombing halt. Heartbreak Hotel had even been renamed "New Guy Village." The first "new guy" was Air Force Captain Mark J. Ruhling, whose RF-4 reconnaissance plane was bagged on November 23, 1968. In October of 1972, three years and 11 months after being taken prisoner, he tapped out a message from Room 2 of Hoa Lo Prison: "Today I've been a prisoner longer than any American held in World War II. Don't call me a 'new guy' anymore."

Later that same month, on October 26, 1972, Henry Kissinger appeared before the White House press corps and announced that "Peace is at hand." Cynics would later comment that Nixon's landslide victory in his campaign for reelection, on November 7, owed a lot to that announcement. It proved to be premature. The North Vietnamese were not yet ready to sign. When Kissinger returned to Washington after another frustrating round of negotiations, he asked JCS Chairman Admiral Thomas Moorer how many B-52s were operational throughout the world. On Sunday, December 17, they were unleashed over Hanoi.

It was December 18, about ten o'clock in the evening, Hanoi time, when the first sticks of 500-pound bombs fell. As Ed Martin would describe that night in Hoa Lo Prison, "The whole world lit up. . . . The North Vietnamese were absolutely frantic, terrified. We cheered; we cried; we hugged each other. We knew the end was close."

For the next 12 days, B-52s, F-111s, and fighter-bombers from Okinawa, Thailand, and the Tonkin Gulf pummeled North Vietnam in an around-the-clock blitz—1,353 B-52 sorties and 3,034 fighter-bombers dropped 36,452 tons of munitions, 11 times as much destruction in 12 days as had fallen on all North Vietnam in the three *years* of 1969, 1970, and 1971. By December 30, 27 American planes and one rescue helicopter had been shot down; 93 airmen would be reported missing; 31 had been taken prisoner.

Seventeen of the planes lost were B-52s, ten of which went down over North Vietnam, the first time any had been lost there. Twenty-eight crewmen perished; 33 others survived but became POWs. Six other B-52s hit over North Vietnam crashed in Laos or while trying to land in Thailand (most so mortally wounded that they had to be stricken from inventory); another plane made it to the Gulf of Tonkin, where the crew bailed out and was rescued by the Navy. Eleven men from these seven planes were killed. Seven more B-52s crashed while en route to their targets. The Air Force called them "operational losses" and omitted them from press communiqués. Fifteen other B-52s received major damage from surface-to-air missile hits. It was a horrible loss rate. Prior to the Christmas raids on Hanoi, only one B-52 had been lost in over 112,000 sorties over Southeast Asia.

The raids had a profound impact on the North Vietnamese. On December 26, the day of one of the biggest raids, Hanoi said that the Paris peace talks could resume as soon as the bombing stopped. The next day Hanoi reaffirmed the message, saying that Le Duc Tho could meet with Henry Kissinger on January 8. The U.S. agreed to stop bombing within 36 hours of agreement on procedural details of the new talks. Kissinger would later write, "Hanoi's reply took less than twenty-four hours—an amazing feat considering the time needed for transmission to and from Paris and the time differences." He and Tho met on January 8.

Kissinger's White House memoirs would recall his cold public reception: ". . . no Vietnamese appeared to greet me at the door. . . . In fact, relations on the inside, out of sight of the press, were rather warm. All the North Vietnamese were lined up to greet us." Major General Dick Stewart, DIA's deputy director, would later remember how Henry Kissinger had become "real impressed with what you can do with B-52 bombers." Kissinger had reported that "he hadn't realized Le Duc Tho could be such a nice guy. He said he walked in to the meeting and Le Duc Tho walked up to him and put his arms around him and was hugging him and squeezing him, and he said that all of a sudden old Le had become the most friendly, warmest guy in the world." Henry said, "He just couldn't keep his hands off me."

At 12:30 P.M. on Tuesday, January 23, 1975, Henry Kissinger and North Vietnam's chief negotiator, Le Duc Tho, initialed the "Agreement on Ending the War and Restoring Peace in Vietnam." On Saturday the 27th, the North Vietnamese and the Viet Cong released a list of 617 American POWs, 55 of whom they said had died in captivity. The list proved to be ludicrously, and in some cases tragically, inaccurate. In the weeks ahead, 566, not 562, American POWs would return home alive.

The first 116 of those men, released in Hanoi, stepped down the ramp of an Air Force medical-evacuation plane at Clark Air Force Base in the Philippines on Monday, February 12, 1973. Millions of Americans, an audience even bigger than had seen Neil Armstrong and Buzz Aldrin land on the moon in July of 1969, watched on TV, choked with emotion, grateful that their ordeal was over, hopeful that the abscess created in the hearts and minds of America by the war in Vietnam would soon heal.

The first man off that plane was Navy Commander Jeremiah A. Denton. He saluted the American flag, hesitated, stepped to a microphone, and told the world: "We are honored to have [had] the opportunity to serve our country under difficult circumstances. We are proudly grateful to our Commander in Chief and to our nation for this day. God bless America." In just 33 words, he summed up eloquently what he had lived for in seven years and seven months of captivity.

In all, 661 military personnel would survive captivity in Southeast Asia: they included 566 men released during "Operation Homecoming" between February 12 and April 1, 1973; two prisoners who had refused repatriation from North Vietnam but returned home later; 30 men who had escaped (28 from South Vietnam and two from Laos); and 64 who had been released early.

A total of 141 civilians and foreign nationals were also released. Of those, 43 were captured after Operation Homecoming in February–March 1973; they included tourists, sailboat crews, and missionaries.

One of the 1973 returnees, Lieutenant Commander Philip A. Kientzler, was the last capture of the Vietnam War. Shot down on January 27, even as the lists of prisoners were being exchanged in Paris, he was released two months later, but was not the last man to be released: that was Army Captain Robert T. White, captured in South Vietnam in mid-November of 1969 and released on April 1, 1973.

Of the 468 military men (and one U.S. civilian) imprisoned in North Vietnam, not one escaped. Eighteen of the POWs who survived captivity there had made escape attempts, but most were short-lived. The CIA's Ernie Brace made four escape attempts. One lasted five minutes. Ben Purcell and John Dramesi each escaped twice. A civilian, Arlo Gay, captured in South Vietnam in April 1975 and moved to North Vietnam, escaped and evaded for 30 days, but had to give up due to starvation.

Only one American military person successfully escaped from North Vietnam, but not from a prison. He escaped just as his capture seemed imminent, so he was never listed as a POW. That was Navy Lieutenant Francis S. "Frank" Prendergast, a bombardier/navigator on an RF-5C who made a little-known but heroic escape from 200 yards offshore from the North Vietnamese coastline after his reconnaissance aircraft was shot down on March 9, 1967. Two soldiers armed with rifles waded out to capture him and took away his standard issue .38-caliber revolver, but failed to find the .25-caliber automatic he carried in a pocket of his survival vest. F-4 escort planes watched the drama as the guards ducked under the water, holding their rifles above their heads, each time one of the planes made a low pass. Prendergast saw a rescue helicopter headed his way, pulled out his automatic, and snatched a rifle away from one of the soldiers. The soldier aimed Prendergast's pistol at him and pulled the trigger, but was unaware that Prendergast always left the first two chambers unloaded. When the pistol clicked empty, Prendergast shot him between the eyes. When the second soldier surfaced, Prendergast knocked him silly with his AK-47, threw it away, got up on a sandbar, and started running toward the inbound helicopter. One of the North Vietnamese soldiers recovered his weapon and trained it on Prendergast, less than a hundred yards away, and started shooting. Prendergast held up his hands as if to surrender, and his would-be captor stopped shooting. Prendergast fired again and resumed running. The same thing happened again before the helicopter arrived, turned broadside, machine-gunned the soldier, rescued Prendergast, and returned him to his aircraft carrier, the U.S.S. *Kitty Hawk*.

His pilot, Commander Charles Putnam, had landed on the beach and was last seen running like mad with the North Vietnamese in hot pursuit. He was never listed as a prisoner of war and presumably was killed on the beach.

At least 84 Americans had died in the prisons and jungle camps of Southeast Asia, usually from torture, untreated wounds, or execution. One POW would relate that 95 percent of the prisoners held by North Vietnam had been tortured, so much so that 80 percent of them finally gave in and made propaganda statements demanded of them. After his release from more than seven years in captivity, Colonel, and soon promoted to Brigadier General, Robinson Risner would give this graphic description of North Vietnamese torture techniques: "I myself screamed all night," explaining how he and others had been forced to comply with their captors' demands. He readily acknowledged being reduced to a state where "I wrote what they told me to write. . . . If they told me the war was wrong, I said it was wrong."

Three years after Operation Homecoming, 763 Americans shot down over North Vietnam were still listed as missing in action in a part of the world their countrymen were trying hard to forget. By March of 2001, 25 years after Vietnam began repatriating the remains of missing U.S. servicemen and 11 years after the U.S. established full diplomatic relations with Vietnam, 528 of those airmen were still unaccounted for; only 235 of the missing Americans had been accounted for.

A year after their release, the prisoners of war were asked to complete a classified "survey of returned prisoners of war." It was a comprehensive 74-page questionnaire, drawn up by Air Force Intelligence and the Monroe Corporation, a small think tank specializing in POW affairs. About 320 of the returnees completed it, including 80 Navy and 20 Marine Corps former POWs.

In one part of the survey, the prisoners were asked how seven events affected their morale while in prison: "Successful resistance (winning); Son Tay raid; Ho Chi Minh's death; attempted escapes; Tet offensive in 1968; December 1972 bombing raids on Hanoi; and Bombing Halts." Their answers to each could range from "Major negative effect" over six options to "Major positive effect" and "Essential to well-being."

Two events aided morale most—by wide margins. They were the 1972 bombing of Hanoi and the Son Tay POW raid. Seventy percent of the POWs said Son Tay had a "Major positive effect" on their morale or was "Essential to well-being." About 60 percent reported the same impact from the 1972 "Linebacker II" bombing resumption. Only 30 percent of the POWs, by comparison, felt that Ho Chi Minh's death had a "Major positive effect," even though many attributed a major relaxation of prison rules and treatment to it. Twice as many POWs called Son Tay "essential" to their well-being as felt that way about the Linebacker II bombing campaign. The difference was striking, given that so many people have attributed North Vietnam's decision to sign the Paris peace accords and finally release the prisoners to the 1972 bombing.

President Nixon would later offer this summary about the operation in a letter to the author: "The Son Tay raid did not succeed in its immediate objective but had a very substantial effect on the morale of our POWs—and also gave the enemy deep concern as to their vulnerability to attack in their own territory."

Dr. Roger Shields was the man coordinating all POW/MIA activities after 1971 and in charge of "Operation Homecoming" when the prisoners were finally released in 1973. He came to his job as Deputy Assistant Secretary of Defense for International Security Affairs a few months after the Son Tay raid, but from hundreds of POW debriefs after 1973 and his own extensive visits with many of the prisoners, Shields would sum up its impact this way:

"A lot of people said it was just a foolish thing to have done, that we really didn't have enough information to succeed, and therefore concluded that it was crazy.

"It *did* succeed. It was a very, very helpful operation. There is just no question whatsoever about it. After the Son Tay raid, they were all brought back to Hanoi. There, they were able to get together and organize, to mount some kind of common defense against their captors. That organization was brought about by the Son Tay raid. The North Vietnamese did feel vulnerable, they became very much concerned about this. As a result, they brought them together. They put them in a situation where the men could communicate, organize, and support each other and care for the sick and wounded. Not only that, the morale boost that these men received was great. Some of them had been held incommunicado for years and didn't know what was going on. They were tremendously boosted to know that their country cared for them."

Shields would add: "Something else should come out of this. The *Mayaguez* raid worked and those men came home. But there was no guarantee before *it* went off that it would work. Just as there was no guarantee that the Son Tay raid would work.

"Son Tay was a very bold and very imaginative operation. Secretary Laird made the statement that had he the decision to make over again, he would do the same thing and I concur with that most heartily. When you think of the difficulties, no matter how much you rehearse, no matter what kind of maps you have, the first time you run through the real thing, there are going to be surprises.

"I would hate to see the day when Americans feel that we have to have a one hundred percent guarantee of success before we try something like this. That would mean if we didn't have the guarantee, we just wouldn't try, we wouldn't do anything. There is a chance of failure in everything we do."

Political cartoonist R. B. Crockett of the *Washington Star* probably said it best, and first, the day after the news of the Son

Tay raid broke. At the top of the *Star*'s editorial page was a drawing of a bearded, gaunt but stooped POW. His ankle was chained to a post outside his hutch. His misty eyes were watching a small flight of American helicopters fade into the distance.

"Thanks for trying."

'THANKS FOR TRYING!'

Epilogue

When Hanoi launched its final offensive in South Vietnam during the spring of 1975, South Vietnam's defenses in the Central Highlands collapsed so quickly that nine more Americans became prisoners of war. They included five missionaries, the six-year-old daughter of a missionary couple, a U.S. consular official, and the chief provincial adviser for the Agency for International Development. For five months, the nine were shifted from one detention camp to another, held captive in leaky huts crawling with scorpions and occasionally snakes. Six of them contracted malaria. There was sufficient rice to nourish them, but little else. They lost an average of 20 pounds each. Finally, they were driven by truck to North Vietnam—and imprisoned at a little compound near Hanoi. It was Son Tay.

The ninth prisoner was James F. Lewis, a fabled CIA operative, who was tortured for six months there and died. On the last day of October 1975, almost five years after the raid on Son Tay, the remaining eight were finally released.

A few weeks before the fifth anniversary of the Son Tay raid, I got a call from Melvin Laird. "Ben, now listen," he said, "about your book. There's one thing you've got to get across: that raid was a *disgrace*. It was a *disgrace*, do you hear me?"

I was stunned and asked, "Why?"

"Because they didn't promote that colonel!" Laird said. He told me that he had tried personally to get the Army's promotion board to pick Bull Simons for brigadier general. When he failed to show up on the list of 80 colonels selected for promotion in the spring of 1971, Laird said he appealed to Westmoreland to add Simons's name to the list. Westmoreland explained to him at great length that it was "impossible"—the Army had a rigid selection system, it worked, the Chief of Staff shouldn't overrule his own promotion boards, not everyone could make general, Simons was a fine colonel but he hadn't even been to one of the war colleges, just because he was an exceptional combat leader didn't mean he'd make a good general, et cetera, et cetera.

Simons retired from the United States Army on July 7, 1971, less than a year after Blackburn asked if he would volunteer for a mission he couldn't describe. Simons and his wife, Lucille, decided to raise pigs for a living on a small farm in the Florida swamps 70 miles west of where he had trained the Son Tay raiders. He once described the pigs to me as "the sweetest God damn things you ever saw."

In all the years following the Son Tay raid, Simons was invited only once to lecture at an Army service school, at the Command and General Staff College. Even though senior retired officers and notable combat leaders are regularly sought out to share their "lessons learned" at such institutions, Simons, who could be a compelling speaker, was never asked to lecture at West Point, at the Infantry School, the Special Warfare Center, or at the Army War College. He was invited to speak at the Air Force Academy and at the Armed Forces Staff College, the latter at a time when its commandant was then Rear Admiral Jeremiah A. Denton, Jr., one of the Navy's first shootdowns. A prisoner of war for seven and a half years, Denton, who became a United States Senator in 1980, once said that the Son Tay raid was the greatest thing that happened in Vietnam.

Simons never fretted about the Army's relative indifference to the combat experience he might have shared with the generation of officers who followed him. Years after Son Tay, I asked him how he felt about it. He said, "When the raid was over, I forgot it, and I haven't thought about it since then." But he was concerned that the Army was decimating its Special Forces capability. "They can produce results that far outweigh their numbers," he said. "You can demand anything of them, any God damn thing you can name, and you can demand it with impunity, without any hesitation. But it takes good leaders, good training, people who know their business."

Simons thought of Special Forces, in a way, as the 20th-century embodiment of the 13th-century Mongolian commandos who served under the legendary Colonel Yasotay, the foremost warrior in Genghis Khan's army. (Khan never promoted Yasotay because he didn't want to ruin Yasotay's warrior qualities.) As Yasotay once told his revered commander, "You do not need another general . . . But when the hour of crisis comes, remember that 40 selected men can shake the world."

Lucille Simons died in 1978; her husband withered into an increasingly lonely recluse surrounded by mementos of his wife, scores of dogs, hundreds of handguns and shotguns, and his beloved pigs. He was atrophying; during a phone visit late that year, he sounded so morose that I told him, "Bull, get off the farm or you'll be dead or nuts in a few months." Two unrelated events got him off the farm.

One was a call from Army Colonel Charles A. Beckwith, the commander of Delta Force, a newly formed, highly classified, small unit created as America's counterterrorist unit—"40 (or so) selected men" who could "shake the world" by rescuing hostages from impossible straits, men trained to "make the impossible possible." Beckwith asked Simons to come to Fort Bragg for four days to critique the unit's progress. Then Beckwith asked Simons to assess a surprise three-day training exercise Delta Force held at Eglin Air Force Base. As Beckwith would recall later, "Simons's wisdom and observations were priceless."

One of his "observations" of that exercise was typical of Simons. It was a live-fire takedown of a hostage-laden aircraft, and Simons had insisted on observing it from inside the passenger cabin. When asked later if he had anything to add to the comments of other, more senior observers, Simons said, in effect: "Charlie, it seems to me you might gain a few seconds' more surprise if your guys didn't charge down the airplane wings in their combat boots. It sounded like a freight train was coming." Delta Force quickly switched footwear for such operations.

Shortly before New Year's Eve of 1978, Simons received another call, one asking if he would consider volunteering to lead another rescue mission—but totally as a private citizen. Two employees of Electronics Data Systems, he was told, had been jailed in Tehran; even though no charges had been filed against them, they were being held on almost thirteen million dollars bail; repeated legal and diplomatic efforts had failed to win their release; finally, efforts to pay the extortionist ransom had come to naught because Iran's banking system was collapsing. H. Ross Perot, the Dallas multimillionaire (some said billionaire) who headed E.D.S., asked Simons if he would mount a private rescue operation.

Simons accepted the mission, went into Iran with a hand-picked team of E.D.S. employees in mid-January as anarchy overtook the country when the Shah fled from power, and brought the two men safely home to their families on February 19, 1979. (In doing so, Simons had helped stage, or at least exploit, what was probably the biggest jailbreak in history, freeing two Americans and 10,998 Iranians from Tehran's Gazre Prison.)

Simons refused to accept any payment for that work. As he watched the two men reunite with their families, he turned to Perot and said simply, "I just got paid." Colonel Arthur D. Simons died three months later of heart failure in a Dallas hospital.

Before he died, I asked Simons if the raid on Son Tay was the most beautiful operation of his Army career. He said, "Son Tay was about the best." But there was one thing about the raid, I had been warned, he would flatly refuse to discuss: landing at the wrong compound. He was adamant about it, until I showed him General Orders Number 32, Headquarters, Department of the Army. Dated July 13, 1971, the document was 23 pages long in single-space type. In it were all of the individual citations for the awards made to the Army Son Tay raiders. It was an unclassified document; six months earlier, I had requested the citations from the Army through normal public information channels. When I read it, I realized that the citations gave a picture of the Son Tay raid that in many respects just didn't "square" with public accounts of it.

Captain Udo H. Walther (Silver Star): "Upon reaching his first objective, Captain Walther realized his force had been landed in an area other than, but resembling the target area. . . ."

Captain Daniel D. Turner (Silver Star): ". . . leader of the command group . . . he noted that one of the assault helicopters had not landed as planned. Realizing that immediate action was required to institute an alternate plan. . . ."

Staff Sergeant Walter L. Miller (Silver Star): "Realizing that the group had landed in an area approximately 400 meters south of the objective. . . ."

Simons read the citations, turning page after page in silence. He was surprised that mention of landing in the wrong place appeared in an unclassified document. Finally, I asked him again to tell me what had really happened at Son Tay. "Let me put it to you this way," he said. "I am not prepared to repudiate what that citation says." We talked about the raid for the next nine hours.

Simons, ironically, was the one who had caused the orders to come out. A week or so before he was to retire, he realized that not one of his men had received the individual citation backing up his award for valor. Simons knew how important the citations were to the men; future promotions could hinge on just such a piece of paper. Simons wanted them in every man's personnel file, before he retired. He called the Pentagon and told some colonel that if those citations weren't on his desk before the end of the week, he was going to call the Chief of Staff personally and have the colonel castrated for taking seven months to process a few pieces of paper. The colonel probably turned to a major and said something like, "Here, get these out fast, will you?" and forgot to remind him that the citations still had to be cleared by "security review."

Simons recalled being only "slightly" miffed at Don Blackburn's odd and somewhat frantic queries from the Pentagon asking if his men had really kidnapped a baby water buffalo. Henry Kissinger put his own spin on that episode in his 1979 White House memoirs:

The raid produced a rather bizarre footnote generated by my warped sense of humor. An officer briefing me on the raid apologized for its failure. I told him not to apologize, joking that no doubt they had brought back a baby water buffalo, and the North Vietnamese were going crazy trying to figure out why we had mounted a big operation for that purpose. The officer, patriotically presuming that the President's security adviser could not be totally mad, reported this to his superiors. His superiors started a hunt for the animal. The troops in the field, convinced by now that Washington had lost its mind, reported they knew nothing about any kidnapped baby water buffalo. The Pentagon refused to believe I had made my comment lightly. Back went a cable asking to make sure by checking the helicopter for buffalo dung. The whole incident has been memorialized in a book.

Kissinger generously cited the first edition of this book. He later wrote me of the incident, "It seems to have caused even more consternation than I was aware of at the time!"

The Air Force participants were equally reluctant to discuss details of the raid on Son Tay, particularly landing at the wrong camp. Over a period of almost a year, I requested from the United States Air Force—verbally and in writing, several times—copies of the Air Force citations equivalent to Army General Orders Number 32, which were also unclassified. I got the silent treatment. Finally, I was advised that the *only* way they might be released was if I wrote a formal petition for them under the new Freedom of Information Act. I decided not to bother; by that time I no longer needed them. But I wondered why the Air Force public information system was so gun-shy about a 400-yard navigation error in the dead of night deep in hostile territory, when that error may have saved half the raiders from being slaughtered, and when men like Warner Britton reacted so swiftly and courageously to pull Bull Simons's chestnuts out of the fire.

Colonel Warner Britton is now retired, living in Mobile, Alabama. Colonel John Allison retired after being Director of Safety for the Aerospace Rescue and Recovery Service. Colonel Frederic M. Donohue went to work in the "Special Operations Division" of the Office, Joint Chiefs of Staff, the group that replaced SACSA; later he headed the special operations division of the U.S. Pacific Command. In his last assignment, he was deputy commander of the forward headquarters element of the U.S. Central Command, organized in 1983 to oversee U.S. security interests in the nineteen Southwest Asia nations bordering the Persian Gulf. He retired in 1984 after more than thirty years of active duty service. Colonel Herb Zehnder also retired; he fishes for an avocation off Ft. Walton Beach, Florida, near Eglin Air Force Base. Norv Clinebell is retired. So are Colonels George J. Iles and Rudolph C. Koller. Claude

Watkins, while also retired, lectures frequently on escape and evasion and POW affairs.

Leroy J. Manor became a two-star general commanding 13th Air Force in the Philippines and then a three-star general as Chief of Staff, U.S. Pacific Command. Since Son Tay, he has been involved in several other rescues: The *Mayaguez* in 1975—swiftly executed, it was a success but cost more lives than were saved; and the evacuation of Hue, Da Nang, and Saigon, when that tragic decade called Vietnam finally collapsed in mid-1975.

After he retired, Manor served as Executive Director of the Retired Officers Association and consulted frequently to the Pentagon on a special, high-level review board overseeing sensitive special operations. He lectured often all over the country at Army and Air Force special operations schools and at military staff, command, and war colleges. After the aborted 1980 mission to rescue American hostages from Iran, Manor served on a special Defense Department commission to "independently appraise the rescue attempt" and recommend how to improve such operations in the future.

Composed of six general or flag rank officers headed by the recently retired Chief of Naval Operations, Admiral James L. Holloway, III, the board cited 23 factors that contributed to the failure. Foremost among them was an overemphasis on operational security that, the Board said, prevented the entire rescue team from undertaking a full dress rehearsal of the operation. It also said that the Air Weather Service had failed to warn the rescue team's eight Marine Corps RH-53 helicopter pilots that huge, suspended, white dust clouds, called "haboobs," often arise over the Iranian deserts and could reduce low-level visibility to zero. The pilots had been assured they would have 40 hours of clear weather during the rescue time frame, but flew into haboobs so thick that one likened them to "a wall of talcum powder." Another described it "like the inside of a bottle of milk." Crews got disoriented; they couldn't keep each other in sight, became separated in the dust, and their leader lost control.

Moreover, the haboob closest to their destination was over 100 miles long. The helicopter part of the mission became so disorganized that one crew turned back from its 600-mile flight and returned to the aircraft carrier *Nimitz* instead of proceeding to the Desert One rendezvous site, where the helicopters were to link up with the 82 men from Delta Force and carry them to Tehran. At the time, the aircraft was only 145 miles from Desert One.

The dust clouds had been little more than an annoyance for the MC-130 Combat Talons that carried Delta Force to Desert One, but mandated radio silence precluded them from alerting the helicopters of poor visibility ahead and telling them that they could gain clear visibility by climbing several hundred feet higher and that, in any case, they would be clear of the chalklike mass in another 25 or 30 minutes. The mission failed when two other helicopters aborted at Desert One because of mechanical problems. That left only five RH-53s for the final leg of the rescue, when at least six were needed to move Delta Force and carry the rescued hostages out of Tehran.

The Holloway Board's report never did satisfactorily answer two questions that nagged special operations experts for years. First, why didn't the rescue force use Combat Talons to guide the helicopters from the *Nimitz* to Desert One, just as they had guided Manor's HH-53s throughout the 675-mile round trip to Son Tay and back to Thailand ten years earlier? Manor would note later that he tried several times to raise the question, but he said the board never pursued the issue. Some Desert One participants, however, have noted that their mission to Desert One was flown in daylight, whereas Son Tay was strictly a nighttime operation. But the tracks of Delta Force's MC-130s and the RH-53 helicopters headed for Desert One from the *Nimitz* were remarkably close to each other; in fact, they even crossed the Iranian coastline within sight of each other. A linkup would have seemed natural, especially since the Marine pilots had so little experience flying at low level in mountainous terrain. Moreover, most of the RH-53s—helicopters normally used for Navy daylight minesweeping operations—lacked the sophisticated navigational systems, forward-looking infrared systems, and terrain-following radars that distinguished the Combat Talons.

Second, how could the CIA and the Air Weather Service have failed to alert flight crews to the haboob phenomenon, which was certainly not uncommon in Southwest Asia? Manor's after-action report to the JCS made clear that weather patterns dominated planning for the Son Tay raid and dictated its timing. Didn't the Iranian planners ever read that report? Not only was the Son Tay raid remarkably similar to their challenge—in size, scope, *and* time/distance factors—but it was probably the most notable rescue attempt of the twentieth century.* Why didn't anyone consult Manor before launching the operation? Surely he would have raised a red flag about weather forecasts, having also been promised (incorrectly, as it turned out) "a 97 percent chance of having clear weather if we did it during those [two] months, [October and November]." As Manor could have reminded them from his December 1970 oral debriefing to Air Force historians, "As for tactical considerations, weather was perhaps the most important."

From 1980 forward, Manor worked faithfully without pay to head a little-known scholarship fund to provide college educations for the 17 children surviving the eight men killed at Desert One. Aptly named the Colonel Arthur D. "Bull" Simons Scholarship Fund, it eventually grew into today's Special Operations Warrior Foundation, which (as of late March 2002) has offered full college scholarship grants to over 400 children surviving the 346 special operations personnel who have lost their lives on real-world missions since 1980 or in accidents while training for them (see Appendix VII). Manor continued to serve as its chairman until mid-1999.

One month after the Son Tay raid, Donald D. Blackburn learned in an almost haphazard way that he would be reassigned from the Office, Joint Chiefs of Staff, to a research and development post on the Army general staff. On his departure from the JCS, he was awarded the Distinguished Service Medal. He retired after 33 years of military service eight months after the Son Tay raid. Brigadier General Leroy J. Manor succeeded him as SACSA.

Blackburn retired to his home in McLean, Virginia, a few miles from CIA headquarters. He too served on the Defense Department review board overseeing special operations. In the

---

*The mission's planners were not illiterate. One has to ask, hadn't *one* of them read *The Raid*? By early 1980 it had been in publication over three years, sold over 50,000 hardbound copies, and was on the recommended reading lists of several Service chiefs of staff, command and staff colleges, and several of the military's war colleges. It had been featured as a prime selection in the Military Book Club and Jeppesen Aviation Book Club and even as a *Penthouse* cover story.

den of the white brick house which he designed and built on a heavily wooded six-acre lot, Blackburn hung the usual memorabilia of a long and colorful military career—citations for a host of medals and decorations, his original commission, crests and badges, plaques from the units he led. Some things in the den, however, went far beyond the realm of usual military nostalgia.

One was a leather sheath housing a six-inch knife-bayonet. It was carried into the middle of the Son Tay Prison compound by Captain Richard J. Meadows when his HH-3 helicopter crash-landed there on November 21, 1970. A leather thong, used to strap the knife to Meadows thigh, is wound around the bayonet's sheath. Stuck in it is a 3-inch piece of rice straw. Meadows found the straw on his combat jacket when he returned from the Son Tay raid. He gave it to Blackburn the day Blackburn retired. That piece of straw, Meadows told Blackburn, was "the only thing living in Son Tay Prison worth bringing home from North Vietnam." Next to the sheathed bayonet, Blackburn framed the Son Tay patch. It sums up his last year in uniform: "Kept In Total Darkness/Fed Only Horse Shit."

Donald V. Bennett retired from the Army in mid-1974 as a four-star general, after serving as Commander-in-Chief of United Nations Forces in Korea, Commanding General of 8th Army and, finally, Commander-in-Chief, United States Army, Pacific. His last act in uniform was to recommend that his entire headquarters, USARPAC in Hawaii, be "dis-established" to save men and money, and eliminate an unnecessary "switchboard" in the Pentagon's worldwide chain of command.

James R. Allen became a four-star general and commander-in-chief of the Military Airlift Command. Lieutenant Colonel John E. Kennedy, the NSA expert who found the "eye of the needle" into North Vietnam, is dead. George Carver became the CIA's station chief in West Germany before his death. Harry D. Train II became a four-star admiral and NATO's Supreme Allied Commander, Atlantic.

Richard J. Meadows was passed over for promotion to major five years after his crash landing inside Son Tay Prison, but his combat arms branch chief—Elliott Sydnor—succeeded in appealing that decision. Meadows went on to join Delta Force and in 1980 volunteered to go into Iran early to gather intelligence in Tehran for the hostage rescue attempt that had to be aborted at Desert One because the Navy/Marine Corps helicopters broke down.

Meadows went on to serve his country as a civilian on clandestine counterdrug and counterterrorist missions in Central and South America. He died of cancer in 1999, the day before the President was scheduled to award him the Medal of Freedom. It was given posthumously to his wife, Pam. A statue of Meadows was erected in 1999 at the Memorial Plaza outside the headquarters of the U.S. Army Special Operations Command at Fort Bragg, North Carolina. Near it is a statue erected the year before of Bull Simons.

Five years after the Son Tay raid, 79 percent of the prisoners of war who finally came home were still in service. One Army POW who was still on active duty in 1983 served in Operation "Just Cause" in Grenada; four airmen and two Navy pilots served in Kuwait and Iraq during Operation "Desert Storm" in 1991. It is not known how many, if any, Vietnam POWs remained on active duty or were in the reserves by 1999 and served in NATO's Operation "Allied Force" over Kosovo and Serbia. One Air Force officer, Captain Charles A. Brown, Jr., a B-52 copilot shot down during the Christmas 1972 Linebacker II bombing raids over Hanoi, was recalled to active duty in November 2001 as a colonel heading a C-5A transport support unit at Westover Air Force Base, Massachusetts, in support of Operation "Enduring Freedom" in Afghanistan.

Thirty-one years after the Son Tay raid, only four Vietnam POWs were still in military service. One was Lieutenant Joseph S. Mobley, a 1968 shootdown who rose to become a vice admiral and retired in mid-April, 2001, as Commander of Naval Air Forces, Atlantic. The second was an Air Force reservist, Major General Edward J. Mechenbier, Jr., captured in 1966 as a captain; he spends six months a year in charge of reserve forces at Air Force Materiel Command and the other six months in his civilian career as a vice president for development at Science Applications International Corporation. In October 2001 he was appointed to the Pentagon's Reserve Forces Policy Board, which serves as the principal policy adviser to the Secretary of Defense on military reserve force matters. The third officer, Air Force Lieutenant William T. Mayall, shot down during the 1972 Linebacker II Christmas bombings of Hanoi, rose to become a colonel and in late 2001 retired as dean of the Industrial College of the Armed Forces, outlasting Mobley on active duty. The fourth was Brown, still commanding the 439th Airlift Wing Logistics Group at Westover Air Force Reserve Base as this book went to press.

Twenty-two other Vietnam POWs became general officers or admirals. One became an Air Force four-star, General Charles G. Boyd, who had been shot down in 1966 as a captain. He retired to become executive director of the Hart-Rudman Commission on National Security for the 21st Century in 2000–2001. Five POWs made three-star rank, one Air Force and four Navy. Six achieved two-star rank, three Navy and three Air Force. Eleven Air Force officers became brigadier generals.

Air Force Major Douglas B. Petersen, shot down in September 1966 and held captive for six and a half years, was elected to Congress and became America's first ambassador to Hanoi in 1997, serving there until mid-2001. Two other POWs became Congressmen (McCain and Air Force Major Samuel E. Johnson). Two POWs became United States Senators (Denton and McCain).

Thirty years after the raid, the POWs held their annual reunion over the Thanksgiving holidays in Destin, Florida, near Hurlburt Field, in conjunction with the 30th reunion of the Son Tay Raiders Association. They invited former Defense Secretary Melvin Laird to be their guest speaker at a banquet honoring the 84 POWs who had died in captivity in Southeast Asia plus the 66 POWs who had died since being returned to U.S. control in 1973 and the 25 Son Tay raiders who had passed away since 1970. Laird spoke briefly about his "Go public" campaign to focus world attention on Hanoi's inhumane treatment of the POWs. He noted that he had been an "unpopular" figure at times for causing so much ruckus over the issue; and he told of the flurry of last-minute messages, doubts, and meetings about whether or not to launch the raid. It was the first time he had ever spoken publicly about his meeting with the President on the morning of November 18, their phone conversation the evening of the 19th, and of the personal note President Nixon had then penned to him expressing his admiration of the "superb" planning behind the operation, his "complete backing" of the men about to undertake the mission, and proclaiming that there would be "no second-guessing if the plan fails." Laird received a standing ovation.

Mo Baker became a colonel. When he stepped off the plane at Clark Air Force Base in the Philippines on March 14, 1973, he was told that his wife had divorced him. In mid-1974 he married the widow of Captain Vincent J. Connolly, missing in action for seven and a half years, an RF-101 pilot shot down by a SAM over Hanoi in 1966. Those who were with him felt it impossible that he could have survived the hit. Mo and Honey Baker each had two children and they get along "famously." It is one of the most beautiful, close-knit families in America. They give can openers to their friends as housewarming presents and now live in Texas.

John P. Flynn, who led the Fourth Allied POW Wing in North Vietnam, became a three-star general and inspector general of the Air Force. He died in 1999. John Dramesi, who escaped North Vietnamese prisons twice but was recaptured, once with Ed Atterbury, went on to become the chief war planner for U.S. Air Forces in Europe and later commanded a Strategic Air Command F-111 wing. Wes Schierman regained perfect health and became a pilot for Northwest Orient Airlines. Ed Martin became a three-star admiral and in 1984 was commanding the Sixth Fleet in the Mediterranean. Bill Lawrence and James Stockdale also became vice admirals. Stockdale was awarded the Congressional Medal of Honor early in 1976 for his heroism as a prisoner of war, as was Air Force Colonel George E. Day. Stockdale retired after serving as President of the Naval War College. He wrote a book in 1984 with his wife, Sybil, about their eight years when he was a POW, and it later was made into a TV docudrama. While most still idolize him, some of his fellow POWs were more than a bit miffed about the book. Among other flaws, Stockdale wrote so much about his own (and considerable) valor and leadership inside the prison camps that he failed even to mention the sacrifices and courage of Air Force leaders like Flynn, who was shot down in late 1967 and took over from Stockdale as senior ranking officer, or "Bud" Day, who was shot down in mid-1967, captured, interrogated, and tortured (even though his arm was broken in three places and his knee badly sprained), but who nevertheless escaped into the jungle and, almost delirious, made his way to within sight of a U.S./South Vietnamese base on the southern side of the DMZ, where he was recaptured. He was brutalized for years in Hanoi for giving his captors false information and resisting their every order.

Day, a veteran of World War II, Korea, and Vietnam, retired, went to law school, and set up practice in northern Florida. He soon engaged in his fourth war—one against the United States. In early 2001, at age 76, he won a landmark lawsuit against the Secretary of Defense. A federal appeals court agreed with him that the government had broken its implied promise to thousands of World War II and Korean War military retirees, or everyone who had entered the service before mid-1956—to give them and their families no-cost health care for life. The government tried to rejoin that retirees who had entered military service before mid-1956 (when the free lifetime benefit effectively ended) were never officially promised free care, claiming that recruiters who had advertised or proffered that benefit had done so without authorization. Day has filed a motion to extend the court ruling to cover more than a million retirees. If the appeals court ruling is upheld, retirees could collect as much as $10,000 each (largely to cover the Medicare premiums they were forced to pay when denied free health care at military installations). Day's fourth war may have won his fellow service members back pay or benefits that could run into billions of dollars.

John McCain went back on flying duty commanding a training wing in Florida and then became Deputy Director of Legislative Liaison for the Navy before retiring as a captain in 1981. In 1982 he was elected to the House of Representatives from Arizona and in 1986 won election to the Senate to replace Barry Goldwater. He ran for the presidency in 2000, lost the Republican nomination to George W. Bush, and returned to the Senate to fight for campaign finance reform and won that battle early in 2002. Bill Lawrence became a vice admiral and Deputy Chief of Naval Operations in charge of all personnel and training matters. Lieutenant Commander Rodney A. Knutson went back on flying duty. He has not been bitter toward those who tortured him so cruelly from the moment of his capture in November 1965. In 1975, in fact, he told the author that he wished he could host his captors for a visit to America and said he would take them to Disney World, the Houston Astrodome, and the John F. Kennedy Center for the Performing Arts. Then he would tell them, "Okay, go home now, if you want to—and enjoy that mind-blowing form of 'civilization' you tried to cram down my throat."

Mike McGrath retired from the Navy as a captain and went on to write a poignantly illustrated book, *Prisoner of War: Six Years in Hanoi,* published in 1975 by the Naval Institute Press and still in print today. A gifted, self-taught artist, he did each of the book's 56 pen-and-ink sketches (two of which are reproduced with his permission in this book). He became the U.S. naval attaché in Ecuador and took up a second career flying seven and a half years for United Airlines, retiring from that job as a First Officer on UAL's 757s and 767s. He also became secretary, treasurer, and eventually president of NAM-POWs, Inc., a nonprofit, tax-exempt veterans' organization chartered by the State of Arizona in 1973. Membership is limited to those who were incarcerated before Operation Homecoming ended in March 1973 and as of early 2001 included 530 military and civilian personnel of the 801 POWs eventually repatriated from the prison camps of North Vietnam, South Vietnam, Cambodia, Laos, and China. McGrath has worked prodigiously to compile what is certainly the most comprehensive database that exists on both civilian and military POWs during the conflict in South Asia, which he updates regularly. He has published 50 bulletins called "MAC's Facts," disseminated periodically to all NAM-POW members via the Internet. He has worked diligently to expose almost 700 scumbags who claimed to have been prisoners of war but never were, and with the Defense Prisoner of War/Missing Personnel Office to reconcile the often conflicting data about Vietnam POW experiences.

Douglas Hegdahl, the young apprentice seaman who fell off a destroyer off the coast of North Vietnam in 1967 and was ordered by senior POWs to accept early release in 1969 to bring home a list of all POWs and make public the real story of their brutal treatment, stayed in the Navy. For more than 25 years he taught survival, evasion, resistance, and escape techniques at a special Navy school near San Diego.

Ensign Gary Thornton stayed in the Navy, got promoted to commander, and retired in Texas after teaching survival, evasion, resistance, and escape activities.

Lieutenant Frank Prendergast, who barely escaped capture from off the coast of North Vietnam in 1967, requested flight training, earned his wings, and was promoted to commander. He died early in 2001 near Los Angeles. The remains of his pilot, Commander Charles Putnam, who was last seen running up the beach with the North Vietnamese in hot pursuit, were returned to the U.S. fifteen and a half years after Operation Homecoming—in late 1988, twenty-one and a half years after his shootdown.

Ernie Brace, who had flown secret civilian resupply missions for the CIA over Laos and became America's longest-held civilian prisoner of war in Vietnam, 1965–73, much of it spent in cages in Laos, became a vice president of Evergreen Helicopters, and then went to work for Sikorsky Aircraft. He became program manager for the firm's successful effort to sell China's army its S-70C helicopter, a civilian version of the U.S. military's UH-60 Black Hawk. He lived in China for two years and returned to the U.S. to become Sikorsky's vice president of international operations, spending most of his time traveling in the Far East. In the late 1990s he became an executive of a U.S. company building electric trucks and buses in Mexico.

Lieutenant (j.g.) Edward Alvarez, the first pilot captured in North Vietnam (in the mid-1964 Tonkin Gulf incidents) but the 23rd POW of the Vietnam War, retired as a Navy commander and served in the Reagan administration as Deputy Director of the Peace Corps and then as Deputy Director of the Veterans Administration.

Army Chief Warrant Officer David Sooter went back on flying duty as an instructor pilot at the Army Aviation Center at Fort Rucker, Alabama. He went on to fly for the Central Intelligence Agency in South America and was killed when his helicopter crashed on a classified mission in 1985. Jon Reynolds became a brigadier general and the U.S. Air Force attaché in Beijing, China, from 1984 to 1988. After his retirement, he served there several more years as a vice president of Raytheon. Dick Dutton became a colonel commanding the U.S. Air Force Special Operations School in Hurlburt Field, Florida. He devoted countless unpaid hours of his time helping to set up and serve as treasurer for and a director of the Bull Simons Scholarship Fund and its successor organization, the Special Operations Warrior Foundation.

A number of POWs have returned to Vietnam since the United States established diplomatic relations in 1997. Senator John McCain was one of them, returning in the year 2000. Some Son Tay prisoners have strayed far from the usual tourist itineraries to revisit Camp Hope. One of them was William Guenon, the pilot of "Cherry One," the lead MC-130, who returned there late in 1994 with an English-speaking guide and trusted driver at the end of a trip to the first Vietnamese Transportation Exposition. He found the Son Tay compound empty, a few featherless chickens and a three-legged pig occupying one of the cells. The four prison buildings were "in disrepair, empty, and needed a fresh coat of whitewash." Their high-positioned windows were boarded over. "Clearly Son Tay had been deserted for some time." Guenon started taking photos of the place when he was abruptly stopped by local town police in faded green uniforms, who pointed angrily at the offending camera. Guenon surmised that the police were using the camp's smaller buildings, formerly guard quarters, for family housing, and they were agitated because strangers were taking pictures of their homes.

"After eternity's longest half hour," Guenon was told he could leave—but only after going to the Son Tay police station and filing a full report. There he was taken to a small upstairs room with a plain wooden table, a shaky bench, and a bare lightbulb dangling from the ceiling—"an interrogation room right out of a Hollywood set." Guenon explained that he was in Hanoi on business and had promised a friend who had been a prisoner of war to take photos of his former quarters. Not a word was mentioned or hinted about the raid Guenon's plane had led twenty-four years earlier. "Everything had to be translated back and forth between two languages, clarified, and then recorded in Vietnamese hieroglyphics." The police then demanded his exposed film, but during the ride to the police station Guenon had deftly switched film, and he turned over a bogus roll while the good one was hidden in his sock. At last he was allowed to leave: "As only a PW can appreciate, it was such a tremendous relief to finally see Son Tay shrinking in the rearview mirror." Guenon got back to Hanoi's airport at dusk, just in time to make Vietnam Airline's final boarding call.

Another returnee was Render Crayton, who visited Son Tay late in the mid-1990s and found that "the Oven" in which he'd spent most of his last two months there was one of the few structures still intact.

Nguyen Van Hoang, the senior official in the North Vietnamese Enemy Proselytizing Office whose pack of Thuoc La Bien cigarettes may have given the U.S. its best fix ever on the number and locations of American POWs, died in a Hanoi hospital of a "sudden [but unexplained] illness" some months after the first edition of this book was published, according to a cryptic mention in a Hanoi newspaper.

I have spoken with many of the men who were imprisoned at Son Tay. Some are bitter about the planning behind the raid. "Why," one of them asked, "did it take six or seven months?" To them, "weather" was a very unsatisfactory explanation. But they have nothing but admiration and gratitude for the men who actually landed at Son Tay. One of them put it this way: "If I ever run into the guys who made that raid, they'll never be able to buy their own drinks."

Author's Note

There is something about a raid that is very primitive. From the days of the caveman, the Viking, and the American Indian, the most dramatic form of military action has been the calculated gamble of small, sharply honed forces on high-risk ventures deep in enemy territory. Many such raids have changed the course of larger battles; some have changed the course of history. Yet the second paragraph of the JCS Son Tay after-action report almost apologized for the raid when it said: "In retrospect, it might appear that excessive forces and resources were committed to the operation." But the 56 men who landed at Son Tay Prison and the $7 million or $70 million which the raid cost are a striking contrast to the 3,091 lives and $21.7 *billion* that Americans spent in 1971, 1972, and 1973 to achieve the same goal—bring our prisoners of war home.

Military men hate criticism as much as anybody else (including authors). But in writing the story of the Son Tay raid it was not my intention to criticize it. No one needs to apologize for the "failure" at Son Tay. On the contrary, when seen in its full perspective, the raid might serve our national planners as a reminder of how much a small, elite, well-trained unorthodox force can accomplish. Nor was it my intention to add fuel to the controversy about the quality of the intelligence behind the raid. The revelation that Son Tay was a dry hole made the phrase "military intelligence" sound like the biggest contradiction in the English language for months afterward. Yet Simons and his men were given the benefit of the best intelligence available, often gathered against great odds; and it would have been impossible to plan—or execute—the raid without it. The story of the raid may also serve to remind critics of military intelligence what might have happened, without it, to the men who had been at Son Tay.

Little of what really happened at Son Tay was ever made public. The Pentagon doesn't like to talk about its "failures": "Other than the absence of prisoners at the objective, there were no major surprises in the operation," its commander wrote in the second paragraph of his official, Top Secret After-Action Report to the Joint Chiefs of Staff. There were other surprises, of course—lots of them. They began to turn up as I quietly started researching the story behind the raid within days of when it happened, not in the "official" accounts, but from interviews with the men who took part in the operation. For 18 months, between August of 1974 and February of 1976, I had 173 such interviews with the men who planned the raid, collected intelligence for it, or executed it—and with many of the prisoners of war they had tried to free. It would be impossible to acknowledge all of them by name. For one thing, there are too many people to thank. For another, some of those interviews were granted with the understanding that they were not for attribution and would have to remain "deniable."

Most of the interviews were tape-recorded: transcripts of just the key ones fill six 3-inch-thick loose-leaf binders. One interview lasted close to nine nonstop hours. Another spanned a period of four days, including an intensive background discussion taped during a four-hour drive from Washington to a hideaway in the mountains of North Carolina where the principal and I could visit undisturbed. Notes from interviews which were not recorded grew to fill 34 "reporter's notebooks," and almost four file drawers of maps, photographs, official documents, news clippings, and correspondence were annotated and cross-referenced to the interviews. Whenever possible, quotations in the book have been taken *verbatim* from interviews, or from notes made by the participants at the time of the raid. But others had to be reconstructed from their recall of a meeting or conversations that took place five or more years before. I tried to interview most of the participants in such meetings, but it was not always possible. President Richard M. Nixon, for instance, chose never to discuss the final anxious moments in which he agreed to let the raid proceed, in the face of mounting evidence that it would be futile. He did, however, write me from San Clemente after the first edition of this book came out to praise the Son Tay raiders:

The men who participated in this project were magnificent in every respect. I am grateful that you have given them the credit they deserve.

Melvin Laird would wait more than 30 years to reveal his several conversations with Nixon in those difficult hours. In 2001 he agreed to let me print Nixon's handwritten note to him reaffirming, "regardless of results," his "complete backing" of the mission and saying, "There will be no second-guessing if the plan fails. It is worth the risk. . . ."

It was also impossible to obtain another very important perspective on the raid. I requested, but never received, permission from the North Vietnamese to visit Son Tay Prison and to interview military officials in Hanoi for their impressions of and reactions to this operation. Nor would the Vietnamese embassy in Washington return phone calls or answer letters asking who was at the Secondary School, even 30 years after the raid.

During my interviews, many of those who planned the raid—and even more of those who participated in it—expressed surprise about things they *still* hadn't been told of an operation to which they dedicated months of their lives or risked their lives to execute. Bull Simons told me in one interview, for instance, "You know, I'm beginning to think you know more about this God damn operation than I do." Some of the officials I interviewed were aghast that I had learned that the largest part of the raiding force had landed in the wrong camp. Others were concerned that I had found out that they knew, before the raid, that Son Tay had been empty of prisoners for four and a half months, and that they had corroboration of that information 24 hours before the raid was launched.

Some "facts" about the raid, of course, are still in dispute. Inevitably, I had to sort out differing recollections, some of them dimmed by time, to determine what really happened.

One example will illustrate how widely recollections of the mission differed, even among those "in the know." Henry Kissinger said of the mission in his 1979 White House memoirs:

The Son Tay raid, carried out on November 20, was meticulously planned and heroically executed but was based on an egregious failure of intelligence: The prison had been closed at least three months earlier. We knew the risk of casualties, but none of the briefings that led to the decision to proceed had ever mentioned the possibility that the camp might be empty. *After* the failure of the raid I was informed of a message sent in code by a prisoner of war that the camp was "closed" on July 14. [Original emphasis.] This was interpreted by military analysts to mean that the gates were locked; it had not been considered of sufficient importance to bring to the attention of the White House.

If Kissinger's recollection is accurate, it must mean that President Nixon felt Kissinger had no need to know what Laird had told him on November 19, just before the raid was launched. Kissinger's suggestion that military analysts interpreted "the camp was 'closed' " to mean "that the gates were locked" reflects an insulting appreciation of military intelligence, which performed superbly in this instance: one has to wonder if Kissinger naively believed that prison gates were usually left open.

In other instances, even highly classified official reports were misleading in important particulars, to put it kindly. On December 30, 1970, for instance, barely a month after the raid, General Manor gave a detailed oral account of the mission at his own Eglin AFB headquarters to the Office of Air Force History and the historian of USAF Special Operations Forces—his own command. The account was taped and transcribed. Originally classified Secret, it was later downgraded to Confidential and fully declassified at the end of 1978. Except for highly compartmented intelligence information requiring special access clearances, the 15-page transcript (plus tables and charts) was an unusually complete, succinct report on the operation. But there was one material omission from Manor's report: he never mentioned that part of the raiding force had landed by mistake at the Secondary School and obliterated the enemy force there.

Yet he had stressed contingency planning "to respond to emergencies on the ground also. For example, we had three troop-carrying helicopters; had we lost one of those, again for mechanical reasons or enemy action, we could still do the job with the two that remained. If we lost more than one, we would have to abort the mission." Toward the end of that interview, Manor said, "In summary, I can unequivocally state that other than the absence of prisoners at the objective, there were no major surprises in the operation." Given the highly classified nature of that account, it was tantamount to a false official statement. Little wonder that his fellow airmen would prove reluctant for years to discuss landing at the wrong camp.

Moreover, Manor made the same exact statement to begin the second paragraph of his signed, five-page "Commander's Comments" or summary introducing his task force's three-volume 1981 Top Secret After-Action Report to the Joint Chiefs of Staff:

> 2. I can unequivocally state that, other than the absence of prisoners at the objective, there were no major surprises in the operation.

I wrote to Manor asking about those omissions, but he declined to reply. Late in 2001 he told retired Colonel John Gargus, his lead MC-130 navigator on the operation, who had just reminded Manor that I still wanted to discuss his categorical statements about "no [other] major surprises," that the landing at the Secondary School "was blown out of all proportion by the media." Considering the calm and valor with which Captain Udo Walther and his team, Bull Simons, and Colonel Warner Britton had obliterated what could have been a devastating threat to the entire Son Tay mission, I found Manor's disclaimer distasteful.

Where such discrepancies were material to the story, I have tried to present both sides. A case in point is the controversy over Operation Popeye and the extent to which it triggered the flood that caused the North Vietnamese to move the prisoners from Son Tay in mid-July of 1970, four and a half months before the raid. In other cases, I found that documentary evidence needed to verify points in dispute no longer existed; some of it, I discovered, was destroyed at the very time I began questioning conflicting versions of the raid. There is some uncertainty, for instance, over just how much detail Air Force intelligence had, at the time SACSA was first briefed on May 25, 1970, on the request by six prisoners in Son Tay to be rescued. In searching for the records of that briefing, I was told in the fall of 1975 that they had been destroyed during an earlier, "routine" purging of sensitive JCS files—even though they had been carefully marked never to be destroyed.

My research was also complicated by the fact that the intelligence behind and planning for the raid was so "compartmentalized" that very few individuals were privy to "the big picture." I am grateful for the candid and lengthy interviews I have enjoyed with those few people who did have that visibility, and were willing to talk about it. One Pentagon official told me jokingly one day, "Maybe you should subtitle the book, 'More About the Son Tay Raid Than We Ever Intended to Make Known.'" The book has not been "censored" by the Pentagon, however, or any other agency or individual. But I am very grateful to several men who gave privately of their time to review parts of the draft manuscript, pointed out errors, inconsistencies or conflicts, and provided leads that made it possible to resolve most of them.

In lieu of thanking by name each individual who contributed to my research, I simply would like to thank all of them—for letting me tell their story. They are a unique group, dedicated military guys who made no big deal about volunteering and risking their lives to rescue their fellow soldiers—men who were strangers to them.

I am particularly indebted to several individuals among the Son Tay raiders and POWs without whose help and information this revised and updated version of *The Raid* might never have gone to press. (As is the case throughout this book, all ranks shown are those each individual held at the time of the raid or when a POW was captured. Among groups of individuals, people are listed in alphabetical order.)

Among the Son Tay raiders, particular thanks go to then SSgt. Thomas E. Powell, who landed with Bull Simons at the Secondary School as part of Udo Walther's Greenleaf element and who has been administrator of the Son Tay Raiders Association since it was formed. He has been diligent over the years in advising me of errors he and his fellow raiders have found either in the original 1976 Harper & Row hardbound edition of *The Raid* or the revised 1986 Avon paperback version. Others from the ground force have provided especially helpful new data for this update: SFC Jake Jakovenko, MSgt. Thomas

J. Kemmer, MSgt. Joe Lupyak, Lt. Col. Bud Sydnor, Capt. Dan Turner (who led Sydnor's Redwine team), and Capt. Udo Walther. Several Air Force members of the strike force were equally helpful in providing new insight. Foremost among them: Maj. Marty Donohue, Maj. John Gargus, Capt. William Guenon, Capt. Ted Lowry, Lt. Col. Larry Ropka, Maj. John Waresh, and Lt. Col. Herb Zehnder.

Thanks to Army CWO3 David Sooter and the many Air Force POWs who gave unselfishly of their time to help me flesh out their story: Col. Mo Baker, Capt. Joe Crecca, Col. Bud Day, Col. John Dramesi, Col. Dick Dutton, Lt. Gen. John Flynn, Col. James Kasler, Brig. Gen. Jon Reynolds, Brig. Gen. Robbie Risner, Maj. Wes Schierman, Col. Robert Stirm, and Brig. Gen. Dave Winn. In the Navy, I owe similar thanks to Capt. Render Crayton, Capt. Jack Ensch, Cdr. Paul Galanti, Capt. Rod Knutson, V. Adm. William Lawrence, Capt. John S. McCain III, Capt. Red McDaniel, Cpt. Mike McGrath, V. Adm. Edward Martin, Capt. Howie Rutledge, and Cdr. Gary Thornton.

Other individuals warrant my thanks as well (most of which is woefully belated because for two and a half decades I have not wanted to suggest they were "sources"): Gen. James Allen, Cdr. Brent Baker of the Navy's Chief of Information staff in 1976; Lt. Gen. Donald V. Bennett and Maj. Gen. Richard Stewart of DIA; retired Brig. Gen. Donald D. Blackburn and retired Col. Ed E. Mayer of SACSA; David E. Coffey, who retired in 1995 from CIA's Science & Technology Directorate and was honored on the Agency's 50th anniversary in 1997 as one of 50 people who had made the "most significant contributions" to its work; retired General Alexander M. Haig, Jr.; JCS Chairman Admiral Thomas E. Moorer; former Secretary of Defense Melvin R. Laird and his senior military assistant, Lt. Gen. Robert Pursley; retired Col. Marty Schiller of DIA; Cdr. Donald Sewell of the OSD public affairs staff in 2001; V. Adm. Harry Train, Director of the Joint Staff in 1976; retired Air Force MSgt. Claude Watkins—and, above all, Col. Arthur D. "Bull" Simons.

I started researching the Son Tay story soon after the 1970 raid took place, but I didn't begin nonstop work on this book until mid-1974, two months after the death of my first wife, Cynthia Blythe Sweatt Schemmer. My son and I were sitting in our living room one evening when we found a note she had written almost two years earlier but somehow knew I would find at that turning point in my life. It was a very beautiful note and read in part, "To my beloved—because he knows the other half that hasn't been printed. Please write it now."

My son, Clinton Howard Schemmer, was 16 and even at that age was becoming a gifted journalist, writing an occasional piece for our local weekly paper. He spurred me on to write this story the way he knew his mother wanted it to be done. When I began to bog down or when answers to certain questions seemed so bizarre that at times I thought I was writing fiction, his excitement over what really happened at Son Tay inspired me to keep working. So did his reaction to interviews we enjoyed together in the year and a half that followed, and then his frequent, enthusiastic question from the University of Montana, "How's the book going, Dad?"

I dedicated the first editions of *The Raid* to his mother and thought of her often in the years that followed, especially when President Nixon wrote me after the book was published: "The men who participated in this project were magnificent in every respect. I am grateful that you have given them the credit they deserve."

This updated and revised version of *The Raid* was inspired by Elizabeth Teresa Rakauskas Schemmer, whom I fortuitously met in 1992 after a number of doctors declared that I had but a month or two to live. She made me realize that I didn't want to die, made me regain my health, married me in 1996, and rekindled my life. Many of the Vietnam POWs and Son Tay raiders have come to love her almost as much as I do, and she has shared my quest to get their story right.

Benjamin F. Schemmer

Naples, Florida
April 2, 2002

APPENDIX I

The Son Tay Prisoners

All of the POWs held at Son Tay were known to have been captured, as opposed to being carried on "missing-in-hostile-action" lists.

United States Air Force

Of the 333 USAF personnel who were captured and later returned to U.S. control by the North Vietnamese, 45, or just over 13½ percent, were imprisoned at Son Tay. The ranks shown below are as of the dates individuals were shot down.

Rank	Name	Date Shot Down or Reported Missing	Date Returned to U.S. Control
Maj.	Elmo C. Baker	23 Aug 67	14 Mar 73
Capt.	Charles G. Boyd	22 Apr 66	12 Feb 73
1st Lt.	Richard C. Brenneman	8 Nov 67	14 Mar 73
1st Lt.	Edward A. Brudno	18 Oct 65	12 Feb 73
Maj.	Alan L. Brunstrom	22 Apr 66	12 Feb 73
1st Lt.	Hubert E. Buchanan	16 Sep 66	4 Mar 73
Maj.	William D. Burroughs	31 Jul 66	4 Mar 73
Dr.	William W. Butler	20 Nov 67	14 Mar 73
Capt.	Larry E. Carrigan	23 Aug 67	14 Mar 73
1st Lt.	Larry J. Chesley	16 Apr 66	12 Feb 73
Capt.	John W. Clark	12 Mar 67	18 Feb 73
Capt.	Thomas E. Collins, III	18 Oct 65	12 Feb 73
Capt.	Thomas J. Curtis	20 Sep 65	12 Feb 73
1st Lt.	Myron L. Donald	23 Feb 68	14 Mar 73
1st Lt.	Jerry D. Driscoll	24 Apr 66	12 Feb 73
Capt.	Richard A. Dutton	5 Nov 67	14 Mar 73
1st Lt.	Leon F. Ellis	17 Dec 67	14 Mar 73
Capt.	Kenneth Fisher	7 Nov 67	14 Mar 73
1st Lt.	Frederic R. Flom	8 Aug 66	4 Mar 73
Capt.	Willis E. Forby	20 Sep 65	12 Feb 73
Capt.	David E. Ford	19 Nov 67	14 Mar 73

1st Lt.	Henry P. Fowler, Jr.	26 Mar 67	18 Mar 73
1st Lt.	David F. Gray, Jr.	23 Jan 67	4 Mar 73
Capt.	Charles E. Greene, Jr.	11 Mar 67	4 Mar 73
Capt.	Carlisle S. Harris	4 Apr 65	12 Feb 73
Capt.	David B. Hatcher	30 May 66	12 Feb 73
Capt.	Julius S. Jayroe	19 Jan 67	4 Mar 73
Capt.	Robert D. Jeffrey	20 Dec 65	12 Feb 73
Maj.	Thomas M. Madison	19 Apr 67	4 Mar 73
Maj.	Louis F. Makowski	6 Oct 66	4 Mar 73
1st Lt.	Ronald L. Mastin	16 Jan 67	4 Mar 73
1st Lt.	Thomas N. Moe	16 Jan 68	14 Mar 73
Capt.	Robert D. Peel	31 May 65	12 Feb 73
Maj.	Ben M. Pollard	15 May 67	4 Mar 73
1st Lt.	James E. Ray	8 May 66	12 Feb 73
Capt.	Jon A. Reynolds	28 Nov 65	12 Feb 73
Capt.	Wesley D. Schierman	28 Aug 65	12 Feb 73
Capt.	Bruce G. Seeber	5 Oct 65	12 Feb 73
Maj.	Richard E. Smith, Jr.	25 Oct 67	14 Mar 73
Maj.	Robert L. Stirm	27 Oct 67	14 Mar 73
Capt.	Thomas G. Storey	16 Jan 67	4 Mar 73
1st Lt.	Leroy W. Stutz	2 Dec 66	4 Mar 73
Capt.	Russell E. Temperley	27 Oct 67	14 Mar 73
Maj.	Irby D. Terrell, Jr.	14 Jan 68	14 Mar 73
1st Lt.	Gerald S. Venanzi	17 Sep 67	14 Mar 73
Capt.	Lawrence D. Writer	15 Feb 68	14 Mar 73

United States Navy

Of the 145 Navy pilots who were captured and later returned to U.S. control by the Vietnamese, 16, or just over 11 percent, were imprisoned at Son Tay.

Rank	Name	Date Shot Down or Reported Missing	Date Returned to U.S. Control
Lt. (j.g.)	Wendell R. Alcorn	22 Dec 65	12 Feb 73
Lt. Cdr.	Claude D. Clower	19 Nov 67	14 Mar 73
Lt. Cdr.	Render Crayton	7 Feb 66	12 Feb 73
Lt. (j.g.)	Michael P. Cronin	13 Jan 67	4 Mar 73
Lt. Cdr.	Robert H. Doremus	24 Aug 65	12 Feb 73
Lt. (j.g.)	Ralph E. Gaither, Jr.	17 Oct 65	12 Feb 73
Lt.	Paul E. Galanti	17 Jun 66	12 Feb 73
Lt.	Danny E. Glenn	21 Dec 66	4 Mar 73
Lt. (j.g.)	Wayne K. Goodermote	13 Aug 67	14 Mar 73
Lt.	John Heilig	5 May 66	12 Feb 73
Lt.	Wilson D. Key	17 Nov 67	14 Mar 73

Lt.	Dennis A. Moore	27 Oct 65	12 Feb 73
Lt.	Robert J. Naughton	18 May 67	4 Mar 73
Lt. (j.g.)	Theodore G. Stier	19 Nov 67	14 Mar 73
Ensign	Gary L. Thornton	20 Feb 67	4 Mar 73
Lt. (j.g.)	William M. Tschudy	18 July 65	12 Feb 73

United States Marine Corps

Of 37 Marine Corps officers who were captured by the North Vietnamese, 4, or just under 11 percent, were imprisoned at Son Tay.

Rank	Name	Date Shot Down or Reported Missing	Date Returned to U.S. Control
Maj.	John H. Dunn	7 Dec 65	12 Feb 73
CWO-4	J. W. Frederick	5 Dec 65	Died in captivity
Capt.	Orson G. Swindle, III	11 Nov 66	4 Mar 73
1st Lt.	James H. Warner	13 Oct 67	14 Mar 73

APPENDIX II

The Son Tay Raiders

United States Army

Support Group

Rank	Name	Parent Organization
Col.	Arthur D. Simons	Hq. XVIII Abn Corps
Capt.	Eric J. Nelson	Co B, 7th SFG
Capt.	Glenn R. Rouse	HHC, 2nd Bn USAIMA
Capt.	Udo H. Walther	Co D, 6th SFG
SFC	Earl Bleacher	2d Bn, USAIMA
SFC	Leroy N. Carlson	Co C, 7th SFG
SFC	John Jakovenko	Co C, 6th SFG
SFC	Jack G. Joplin	HHC, 6th SFG
SFC	Daniel Jurich	Co B, 7th SFG
SFC	David A. Lawhon, Jr.	Co C, 7th SFG
SFC	Salvador M. Suarez	Co B, 6th SFG
SFC	Donald E. Taapken	Co C, 6th SFG
SFC	Richard W. Valentine	Co B, 7th SFG
SSgt.	Walter L. Miller	Sig Co, 6th SFG
SSgt.	Robert L. Nelson	Co B, 6th SFG
SSgt.	David S. Nickerson	Sig Co, 6th SFG
SSgt.	Thomas E. Powell	Co D, 7th SFG
SSgt.	John E. Rodriquez	Co C, 6th SFG
Sgt.	Gary D. Keel	Co C, 6th SFG
Sgt.	Keith R. Medenski	Co B, 6th SFG
Sgt.	Franklin D. Roe	Co B, 6th SFG
Sgt.	Marshall A. Thomas	Co D, 6th SFG

Assault Group

Rank	Name	Parent Organization
Capt.	Richard J. Meadows	Det 1, USAIS
Capt.	Thomas W. Jaeger	Co A, 7th SFG
Capt.	Dan H. McKinney	Co D, 7th SFG
1st Lt.	George W. Petrie	Co D, 6th SFG
MSgt.	Thomas J. Kemmer	Co B, 6th SFG
MSgt.	Billy K. Moore	Co C, 6th SFG

MSgt.	Galen C. Kittleson	Co B, 6th SFG
SFC	Anthony Dodge	2d Bn, USAIMA
SFC	Lorenzo O. Robbins	Co B, 6th SFG
SFC	William L. Tapley	Co C, 6th SFG
SFC	Donald R. Wingrove	Co D, 6th SFG
SSgt.	Charles G. Erickson	Co B, 7th SFG
SSgt.	Kenneth E. McMullin	HHC, 6th SFG
Sgt.	Patrick St. Clair	Co C, 6th SFG

Command Group–Security

Rank	Name	Parent Organization
Lt. Col.	Elliott P. Sydnor, Jr.	Det 1, USAIS
Lt. Col.	Joseph R. Cataldo	Surgeon General, Hq DA
Capt.	James W. McClam	Co A, 6th SFG
Capt.	Daniel D. Turner	Co A, 6th SFG
MSgt.	Joseph W. Lupyak	Co D, 7th SFG
MSgt.	Herman Spencer	Co C, 7th SFG
SFC	Tyrone J. Adderly	Co A, 6th SFG
SFC	Donald D. Blackard	Co B, 7th SFG
SFC	Freddie D. Doss	HHC, 6th SFG
SFC	Jerry W. Hill	2d Bn, USAIMA
SFC	Marion S. Howell	Co A, 6th SFG
SFC	Billy R. Martin	Co A, 6th SFG
SFC	Gregory T. McGuire	Co A, 6th SFG
SFC	Charles A. Masten, Jr.	Co D, 6th SFG
SFC	Joseph M. Murray	Co A, 6th SFG
SFC	Noe Quezada	Co D, 7th SFG
SFC	Ronnie Strahan	Co B, 6th SFG
SSgt.	Paul F. Poole	Co B, 6th SFG
SSgt.	Lawrence Young	2d Bn, USAIMA
Sgt.	Terry L. Buckler	Co D, 7th SFG

Support Personnel

Rank	Name	Parent Organization
Lt. Col.	Bill L. Robinson	Co D, 6th SFG
Lt. Col.	Gerald Kilburn	HHC, JFKCMA
Capt.	Randle L. Smith	HHC, JFKCMA
Sgt. Maj.	Minor B. Pylant	Co A, 6th SFG
MSgt.	Jesse A. Black	Co A, 7th SFG
MSgt.	Edgar C. Britt	Co A, 6th SFG
MSgt.	Bernard L. Rauscher	Co D, 6th SFG
SFC	Franklin B. Abramski	Co B, 7th SFG
SFC	James A. Bass	HHC, 6th SFG
SFC	Archie Batrez, Jr.	Co D, 6th SFG
SFC	Robert L. Dodd	Co A, 7th SFG
SFC	Charles M. Erwin	Co D, 6th SFG
SFC	James A. Green	Co A, 6th SFG

SFC	Bobby R. Hansley	Co B, 7th SFG
SFC	Roswell D. Henderson	Co D, 7th SFG
SFC	Frederick L. Hubel	Co B, 7th SFG
SFC	Bruce M. Hughes	Co D, 7th SFG
SFC	John R. Jourdan	Co B, 7th SFG
SFC	Ernest R. Pounder	Co A, 7th SFG
SFC	Aaron L. Tolson, Jr.	Co D, 6th SFG
SFC	Burley W. Turner	Co D, 7th SFG
SFC	Grady C. Vines	Co C, 7th SFG
SSgt.	Elmer D. Adams	Co D, 6th SFG
SSgt.	Rodger D. Gross	HHC, 7th SFG
SSgt.	Larry G. Stroklund	Co A, 6th SFG
SSgt.	David L. Wilson	Co C, 6th SFG
Sgt.	Brian J. Budy	Co B, 6th SFG
Sgt.	Michael G. Green	Co C, 6th SFG
Sgt.	Robert R. Hobdy	Sig Co, 6th SFG
Sgt.	John J. Lippert	Co D, 7th SFG
Sgt.	Arlin L. Olson	Co D, 6th SFG
Spec. 5	Willard F. Dezurik	Co D, 6th SFG
Spec. 5	Lawrence C. Elliott	HHC, 6th SFG
Spec. 5	Gary R. Griffin	Co D, 6th SFG
Spec. 4	Christopher Casey	Co B, 6th SFG
Spec. 4	Frank J. Closen	Co B, 6th SFG

UH-1 Aircraft Crew Members

Rank	Name	Parent Organization
1st Lt.	George W. Williams	6th SFG
CWO-2	Ronald J. Exley	6th SFG
CWO-2	Jackie H. Keele	6th SFG
CWO-2	John J. Ward	6th SFG
Spec. 6	Larry C. Boots	6th SFG
Spec. 4	Alan H. Wood	82nd Abn Div

United States Air Force

Assault Force

Aircraft	Code Name	Rank	Name	Parent Organization
HH-3	Banana 1	Lt. Col.	Herbert R. Zehnder	ARRTC
		Maj.	Herbert D. Kalen	ARRTC
		TSgt.	Leroy M. Wright	ARRTC
HH-53	Apple 1	Lt. Col.	Warner A. Britton	ARRTC
		Maj.	Alfred C. Montrem	ARRTC
		MSgt.	Harold W. Harvey	ARRTC

		MSgt.	Maurice F. Tasker	ARRTC
		SSgt.	Jon K. Hoberg	40th ARRS
HH-53	Apple 2	Lt. Col.	John V. Allison	ARRTC
		Maj.	Jay M. Strayer	40th ARRS
		TSgt.	William E. Lester	ARRTC
		TSgt.	Charlie J. Montgomery	ARRTC
		SSgt.	Randy S. McComb	40th ARRS
HH-53	Apple 3	Maj.	Frederic M. Donohue	ARRTC
		Capt.	Thomas R. Waldron	ARRTC
		SSgt.	Aron P. Hodges	ARRTC
		SSgt.	James J. Rogers	ARRTC
		SSgt.	Angus W. Sowell, III	ARRTC
HH-53	Apple 4	Lt. Col.	Royal C. Brown	37th ARRS
		Maj.	Roy R. Dreibelis	37th ARRS
		TSgt.	Lawrence Wellington	ARRTC
		SSgt.	Wayne L. Fisk	40th ARRS
		SSgt.	Donald Labarre	ARRTC
HH-53	Apple 5	Maj.	Kenneth D. Murphy	703d SO Sqdn
		Capt.	William M. McGeorge	40th ARRS
		TSgt.	David F. McLeod	ARRTC
		SSgt.	John J. Eldridge	40th ARRS
		SSgt.	Daniel E. Galde	ARRTC
HC-130P	Lime 01	Maj.	William J. Kornitzer, Jr.	ARRTC
		Capt.	Richard E. Frank	39th ARRS
		Maj.	Jerry T. Felmley	39th ARRS
		Capt.	Charles P. McNeff	39th ARRS
		SSgt.	Aaron Swimson	39th ARRS
		MSgt.	Johnie Bomans	39th ARRS
		MSgt.	Holley V. Keel	39th ARRS
		Sgt.	Samuel L. Waters	39th ARRS
HC-130P	Lime 02	Capt.	Clyde O. Westbrook, Jr	39th ARRS
		Capt.	John H. Pletcher, Jr.	39th ARRS
		Capt.	Bruce J. Host	39th ARRS
		SSgt.	Luther F. Hollums	39th ARRS
		MSgt.	Richard D. Klasser	39th ARRS
		MSgt.	Lawrence Durbin	39th ARRS
MC-130	Cherry 1	Maj.	Irl L. Franklin	7th SO Sqdn
		Maj.	Thomas L. Mosley	7th SO Sqdn
		Capt.	Randal D. Custard	7th SO Sqdn
		Capt.	Thomas K. Eckhart	7th SO Sqdn
		Capt.	William A. Guenon, Jr.	7th SO Sqdn
		Capt.	James F. McKenzie, Jr.	7th SO Sqdn
		Capt.	Thomas L. Stiles	7th SO Sqdn
		MSgt.	Leslie G. Tolman	7th SO Sqdn
		TSgt.	William A. Kennedy	7th SO Sqdn

		TSgt.	Kenneth C. Lightle	7th SO Sqdn
		TSgt.	James M. Shepard	7th SO Sqdn
		SSgt.	Earl D. Parks	7th SO Sqdn
MC-130	Cherry 2	Lt. Col.	Albert P. Blosch	Det 2, 1st SOW
		Maj.	John Gargus	Det 2, 1st SOW
		Maj.	Harry L. Pannill	Det 2, 1st SOW
		Capt.	John M. Connaughton	Det 2, 1st SOW
		Capt.	David M. Kender	Det 2, 1st SOW
		Capt.	Norman C. Mazurek	Det 2, 1st SOW
		Capt.	William D. Stripling	Det 2, 1st SOW
		TSgt.	Dallas T. Criner	Det 2, 1st SOW
		TSgt.	Billy J. Elliston	Det 2, 1st SOW
		TSgt.	Jimmie O. Riggs	Det 2, 1st SOW
		TSgt.	Paul E. Stierwalt	Det 2, 1st SOW
		SSgt.	Melvin B. D. Gibson	Det 2, 1st SOW

Assault Force Alternates Who Did Not Fly

Aircraft	Code Name	Rank	Name	Parent Organization
HH-3	Banana 1	Maj.	David E. Vaughn	37th ARRS
MC-130	Cherry 1	SSgt.	Robert L. Renner	7th SO Sqdn
MC-130	Cherry 2	Lt. Col.	Cecil M. Clark	Det 2, 1st SOW
		Capt.	Ronald L. Jones	Det 2, 1st SOW
MC-130	Cherry 2	TSgt.	Failus Potts	Det 2, 1st SOW
		SSgt.	William J. Brown	Det 2, 1st SOW

Attack Group

Aircraft	Code Name	Rank	Name	Parent Organization
A-1	Peach 1	Maj.	Edwin J. Rhein, Jr.	1st SOW
		Maj.	John C. Waresh	56th SOW
A-1	Peach 2	Maj.	James R. Gochnauer	1st SOW
		Capt.	Robert M. Senko	56th SOW
A-1	Peach 3	Maj.	Richard S. Skeels	1st SOW
		Lt.	James C. Paine	56th SOW
A-1	Peach 4	Maj.	Eustace M. Bunn	1st SOW
		Capt.	Robert H. Skelton	56th SOW
A-1	Peach 5	Maj.	John C. Squires	1st SOW
		Capt.	William R. Sutton	56th SOW

MIG Combat Air Patrol Group

Aircraft	Code Name	Rank	Name	Parent Organization
F-4	Falcon 1	Maj.	Kenneth L. Gardner	13th TFS
		Maj.	Roger L. Henry	13th TFS
F-4	Falcon 2	Capt.	John D. Landin, Jr.	13th TFS

Aircraft	Code Name	Rank	Name	Parent Organization
		Capt.	George E. McKibben	13th TFS
F-4	Falcon 3	Capt	Stuart B. McCurdy	555th TFS
		Maj.	George E. Coats	555th TFS
F-4	Falcon 4	Capt.	Michael E. Golas	555th TFS
		Capt.	Charles E. Smith	555th TFS
F-4	Falcon 5	Capt.	Russell G. Wright	13th TFS
		Maj.	James C. Malaney	13th TFS
F-4	Falcon 11	Maj.	Orville B. Baird	555th TFS
		Maj.	Hubbard W. Lee	555th TFS
F-4	Falcon 12	Capt.	Douglas P. Brown	555th TFS
		Capt.	Carl Paladino	555th TFS
F-4	Falcon 13	Capt.	John L. Cantwell	13th TFS
		Capt.	Lawrence L. Henry	13th TFS
F-4	Falcon 14	Capt.	Ronald M. Hintze	13th TFS
		1st Lt.	Joseph R. Preston	13th TFS
F-4	Falcon 15	Maj.	Jimmy C. Pettyjohn	555th TFS
		1st Lt.	Thomas A. Wagner	555th TFS

Wild Weasel Decoy Group

Aircraft	Code Name	Rank	Name	Parent Organization
F-105	Firebird 1	Lt. Col.	Robert J. Kronebush	388th TFW
		Maj.	John Forrester	388th TFW
F-105	Firebird 2	Maj.	Raymond C. McAdoo	388th TFW
		Maj.	Robert J. Reisenwitz	388th TFW
F-105	Firebird 3	Lt. Col.	William J. Starkey	388th TFW
		Maj.	Everett D. Fansler	388th TFW
F-105	Firebird 4	Maj.	Murray B. Denton	388th TFW
		Capt.	Russell T. Ober	388th TFW
F-105	Firebird 5	Maj.	Donald W. Kilgus	388th TFW
		Capt.	Clarence T. Lowry	388th TFW

College Eye Crew Members

EC-131T Frog One	Frog Two
Lt. Col. John B. Mulherron	Maj. Richard T. Weber
Lt. Col. Dewitt H. Barwick	Maj. Irvin M. Gipsom
Capt. Herbert T. Bornhoff	Capt. Bobby G. Edney
Capt. Bruce W. Rogers	Capt. Lawrence R. Lausten
Lt. Samuel E. O'Briant	Lt. Lawrence R. Conover
Lt. Ronald D. Turner, Jr.	Lt. Robert S. Craig
SMSgt. Darrel R. Crossman	MSgt. Clarence R. Helm
CMSgt. Forrest G. Wright	MSgt. Robert H. Mansfield
MSgt. Jimmie A. Chevrier	MSgt. Donald P. Roy
MSgt. Edgar C. Howard	MSgt. Gary L. Walker
MSgt. Gary T. Igo	TSgt. Henry A. Moore
TSgt. James H. Bleecker	TSgt. Joel S. Rosenow
TSgt. James M. Russell	TSgt. James H. Lippert

SSgt. Charles A. Drowns
SSgt. Bruce A. Griffin
SSgt. Michael J. McConnell
SSgt. Alfred G. Scipio
SSgt. Roy A. York

TSgt. Nicholas J. Zeri
SSgt. Ronald G. Clark
Sgt. Charles E. Russ
A1C Davis O. Jiminez
A1C Charles E. Martin

Maintenance Support Group

Rank	Name	Parent Organization
Capt.	Gerard M. Carroll	Det 2, 1st SOW
Capt.	Lionel E. Faggard	AFLC
MSgt.	Thomas E. Hogan	1198 OE&T Sq
TSgt.	David L. Brookover	1198 OE&T Sq
TSgt.	Ronald H. Casey	1198 OE&&T Sq
TSgt.	Gerald Crisp	Det 2, 1st SOW
TSgt.	Charles W. Duff	1198 OE&T Sq
TSgt.	Billy R. Frederick	Det 2, 1st SOW
TSgt.	Tommy C. Moseley	1198 OE&T Sq
TSgt.	Bradley A. Whittier	1198 OE&T Sq
TSgt.	Richard W. Yates	1198 OE&T Sq
SSgt.	George T. Butler	1198 OE&T Sq
SSgt.	Raymond L. Chalkley	1198 OE&T Sq
SSgt.	George R. Kendall	1198 OE&T Sq
SSgt.	Donald R. Skidmore	1198 OE&T Sq
Sgt.	Robert W. Cleeland	Det 2, 1st SOW
Sgt.	Dale E. Dalton	Det 2, 1st SOW
Sgt.	David N. Dierking	Det 2, 1st SOW
Sgt.	Elliot L. Rothman	Det 2, 1st SOW
Sgt.	Kenneth A. Ruud	Det 2, 1st SOW
Sgt.	Robert D. Werner	Det 2, 1st SOW
A1C	Richard A. Bacon	Det 2, 1st SOW
A1C	Stephen P. Goodson	Det 2, 1st SOW
A1C	James R. Holder	Det 2, 1st SOW
A1C	Jerry D. Melcher	1198 OE&T Sq
CIV	Walter R. Fuller	Texas Instruments
CIV	Garry L. Hesse	Hallicrafters
GS-13	Hubert J. Hildreth	Air Force Logistics Command
CIV	Gene L. Pyle	Texas Instruments

Security Police Support Group

Rank	Name	Parent Organization
SSgt.	Wilbert Bell	464 SP Sq
AIC	Steven L. Berg	464 SP Sq
AMN	Stanley W. Crouch	464 SP Sq
AMN	Joseph T. Jernigan, Jr.	464 SP Sq
Sgt.	Clarence A. Ratcliff	464 SP Sq

Munitions Group

Rank	Name	Parent Organization
TSgt.	Teddie R. Goss	1st SOW
TSgt.	Giles C. Rose	1st SOW
Sgt.	William H. Mowder	1st SOW

APPENDIX III

The Son Tay Awards for Valor

*Decorated by President Richard M. Nixon at the White House on November 25, 1970. All others were decorated by Secretary of Defense Melvin R. Laird at Fort Bragg, North Carolina, on December 9, 1970.

United States Army

Distinguished Service Cross

Col. Arthur D. Simons*
Lt. Col. Elliott P. Sydnor, Jr.
Capt. Richard J. Meadows

MSgt. Thomas J. Kemmer
SFC Tyrone J. Adderly*
SSgt. Thomas E. Powell

Silver Star

Lt. Col. Joseph R. Cataldo
Capt. Thomas W. Jaeger
Capt. James W. McClam
Capt. Dan. H. McKinney
Capt. Eric J. Nelson
Capt. Glenn R. Rouse
Capt. Daniel Turner
Capt. Udo H. Walther
1st Lt. George W. Petrie, Jr.
MSgt. Calen C. Kittleson
MSgt. Joseph W. Lupyak
MSgt. Billy K. Moore
MSgt. Herman Spencer
SFC Donald D. Blackard
SFC Joseph M. Murray
SFC Noe Quezada
SFC Lorenzo Robbins
SFC Ronnie Strahan
SFC Salvador M. Suarez
SFC Donald E. Taapken
SFC William L. Tapley

SFC Earl Bleacher, Jr.
SFC Leroy N. Carlson
SFC Anthony Dodge
SFC Freddie D. Doss
SFC Jerry W. Hill
SFC Marion S. Howell
SFC John Jakovenko
SFC Jack G. Joplin
SFC Daniel Jurich
SFC David A. Lawhon, Jr.
SFC Gregory T. McGuire
SFC Billy R. Martin
SFC Charles Masten
SFC Donald R. Wingrove
SSgt. Robert F. Nelson
SSgt. David Nickerson
SSgt. Paul F. Poole
SSgt. John E. Rodriguez
SSgt. Lawrence Young
Sgt. Terry L. Buckler
Sgt. Gary D. Keel

SFC Richard W. Valentine
SSgt. Charles G. Erickson
SSgt. Kenneth E. McMullin
SSgt. Walter L. Miller

Sgt. Keith R. Medenski
Sgt. Franklin D. Roe
Sgt. Patrick St. Clair
Sgt. Marshal A. Thomas

Distinguished Flying Cross

1st Lt. George W. Williams
CWO Ronald J. Exley

CWO Jackie H. Keele
CWO John J. Ward

United States Air Force

Distinguished Service Medal

Brig. Gen. Leroy J. Manor

Air Force Cross

Lt. Col. John V. Allison
Lt. Col. Warner A. Britton
Maj. Frederic M. Donohue

Maj. Herbert D. Kalen
TSgt. Leroy M. Wright

Silver Star

Lt. Col. Albert P. Blosch
Lt. Col. Royal A. Brown, Jr.
Lt. Col. Herbert E. Zehnder
Maj. Eustace M. Bunn
Maj. Ryland R. Dreibelbis
Maj. Irl L. Franklin
Maj. John Gargus
Maj. James R. Gochnauer
Capt. David M. Kender
Capt. Norman C. Mazurek
Capt. William M. McGorge
Capt. Robert M. Senko
Capt. Robert H. Skelton
Capt. Thomas L. Stiles
Capt. William D. Stripling
Capt. William R. Sutton
Capt. Thomas R. Waldron
Lt. James C. Paine
MSgt. Harold W. Harvey
MSgt. David V. McLeod, Jr.
MSgt. Maurice F. Tasker
Sgt. Dallas R. Criner
TSgt. Billy J. Elliston

TSgt. William E. Lester
Maj. Alfred C. Montrem
Maj. Kenneth D. Murphy
Maj. Harry L. Pannill
Maj. Edwin J. Rhein
Maj. Richard S. Skeels
Maj. John C. Squires
Maj. John C. Waresh
Capt. John M. Connaughton
Capt. Jay M. Strayer
SSgt. Jack J. Eldridge
SSgt. Wayne L. Fisk
TSgt. Charles J. Montgomery, Jr.
TSgt. Jimmy O. Riggs
TSgt. Paul W. Stierwalt
TSgt. Lawrence Wellington
SSgt. Daniel E. Galde
SSgt. Melvin B. D. Gibson
SSgt. Aron P. Hodges
SSgt. Jon K. Holberg
SSgt. Donald LaBarre
SSgt. James J. Rogers
SSgt. Angus W. Sowell, III

Distinguished Flying Cross

Maj. Kenneth L. Gardner

Maj. Roger L. Henry

Capt. John D. Landin, Jr.

Capt. George E. McKibbin

Capt. Stuart B. McCurdy

Maj. George E. Coats

Capt. Michael G. Golas

Capt. Charles E. Smith

Capt. Russell G. Wright

Maj. James C. Malaney

Maj. Orville B. Baird

Maj. Hubbard W. Lee

Capt. Douglas P. Brown

Capt. Carl Paladino

Capt. John L. Cantwell

Capt. Lawrence L. Henry

Capt. Ronald M. Hintze

1st Lt. Joseph R. Preston

Maj. Jimmy C. Pettyjohn

1st Lt. Thomas A. Wager

APPENDIX IV

The Son Tay Planners

Feasibility Study Group (convened by SACSA, June 10, 1970)

Rank	Name	Service	Parent Organization
Col.	Norman H. Frisbie	USAF	Hq USAF
Col.	William C. Norman	USA	SACSA
Lt. Col.	Warner A. Britton	USAF	ARRTC
Lt. Col.	Keith R. Grimes	USAF	Air Univ
Lt. Col.	Thomas F. Minor	USA	DCSOPS
Lt. Col.	Lawrence Ropka, Jr.	USAF	Hq USAF
Maj.	Arthur A. Andraitis	USAF	Hq USAF
Maj.	Boyd F. Morris	USA	USAJFKCEN, Ft. Bragg
Capt.	James A. Jacobs	USAF	DIA
Capt.	John H. Knops	USAF	Hq USAF
Lt.	Theodore A. Grabowsky	USN	CNO
1st Lt.	James A. Brinson	USMC	DIA
SGM	Donald M. Davis	USA	6th SFGA, Ft. Bragg
GS-8	Frances L. Earley	DA	SACSA
GS-6	Barbara L. Strosnider	DAF	Hq USAF

Planning Group (convened by SACSA, August 10–14, 1970)

Rank	Name	Service	Parent Organization
Brig. Gen.	Leroy J. Manor	USAF	USAFSOF
Col.	Arthur D. Simons	USA	Hq XVIII Abn Corps
Col.	Norman H. Frisbie	USAF	Hq USAF
Capt.	William M. Campbell	USN	CNO
Lt. Cdr.	Clair R. Hershey	USN	CNO
Lt. Col.	James V. Bailey	USA	Hq DA AC/S COMELEC

Lt. Col.	Joseph R. Cataldo	USA	Hq DA SG
Lt. Col.	Keith R. Grimes	USAF	Air Univ
Lt. Col.	Benjamin N. Kraljev, Jr	USAF	Hq USAF
Lt. Col.	Richard A. Peshkin	USAF	Hq USAF
Lt. Col.	Lawrence Ropka, Jr.	USAF	Hq USAF
Lt. Col.	Homer Willett	USAF	Hq USAF
Maj.	Arthur A. Andraitis	USAF	Hq USAF
Maj.	Richard S. Beyea, Jr.	USAF	Hq USAF
Maj.	Thomas E. Macomber	USAF	Hq USAF
Maj.	Boyd F. Morris	USA	USAJFKCEN, Ft. Bragg
Maj.	James H. Morris	USA	7th SFGA, Ft. Bragg
Maj.	Max E. Newman	USA	USAFNTC-USAFAC
Capt.	James A. Jacobs	USAF	DIA
Capt.	John H. Knops	USAF	Hq USAF
Capt.	Richard J. Meadows	USA	Det 1, USAIS
1st Lt.	James A. Brinson	USMC	DIA
SGM	Donald M. Davis	USA	6th SFGA, Ft. Bragg
MSgt.	William S. Gann	USA	6th SFGA, Ft. Bragg
SFC	Jesse E. Sherrod	USA	6th SFGA, Ft. Bragg
GS-8	Frances L. Earley	DA	SACSA
GS-6	Barbara L. Strosnider	DAF	Hq USAF

SACSA's Administrative Support/Augmentation Group

Rank	Name	Service	Parent Organization
Capt.	John S. Harris	USN	DIA
Col.	Franklin C. Rice	USAF	NMCC
Lt. Col.	John E. Kennedy	USAF	PDAF
Maj.	Harvey D. Hallman	USAF	USAFSOF
Maj.	Frank C. Vogel	USAF	Hq USAF
1st Lt.	Michael L. Batsell	USAF	USAFSOF
MSgt.	Billy B. Baber	USAF	USAFSOF
DM 1	Larry Downing	USN	OJCS
SSgt.	Stanley G. Graves	USA	DIA
SSgt.	John J. Martin	USAF	USAFSOF
GS-8	Elneita S. Russell	USAF	USAFSOF

APPENDIX V

Who *Was* at the "Secondary School"?

Thirty-one years after the Son Tay raid, many of the raiders, planners, and POWs have still been asking, "Who *were* those people at the 'Secondary School'?" where Bull Simons's force landed by mistake and left the compound a blazing inferno after Bull's nine-minute "preemptive strike." Were they North Vietnamese, North Korean, Russian, or Chinese—possibly even Cubans? And, some raiders wondered, "Did we really land there by mistake?"

For six years, from 1970 to 1976, the fact that part of the raiding force had landed by error at the Secondary School was a well-kept secret. It became public knowledge only when the first edition of this book was published. In his first official, oral debriefing late in 1970 for the Air Force historical office and the historian of his own command, General Leroy Manor never mentioned that part of the raiding force had landed there by mistake. Although that account of the raid was classified Secret, Manor said: "In summary, I can unequivocally state that other than the absence of prisoners at the objective, there were no major surprises in the operation." He said exactly the same thing to begin the second paragraph of his five-page "Commander's Comments" introducing his task force's official after-action report to the Joint Chiefs of Staff. Buried far back in the Top Secret report, Manor's staff recommended that the "Secondary School be reclassified as a 'military installation,' as numerous armed personnel were encountered at this location." It said of the enemy troops there that they were "5 feet 10 inches to 6 feet, Oriental, not wearing the normal NVA dress, but instead . . . T-shirts and fitted dark undershorts" and of lighter skin. All of them, it noted, were "much better equipped" than the guards at Son Tay. But, Manor's report said, "Ground forces personnel were unable to determine their nationality."

During an eighteen-month period between 1974 and 1976, I interviewed 173 men who planned the raid on Son Tay, collected intelligence for it, or executed it—along with many of the POWs they tried to bring home. Not one person professed to have any idea who was in that school.

Bull Simons never wanted to discuss the Secondary School firefight. He adamantly refused to entertain questions about it until we met one afternoon in 1975 in a motel near Eglin Air Force Base and visited over room service steaks and a bottle of scotch (or bourbon, I forget which). This was months before two parts of the three-part JCS after-action report were declassified and made available to me. I showed Simons a 23-page, single-spaced unclassified document from the Department of the Army. Dated July 31, 1971, it detailed every citation for the awards belatedly made to the Son Tay raiders. Some of the citations, especially those for the Silver Stars earned by Udo Walther, Dan Turner, and Walter Miller, didn't square with the sparse accounts of the raid that the Defense Department had made public, none of which had hinted at the Secondary School foray or that helicopters landed anywhere other than at their intended targets. One of the citations read, for instance, "Captain Walther realized his force had been landed in an area other than, but resembling the target area . . ." Turner's citation said that "one of the assault helicopters had not landed as planned." Miller's had this entry: "Realizing that the group had landed in an area approximately 400 meters south of the objective . . ."

Bull studied the pages in silence, chewing on his cigar, slowly rolling it over in his mouth. "Where'd you get these, Sonny?" he asked me. (He called me "Sonny" whenever he was slightly miffed or thought I was pressing him too hard, but eventually he used it almost endearingly, just to pull my chain.) "I asked for them six months ago," I told him, "through public information channels. They arrived a few weeks ago." Chagrined that the Secondary School information was in an unclassified document and now in the public domain, Bull just shook his head when I told him that he was probably the one who had caused the orders to come out. I reminded him that a week or so before he retired, Bull had gone ballistic because none of his men had yet received the citations backing their awards for valor. He threatened to call the Army Chief of Staff and have a certain colonel castrated for taking seven months to prepare that paperwork. The citations materialized in quick order, but someone obviously forgot to have them vetted first by security review.

Bull finally responded, pointing to one of the pages: "Let me put it to you this way. I am not prepared to repudiate what that citation says."

We talked about the raid for the next nine hours; it was one of the most exhausting but exhilarating interviews I've ever done, all tape-recorded. As for who was at the Secondary School, Bull said he didn't know and didn't particularly care: he just considered it fortuitous that his support group had been landed there by mistake, for that error allowed Udo Walther's 22-man team to obliterate the one threat that, as events turned out, could have turned the mission into a disaster. And he expressed quiet but moving admiration for the way Lieutenant Colonel Warner Britton had wracked his HH-53, Apple 1, into a tight turn to land there again and extract him and his team from the encounter while ammunition was exploding all over the compound.

For reasons that long baffled me, the Pentagon and the Nixon administration seemed to have gone out of their way never to find out who was in that compound 400 yards south of Son Tay Prison. At CIA, George Carver, who in 1970 was the Director's Special Assistant for Southeast Asia Matters, later told me categorically in an on-the-record interview that he had never been told who was in the school and, after he checked his agency's records, that he "could not find out." Carver deferred further questions to the Defense Intelligence Agency, calling it strictly a "military matter." (God rest his soul, he had always been good at fending off difficult issues.) I had already interviewed scores of people at DIA, many of them four or more times, including the director at the time, then Army Lieutenant General Donald V. Bennett, and DIA's deputy director, then Air Force Major General Richard R. Stewart; but given Carver's denial, I ran the DIA trap line again. DIA checked its records carefully and finally told me, on the record, that no entry could be found indicating that the question—"Who were those troops at the Secondary School?"—had ever been entered as an intelligence collection requirement. Did no one care, or want to know?

In 1979, I thought I had finally unraveled the mystery. Visiting Ross Perot in his Dallas office, I noticed an unusual shadow box on the wall near his desk. Inside it was a leather belt with a Chinese officer's belt buckle—the only bit of uniform that in those days distinguished Chinese officers from enlisted men. A small brass plaque beneath the belt read,

"CAPTURED"
NOV. 30 [sic], 1970
0220 HRS
SON TAY NORTH VIETNAM

Perot told me that Udo Walther had given it to him, and he let me take the photo of the display case printed in the photo insert. Walther later told me that about the time he ran out of ammunition, his belt broke, so he stripped a belt from a nearby body, one of the 100 or 200 Bull estimated had been killed there. "I just wanted to hold my pants up," Udo told me. "It wasn't a secret that there were Chinese there, and it wasn't a secret that there were a bunch of them. I communicated that and I took some photographs. Now, what happened to [them], I don't know."

Both the Pentagon and the Chinese embassy declined comment when I queried them about this new "evidence." I asked Roy Manor, "When did you find out the occupants were Chinese?" He told me in a phone interview, "We never did find out." Manor insisted that he had "never heard of any photographs" such as those Walther had mentioned; nor, he said, had any specific information unfolded about occupants of the school when the raiders were all debriefed at Eglin AFB soon after their return home. Manor speculated, "I'm pretty convinced they were either Russian or Chinese," but then told me of a persuasive disclaimer from the Chinese. Some time after Manor had retired and became head of the Retired Officers Association, he was invited to a reception at the Chinese embassy, where he talked about the Son Tay raid with a Chinese officer. He mentioned the possibility of an encounter there with Chinese troops. He asked the Chinese officer if he would check into it. Several months later the officer called Manor and reported they could find nothing. Manor said, "It was, I thought, rather convincing."

Manor suggested a way to resolve the question: he hoped someday to ask Pete Petersen, our ambassador to Vietnam in 1998–2000 and a former POW (although never at Son Tay), to have the Vietnamese tell him: Who was at the Secondary School?

An answer to that question, however, would still leave hanging the question: Had the United States gone out of its way not to find out who was in that compound? I asked that question of Alexander Haig, who in 1970 had been Deputy Assistant to the President for National Security Affairs under Henry Kissinger and who had carefully monitored planning for and after-action reports of the raid for President Nixon: Did the Nixon White House did not want to know who was in the school because, at that time in history, Haig and Kissinger were massaging every diplomatic opening they could think of, hoping to open a dialogue with China? Or did they fear finding out that the troops might have been Russian, scores of them killed by American troops almost one year to the day after Moscow and Washington began their first round of the Strategic Arms Limitation Talks?

Haig reaffirmed the "great satisfaction" that everyone at the White House, including President Nixon, had felt about the Son Tay operation. He said the raid "put the North on notice that theirs was no longer sacrosanct territory." He spoke of the guts it took to try rescuing the POWs there in spite of last-minute intelligence that the camp might prove empty, noting that even at that late moment the operation "could have been recalled." He is convinced that Bull Simons's team landed by mistake at the Secondary School: "There was never any discussion of an alternate or secondary target." Moreover, Haig said, "I don't think anybody had any idea the Secondary School was an enemy compound."

As for the school's occupants, Haig said, "I'm not so sure they were Chinese." The U.S., he said, had learned later that most of the air defenses around Hanoi were manned by Russians—a fact confirmed when Soviet soldiers who had served in Vietnam later applied for their wartime veterans benefits. Haig also pointed out that Russia typically used troops from its Asian or Far Eastern provinces for duty in Vietnam, which could have accounted for the "Oriental" appearance of the soldiers in the compound. Finally, Haig noted the animosity between China and North Vietnam, remarking that Chinese troops who did help North Vietnam during the war had served mostly in Laos.

I asked Haig if the Secondary School firefight had ever come up in his discussions with the Chinese or Russians or if the U.S. had ever apologized to either nation for "inadvertently" killing so many of their soldiers. Haig says the U.S. never raised the issue, nor did the Chinese or Russians. He totally discounted any suggestion that the U.S. went out of its way not to find out who was in the school. "It was a non-event in the White House," he explained, in part because the White House didn't learn of the firefight for some time. Roy Manor had described it in the short after-action summary he cabled to the Pentagon Command Center just before he and Bull Simons left Udorn, but that message got lost and didn't reach Washington until a week after the raid. The Secondary School never came up when Manor and Simons visited with Defense Secretary Melvin Laird and JCS Chairman Admiral Thomas Moorer, and later with the President. Simons told me he assumed that Laird and Moorer knew of the fortuitous mistake that landed the biggest part of his raiding force at the wrong spot, but his discussion with them never got into "tactical details." But Laird and Moorer, it so happened, knew nothing of the Secondary School encounter; they had no idea. In fact, columnist Jack Anderson somehow got part of Manor's message before Laird got to see any of it.

The firefight was a non-event in the diplomatic sense as well, Haig explained. There was no reason to fear any repercussions from the Russians because "they would never have admitted it" [having troops there] in any case.

Haig discounted any richochet effects from the Chinese because the Son Tay raid happened "well before we were far down the trail" toward opening Nixon's door to China.

So who *was* at the Secondary School? As Ben Bradlee, editor of the *Washington Post,* used to explain, "The truth doesn't just happen; it emerges; it unfolds." Thirty years after the Son Tay raid, the truth about the Secondary School had yet to emerge.

By the year 2001, of course, the U.S. and the government of Vietnam had enjoyed normal diplomatic relations for over five years; the U.S. ambassador in Hanoi, Douglas B. "Pete" Petersen, had been a POW for six and a half years. Unwilling to let the matter go unresolved, early in 2001, I contacted the Pentagon spokesman on Defense Intelligence Agency matters with a formal press query:

> Has the Department of Defense or Defense Intelligence Agency ever ascertained who, or what units and of which nationality, were located at the "Secondary School" 400 meters south of Son Tay Prison where part of the POW rescue landed by mistake on November 20/21, 1970, during the attempt to rescue American POWs from Son Tay?
> If DIA does not yet know who was at the Secondary School, may I ask if DIA could have our defense attachés in Hanoi query the Vietnamese and try to ascertain the identity and nationality of the troops who were at that installation?

I telephoned a similar query to the Vietnamese embassy in Washington, but the calls were never returned. When no answer was forthcoming from the Pentagon after five weeks, I asked again. Lieutenant Commander Donald Sewell told me that DIA had lost my query, and he resubmitted it. A week later he told me that his point of contact at DIA, a Captain Stainbrook, "has exhausted his means of finding out who may have been at the school . . . He does not know who was at the school." I asked again if DIA had queried its attachés in Hanoi. On March 21st, Commander Sewell advised me, "Captain Stainbrook has informed me that neither DIA nor the Defense Attaché's [sic] have the answer to your question."

With military channels thus exhausted, I wrote Ambassador Petersen asking if he would query the Vietnamese about the identity of those troops. He never replied; Roy Manor, it turned out, had also followed through on his idea about asking him, but never heard back. I finally contacted the Counselor for Public Affairs of the U.S. Embassy in Hanoi, David B. Monk. With help from his assistant, Pham Trong Thuc, he alerted me that a series of articles on the Son Tay raid had been published in a Vietnamese journal, *An Ninh The Gioi Review,* in 1998 by one of its editors, Mr. Dang Verong Hung.

It proved impossible to find copies of or references to the magazine in any of the U.S. or British libraries, universities, and translation services I then contacted. I finally wrote the journal's editors, who quickly offered for $1,500 translations of parts of their 30,000-word series about "the massacre" and "the story about two Vietnamese intelligences [sic] who had known about the raid before it happened," plus fifteen "valuable, documental photographs" related to the raid. I sent the journal a $100 good faith deposit, asking if it would be possible to see two samples of the photos to make sure they would reproduce well, and also asked if the articles indicated who had occupied the Secondary School.

I wanted to provide the Vietnamese perspective of the raid, but the photos proved not worth printing: "Bullet traces on the walls of Son Tay prison (photo made in the morning of September 21, 1970 [sic])"—that was two months before the raid; blurred images of the wreckage of the "helicopter HH-53 [sic] . . . that American Rangers left in the Son Tay prison ground right after the raid (photo made in the morning of September 21, 1970)"—it was an H-3, and the raid took place on November 21, 1970; and three photos of weeping family members of "victims killed by the American Rangers on the eve of September 21, 1970."

The only article that Mr. Hung forwarded was one about 6,500 words long that claimed that "each American pilot POW" in Son Tay "was provided with food at the rate as high as 7 dongs a day." By comparison, the article said, officers of the provincial security service in that region were fed in a collective dining hall "with the rate of only . . . 0.5 dong/day; this was only ¼th of the rate enjoyed by an American POW." To put the POW ration allowance in perspective, he said that "The Chief of the Son Tay Public Security Service was paid a total monthly income of just . . . 115 dongs!"

The official exchange rate for the dong compared to the U.S. dollar has varied wildly over the years, from 2.9 dongs per U.S. dollar in 1976, for instance, to 14,530 dongs per dollar in 2001, according to the Central Intelligence Agency's *World Factbooks* for those years. Mr. Hung's statement that POWs in Son Tay were fed at the rate of 7 dongs per day suggests (using the 1976 exchange rate, the earliest year for which CIA could quickly find data), that they were supposed to have been fed as much as $2.41 worth of food a day, roughly two-thirds of the U.S. military daily ration allowance at the time. That would have been news, indeed, to American POWs.

The only information in the article about the Secondary School said that, "In fact, this had been a Party School of Son Tay Province; after the foundation of Ha Tay province, this school was changed to a sanatorium for cadres." The article then claimed, "Simon [sic] ordered his soldiers to break through the fence and assault. And right here, before withdrawing to the outside, the American Rangers committed a barbarous crime: They fired [shot] dead 5 patients of the sanatorium while they were sleeping. Within 5 minutes, they burned this sanatorium into a large torch and destroyed it." (The mention that five patients had been shot dead conflicted slightly with one of the captions Mr. Hung had sent me. It was for a photo of a "three-way crossroads 500 meters to the south of Son Tay, where the helicopter of Simon [sic] landed by mistake and killed 6 civil servers on their convalescent leave on the eve of September 21, 1970.")

Sitll wondering who those foreign troops might have been at the Secondary School, I wrote the Vietnamese embassy in Washington for a second time and asked its defense attache, Colonel Giao Ngoc Nguyen, for his assistance in finding out. He never replied. Instead, three weeks later I received another communique from Mr. Hung, who said that Colonel Nguyen had sent him my query and that he was writing "to clarify" the questions I had asked of Colonel Nguyen.

First, he said, the "secondary school was one of the places where . . . members of the communist party of Vietnam" were schooled. He noted that "each province in Viet Nam had a place like it," assuring me that "it was not a 'military installation' and there were no troops in it." (He pointed out, however, that all provincial installations throughout the country—whether hospitals, factories, or schools—"were equipped with small arms." This communique seemed to conflict with Mr. Hung's 1998 article, which had claimed that the secondary school was a "sanatorium," some of whose "patients" Bull Simons's men had shot dead while they were sleeping.

Second, Mr. Hung wrote, "there were no foreign soldiers" at the Secondary School. Apparently referring to my query of Colonel Nguyen about the Chinese officer's buckle from the belt Capt. Udo Walther had used to hold up his pants, Mr. Hung said that during the war Vietnam had received supplies or aid from Russia and China, specifically mentioning, as examples, "Russian shoes" and "Chinese clothes [and] buckels." "Because we were very poor," Mr. Hung wrote, the Vietnamese people, both commoners and officers, liked to use such army uniforms; "these things were good, hard-wearing, durable" and "it was really an economic use." But, he said, the uniforms which commoners wore "did not have chevrons like army officer's dress."

The significance of Mr. Hung's information about Chinese uniforms escaped me until months later, just as this edition was going to press. Retired Air Force Brigadier General Jon Reynolds, the Son Tay POW who had become the U.S. defense attache in China for years, and who had been trying to help me solve the riddle of the foreign troops at the Secondary School, sent me a revealing message. He said that he had just found out from a former Chinese staff officer something apparently not known before to the United States: "Chinese units in Vietnam wore Vietnamese uniforms, except for hats. In fact, all foreign units in Vietnam wore Vietnamese uniforms. Interestingly, Vietnamese uniforms were made in China—to include belts and belt buckles. Vietnamese troops in Vietnam wore the same belt buckle that Chinese troops wore in China (or Vietnam). In short, because a guy had a Chinese belt buckle didn't mean he was Chinese."

That doesn't explain, however, the taller height, Oriental appearance, and lighter skin of the troops Simons encountered at the Secondary School, or the fact that they were "not wearing the normal NVA dress, but instead T-shirts and fitted dark under shorts" and were "much better equipped" than the guards at Son Tay.

Some day, the truth *may* emerge.

APPENDIX VI

Nagging Questions

Other questions about the Son Tay raid remain unanswered. Why was America totally unprepared to attempt any meaningful rescue of our POWs until more than *six years* after the first American was taken prisoner in North Vietnam, when Navy Lieutenant Everett Alvarez, Jr., was shot down over Haiphong Harbor on August 5, 1964? Why was there no trained, standing rescue force ready by the time Son Tay Prison was discovered in the spring of 1970? In January 1968, after all, America had found itself unprepared to even attempt rescuing 82 seamen taken captive and tortured for eleven months by North Korea after it seized the U.S.S. *Pueblo*. By the beginning of 1970, 356 Americans were prisoners in North Vietnam, and their inhumane treatment had been public knowledge since the preceding August.

One's stomach turns just asking: Why did the Pentagon have to start from scratch? Perhaps there is no answer—or possibly only one answer. New cadets at the U.S. Military Academy learn their first day at West Point that there are only three acceptable answers a Plebe can give to a question asked by an officer or member of an upper class: "Yes, Sir"; "No, Sir"; and "No excuse, Sir." If there is an answer to the question posed here, only "No excuse" seems to fit.

Then one wonders: Why did it take another *two months* to devise the outline of a plan, name a commander for the rescue task force, and pick a leader for the ground operation—five years and eleven months after Alvarez's capture? Why did it then take four *more* months to select and train the men who would undertake the mission? Why did it take over *six months,* in all, to launch the raid? And why was the rescue task force disbanded immediately after the Son Tay rescue attempt, allowing *two and a half more years* to pass before the first POWs were released in February 1973, a time during which hundreds more Americans became prisoners.

Shouldn't the Joint Contigency Task Force have been kept intact, ready to mount (or serve as the nucleus of) another rescue, should such an opportunity have arisen? Might it not have handled the 1975 SS *Mayaguez* incident with fewer casualties than the 41 American airmen and Marines who were killed in a helicopter crash and fighting on Koh Tang Island?

Why did it take more than two years after the *Mayaguez* for the American military to finally decide it needed a permanent, highly trained rescue force ready to deploy "wheels up" on four hours' notice? Might the 1980 Iranian rescue attempt have gone better had Delta Force been organized earlier and allowed those extra years to rehearse and train with the Air Force special operations crews on whom they would eventually depend to get them to their targets? Might the Air Force's new MH-53 Pave Low helicopters have been ready in time for Desert One, instead of the rescue force having to use hastily modified Navy minesweeping helicopters flown by Marine pilots who were relatively inexperienced in nighttime, low-level flight operations in radio silence over mountainous terrain? Why did it then take the failure at Desert One for the Joint Chiefs of Staff to realize that a standing joint task force headquarters was needed—the Joint Special Operations Command—to integrate training and harmonize standard operating procedures for such high-risk, multiservice operations? Why did it take the high special operations casualties incurred on Grenada three years later for Congress to mandate in 1986, over vociferous objections from the Joint Chiefs of Staff and the Secretary of Defense, that the U.S. Special Operations Command be created to assure the proper funding for and employment of America's elite units when operating with conventional forces.

Thanks in part to the law of unintended consequences, but mostly due to the calm courage and resourcefulness under fire of American soldiers and airmen who mounted the Son Tay raid, an operation that much of Congress and many in the press labeled a "failure" turned out to be an unmitigated blessing for U.S. prisoners of war. Thirty-one years later, their successors are quiet professionals ready to mount the next rescue, wheels up, in four hours.

Why did it take so long? One doubts that the truth will *ever* emerge.

The Special Operations Warrior Foundation

Ten years after the Son Tay raid, eight American airmen died in a valiant but ill-fated attempt to rescue 52 Americans held hostage by militants who had seized the American embassy in Tehran. Those men left behind 17 fatherless children. Family members from the rescue team passed the hat to help start a scholarship program to ensure that those children could obtain the college educations their fathers surely would have wanted for them. That effort, which I had the honor of cofounding, was called the Colonel Arthur D. "Bull" Simons Scholarship Fund.

Sixteen years after the Son Tay raid and six years after the 1980 Iranian rescue mission, two visionaries in the United States Senate, Sam Nunn and William S. Cohen, created legislation forming the United States Special Operations Command. America owes them a debt of gratitude, for never again will ad hoc rescue forces have to be cobbled together to meet the kind of time-urgent crisis that the Son Tay and Iranian rescue missions represented. We now have superbly trained standing units to handle such contingencies as well as to lead the wars on drugs, terrorism, and transnational unrest and to help stem the proliferation of weapons of mass destruction. But this is dangerous work, and by its very nature, training for it is even more hazardous.

Even though they comprise barely 2 percent of all America's armed forces, the volunteers who serve in its elite Special Operations units suffer over 31 percent of all combat casualties. Since 1980, 346 of these soldiers, airmen, sailors, and Marines have made the ultimate sacrifice for our country. Even before Operation "Enduring Freedom" began in Afghanistan late in 2001, one hundred and eleven special operators had died on real-world missions in seventeen countries, suffering over fifteen times the combat casualty rate of America's conventional forces. Yet there are no special survivors' benefits for Special Operations families. Thus, there is an urgent need to relieve these courageous volunteers of the one concern—their families—that could distract them from peak performance when they need to be—and when America needs them—at their very best.

The brave men and women in our Special Operations units have left behind over 400 children, most of whose families cannot afford them a college education. Today the Bull Simons Scholarship Fund continues on a far larger scale as the Special Operations Warrior Foundation, a nonprofit, tax-exempt, 501(c)(3) educational organization. Its sole mission is to provide college educations, based strictly on need, for children surviving Special Operations personnel killed on real-world missions or in training accidents.

All of the Foundation's scholarships are grants, not loans, and cover full college costs—not just tuition and books, but room, board, and, where necessary, even travel and living expenses. Through a unique financial aid counseling program provided free to all surviving families as children approach college age, the Foundation helps qualify each student for every other form of scholarship aid available. On average, the Foundation finds each child almost four dollars in outside aid for every scholarship dollar it lays out. In 2001, for instance, the Foundation qualified the average student for $8,337 in federal, state, and college grants plus scholarships from other philanthropies, leaving $3,492 to be paid by the Warrior Foundation, a 2.4-to-1 ratio. With its donor dollars doing more than double duty, the Foundation offers a rare philanthropic bargain that lets more deserving youngsters obtain the education their fallen parent surely would have wanted for them.

To donate, please send your tax-deductible contribution to:

The Special Operations Warrior Foundation
Post Office Box 14385
Tampa, FL 33690

The Warrior Foundation's tax-exempt number is 52–1183585. It is accredited as part of the Combined Federal Campaign under Donor #2124. You may contact the Foundation by phone at 813–805–9400, by fax at 813–805–0567, by e-mail at *warrior@specialops.org* or check it out on the Internet at *http://www.specialops.org*.

APPENDIX VIII

Fallen Warriors

In the thirty-one years that have passed since the Son Tay raid, 24 members of the raiders have gone on to their own Valhalla, as have five of the prisoners they tried to rescue.

Son Tay Rescue Force
Col. Arthur D. Simons, USA
Lt. Col. Keith Grimes, USAF
Lt. Col. Gerald Kilburn, USA
SSgt. Earl D. Parks, USAF
Lt. Col. Richard Skeels, USAF
MSgt. David A. Lawhorn, Jr., USA
Maj. Richard A. Meadows, USA
Lt. Col. William J. Starkey, USAF
SMSgt. Randy S. McComb, USAF
Col. Donald W. Kilgus, USAF
Lt. Col. Charles McNeff, USAF
TSgt. Billy Joe Elliston, USAF
TSgt. James M. Sheppard, USAF
MSgt. Aaron L. Tolson, USA
Sgt. Marshall A. Thomas, USA
Capt. William M. McGeorge, USAF
Maj. Alfred C. Montrem, USAF
TSgt. Lawrence Wellington, USAF
CSM Billy K. Moore, USA
MSgt. Harold W. Harvey, USAF
Col. John Forrester, USAF
Col. Norman Frisbie, USAF
TSgt. Leroy M. Wright, USAF
MSgt. Jesse A. Black, USA

Son Tay POWs
Col. John H. Dunn, USMC
CWO-4 John W. Frederick, USMC
Maj. Edward A. Brudno, USAF
Col. William D. Burroughs, USAF
Col. Richard Dutton, USAF

Bibliography

Books

American Enterprise Institute for Public Policy Research, *Vietnam Settlement: Why 1973, Not 1969?* Washington, D.C.: 1973.

Arnold, James R. *The First Domino: Eisenhower, The Military, and America's Intervention in Vietnam.* New York: William Morrow and Company, 1991.

Brace, Ernest C. *A Code to Keep.* New York: St. Martin's Press, 1988.

Buttiner, Joseph. *Vietnam: A Dragon Embattled.* Vol. II. New York: Praeger, 1967.

David, Heather. *Operation Rescue.* New York: Pinnacle Books, 1971.

Davis, Vernon E. *The Long Road Home: U.S. Prisoner of War Policy and Planning in Southeast Asia.* Washington, D.C.: Historical Office, Office of the Secretary of Defense, 2000.

Day, George E. *Return With Honor.* Mesa, Ariz.: Chaplin Fighter Museum Press, 1989.

Denton, Jeremiah A., Jr. *When Hell Was in Session.* New York: Reader's Digest Press, 1976.

Department of the Army. *Vietnam Studies: U.S. Army Special Forces, 1961–1971.* Washington, D.C.: Government Printing Office, 1973.

Dramesi, John A. *Code of Honor.* New York: Norton, 1975.

Effros, William G., ed. *Quotations, Vietnam: 1945–1970.* New York: Random House, 1970.

Gaither, Ralph. *With God in a POW Camp.* As told to Steve Henry. Nashville, Tenn.: Broadman Press, 1973.

Gallucci, Robert L. *Neither Peace Nor Honor, The Politics of American Policy in Vietnam.* Baltimore, Md.: The Johns Hopkins University Press, 1975.

Gup, Ted. *The Book of Honor: Covert Lives and Classified Deaths at the CIA.* New York: Doubleday, 2000.

Harkins, Philip. *Blackburn's Headhunters.* New York: Norton, 1956.

Kalb, Bernard, and Marvin Kalb. *Kissinger.* Boston: Little, Brown, 1974.

Kiley, Frederick and Stuart I. Rochester. *Honor Bound: The History of American Prisoners of War in Southeast Asia, 1961–1973.* Annapolis, Md.: Naval Institute Press, 2001.

Kissinger, Henry A. *The White House Years.* New York: Little Brown, 1979.

Kyle, Colonel James H. with John Robert Eidson. *The Guts to Try.* New York: Orion Books, 1990.

Lenahan, Rod. *Crippled Eagle: A Historical Perspective of U.S. Special Operations, 1976–1996.* Charleston, S.C.: Narwhal Press, 1998.

Littauer, Ralph, and Norman Uphoff, eds. *The Air War in Indochina.* Revised ed. Boston: Beacon Press, 1972.

Marquis, Susan L. *Unconventional Warfare: Rebuilding U.S. Special Operations Forces.* Washington, D.C.: Brookings Institution Press, 1997.

McCain, John with Mark Salter. *Faith of My Fathers: A Family Memoir.* New York: Random House, 1999.

McGrath, John M. *Prisoner of War: Six Years in Hanoi.* Annapolis, Md.: Naval Institute Press, 1975.

New York Times. *The Pentagon Papers.* New York: Bantam Books, 1971.

Plumb, Charles. *I'm No Hero—A P.O.W. Story as Told to Gwen de Werff.* Independence, Mo.: Independence Press, 1973.

Risner, Robinson. *The Passing of the Night: My Seven Years as a Prisoner of the North Vietnamese.* New York: Ballantine Books, 1973.

Rochester, Stuart I. and Frederick Kiley. *Honor Bound: American Prisoners of War in Southeast Asia, 1961–1973.* Annapolis, Md.: Naval Institute Press, 1999.

Rowan, Roy. *The Four Days of the Mayaguez.* New York: Norton, 1975.

Rowan, Stephen A. *They Wouldn't Let Us Die: The Prisoners of War Tell Their Story.* New York: Jonathan David Publishers, 1973.

Rowe, James N. *Five Years to Freedom.* Boston: Little, Brown, 1971.

Ryan, Paul B. *The Iranian Rescue Mission: Why It Failed.* Annapolis, Md.: Naval Institute Press, 1985.

Schemmer, Benjamin F., and the Editors of *Armed Forces Journal. Almanac of Liberty.* New York: Macmillan, 1974.

Stockdale, James B. and Sybil. *In Love & War.* New York: Harper & Row, 1984.

The Council on Foreign Relations. *American Hostages in Iran: The Conduct of a Crisis.* New Haven: Yale University Press, 1985.

The New York Times Almanac, 2000, edited by John W. Wright. New York: Penguin Reference, 1999.

Trest, Warren A. *Air Commando One: Heinie Aderholt and America's Secret Wars.* Washington, D.C.: Smithsonian Institution Press, 2000.

Van Dyke, Jon M. *North Vietnam's Strategy for Survival.* Palo Alto, Calif.: Pacific Books, 1972.

Veith, George J. *Code-Name Bright Light: The Untold Story of U.S. POW Rescue Efforts During the Vietnam War.* New York: The Free Press, 1998.

Westmoreland, William C. *A Soldier Reports.* Garden City, N.Y.: Doubleday, 1976.

Zapinski, Leonard E. *10 Days in November 1970: An Incredible Story.* (Unpublished manuscript, copyright 1984.)

Hearings

"Bombing Operations and the Prisoner-of-War Rescue Mission in North Vietnam," *Hearings Before the Committee on Foreign Relations, United States Senate, Ninety-First Congress, Second Session,* Washington, D.C.: Government Printing Office, 1971.

"American Prisoners of War in Southeast Asia, 1971," *Hearings Before the Subcommittee on National Security Policy and Scientific Developments, Committee on Foreign Relations, Ninety-Second Congress, First Session,* Parts 1 and 2, Washington, D.C.: Government Printing Office, 1971 and 1972.

"Weather Modifications," *Hearings Before the Subcommittee on Oceans and International Environment of the Committee on Foreign Relations, Ninety-Third Congress, Second Session,* Washington, D.C.: Government Printing Office, 1974.

"Americans Missing in Southeast Asia," *Hearings Before the House Select Committee on Missing Persons in Southeast Asia, Ninety-Fourth Congress, First Session,* Parts 1 and 2, Washington, D.C.: Government Printing Office, 1975 and 1976.

Periodicals

Armed Forces Journal, "Better Deal for Service Spooks?", December 1971.

———, "Dissent," July 1974.

———, "Last Medals of Honor of the Vietnam War," March 1976.

———, "Our Outgunned Spies," December 1971.

———, "POW Profile: The Upward Trend in Letter-Writing," October 5, 1970.

———, "There's Always a Chance," March 1973.

———, "U.S. Raiders Killed 100–200 Chinese Troops in 1970 North Vietnam Foray," January 1980.

Doyle, Robert C. in *Proceedings,* book review, *The Long Road Home: U.S. Prisoner of War Policy and Planning in Southeast Asia,* March 2001.

Hung, Dang Vuong, *An Ninh The Gioi Review,* "The Truth of the Raid on the Son Tay Prison to Rescue American Pilots in 1970," multiple-part series, 1998.

Ruhl, Robert K. *Airman,* "Raid at Son Tay," August 1975.

Schwanhausser, Robert R. in *Armed Forces Journal,* "RPV's: Angel in the Battle, Victim in the Budget," November 1974.

Steinhauser, Thomas C. in *Armed Forces Journal,* "How to Make Flag Rank," July 1972.

Thomas, William C., Capt., USAF. *Joint Forces Quarterly,* "Operation Kingpin: Success or Failure?" Spring 1997.

Waresh, John C., Col., USAF-Ret. *Ivory Coast* [newsletter, Son Tay Raiders Association], "A-1s and the Son Tay Raid," Spring 2000.

Weaver, Robert A. in *Armed Forces Journal,* "A New Expanded 1975 Version of the Army Writer's Dictionary (6th Edition)," May 1975.

Weiss, George in *Armed Forces Journal,* "Battle for Control of the Ho Chi Minh Trail," February 15, 1971.

Transcripts of Briefings

Transcript of Secretary of Defense's Press Conference on the Son Tay Prisoner of War Raid, Office, Assistant Secretary of Defense (Public Affairs), November 23, 1970.

Operation Kingpin, Briefing Book for the Joint Chiefs of Staff and National Command Authorities, Office, Joint Chiefs of Staff, November 1970.

Briefing on the Son Tay Raid, Brigadier General Leroy J. Manor, USAF, 1971: untitled, undated.

Letters, Memorandums, Monographs, Newsletters, and Reports

Report on the War in Vietnam, Admiral U.S.G. Sharp and General W. C. Westmoreland. Washington, D.C.: Government Printing Office, 1968.

General Orders No. 32, Headquarters, Department of the Army, Washington, D.C., July 13, 1971.

"Report on the Son Tay Prisoner of War Rescue Operation," Parts I and II, Brigadier General Leroy J. Manor, USAF, Commander, JCS Joint Contingency Task Group, Office, Joint Chiefs of Staff, Washington, D.C., 1971.

"Chronology of the Vietnam War," Office of the Joint Chiefs of Staff, Historical Office, 1955–1972.

"Southeast Asia Statistical Digest," Table 6, Office, Assistant Secretary of Defense (Comptroller), Washington, D.C., 1966 through 1973.

"Written Report of Lieutenant General Vernon A. Walters, USA, Deputy Director, Central Intelligence Agency," submitted for the record to the Select Committee on Missing Persons in Southeast Asia of the U.S. House of Representatives, March 17, 1976.

"Foreign and Military Intelligence," Book 1, *Final Report of the Select Committee to Study Governmental Operations with Respect to Intelligence Activities, United States Senate, Ninety-Fourth Congress, Second Session,* Washington, D.C.: Government Printing Office, 1976.

"Intelligence Activities and the Rights of Americans," Book 2, *Final Report of the Select Committee to Study Governmental Operations with Respect to Intelligence Activities, United States Senate, Ninety-Fourth Congress, Second Session,* Washington, D.C.: Government Printing Office, 1976.

Letter, Henry Kissinger to the author, October 19, 1999.

Letter, Melvin R. Laird to the author (with enclosures), February 20, 2001.

Letter, Richard Nixon to the author, February 27, 1978.

"MAC's Facts No. 2, Escapes in NVN," by Capt. John M. McGrath, USN-Ret., unpublished monograph, December 27, 1999.

"MAC's Facts No. 5, POW Facts," by Capt. John M. McGrath, USN-Ret., unpublished monograph, February 2, 1998.

"MAC's Facts No. 6, (More POW Facts)," by Capt. John M. McGrath, USN-Ret., unpublished monograph, December 1, 1999.

"MAC's Facts No. 46 (B-52 crewmembers: Linebacker II)," by Capt. John M. McGrath, USN-Ret., unpublished monograph, January 24, 2001.

Memorandum for the Record, Subject: Discussion with the President, Melvin R. Laird, The Secretary of Defense, November 6, 1970.

Memorandums to the author with comments on the draft manuscript: Lt. Col. Richard Brenneman, USAF-Ret., September 6, 2001; Mr. Joseph Crecca, April 25, 2001; Col. Frederic M. Donohue, USAF-Ret., March 20 and 21, 2001; Frederick Kiley, February 21, 2002; Col. John Gargus, USAF-Ret., March 18, 2002; Sherge Keirn McKenzie, May 26, 2001; Maj. Tom Powell, USA-Ret., March 22, 2002; Brig. Gen. Jon Reynolds, USAF-Ret., March 29 and April 2, 2002; Col. Elliott P. Sydnor, Jr., USA-Ret., March 20, 2002; Maj. Dan D. Turner, USA-Ret., January 22, 2001; Col. John C. Waresh, USAF-Ret., January 22, 2001.

Note, Richard Nixon to Melvin R. Laird, November 19, 1970.

Ivory Coast, quarterly newsletter of the Son Tay Raid Association.

The Free Press, quarterly newsletter of the NAM-POWs, Inc.

"Prelude to the Son Tay Raid," Col. John Gargus, USAF-Ret., unpublished monograph, 2001.

"COLLEGE EYE—The Rest of the Story," Col. John Gargus, USAF-Ret., unpublished monograph, 2001.

"Return to Son Tay—One More Time," Col. William A. Guenon, Jr., USAF-Ret., unpublished monograph, October 21, 2000.

"Corrections," numbers 1–7, Capt. Mike McGrath, USN-Ret., e-mail messages of March 17, 18, and 19, 2002.

"Room 7," Capt. Mike McGrath, USN-Ret., e-mail message of March 12, 2001.

"Son Tay Raid," Roy Dreibelbis, e-mail message of April 17, 2001.

"Vignette," Joe Crecca, e-mail messages of April 25, 2001.

"Son Tay Raider Leroy Wright," Tom Powell, e-mail of November 2, 2001.

"NAM-POW member KIA," Capt. Mike McGrath, USN-Ret., e-mail of November 3, 2001.

"Son Tay articles," Dang Vuong Hung, *An Ninh The Gioi Review,* e-mail messages of November 6, 9, and 14 and December 28, 2001.

"The Son Tay Prisoner of War Search and Rescue Operation," TSgt. Harold Newcomb, monograph from history of 432nd Tactical Fighter Wing, vol. IV, October 1, 1970 to December 31, 1970.

"The Son Tay POW Camp Raid," draft chapter 11 from "History of the 552d AEW&C Wing (ADC) [Airborne Early Warning and Control Wing (Air Defense Command)], 1 October 1970–1 December 1970."

"Thuds at Son Tay," unpublished, undated monograph by Col. Clarence T. "Ted" Lowry, USAF-Ret.

"Transcript of Oral Account: Son Tay Search and Rescue Mission," USAF Oral History, interview with Brig. Gen. Leroy J. Manor by Dr. Charles Hildreth, Office of Air Force History, and William J. McQuillen, USAFSOF historian, 30 December 1970.

Index

Abbott, Wilfred "Will" K., 294
Aberdeen Proving Ground, Maryland, 97, 117
Abrams, Creighton, 144, 145, 157, 181
Acoustic and seismic sensors, 96–98
Adderly, Tyrone J., 255, 259
Agnew, Spiro, 256, 287
Aiken, Larry D., 253
Air Force Systems Command (AFSC), 124–25
Air Weather Service, 124, 189–90, 309, 310
"Alfred," 96, 174–76
Allen, James R., 33–40, 170, 171, 312
Allison, John, 78, 79, 215, 226, 227, 231, 261, 308
Alvarez, Everett, Jr., 6, 47, 318
Anderson, Jack, 242, 264, 278
Andraitis, Arthur A., 58, 59, 145, 154, 155, 212
Ap Lo, 18–19, 30, 35, 36, 39, 49, 50, 62, 280, 292
Arlington Hall Station, Virginia, 52–60
Armalite Corporation, California, 119–20
Armstrong, Neil, 17
Army Special Forces, 1, 13, 35, 39, 43
   SOG (Special Operations Group), 43–47, 52, 74, 75, 96, 142, 265
   White Star teams, 43, 44, 73, 82

Arnold, James R., 168n
Atterbury, Edwin L., 166, 315

Baker, Elmo C. "Mo," 14–17, 20–21, 93, 282, 284, 290–91, 293–95, 315
Baldwin, Clarke T., 125
BARCAP missions, 140
Bardshar, Frederick A., 150–51, 192, 203–8
Bayh, Birch, 187
Bean, James E., 290
Beckwith, Charles A., 305
Bennett, Donald V., 48, 49, 51, 53–55, 62–64, 76, 94–95, 136, 140, 173–74, 176, 177, 181–85, 233–34, 237, 312
Big Bird reconnaissance satellite, 56, 87, 172
Blackburn, Donald D., 34–52, 57–60, 62, 63, 65–70, 72–75, 77, 81, 82, 85, 86, 88, 89, 92, 95–98, 107, 109, 124–27, 132, 135–45, 150–61, 168–74, 176–85, 198, 233, 234, 236, 237, 239, 251, 254, 258, 263–66, 272, 273, 279–81, 304, 307, 311–12
Black River, 88, 201, 209
Blosch, Albert P., 101–103
"Blueboy" call sign, 105
Borman, Frank, 133
Boyd, Charles G., 314
Boyer, Terry L., 295

Brace, Ernie, 289–90, 298, 318
Brenneman, Richard C. "Dog," 21, 65
Briarpatch (*see* Ap Lo)
Brinson, James A., 57
Britton, Warner A., 58, 78, 79, 99, 214, 217–20, 261, 308, 325
Brock, Ken, 62–63
Brown, Charles A., Jr., 313
Brown, Royal C., 150, 235
Bruce, David K. E., 60, 63, 133, 134
Buffalo Hunter reconnaissance. drone, 56, 63, 77, 92–94, 96, 137, 140, 172, 184
Burns, Michael T., 295

C-130 Combat Talons, 79, 80, 99–102, 122, 123, 125, 147, 199–201, 209–11, 221, 222, 224
C-141 Starlifters, 124, 125, 171, 199, 202, 269
Cambodia, 7, 25, 29, 39, 43, 47, 152, 167, 247, 249
Campbell, William M., 86
Camp Faith (*see* Dong Hoi)
Camp Hope (*see* Son Tay Prison)
Camp Unity (*see* Hoa Lo Prison)
Cam Ranh Bay, 146, 149
Carrier Task Force 77, 132, 140, 150, 172, 182, 192, 204–6, 208
Carrigan, Larry E., 15–16, 93
Carver, George, 52, 141–43, 272, 278, 312
CAS (Controlled American Sources) teams, 37–38, 81, 94–95, 141–42, 197, 279
Cataldo, Joseph R., 83–86, 104, 107, 110–12, 124, 187, 197–98, 200, 261–62
Ceauşescu, Nicolae, 135
Central Intelligence Agency (CIA), 27, 29–31, 35, 43, 44, 50, 53–56, 59–61, 66, 73, 76, 81, 86, 88–90, 95, 98, 118, 123, 129, 141–43, 151–52, 157, 256, 257, 272, 276–77, 310

Church, Frank, 250
Cienfuegos, Cuba, 99, 100
Clancey, John, 172
Clark, Cecil, 80
Clark, Ramsey, 33
Clark Air Force Base, Philippines, 171, 172, 202, 269
Clay, Lucius, 145, 189
Cleaver, Eldridge, 178
Clinebell, Norman, 24, 29–33, 49, 308
Clower, Claude D. "Doug," 20, 164
Colby, William, 44
Coleman, J. L., 205
Colt Arms, 120
Committee of Liaison with Families of Servicemen Detained in North Vietnam, 28
Committee of Solidarity with the American People, 156
Congressional debate on Son Tay raid, 246–54, 257
Corcoran, Charles A., 141, 268, 271
Cosmos 355, 87, 88, 159
Crayton, Render, 17, 21, 22, 65, 319–20
Crecca, Joseph, Jr., 283, 294–95
Cuba, 56, 99–100
Czechoslovakia, 53

Dale, John, 93
Da Nang, 43, 46, 80, 121, 146, 147
Dat, Nguyen Guoc, 291
Davis, Donald M., 57, 58
Day, George E., 9, 315–16
D-Day, 192
Defense, Department of, 3, 49, 89, 91, 128–31, 247, 309, 311–12
Defense Intelligence Agency (DIA), 27–32, 40, 49, 52–57, 62, 64, 65, 76, 88, 91, 94–96, 100, 110, 137, 154, 155, 166, 174–80, 183, 210, 233, 256, 270, 272, 276
Denton, Jeremiah A., Jr., 130, 290, 292, 297, 304, 314

Deputy Chiefs of Staff for Operations (DCSOPS), 52, 183
Dirty Bird camp, 19
DMZ (Demilitarized Zone), 7, 9, 31, 46
Dole, Robert, 246
Dolvin, Welborn, 145
Donaldson, James C., 161, 171–72
Dong Hoi ("Camp Faith"), 74, 177, 180, 282–84
Donohue, Frederic M. "Marty," 79, 99–100, 106, 107, 208, 209, 211–12, 214, 225, 230–32, 235, 238, 259, 261, 308
Donohue, Robert, 86
Doolittle Raiders, 87
Dougherty, Russell E., 34
Downing, Larry, 157–58, 160
Dramesi, John, 298, 315
Droge, Dolf, 62–64
Dunn, John H. "Howie," 20
Dutton, Dick, 318

"Eagle," 83
Earley, Frances L., 58
EC-121T College Eye test aircraft, 148–49, 202
Eglin Air Force Base, Florida, 68, 69, 78–80, 87–89, 99–108, 114, 115
82nd Airborne Division, 69, 276
Eisenhower, Dwight D., 192
1127th Field Activities Group, 24, 27, 29–32, 35, 40, 49, 52, 59, 236
11th Airborne Division, 41, 42, 72
Elliott, Richard, 52, 59, 62, 86, 136
Engen, Don, 170, 171

Federal Bureau of Investigation (FBI), 27, 54
56th Special Operations Squadron, 150
Finger Lake, 209, 212, 230, 259
Flora, Carroll, 12–13
Flynn, John P. "Jack," 288–90, 315

Fonda, Jane, 33, 177
Fontaine, Sully, 264–68, 272
Forby, Willis E., 27
Ford, Gerald R., 246
Fort Belvoir, Virginia, 24, 27, 29, 38, 59, 236
Fort Bragg, North Carolina, 43, 58, 67–69, 72–74, 116, 117, 260
Fort Stewart, Georgia, 117
Franklin, Irl L., 102–103, 200–201, 210
Frederick, John, 19
Frisbie, Norman, 33, 36, 57, 63–65, 147, 159
Frishmann, Robert F., 130
Fulbright, J. William, 168, 245–49, 254, 257, 278

Gaddis, Norman C., 290
Gaither, Ralph, 18–21, 285–86
Gamma intercepts, 177–78, 185, 249, 250
Gargus, John, 80, 108, 146, 150, 202, 209, 221, 222, 325
Gay, Arlo, 298
Gayler, Noel, 135–36
Gee, Samuel E. "Ned," 419
Geneva Accords of 1962, 128–29
Geneva Convention, 10, 19, 27, 128, 129, 133, 243
Gia Lam airport, 174
Giap, Vo Nguyen, 49
Gochnauer, James R., 202, 222, 223
Goforth, Pat E., 270
Gore, Albert, 250
"Greenleaf" call sign, 105, 200
Grimes, Keith, 58, 146
Grubb, Wilmer N. "Newk," 166–67
Guenon, William A., Jr., 80, 319
Gulf of Tonkin, 7, 51, 140, 148, 189, 204, 207, 228
Guy, Theodore W. "Ted," 289, 290

Haak, Frank S., 205
Habib, Philip, 134
Haig, Alexander M., 2, 127, 137, 138, 163, 164, 168, 169, 234, 236

Haiphong, 7, 51, 188
Haiphong Harbor, 6, 38, 163, 210, 275
Hanoi Hilton (*see* Hoa Lo Prison)
Harkins, Philip, 42*n*
Harriman, W. Averell, 127–30
Harris, John S. "Spots," 32, 55–56, 76, 86, 178–79, 182, 184, 234
Hayden, Tom, 15, 178
Heartbreak Hotel (*see* Hoa Lo Prison)
"Heavy Chain" program, 147
Hegdahl, Douglas B., 130, 131, 316
Helms, Richard, 54, 60, 127, 152, 162, 185, 186
Helms, Richard A., 1
Henkin, Daniel Z., 152, 240–42, 244
Henry, Steve, 19*n*
HH-3 helicopter, 79, 80, 99–101, 107–10, 124, 126, 149, 208, 212–13, 220, 226
HH-53 helicopter, 99, 100, 106, 107, 110, 123, 124, 146, 148, 157, 171, 208, 220, 222, 226
Hill, Alan "Boot," 151, 206
Hoa Lo Prison ("Camp Unity," "Hanoi Hilton," "Heartbreak Hotel"), 6–7, 10–14, 18, 274, 275, 283–96
Hoang, Nguyen Van, 96–97, 174–76, 179, 279, 320
Ho Chi Minh, 19, 96, 131, 292, 300
Ho Chi Minh Trail, 90, 96–97, 129, 292
Holloway, James L., III, 309
Hoskins, P.D., 151, 205, 206
Hughes, John T., 56

Iles, George J., 30, 31, 33–35, 49, 308
Interagency Prisoner of War Intelligence Committee (IPWIC), 27–28, 32, 52, 56
International Control Commission, 129, 174, 175
International Red Cross, 133
"Ivory Coast" (*see* Son Tay raid)

Jackson, Henry, 246
Jacobs, James A., 57, 212
Jakovenko, John "Jake," 217–18, 219, 223, 224
Javits, Jacob, 252, 254
Jayroe, Julius, 19–20
Johnson, Lyndon B., 6, 7, 35, 37, 38, 45, 90
Johnson, Samuel E., 314
Johnson, T.C., 205
Joint Chiefs of Staff, 36, 48, 51–53, 54, 60, 76, 91, 126–27, 275
Joint Contingency Task Group (JCTG), 69–70, 85, 94, 124, 143–46, 158 (*see also* Son Tay raid)
Joint Personnel Recovery Center (JPRC), 253

Kadena Air Force Base, Okinawa, 94, 154
Kalen, Herb, 109, 110, 212, 214, 220, 261
Kasler, James H., 287–88
KC-135 refueling aircraft, 148, 172
Keirn, Richard P. "Pop," 11
Kemmer, Thomas J., 213
Kennedy, Edward M., 246
Kennedy, John E., 86, 312
Kennedy, John F., 43, 128
Kennedy, Robert, 129
Kent State University, 25
Kep airfield, 164
Khan, Yahya, 135
Kientzler, Philip A., 298
Kilgus, Donald W., 225–27, 235, 238
"Kingpin" (*see* Son Tay raid)
Kissinger, Henry A., 1, 2, 25, 66, 127, 133, 134, 136–39, 153, 162, 165, 232, 251, 258, 259, 272, 273, 295, 307–8, 323–24
Knops, John H., 58, 59, 146
Knowles, Richard T., 126
Knutson, Rodney A., 315–16
Koller, Rudolph C., 30–34, 36, 49, 59, 309
Korat, Thailand, 147, 149–50, 228

Kornitzer, William J., Jr., 146, 149
Kraljev, Benjamin N., Jr., 146, 149–50, 263–64
Ky, Nguyen Cao, 49, 291

Laird, Melvin R., 1, 3–4, 53, 127–31, 134, 135, 140, 153, 156, 161, 162, 163, 165, 168–70, 179–85, 233, 236, 237, 239–57, 259–62, 264, 271, 275, 278, 280, 284, 301, 303, 313–15, 323, 324
Lang Chi Dam, 48, 266–68, 273, 274
Laos, 7, 13, 16, 29, 32, 35, 37, 43–45, 50, 59, 66, 73, 81, 89–92, 96–97, 102, 108, 109, 129, 136, 152
Lavelle, John P., 270–72
Lawrence, William P., 61–62, 288, 315, 316
Leggett, Robert, 246
Lewis, James F., 303
Long Than, 43
Lowry, Clarence T., 225–27, 235, 238

M-14 rifle, 119–21
M-16 rifle, 104
M-60 machine gun, 105
M-79 grenade launcher, 114, 116, 220
Manor, Leroy J., 3–4, 75–80, 85–87, 89, 92, 93, 98, 99, 102, 107, 109, 110, 112, 113, 121–27, 131, 135–39, 143–48, 150, 151, 152, 155–58, 161–66, 170–73, 181–85, 186–89, 191, 198, 200, 206, 208, 209, 217, 227–29, 231, 232, 234, 235, 237–44, 247, 248, 254, 255, 262, 279, 309, 310, 311, 324–25
Mao Tse–tung, 134
Martin, Edward H., 286–88, 296, 315
Mayaguez raid, 301, 309
Mayall, William T., 313–14

Mayer, E. E. "Ed," 34, 36–40, 48–52, 57, 59, 60, 66–70, 76, 82, 85, 86, 87, 98, 107, 124, 126, 132, 142, 152, 153, 157–62, 169–71, 173, 178–80, 182, 187, 232, 236, 237, 240–41, 251, 254, 261, 262, 272, 273, 279, 280
McCain, John S., III, 13–14, 130, 132, 143, 156, 291, 314, 316, 319
McCain, John S., Jr., 13, 131–33, 143, 156, 239, 256, 268, 271
McClam, James W., 229
McGrath, John M., 12
McGrath, Mike, 176, 282–83, 317
McKinney, Dan H., 214
McKnight, J. E., 205
McMullin, Kenneth E., 213, 214
McNamara, Robert, 39, 46, 54, 96
Meadows, Richard J. "Dick," 45–46, 68, 80–82, 86, 104, 106, 108–10, 118, 141, 187, 197, 200, 212–14, 216, 217, 219, 220, 226, 229, 230, 237, 261, 312–13
Mechenbier, Edward J., 294, 313
Medical equipment, 111–12
Mekong Delta, 42–43, 90
Meo tribesmen, 73, 157
Military Airlift Command (MAC), 124, 125, 148
Miller, Walter L., 217, 307
Miller, William, 62
Milligan, Joseph E. "Mike," 294, 295
Minor, Thomas F., 57–58
Mobley, Joseph S., 313, 314
Momyer, William W. "Spike," 75
Monkey Mountain, 121, 146–48, 183, 190, 191, 200, 227, 228, 232
Moorer, Thomas H., 1–3, 39, 51, 60–63, 69, 85, 94–96, 134, 135, 140, 144, 151–53, 156–58, 160–70, 173, 176, 177, 179–86, 233, 236, 238–40, 242, 248, 251, 256, 264, 275, 279, 288, 296

Morris, Boyd F., 58
Morton, George, 197
Mount Ba Vi, 32, 34–39, 49
Mow, Douglas F., 204
Murphy, Kenneth, 235

Nakhon Phanom, Thailand, 97, 146, 150, 201
Nasser, Gamal Abdel, 134
Natick Laboratories, 112, 113
National Reconnaissance Office, 49, 53, 55, 76
National Security Agency, 53–56, 76–77, 100, 135–36, 154, 155, 158–59, 177, 178
National Security Council, 25, 29, 264, 278
Nelson, Robert L., 223
Newman, Max E. "Blue Max," 86, 125, 151, 152, 155–56, 262
Nha Trang, 43
Nickerson, David S., 216–17, 219
Nixon, Richard M., 1–3, 25, 39, 47, 60, 94, 127, 133–35, 139, 145, 157–58, 160–69, 180, 181–82, 186, 236, 240, 244, 245, 249, 254–57, 262, 272, 280, 295, 300, 314, 322–24
Norman, William C. "Clint," 57
North Vietnamese Enemy Proselytizing Office, 95–96, 175, 320

Operation Homecoming, 297–98, 300, 317
Operation Igloo White, 97
Operation Litterbug, 140
Operation Popeye (Compatriot, Intermediary), 89–92, 190, 277–78, 325

Palmer, Bruce, 66, 70, 159, 233, 260–61, 266, 280
Palmer, G.H., 205
Paris peace negotiations, 12, 36, 60, 63, 66, 127, 128, 130, 133,
138, 153, 245, 257, 289, 295–97
Patton, George, 55, 277
Paul VI, Pope, 133
Peace activists and war protesters, 14–15, 25, 28, 33, 156, 166, 177, 178, 186, 249
Pell, Claiborne, 254
Perot, H. Ross, 273, 306
Peshkin, Richard A., 147, 202
Petersen, Douglas B., 314
Petrie, George L., 68, 213
Philippines, 41–42, 70, 72
Phoenix Island, 46
"Phoenix" operations, 44
Photo reconnaissance, 31, 32, 49, 56, 63, 65, 77, 78, 93–94, 96, 137, 140, 154–55, 183
Phu Cat, 76
Phuc Yen, 136, 164, 208
Plantation, the, 15, 275, 284, 289, 290, 292
Plumb, Charles, 284–85, 295
"Polar Circle" (see Son Tay raid)
Poole, Paul, 215
Porth, Andrew, 269–72
POW/MIA League of Families, 132
Prendergast, Francis S. "Frank," 298–99, 317–18
Proxmire, William, 255
Pueblo (spy ship), 53, 152
Purcell, Ben, 298
Pursley, Robert E., 181, 185, 233
Putnam, Charles, 299, 318

Rainmaking operations, 89–92, 277–78
Ralston, Loyal E., 190, 191
RC-135Ms, 147–48, 172, 228
Red River, 31, 38, 47, 223
Red River Valley, 189, 191, 203, 209, 210, 214, 274
"Redwine" call sign, 105, 200
Reynolds, Jon A., 74, 318
RF-4 reconnaissance plane, 56, 93, 192, 250
RF-101 reconnaissance plane, 93

Rice, Franklin C., 172
Risner, Robinson, 11, 290, 299
Rodriguez, John E., 218
Rogers, James J., 212
Rogers, William P., 1, 157, 162, 163
Ropka, Lawrence, Jr., 33, 58–59,
  145–49
Ross, Franklin A., 192
Ruhling, Mark J., 295
Rumble, Wesley L., 26
Ryan, John D., 76, 146, 147
Ryan, William P. "Pat," 158

SACSA (Special Assistant for
  Counterinsurgency and
  Special Activities), 34–41,
  75, 175 (see also Blackburn,
  Donald D.)
Scali, John, 256
Schierman, Wes, 6, 17–19, 22, 112,
  315
Secondary School, 63, 64, 154,
  214–17, 242, 250, 272–73,
  306–7, 323, 324, 326, 345
Secret Service, 27
Sevareid, Eric, 256
7th Air Force, 93, 146
7th Operations Squadron, 79
77th Special Forces Group, 43
Shields, Roger, 300–1
Shively, James R. "Jim," 294
Shultz, Richard H., Jr., 129
Simons, Arthur D. "Bull," 3–4,
  43–45, 67–89, 92, 98, 103–7,
  109, 110, 112–22, 124–27,
  135–39, 143–45, 150,
  151–53, 155–58, 161–63,
  165, 166, 180–83, 187–89,
  191, 197, 200, 206, 212,
  214–20, 222–24, 226, 227,
  229–31, 237–44, 246–48,
  254, 255, 258–60, 262, 266,
  272, 274, 277, 279, 303–6,
  313, 321, 323, 325
Simons, Lucile, 67, 304, 305
Site 32, 142, 143, 152
Smith, Wayne O., 283

Snow, Edgar, 134
SOG (Special Operations Group),
  43–47, 52, 74, 75, 96, 142,
  265
Song Con River, 22, 31, 74, 138,
  198, 209, 214, 231
Son Tay Army Supply Depot, 64
Son Tay city, 63, 64
Son Tay Prison ("Camp Hope"), 6,
  17–23
  condition of POWs in, 110–11
  discovery of, 30–31
  layout of, 64–65
  list of prisoners in, 62
  location of, 31
  POWs appeal for rescue, 31–32
  POWs moved from, 74, 89, 91–92,
    137, 174, 177–86, 278–79
  raid on (see Son Tay raid ["Polar
    Circle, "Ivory Coast,"
    "Kingpin"])
  reconnaissance photos of, 31, 32,
    49, 56, 63, 65, 77, 78, 93–94,
    96, 137, 140, 154–55, 184
Son Tay raid ("Polar Circle, "Ivory
    Coast," "Kingpin"), 1–5
  Abrams briefing, 144, 145
  after–action reports, 89, 92, 112,
    137, 218, 247, 263, 264, 310,
    321, 322, 325
  aircraft cover, 220–22, 224–26,
    234, 235
  alternate plans, 104–6, 215
  approach to compound, 208–11
  awards and citations, 240–41,
    254–55, 259–62, 306–7
  beginning of plan, 32–52
  CAS agent insertion, 94–96
  Chinese reaction, 267, 272
  choice of commander for, 67–68,
    70–71
  communication problems, 161–62,
    170, 228–29
  Congressional debate on, 246–54,
    257
  cover stories, 165–66
  debriefings, 238

effect on POWs morale, 282–96, 300–1

"Execute" message, 169–70, 174

feasibility study group, 51, 52, 57–60

final briefing, 198

Fontaine investigation, 266–68

helicopter crews, 78–80

intelligence, 55–60, 63–64, 76, 77, 88, 89–95, 136, 137, 154–57, 245, 248–49, 264, 277–79

Ivory Coast planning group, 86–88

Joint Chiefs of Staff briefings, 51–52, 60–66, 127

Kissinger briefing, 137–39

medical equipment, 111–12

mock–up of compound, 87–89, 98–99, 159, 211–12

Navy diversionary strike, 140–41, 151, 163, 164, 189, 203–8, 221

Nixon and, 134, 135, 157–58, 160–69

North Vietnamese reaction to, 257–58, 281

Pentagon press briefing, 241–45, 271

Porth incident, 269–72

POWs removal, 219–20, 236–38

rehearsals, 99–110, 116, 118, 124–38

return flight, 227, 229–30

route of assault force, 194–96

Russian reaction, 268, 273

Secondary School landing, 214–17, 242, 250, 272–73, 306–7, 323, 324, 326, 345

supplies and weapons, 112–23, 199–200

training site, 69, 78, 87

volunteers, 78–85

weather, 39–40, 50, 58, 66, 77, 78, 170, 173, 184–85, 187–91

Sooter, David, 291–92, 318

Sowell, Angus, 212

Special Operations Division, 34–35

SR-71 reconnaissance plane, 56, 63, 77, 89, 92, 94, 137, 154, 155, 172, 182, 184

Stackhouse, Charles D., 294

Starkey, William J., 225

State, U.S. Department of, 27, 128

Steinhauser, Thomas C., 55

Stevens, Walter, 271

Stewart, Richard R. "Dick," 55, 76, 94, 98, 136, 297

Stilwell, Richard, 153–54

Stockdale, James B., 290, 315

Stoner, Gene, 119–20

Strategic Air Command (SAC), 92–93, 147, 148, 154, 171–73, 228

Stratton, Richard A., 129, 130

STRICOM (Strike Command), 127

Strosnider, Barbara L., 57

Swindle, Orson, 19

Sydnor, Elliott P. "Bud", Jr., 68, 80–82, 85–86, 103–6, 121, 124, 187, 188, 198, 200, 214, 215, 217, 218n, 219–21, 224, 226, 229, 238, 239, 245, 255, 261

Symington, Stuart, 247, 252

Tactical Air Command (TAC), 93, 100, 124

Takhli Royal Thai Air Force Base, 107, 146–49, 155, 158, 161, 172, 173, 187–92, 239

Tan Son Nhut Air Base, 189, 191

Terrell, Irby D., Jr., 16

Tet offensive, 152

Thang, Ton Du, 132

3rd Army, 55

37th Air Rescue and Recovery Squadron, 149

39th Air Rescue and Recovery Squadron, 149

Tho, Le Duc, 133, 296–97

Thompson, Floyd J., 47, 295

Thornton, Gary L., 283, 317

Thurmond, Nancy, 132

Thurmond, Strom, 132

Tonkin Gulf incidents, 6, 39, 44, 318
Train, Harry D., II, 153, 157, 158,
160, 168–69, 312
Treasury, U.S. Department of, 27
Triantafellu, Rockly "Rocky," 31–33,
35
Trinh, Mr., 49
Tripler Army General Hospital,
Hawaii, 125, 171
Turner, Daniel D., 85, 105, 200, 215,
223, 224, 306
Typhoon Patsy, 170, 188, 191, 192,
203

Udorn Royal Thai Air Base, 107,
146, 148, 149, 192, 197–98,
202, 227, 237
UH-1 Huey helicopter, 99–101, 107,
108, 109, 126
Union of Soviet Socialist Republics,
28, 45, 48, 53, 56, 87–88
United States Post Office, 27–28
U.S.S. *America*, 140–41
U.S.S. *Hancock*, 141, 205, 206
U.S.S. *Maine*, 162
U.S.S. *Oriskany*, 141, 203, 205–7
U.S.S. *Ranger*, 140–41, 205, 206
U–Tapao, Thailand, 146–48

Van Houdt, Dennis H., 190, 192
Vanik, Charles, 246
Venanzi, Gerald, 21
Viet Cong, 28, 44, 45, 48
Vietnamization, 47, 129
Vinh airfield, 46, 164
Vogt, John, 40, 48, 49, 51, 66–67,
125–27, 137–41, 153, 170,
188, 233, 234, 236, 248

Waldron, Tom, 211, 212, 230–32
Walther, Udo H., 105, 200, 216, 218,
224, 273, 306, 325

Waresh, John C., 201, 202, 222–23,
226, 237–38
Watkins, Claude, 30–35, 37, 49, 59,
236, 309
Weather intelligence, 39–40, 50, 58,
66, 77, 78, 170, 173, 185–86,
188–92
Weather modification activities,
89–92, 277–78
Weiss, Cora, 28, 33, 156, 166,
177–78, 186, 249
Weiss, Peter, 175, 186
Westmoreland, William C., 44–46,
81, 144, 233, 236, 260, 303
Wheeler, Earle G., 38–40, 51, 60
White, Bob, 14
White, Robert T., 298
White Star teams, 43, 44, 73, 82
"Wildroot" call sign, 105
Winn, David W., 290
Women's Strike for Peace, 15
World War II, 11, 36, 41–42, 55, 61,
72–73
Wright, Leroy M., 213, 220, 255

Yankee Station, 7, 189
Yokota Air Force Base, Japan, 94,
155, 156, 184

Zais, Melvin R., 125–26, 236
Zapinski, Leonard E., 189–90
Zaslov, Milt, 88, 136, 158
Zehnder, Herbert R., 78–79, 109,
110, 212, 220, 308
Ziegler, Ronald, 133
Zion, Roger, 133
Zoo, the, 18, 275, 284, 287
Zumwalt, Elmo R., Jr., 60, 66

*Don't miss this thrilling insider's account
of how special operations are changing the
way modern wars are fought. . . .*

NO ROOM FOR ERROR
The Covert Operations of America's Special
Tactics Units from Iran to Afghanistan

by Col. John T. Carney Jr.
and Benjamin F. Schemmer

When the U.S. Air Force decided to create an elite
"special tactics" team in the late 1970s to work in
conjunction with special-operations forces combat-
ing terrorists and hijackers and defusing explosive
international emergencies, John T. Carney was the
man they turned to. Since then Carney and the U.S.
Air Force Special Tactical units have circled the
world on sensitive clandestine missions. Now, for
the first time, Col. Carney and Schemmer lift the
veil of secrecy and reveal what really goes on inside
the special-operations forces that are at the forefront
of contemporary warfare.

**New in hardcover from Ballantine Books.
Available wherever books are sold.**